Fodor's

BELIZE

WELCOME TO BELIZE

It's easy to become immersed in the natural beauty of Belize. Broadleaf canopies shelter exotic birds, and ancient Mayan ruins are wrapped in vines. Underwater caves and the chute of the Blue Hole offer some of the world's best diving, and the Belize Barrier Reef astounds snorkelers with a lavish medley of coral and fish. Belize's secluded resorts embrace these surroundings: here, you can sleep under a palm-thatched roof in a lush jungle lodge and escape to a dreamy overwater bungalow with turquoise sea views all on the same trip.

TOP REASONS TO GO

★ **Mayan Ruins:** Evidence of the ancient Mayan empire is everywhere in Belize.

★ **Snorkeling:** The Belize Barrier Reef presents amazing underwater vistas.

★ **Diving:** Reefs and atolls provide many of the world's greatest dive sites.

★ **Bird-Watching:** Belize has more than 500 species of birds, many rare or endangered.

★ **Beach Stays:** Often remote or removed, and nearly always right on the water.

★ **Jungle Lodges:** For an unforgettable close-to-nature experience in comfort.

12
TOP EXPERIENCES

Belize offers terrific experiences that should be on every traveler's list. Here are Fodor's top picks for a memorable trip.

1 Belize Barrier Reef

Widely considered one of the world's best sites for diving and snorkeling, the Belize Barrier Reef is home to more than 300 species of fish and 65 kinds of coral. It's the longest barrier reef in the Western or Northern hemispheres. *(Ch. 3, 6)*

2 Cave Tubing

Overland journeys and undersea adventures are just part of the Belize experience. Underground, you'll find subterranean rivers that provide thrilling passage through spooky caves. *(Ch. 5, 6, 7)*

3 Bird-watching

Belize's jungles teem with wild birds—nearly 600 species. Endangered beauties such as the scarlet macaw and keel-billed toucan roam freely in the country's interior. *(Ch. 4–7)*

4 Kayaking

The Belize Barrier Reef blocks big swells, so the country has some of the region's best open-water kayaking. Inland, there are rivers for all levels of paddlers. *(Ch. 3, 5, 6, 7)*

5 Jaguar Trekking

Jaguars are shy and nocturnal, so sightings are rare. But Belize has the highest concentration of them in the world. With patience and luck, you might spot one in the wild. *(Ch. 4, 5, 6)*

6 Ziplining

One of the most thrilling ways to explore Belize is from its treetops. Canopy tours zip you through a network of suspended platforms high in the trees. *(Ch. 5, 6, 7)*

7 Remote Escapes

Private islands are the stuff of dream vacations, and Belize's cayes and atolls have a number of these fantasy getaways—some with surprisingly down-to-earth prices. *(Ch. 3)*

8 Mayan Ruins

For 5,000 years the Mayans inhabited this region. Caracol and more than a dozen sites are open to visitors for climbing, exploring, and general ogling of astounding architectual ingenuity. *(Ch. 2–8)*

9 Staying at a Jungle Lodge

In Belize there's a jungle lodge for every budget, from simple cabins to the deluxe Caves Branch Lodge. Included free each night is the jungle music of birds, monkeys, and tree frogs. *(Ch. 4–7)*

10 Hummingbird Highway

A drive on this scenic roadway winds through limestone hill country, deep-green mountains, and citrus country with groves of Valencia oranges. *(Ch. 5)*

11 Actun Tunichil Muknal (ATM)

More than a cave system, ATM is a visit to a Mayan underworld filled with eerie chambers where ancient artifacts and human skeletons remain undisturbed. *(Ch. 5)*

12 Ambergris Caye/Caye Caulker

Belize's largest island and its "little sister" attract divers and beachcombers, sunbathers and snorkelers, with the most water sports, beach resorts, and restaurants in the country. *(Ch. 3)*

CONTENTS

MAPS

ABOUT THIS GUIDE

Fodor's Recommendations

Everything in this guide is worth doing—we don't cover what isn't—but exceptional sights, hotels, and restaurants are recognized with additional accolades. Fodor'sChoice★ indicates our top recommendations. Care to nominate a new place? Visit Fodors.com/contact-us.

Trip Costs

We list prices wherever possible to help you budget well. Hotel and restaurant price categories from **$** to **$$$$** are noted alongside each recommendation. For hotels, we include the lowest cost of a standard double room in high season. For restaurants, we cite the average price of a main course at dinner or, if dinner isn't served, at lunch. For attractions, we always list adult admission fees; discounts are usually available for children, students, and senior citizens.

Hotels

Our local writers vet every hotel to recommend the best overnights in each price category, from budget to expensive. Unless otherwise specified, you can expect private bath, phone, and TV in your room. For expanded hotel reviews, facilities, and deals visit Fodors.com.

Top Picks		Hotels & Restaurants	
★ Fodor'sChoice			
		🏨	Hotel
Listings		🛏	Number of rooms
✉	Address		
✉	Branch address	⚟	Meal plans
☎	Telephone	✕	Restaurant
🖷	Fax	🖉	Reservations
⊕	Website	🏛	Dress code
✒	E-mail	▭	No credit cards
🎫	Admission fee	Ⓢ	Price
☺	Open/closed times		
		Other	
Ⓜ	Subway	⇨	See also
✛	Directions or Map coordinates	☞	Take note
		🏌	Golf facilities

Restaurants

Unless we state otherwise, restaurants are open for lunch and dinner daily. We mention dress code only when there's a specific requirement and reservations only when they're essential or not accepted. To make restaurant reservations, visit Fodors.com.

Credit Cards

The hotels and restaurants in this guide typically accept credit cards. If not, we'll say so.

EUGENE FODOR

Hungarian-born Eugene Fodor (1905–91) began his travel career as an interpreter on a French cruise ship. The experience inspired him to write *On the Continent* (1936), the first guidebook to receive annual updates and discuss a country's way of life as well as its sights. Fodor later joined the U.S. Army and worked for the OSS in World War II. After the war, he kept up his intelligence work while expanding his guidebook series. During the Cold War, many guides were written by fellow agents who understood the value of insider information. Today's guides continue Fodor's legacy by providing travelers with timely coverage, insider tips, and cultural context.

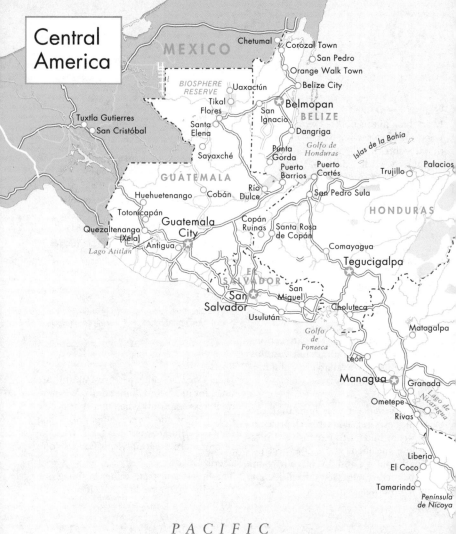

Central America

MEXICO

Chetumal
Corozal Town
San Pedro
Orange Walk Town
Belize City

BIOSPHERE
RESERVE

Uaxactún

Tikal
Flores

San
Ignacio

Belmopan

BELIZE

Santa
Elena

Dangriga

Sayaxché

Punta
Gorda

Golfo de
Honduras

Islas de la Bahía

Puerto
Barrios

Puerto
Cortés

Trujillo

Palacios

GUATEMALA

Huehuetenango

Cobán

Río
Dulce

San Pedro Sula

HONDURAS

Totonicapán

Guatemala
City

Copán
Ruinas

Santa Rosa
de Copán

Comayagua

Quezaltenango
(Xela)

Antigua

Tegucigalpa

Lago Atitlán

EL
SALVADOR

San
Miguel

San
Salvador

Usulután

Choluteca

Matagalpa

Golfo
de
Fonseca

León

Managua

Granada

Lago de
Nicaragua

Ometepe

Rivas

Liberia
El Coco

Tamarindo

Península
de Nicoya

*PACIFIC
OCEAN*

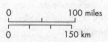

| 0 | | 100 miles |
| 0 | | 150 km |

JAMAICA

CARIBBEAN
SEA

Puerto
Lempira
Mosquitia

La Rosita
Puerto
Cabezas

NICARAGUA

Laguna de
Perkis

Isla de
San Andrés

Rama
Islas del
Maíz (Corn
Islands)

Bluefields

Bahía
Punta Gorda

Tortuguero

COSTA
RICA
Turrialba
Puerto Limón

San
José
Cartago
El Porvenir
San Blas
Islands

Golfo
de
Nicoya
Quepos
Bocas
del Toro
Panama
Canal
Ciudad de
Panama

Bahía de
Coronado
Boquete
Golfo de los
Mosquitos
Puerto
Obaldia

La Palma
David
PANAMA
Bahía de
Panamá

Sirena
Santiago
Yaviza

Matapalo
Chitré
Isla del
Rey

Península
de Osa
Golfo de
Chiriquí
Las Tablas
Golfo de
Panamá

Isla de
Coiba
COLOMBIA

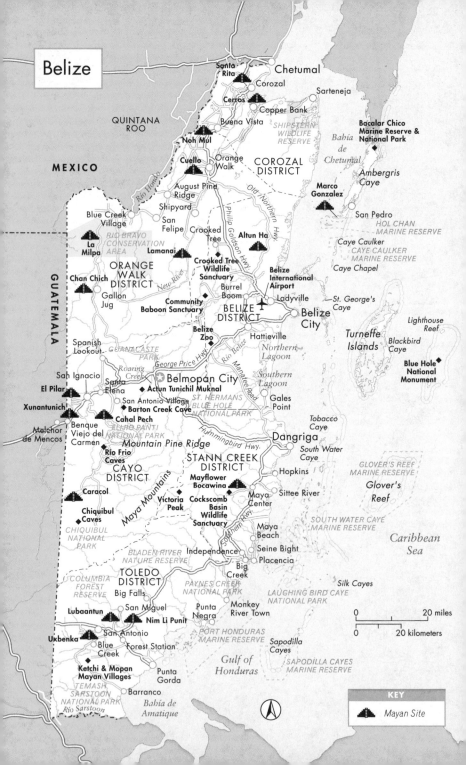

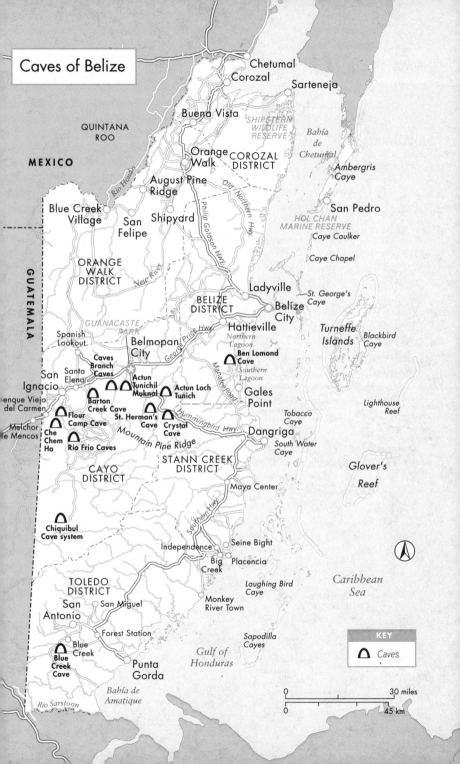

Caves of Belize

MEXICO

QUINTANA
ROO

Rio Hondo

Blue Creek
Village

San
Felipe

August Pine
Ridge

Shipyard

ORANGE
WALK
DISTRICT

New River

Chetumal
Corozal

Buena Vista

Orange
Walk

COROZAL
DISTRICT

SHIPSTERN
WILDLIFE
RESERVE

Sarteneja

Bahía
de
Chetumal

Ambergris
Caye

San Pedro

HOL CHAN
MARINE RESERVE

Caye Caulker

Caye Chapel

Philip Goldson Hwy.

Old Northern Hwy.

Ladyville

BELIZE
DISTRICT

Hattieville

Belize
City

St. George's
Caye

Turneffe
Islands

Blackbird
Caye

GUATEMALA

GUANACASTE
PARK

Spanish
Lookout

Santa
Elena

San
Ignacio

enque Viejo
del Carmen

Melchor
e Mencos

Caves
Branch
Caves

Belmopan
City

George Price Hwy.

Actun
Tunichil
Muknal

Barton
Creek Cave

Flour
Camp Cave

St. Herman's
Cave

Che
Chem
Ha

Río Frio Caves

Mountain Pine Ridge

Actun Loch
Tunich

Crystal
Cave

Ben Lomond
Cave

Northern
Lagoon

Southern
Lagoon

Manatee Road

Hummingbird Hwy.

Gales
Point

Dangriga

Tobacco
Caye

South Water
Caye

Lighthouse
Reef

Glover's
Reef

CAYO
DISTRICT

STANN CREEK
DISTRICT

Maya Center

Southern Hwy.

Chiquibul
Cave system

Independence

Big
Creek

Seine Bight

Placencia

Laughing Bird
Caye

Monkey
River Town

Caribbean
Sea

TOLEDO
DISTRICT

San
Antonio

San Miguel

Forest Station

Blue
Creek

Blue
Creek
Cave

Punta
Gorda

Bahía de
Amatique

Rio Sarstoon

Sapodilla
Cayes

Gulf of
Honduras

KEY
⌂ Caves

0   30 miles
0   45 km

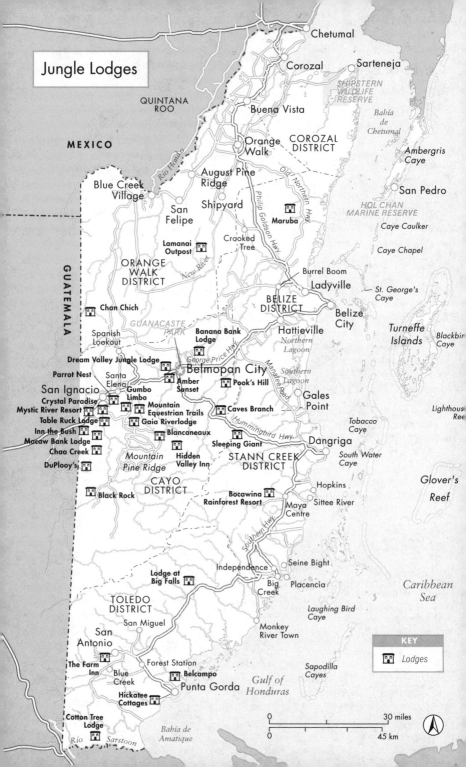

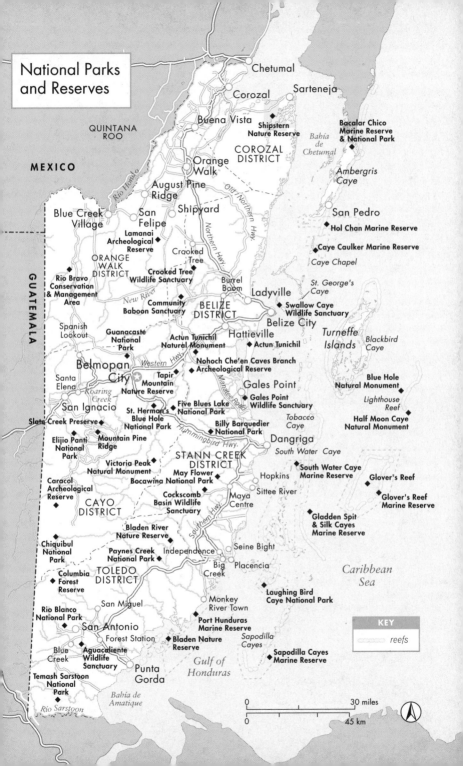

National Parks and Reserves

MEXICO

QUINTANA ROO

Chetumal

Corozal

Sarteneja

Buena Vista

Shipstern Nature Reserve

Bahía de Chetumal

Bacalar Chico Marine Reserve & National Park

COROZAL DISTRICT

Orange Walk

Ambergris Caye

Blue Creek Village

San Felipe

Shipyard

San Pedro

August Pine Ridge

Hol Chan Marine Reserve

Lamanai Archeological Reserve

Crooked Tree

Caye Caulker Marine Reserve

ORANGE WALK DISTRICT

Crooked Tree Wildlife Sanctuary

Caye Chapel

Rio Bravo Conservation & Management Area

New River

Burrel Boom

Ladyville

St. George's Caye

Spanish Lookout

Community Baboon Sanctuary

BELIZE DISTRICT

Swallow Caye Wildlife Sanctuary

Guanacaste National Park

Actun Tunichil Natural Monument

Hattieville

Belize City

Turneffe Islands

Blackbird Caye

GUATEMALA

Belmopan City

Western Hwy.

Actun Tunichil

Nohoch Che'en Caves Branch Archeological Reserve

Santa Elena

Roaring Creek

Tapir Mountain Nature Reserve

Gales Point

Blue Hole Natural Monument

San Ignacio

St. Herman's Blue Hole National Park

Five Blues Lake National Park

Gales Point Wildlife Sanctuary

Manatee Road

Lighthouse Reef

Slate Creek Preserve

Elijio Panti National Park

Mountain Pine Ridge

Billy Barquedier National Park

Hummingbird Hwy.

Tobacco Caye

Half Moon Caye Natural Monument

Victoria Peak Natural Monument

Dangriga

South Water Caye

Caracol Archeological Reserve

May Flower Bocawina National Park

STANN CREEK DISTRICT

Hopkins

South Water Caye Marine Reserve

Glover's Reef

CAYO DISTRICT

Cockscomb Basin Wildlife Sanctuary

Maya Centre

Sittee River

Glover's Reef Marine Reserve

Chiquibul National Park

Bladen River Nature Reserve

Paynes Creek National Park

Independence

Seine Bight

Big Creek

Placencia

Gladden Spit & Silk Cayes Marine Reserve

Caribbean Sea

Columbia Forest Reserve

TOLEDO DISTRICT

Rio Blanco National Park

San Miguel

Monkey River Town

Laughing Bird Caye National Park

San Antonio

Forest Station

Port Hunduras Marine Reserve

Sapodilla Cayes

Blue Creek

Aguacaliente Wildlife Sanctuary

Bladen Nature Reserve

Sapodilla Cayes Marine Reserve

Temash Sarstoon National Park

Punta Gorda

Gulf of Honduras

Bahía de Amatique

Rio Sarstoon

0   30 miles

0   45 km

KEY

reefs

EXPERIENCE
BELIZE

WHAT'S WHERE

The following numbers refer to chapters.

2 Belize City. Depending on your perspective, Belize's commercial, transportation, and cultural hub is either a lively Caribbean port city of raffish charm or a crime-ridden, edgy backwater best seen through the rearview mirror.

3 The Cayes and the Atolls. Hundreds of cayes (pronounced *keys*) dot the Caribbean Sea off Belize, both inside and outside the Barrier Reef. The largest are Ambergris, Belize's most popular visitor destination, and Caulker. Farther out are three South Pacific–style atolls.

4 Northern Belize. This is the land of sugarcane and sweet, off-the-beaten-path places to visit. Corozal Town, up against the Mexican border, has a lovely bay-side setting, and Sarteneja is a fishing village just waiting to be discovered.

5 The Cayo. The rolling hills of western Belize, anchored by San Ignacio, offer outdoor activities aplenty—caving, canoeing, hiking, horseback riding, and mountain biking. Several remarkable Mayan sites also await you, including Caracol, Xunantunich, and Actun Tunichil Muknal.

6 The Southern Coast. Want beaches? The best on the mainland are on the Placencia Peninsula, especially in the Maya Beach area, and in Hopkins.

7 The Deep South. Rainy and lush, beautiful and remote, Punta Gorda in far southern Belize is the jumping-off point for the unspoiled Mayan villages of Toledo District and for onward travel to Guatemala and Honduras.

8 El Petén. This part of Guatemala, easily visited from the Cayo District of Belize, is home to the most spectacular of all Mayan sites, Tikal, and the remains of many other ancient cities.

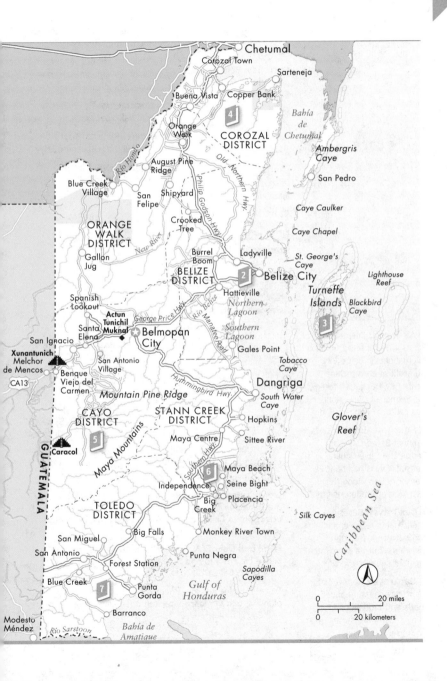

NEED TO KNOW

Belmopan

BELIZE

Caribbean Sea

AT A GLANCE

Capital: Belmopan

Population: 375,000

Currency: Belize dollar; pegged to U.S. dollar at 2BZ$ to 1US$

Money: ATMS in most areas; credit cards accepted at resorts; U.S. dollars accepted everywhere.

Language: English, Spanish, Kriol, several Mayan languages, and Garifuna.

Country Code: 501

Emergencies: 911

Driving: On the right

Electricity: 120v/60 cycle; plugs are U.S. standard two- and three-prong

Time: Two hours behind EST during daylight savings; one hour behind otherwise

Documents: Up to 30 days with valid passport

Mobile Phones: GSM (850 and 1900 bands) and CDMA

Major Mobile Companies: DigiCell, Smart

WEBSITES

Belize Tourism Board:
🌐 www.travelbelize.org

Ambergris Caye:
🌐 www.ambergriscaye.com

GETTING AROUND

✈ **Air Travel:** International flights arrive at Philip Goldson International in Belize City. Domestic airports include Belize City, Dangriga, Placencia, Belmopan, Maya Flats, Corozal Town, and San Pedro.

🚢 **Boat Travel:** Water taxis connect Belize City, San Pedro, and Caye Caulker. Coastal Xpress has boat transportation along the east side of Ambergris Caye.

🚌 **Bus Travel:** Buses are cheap, fairly reliable, and can get you just about anywhere, but be prepared for tight squeezes.

🚗 **Car Travel:** Rent a 4x4 vehicle because unpaved roads and mudslides in rainy season are status quo in Belize.

PLAN YOUR BUDGET

	HOTEL ROOM	MEAL	ATTRACTIONS
Low Budget	BZ$250	BZ$16	Crooked Tree Wildlife Sanctuary, BZ$8
Mid Budget	BZ$500	BZ$30	Snorkel Trip with Ambergris Divers, BZ$80
High Budget	BZ$700	BZ$50	Caracol day trip, BZ$180

WAYS TO SAVE

Eat local seafood. On the coast and cayes, seafood is fresh, inexpensive, and delicious.

Clarify currency. Most hotels, tours, and car-rental prices are quoted in U.S. dollars, while restaurant and store prices are in Belize dollars. Always ask which currency is being used.

Fly to and from TZA. Save 10% to 40% on flights within Belize by flying to and from the municipal airport near downtown Belize City.

Travel in value season. Prices are lower, hotel rooms plentiful, and the landscape lush after rains. Water visibility is better.

Hassle Factor	Medium. Flights to Belize City are frequent but most sights of interest require a puddle jumper, land transfer, or boat transfer.
3 days	Base yourself on Ambergris Caye or Caye Caulker and explore the amazing Belize Barrier Reef. Take a boat to atolls to experience exceptional dive sites.
1 week	Combine a longer trip to Belize islands and atolls with a few days inland at a forest lodge in the Cayo district, where you'll have easy access to caves, bird-watching, and Mayan ruins (don't miss Caracol).
2 weeks	Spend a full week between coastal Belize (Placencia Peninsula or culture-rich Punta Gorda and Toledo) and the cayes and atolls surrounding the Belize Barrier Reef. Spend a few days in Cayo District, and search for wildlife in the Mountain Pine Ridge and in other forest reserves and national parks. Then head to Tikal in neighboring Guatemala.

WHEN TO GO

High Season: The busiest time is from Christmas through New Year's, followed by Easter. Hotel rates spike from mid-November through April. February through May is the best time to visit the coast and cayes.

Low Season: Rainy season is roughly June through October, with fewer crowds and lower prices, but some restaurants close and hotels offer limited facilities.

Value Season: May through November has some of the most bearable temperatures and the best rates for hotels are in late spring, September and October.

BIG EVENTS

February and March: Carnival festivities begin the week prior to Lent.

May: Celebrate Toldeo's Chocolate Festival. ⊕ www.toledochocolate.com

June: Lobster festivals are in San Pedro, Placencia, and Caye Caulker. ⊕ www.sanpedrolobsterfest.com

READ THIS

■ *Wanderlove,* Kirsten Hubbard. Young backpacker searches for her self-identity in Belize.

■ *How to Cook a Tapir,* Joan Fry. Memoir of a young woman's "working honeymoon" among the Maya in Toledo.

■ *No Souvenirs,* K.A. Mitchell. Unexpected romance between two men: a doctor on vacation and a dive instructor.

WATCH THIS

■ *The Dogs of War.* Fictional war film shot in Belize.

■ *Mega Piranha.* Over-the-top sci-fi movie about enormous man-eating piranhas.

■ *The Mosquito Coast.* American family swaps suburbia for jungles of Central America (filmed in Belize, set in Honduras).

EAT THIS

■ *Garnaches*: fried tortillas with refried beans, cabbage, and cheese

■ *Cow-foot soup*: a Creole specialty made with real cows' feet

■ *Salbutes*: fried corn tortillas with chicken and a topping of tomatoes, onions, and peppers

■ *Boil up*: a stew of fish, potatoes, plantains, cassava and other vegetables, and eggs

WHAT'S NEW IN BELIZE

Belize's Own Politics of Change

Like the United States, Belize held national elections in 2012, and, also like the United States, Belize re-elected its first black leader in history. Dean Barrow, a lawyer by profession, educated in Jamaica and Miami, became prime minister in general elections in 2008. His party, the United Democratic Party (or UDP), swept into office then with about 57% of the popular vote. In its first years in office, the UDP generally took a low-key approach to governing. It followed a reform-oriented agenda in an effort to mitigate charges of high-level corruption levied against the former government. Seeking greater diversity in government, the UDP tapped Mayans and Mennonites for high office, in addition to the traditional core of Creole and Mestizo politicians. However, as the years since the 2008 election passed, Belize's UDP government has faced growing challenges and increasing popular discontent. The 2012 election against the People's United Party, the main opposition party, was much closer. Rising prices and a slow economy (when the United States sneezes, Belize catches a bad cold) cost Prime Minister Barrow some popularity, as has increasing crime, especially in Belize City. The government has become mired in new charges of corruption. Despite this, in late 2015 PM Barrow was reelected again, for his third, and, he says, his final term.

Old Tensions Flare

In 2016, old tensions between Guatemala and Belize resurfaced, with occasional firefights between Guatemalan and Belize forces in the far south and west of the country. Observers, however, expect the flag-waving to give way to more rational discussions.

Tourism Rebounds

The tourism industry in Belize, the largest sector of the economy with revenues of more than BZ$700 million, was buffeted in 2008–2010 by the global financial and economic crisis. Belize tourism has since rebounded, with record revenue. Overnight, visitor arrivals reached 341,000 in 2015, a record, and cruise ship passengers totaled almost 1 million. New air service to Belize by Southwest, Copa from Panama, and Canada's WestJet, and expanded service by American and United have helped. A new US$50 million cruise port on an island off Placencia, while controversial and opposed by many Belizeans, is expected to boost cruise tourism in southern Belize beginning in 2017.

Milestones

April the tapir (the tapir is Belize's national animal) celebrated her 30th birthday at the Belize Zoo in 2013—in April, of course. In October of that year April passed on to tapir heaven, where she has no natural predators.

In mid-2016, after a lengthy court process, thanks to the efforts of Caleb Orozco, a modern Belize hero who survived threats and personal attacks, the Belize Supreme Court at long last laid to rest a homophobic colonial-era law that called for up to 10 years in prison for "unnatural sexual acts." The Belize government declined to appeal, and the anachronistic law is expected to be erased from the books. Some Belizeans, however, still hold negative views of LGBTQ rights and changing a mind-set is difficult.

WHEN TO GO

Belize, like much of Central America and the Caribbean, has two basic seasons: the rainy season and the dry season. The rainy season is roughly June through October, extending in some areas through November or even December and later. The dry season usually runs from February, when temperatures inland may reach 100°F. April is usually the hottest month of the year.

If you want to escape crowds and high prices and don't mind getting a little wet, visit in the rainy—or green—season. Though some restaurants may close and hotels may offer limited facilities, especially in September and October, reservations are easy to get, even at top establishments, and you'll have the Mayan ruins and beaches to yourself. And the rains, which most often come at night, do make the entire country lush and green.

The dry season can be a less attractive time for inland trips, with dusty roads and wilting vegetation, but this is a good time to visit the coast and cayes, with their cooling winds from the sea.

Scuba enthusiasts can dive all year, but the water usually is clearest from March to June. Between November and February, cold fronts from North America can push southward, producing blustery winds known as "northers" that bring rain and rough weather and tend to churn up the sea, reducing visibility. Water temperatures, however, rarely stray far from 80°F, so many dive without a wet suit.

Climate and Hurricane Season

Belize is a small country, but there's considerable variation in climate from north to south, and also from the cayes to the mainland. Rainfall, for example, varies dramatically depending on where you are:

the Deep South gets as much as 160 to 200 inches of rain each year, but the rest of the country gets a lot less, as little as 50 inches in Corozal. The cayes generally get less rain than the mainland. The rainy season doesn't mean monsoons, but rather seasonal rains that green the countryside.

Belize's Caribbean coast often gets sweltering, humid weather, especially in summer, while the Mountain Pine Ridge, with elevations up to almost 3,700 feet, is cooler and less humid. Overall, Belize's subtropical temperatures generally hover between 70°F and 85°F (21°C and 29°C).

The western Caribbean's hurricane season is from June through November. September and October are the two prime months for tropical storms and hurricanes in Belize. Over the past century, about 85% of storms to hit Belize arrived in those two months; hurricanes, however, are relatively rare.

Rainy season. Northern Belize gets about a third as much rain as the Deep South, which can get 160 inches or more. The seasonal rains begin in Toledo in early May, progress north over the next couple of months, and usually start in Corozal in late June. The cayes have different microclimates than the mainland and generally get less rain. The rainy season typically peaks from June through September. By November, rainfall in nearly all areas of Belize averages 8 inches or less a month. Many old Belize hands say they prefer traveling in summer or fall. Prices are lower, hotel rooms are plentiful, and the landscape is lush after rains. It's also a little cooler than in the dry season months of April and May, and water visibility is usually very good.

QUINTESSENTIAL BELIZE

The Jewel

Belizeans frequently talk about "the Jewel." They say, "Get yourself a piece of the Jewel." Or, "When are you coming back to the Jewel?" By Jewel, they simply mean Belize. And Belize is a jewel. It's a place of incredible natural beauty, of mint-green seas and emerald-green forests, of the longest Barrier Reef in the Western or Northern hemisphere, with more kinds of birds, butterflies, flowers, and trees than in all of the United States and Canada combined. Massive ceiba trees and graceful cohune palms stand guard in rain forests where jaguars still roam free and toucans and parrots fly overhead. Rivers, bays, and lagoons are rich with hundreds of different kinds of fish. And Belizeans themselves are jewels. The country is a gumbo of cultures—African, Hispanic, Mayan, Asian, European, and Caribbean. Belize? It's a Jewel.

Passing the Time

Nearly every country claims to be full of friendly, smiling, welcoming people, but in the case of Belize it's really true. The vast majority of Belizeans are open and gracious, and they're happy, even eager, to spend a few minutes chatting with you about nothing in particular—the weather, the beautiful morning, how you're enjoying the Jewel. In most cases they don't want anything from you, except to pass the time of day. So let your guard down a little, relax, smile, and share a few rewarding moments with the shopkeeper, the waitress, the fellow you meet in the bar, or the lady you sit next to on the bus.

If you want a sense of life in Belize, familiarize yourself with some of its simple pleasures. There are a few highlights that will send you home saying, "Ah mi gat wahn gud guf taim" ("I had a good time" in Creole).

Bird-Watching

Once you see toucans at Tikal or the hard-to-find motmot in the Cayo, you too might get caught up in the excitement of searching for some of Belize's 600 species of birds. Many Belizeans know all their local birds (although the names they have for them may differ from those in your birding guide) and where the best places are to find them. Crooked Tree, Chan Chich at Gallon Jug, the New River and New River Lagoon near Lamanai, the Mountain Pine Ridge, and much of the Toledo District in the Deep South are wonderful areas for bird-watching; keep your eyes peeled to the treetops and don't forget your binoculars.

Archaeological Treasures

Though the ancient Mayan empire—which once occupied much of present-day Guatemala and extended into Belize, Mexico, Honduras, and El Salvador—began to collapse around AD 900, it still left one of the richest cultural and archaeological legacies in the world. Only a fraction of the thousands of Mayan ruins have been excavated from the jungle that over the centuries has swallowed the splendid temples and sprawling cities. Evidence of the Maya is everywhere in Belize, from the lagoon-side temples of Lamanai to the caves of Actun Tunichil Muknal. All together, Belize has more than 600 Mayan sites, most small and unexcavated, with likely hundreds or even thousands still to be discovered. A short day or overnight trip from western Belize is Tikal, arguably the most impressive of all Mayan sites, along with many other ruins in Guatemala's Petén.

IF YOU LIKE

Luxury Resorts

Deluxe duvets. 1,200-thread-count sheets. Your own villa on a private island or a jungle hideaway with fine wines and gourmet dinners. You may be traipsing around Mayan ruins or diving the Blue Hole during the day, but at night you can look forward to pampering at Belize's luxury jungle lodges and beach resorts.

■ **Victoria House, South End, Ambergris Caye.** This long-established resort remains one of the best-run and most enjoyable beach resorts in all of Belize.

■ **Blancaneaux Lodge, Mountain Pine Ridge.** Francis Ford Coppola's riverside jungle lodge hints of Beverly Hills in the bush.

■ **El Secreto, North Ambergris Caye.** Thirteen splendid thatch villas line the beachfront, a small lagoon, and beautiful gardens at this property far enough north of San Pedro to feel like a secret island, especially for honeymooners.

■ **The Lodge at Chaa Creek, Cayo.** Soak up the carefully tended landscaping, deluxe garden suites, spa, Cuban cigars, and expensive cognac.

■ **Villa Margarita, Hopkins.** Six new luxury suites on the best beach in Hopkins, and within strolling distance of good restaurants.

■ **Turtle Inn, Placencia.** Francis Ford Coppola hand-picked the Balinese furniture and art in the thatch cabanas, but that's not the best part. Wait until you see the garden showers.

■ **The Phoenix, San Pedro.** At the site of one of the caye's oldest hotels, The Phoenix rose from the sands, offering stunning suites, convenience to all the in-town restaurants, clubs, and shops, and its own excellent restaurant.

Fishing

Some of the world's most exciting sport-fishing lies off Belize's coast and cayes. Go for the "grand slam" of tarpon, bonefish, permit, and snook on the shallow flats between the mainland and the reef. Sailfish, wahoo, marlin, and barracuda abound farther out to sea. Several specialty resorts and fishing camps, such as Turneffe Flats and El Pescador, cater to the angler, but most hotels can help you organize excellent fishing trips. You'll need a fishing license for most sportfishing in Belize (except off piers and shores); your hotel or fishing guide can arrange it for you. In some marine reserves where fishing is allowed usage fees are also charged.

■ **Ambergris Caye and Caye Caulker.** There's good saltwater fishing on the northern cayes—look for bonefish, permit, and tarpon.

■ **Glover's Atoll.** Shallow tidal flats around the atoll make for plenty of bonefish; there's also permit, jack, and barracuda.

■ **Placencia.** If you don't want to pay the big bucks that the resorts charge farther north, head here. Budget hotels start around BZ$50 a night. Permit's the number one catch inside the reef, or cast a line in the lagoon or the deep sea beyond the reef.

■ **Punta Gorda.** If you're serious about fishing, this is a great place to be. There's world-famous permit fishing.

■ **Turneffe Atoll.** Bonefish, tarpon, permit, snappers, jacks, barracuda, wahoo, dorado, and billfish all ply the waters.

Caving

One of the most exciting ways to tour Belize is to head underground—there are hundreds of caves all over the country. You can canoe down subterranean rivers in some, ducking under low-hanging stalactites while keeping your eyes trained for Mayan artifacts. The easiest caves to visit are in Cayo; you don't need a guide to visit open caverns such as Rio Frio and the entrance to St. Herman's. Before you head out to cave, make sure to find out whether it's open to the public, whether you need a guide, and, if the cave has a river, whether the water level is low enough for visitors.

■ **Actun Tunichil Muknal.** Go here for amazing limestone formations, many undisturbed Mayan artifacts, and calcified human remains. It's the top caving experience in Belize. A specially licensed guide must accompany you.

■ **Barton Creek Cave.** Canoe about a mile on an underground river through Barton Cave, which has some Mayan artifacts and skeletal remains.

■ **Caves Branch Caves.** The Caves Branch River cave system has become a popular place for cave tubing.

■ **Che Chem Ha.** This cave, once used by the Maya for grain storage and ceremonial rituals, is on private land about 25 minutes from San Ignacio in the Vaca Plateau.

■ **Hokeb Ha.** Blue Creek Cave (as it's known in English), near Blue Creek village, is Toledo's answer to Actun Tunichil Muknal, with vaulted limestone chambers and underground waterfalls.

■ **Rio Frio Cave.** Though it's more a natural tunnel than a cave, it's still worth a visit for its large entryway and path above the Cold River.

Scuba Diving and Snorkeling

Don your scuba or snorkeling gear and soak up the cast of aquatic characters offshore and around the Barrier Reef. One moment you may come upon an enormous spotted eagle ray; the next you may find the feisty little damselfish, a bolt of blue no bigger than your little finger. Bloated blowfish hover in their holes; barracuda patrol the depths; and queen angelfish shimmy through the water with puckered lips and haughty self-assurance. Graceful sea fans and great chunks of staghorn coral add to the exhilarating underwater experience.

■ **Blue Hole.** The underwater sinkhole, one of the most famous dives in Belize, forms a perfectly round, deep blue circle.

■ **Glover's Reef.** This is probably the least visited yet arguably most pristine dive and snorkel area in Belize. You can see nurse sharks and manta rays and go wreck diving.

■ **Hol Chan Marine Reserve.** Snorkel with nurse sharks and stingrays at Shark-Ray Alley and keep your eyes peeled for moray eels in the reserve.

■ **Sapodilla Cayes.** Fringe reefs and patch reefs in shallow water around the cayes support tropical fish like spadefish and parrot fish.

■ **South Water Caye.** If you want to shore snorkel, come here. The beach is sandy, and the island is one of Belize's most beautiful.

■ **Turneffe Islands.** Mangroves line a shallow lagoon, creating a rich nursery for sea life where snorkelers and divers alike can see reef sharks, dolphins, eagle rays, moray eels, and turtles.

GREAT ITINERARIES

RUINS, RAIN FORESTS, AND REEF

Sample the best of all that Belize offers—ruins, rain forests, and reef—in only seven or eight days. If you have only five days, shave off some time in the Cayo and head to Actun Tunichil Muknal on Day 2 instead of Day 3.

Day 1: Arrival

Fly into the international airport near **Belize City** and immediately head out to the **Cayo** in western Belize, about two hours by road from the airport. Stay at one of the superb jungle lodges, such as the Lodge at Chaa Creek, Mystic River Resort, or duPlooy's, or, for less money, Black Rock, Table Rock, or Crystal Paradise.

Logistics: The best way to see the mainland is by rental car. Pick up a car at one of the car-rental agencies in kiosks just across the main parking lot at the international airport. If you'd rather not drive, you can arrange a shuttle van, take a bus, or ask your hotel in the Cayo to pick you up. Buses don't come to the international airport—if you're taking one, you have to take a taxi into town (BZ$50 for two persons). Tropic Air has service from Belize City to the Maya Flats airstrip between San Ignacio and Benque Viejo.

Day 2: Exploring the Cayo

On your first full day in Belize, get out and explore San Ignacio and the beautiful hill country around the Cayo. Among the top attractions are the small but interesting Mayan ruins at Xunantunich and Cahal Pech, Green Hills Butterfly Farm, the Rainforest Medicine Trail at Chaa Creek, and the Belize Botanical Gardens at duPlooy's. Save a little time for walking around and shopping in San Ignacio.

After a full day of exploring, have cocktails and dinner at your lodge.

Logistics: You can do all the main attractions and San Ignacio in one day if you have a rental car and if you don't dawdle. Sans car, you can hire a taxi for the day, or opt for your hotel's tours.

Day 3: Actun Tunichil Muknal (ATM)

Prepare to be wowed by the ultimate cave experience. Go into the mysterious and beautiful Mayan underworld and see untouched artifacts dating back thousands of years.

Logistics: You must have a guide for ATM, so book your trip the day before with an authorized tour guide company. It's an all-day event, and you'll get wet—bring a change of clothes and wear walking shoes, not sandals. Also, bring socks for walking through the cave. If you're badly out of shape or have mobility or claustrophobia issues, this isn't a tour for you. You have to hike several miles, swim a little, and clamber through the dark. Photography in the cave is not permitted.

Day 4: Tikal

Tikal, very simply, is the most awe-inspiring Mayan site in all of Central America, rivaling the pyramids of Egypt and the ruins of Angor Wat in Cambodia. It's well worth at least two days and nights, preferably staying in one of the three lodges at the park, but even on a day tour you'll get a sense of the majesty of this Classic-period city.

Logistics: Although you can go on your own, the easiest and most stress-free way to see Tikal is on a tour from San Ignacio—you'll leave around 6:30 am and return in the late afternoon; lunch is usually included. Overnight and multinight tours also are available.

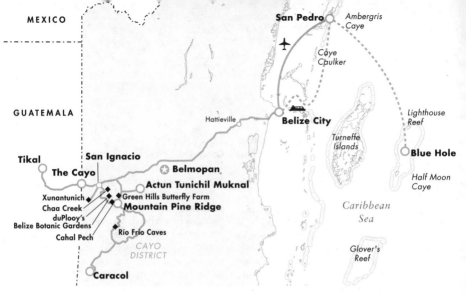

Day 5: Caracol and the Mountain Pine Ridge

A terrific day trip is to Caracol, the most important Mayan site in Belize. The trip there is part of the fun—you bump along winding roads through the Mountain Pine Ridge, past the Macal River, and through broadleaf jungle. If you've seen enough Mayan ruins, skip Caracol and spend the day exploring the Mountain Pine Ridge—there's the Río Frio cave and numerous waterfalls. A bonus: the higher elevation here means it's cooler and less humid than other parts of Belize. If you don't mind packing and unpacking again, for your last night in Cayo consider switching to one of the four lodges in the Pine Ridge. Our favorites are Blancaneaux and Hidden Valley Inn.

Logistics: From Blancaneaux or Hidden Valley it's less than a two-hour drive to Caracol, and about an hour longer from most lodges around San Ignacio. The road can be near-impassable after heavy rains, and there have been some incidents with bandits from Guatemala, so check locally for the latest conditions and cautions.

Alternative: If you tire of rain forest and ruins, and long for the sea, head a day early to San Pedro or Caye Caulker.

Day 6: San Pedro

Return to Belize City by plane, car, bus, or shuttle van. Then fly or take a water taxi to San Pedro (Ambergris Caye) for fabulous eating (our favorites include El Fogon, Finn and Martini, Rain, Casa Picasso, Robin's Kitchen for low-cost local cooking, and, for breakfast with your feet in the sand, Estel's). Try to arrive early enough to do a snorkel trip to Hol Chan/Shark-Ray Alley.

Alternative: San Pedro's a bustling town, so if you want a more laid-back and less-expensive experience on the water, stay on Caye Caulker instead. You still have access to the same snorkel and dive sites, with less costly hotels and restaurants, and sandy streets with no cars.

Day 7: Blue Hole

Take a day trip to dive or snorkel the Blue Hole at Lighthouse Reef atoll. Dive boats also stop at Half Moon Caye for other dives (or snorkeling) besides the Blue Hole.

Logistics: A trip to the Blue Hole involves a full day on the water, so bring seasickness medicine, a hat, and plenty of sunscreen. Dive boats to Lighthouse leave early, usually before 7 am.

Alternative: If you're not up to the time and expense required for a trip to the Blue Hole, there's excellent diving on the Barrier Reef just a short boat ride from San Pedro or Caye Caulker.

■TIP→ **Some dive organizations recommend a minimum 24-hour interval between a dive and a flight, so if you're flying out early the next day consider diving earlier in your trip, or snorkel instead. Also, the Blue Hole is a deep dive recommended only for more experienced divers.**

Day 8: Departure
Return to Belize City by plane or water taxi for your international flight.

Logistics: Plan on arriving at least two hours ahead of your international flight. There's often long lines at security.

MAYAN SITES BLITZ

If you want to see the top Mayan sites in one trip, base yourself in the Cayo. If after a few days in western Belize and Guatemala you still haven't had your fill, you can add extensions to northern Belize and to Punta Gorda in southern Belize. *Information on tour operators and guides, and on admissions to specific sites, is in destination chapters.*

Day 1: San Ignacio
San Ignacio is an easy jumping-off spot for seeing several small but fascinating nearby ruins. If you get an early start, you can take in **Xunantunich, Cahal Pech,** and **El Pilar.** Both Cahal Pech and Xunantunich can be reached by bus (albeit with a short hike after the bus ride in both cases), but a taxi or rental car is needed to get to El Pilar. Guided tours of all these sites can be arranged in San Ignacio or at lodges and hotels in the area. *(See The Cayo,* ⇨ *Chapter 5)*

Day 2: Caracol
Caracol, the most important Mayan site in Belize, deserves a full day. You can drive yourself—or go on a tour. There is no bus transportation in the Mountain Pine Ridge. Even if you arrive independently, you can hire a guide to show you around once you're at the site, or you can tour it on your own. There's an informative museum and visitor center. Due to a series of bandit incidents, trips to Caracol are being done in convoys, protected by Belize Defence Forces soldiers. Check locally for updates. *(See The Cayo,* ⇨ *Chapter 5)*

Days 3 and 4: Tikal
Tikal is by far the most impressive Mayan site in the region and shouldn't be missed (check in advance about travel warnings to the area). Many operators offer day tours of Tikal from the San Ignacio area. *(See El Petén,* ⇨ *Chapter 8)*

Tips
Altun Ha, the ruin closest to Belize City, gets crowds of cruise-ship day-trippers; try to avoid days when there are several cruise ships in port.

Before heading anywhere remote by yourself, check with the locals to find out if there have been any recent safety issues.

On your visit to Tikal, stay at one of the three lodges at the park—you'll be able to visit the ruins early in the morning or late in the afternoon, when howler monkeys and other animals are active and most day visitors have left. If you can't overnight at Tikal, do a day tour from San Ignacio; there also are daily flights from Belize City to Flores near Tikal.

Bring bug repellent. Mosquitoes are especially bad around **Cerro Maya** in northern Belize, at **Marco Gonzalez** on Ambergris Caye, and at the ruins near Punta Gorda.

FAQ'S

Is Belize a safe place to visit? The best answer is "Yes, but." Most visitors say they feel quite safe in Belize (except, they say, in some areas of Belize City's South Side, especially after dark). Tourist Police patrol areas of Belize City, Placencia, Ambergris Caye, and elsewhere, and many hotels and jungle lodges have security guards. Out of the hundreds of thousands of visitors annually, the number who are victims of any kind of crime, mostly petty theft, is perhaps a few hundred. So, while this is still a developing country, enjoy yourself and follow standard travel precautions: Don't wander into areas that don't feel safe; avoid deserted beaches and streets after dark; and don't flash expensive jewelry or cash. Be aware that there have been a few carjackings and robberies on remote roads or at little-visited parks and Mayan sites; travel in a group or with a guide to less popular places.

Should I stay at an all-inclusive? Although Belize is not an all-inclusive kind of destination, some beach resorts and jungle lodges offer a tweaked version of the sort of all-inclusive you often find in Mexico or Jamaica: optional packages that include nearly everything, such as all meals, guided tours, and sports (fishing, diving, or snorkeling). So when is it worth your money to choose one of these over selecting room, meals, and activities à la carte?

The answer is: It depends. If you're going to a remote caye resort or jungle lodge, you may not have a choice. When you're two hours away from the nearest restaurant, you're pretty much stuck eating at your hotel. On the other hand, at a destination such as Ambergris Caye, Caye Caulker, Placencia, Hopkins, or San Ignacio, there are many excellent restaurants to choose from. Even in less-visited areas such as Corozal and Punta Gorda, you'll find good, affordable food. It would be a shame to lock yourself into a single dining experience. A few resorts on Ambergris Caye, mainly those located on the far north end of the island (a long boat ride away from San Pedro), do offer all-inclusive or near all-inclusive packages; however, for most people, one of the main reasons for coming to Ambergris Caye is the opportunity to sample the variety of restaurants.

The main advantage of an all-inclusive or mostly inclusive package is that you don't have to worry about the details of travel planning. Once you've paid your fixed price, all you have to do is show up at the airport with your bags packed. The resort or lodge picks you up at the Belize International Airport, takes you on guided tours, provides your meals, and practically holds your hand. It's almost like being on a cruise, with few decisions to make. If you're the type of person who likes an organized travel experience, an AI or semi-AI package could be a good bet for you.

Before you book, be sure to total up the value of what you expect to get at the all-inclusive, and compare that with what you probably would pay on an à la carte basis.

Are the beaches in Belize nice? Although there are lovely stretches of beaches, many of them are not as good for swimming or sunbathing as the wide, sandy beaches of the main Caribbean or of Mexico's Yucatán. Belizean beaches are usually narrow ribbons of sand with clear but shallow water, sea grass, and an often-mucky sea floor. The best beaches on the mainland are on the Placencia Peninsula and in the

Hopkins area. Ambergris Caye has some beautiful beaches, though swimming isn't always good. South Water Caye and Belize's three atolls have excellent (nearly deserted) beaches as well. Beach resorts keep their beach areas clean, but elsewhere you may see garbage on the beach, brought in by the tides from other areas and from boats.

Why are airfares to Belize so high, and how can we find cheaper flights? Belize is not a mass-market tourist destination. While new carriers have begun serving Belize, air service is still limited, and it is mostly from a few hubs in the United States. Charter flights are rare, so fares tend to stay high. To find the most affordable flights, stay flexible on your dates, check the meta-fare comparison websites such as Kayak.com, avoid peak holiday travel (around Christmas and Easter), and sign up for Internet specials and email fare alerts on the airlines flying internationally to Belize—currently United, American, Delta, Avianca, Southwest, Copa, WestJet, and a small Belize carrier, Tropic Air. Another option is to fly into Cancún, which usually has good air deals, bus to Chetumal at the Mexico-Belize border, and water taxi or bus from there, or alternatively fly Tropic Air from Cancun International to Belize International. The other option is the ADO Express overnight service from Cancún to Corozal Town, Orange Walk Town, and Belize City.

While traveling around the country, should we rent a car, take a bus, fly, or hire a taxi? Each has advantages and disadvantages. With a rental car you go when and where you want, including remote areas that don't have air or bus service or to sites that would otherwise require an expensive guided tour. However, auto rental costs are high, and gas is around BZ$10–BZ$12 a gallon. Buses provide a true local experience, and fares are dirt cheap, but buses mainly run on the major roads and stop frequently to pick up and drop off passengers. Buses—usually old U.S. school buses—take up to twice as long as a private car. Flying is the fastest way to get around the country; service is frequent on most routes, and the views from low altitudes are often dramatic. The downside? Fares—especially if you're traveling with a family—can add up, and not all destinations have service. In some cases, transfers by taxi can be an option, although taxis generally are quite expensive. For most long-distance trips there are no set fares, so the rate is a matter of negotiation and can vary considerably, depending on your bargaining skills. Drivers may also ask a little more if there are three or four going together, rather than just one or two. Expect to pay around BZ$3 a mile for longer taxi trips in Belize. Shuttles are another option, especially on popular routes such as between the international airport and San Ignacio, where shared shuttles operating on a fixed schedule are BZ$70 per person and up, and private shuttles leaving anytime range from around BZ$180 to BZ$200, and up, for up to three persons.

We want to spend time at the beach and also in the jungle. Where should we go? On a first and relatively brief visit to Belize, sample the best "surf and turf" by splitting your time between one of the popular beach areas—Ambergris Caye, Caye Caulker, Hopkins, or Placencia—and the rest in the Cayo, which has the largest concentration of popular mainland activities.

TOP MAYAN SITES

The following are our picks for the most notable Mayan sites in Belize. *See the destination chapters for detailed information on the sites, including hours and admission fees.* Fees at most sites for non-Belizeans are BZ$10–BZ$20, and Actun Tunichil Muknal is BZ$50. Admission fees are in addition to any fees for guides, tours, or transportation.

Northern Belize

Altun Ha. The most visited Mayan site in Belize, though not the most impressive, is popular with cruise-ship passengers and for those staying on Ambergris Caye or Caye Caulker. It's a little more than an hour's drive north of Belize City. One of the temples at Altun Ha is prominently pictured on Belikin beer bottles.

Cerro Maya. Although the few remaining original structures here are weathered, Cerro Maya—like Tulum in the Yucatán—enjoys a glorious location right beside the water. There's now a visitor center here.

Chan Chich. The lodge of the same name was built literally on top of this minor ceremonial site. It can be reached by car or charter flight and is best visited in connection with a stay at the lodge.

Nim Li Punit. This site, just off the Southern Highway north of Punta Gorda, has more than two dozen stelae, some unfinished, raising the mystery of why the site was abandoned suddenly.

Marco Gonzalez. This 2,100-year-old site on the southern end of Ambergris Caye, 5.5 miles (9 km) south of San Pedro, is the first Mayan site national park on a Belize island. There's a small education and visitor center. Access to the site is via a rough boardwalk over mangrove swamp—bring lots of mosquito spray.

La Milpa. The third-largest Mayan site in Belize (only Caracol and Lamanai are larger), La Milpa is in the early stages of exploration and excavation. It can be visited through advance arrangement with Programme for Belize, on whose land it sits.

Lamanai. Boat your way up the New River to the shores of the New River Lagoon to see this ruin, which has the most beautiful setting of any Mayan site in Belize. You also can reach it by road from Orange Walk Town. Lamanai has a small museum and a resident troop of howler monkeys.

Caracol. You simply can't miss the largest and most important Maya site in Belize. It's an all-day trip from San Ignacio through the Mountain Pine Ridge, but it's well worth the time. There's a museum and visitor center, and extensive excavations have been under way for more than 30 years. Hurricane Earl in 2016 knocked down a lot of trees but didn't damage the main structures.

Santa Rita. Corozal Town is built on what was the large Mayan trading center known as Chactemal (or Chetumal, as the capital of Quintana Roo, Mexico, is known today). A part of the ruins, now called Santa Rita, is on a hill on the outskirts of Corozal. The Belize government is trying to promote Santa Rita by transforming it into the "Official Mayan Wedding Garden of Belize."

The Cayo

Actun Tunichil Muknal. "ATM," near Belmopan, provides the most rewarding Mayan cave experience in Belize, and indeed in the entire region. Many visitors say it is the highlight of all their travels in Central America. To see the cave, you have to take a 45-minute hike and a brief swim, and be a part of a guided tour. Only about 30 guides are certified to lead trips to ATM. Photography is no longer permitted.

Barton Creek Cave. You can canoe through part of this 7-mile (11-km) wet-cave system once used by the Maya for human sacrifices. It's about a half hour off the Chiquilbul Road on the way to the Mountain Pine Ridge.

Cahal Pech. This small Late Classic site, with a lovely location on a hill overlooking San Ignacio, is easily accessible from town. It has a little museum.

Caracol. The largest and most significant site in Belize is a must if you're in the Cayo. One of its temples remains the tallest human-made structure in all of Belize. There's a museum and visitor center, and extensive excavations have been under way for decades.

Che Chem Ha. This cave on private land south of Benque Viejo has artifacts dating back 2,000 years.

El Pilar. Set on low hills above the Mopan River at the Guatemalan border is one of the largest sites in Belize, but little of it has been excavated.

Pacbitun. Near San Antonio village on the road to the Mountain Pine Ridge, Pacbitun dates back to at least 1000 BC. It's on private land but is open to the public.

Xunantunich. Although it's not one of the largest sites in Belize, Xunantunich is one of the easiest and most pleasant to visit. To reach it, you cross the Mopan River on a quaint, hand-pulled ferry. There's a well-done museum and visitor center. It's off the Western Highway, west of San Ignacio.

Southern Belize

Lubaantun. Occupied for less than 200 years in the Late Classic period, Lubaantun is unusual in that no stelae were ever found here, and the precisely fitted building stones, laid without mortar, have rounded corners. The controversial "Crystal Skull" supposedly was found here. Lubaantun is near San Pedro Columbia village, about 20 miles (32 km) from Punta Gorda.

Mayflower. This Classic-period site, off the Southern Highway just south of Dangriga, is in the early stages of excavation. Waterfalls nearby make the setting appealing.

Nim Li Punit. Off the Southern Highway north of Punta Gorda is Nim Li Punit ("Big Hat" in Ketchi), a small but pretty site. There's a visitor center.

Uxbenká. The paving of the San Antonio Road, which passes nearby, now makes this site much more accessible.

Pusilha. At a site near Aguacate Village on the Moho River is this collection of extensive but low-lying structures on a small hill. Also visible are the remains of a stone bridge. It is officially closed to the public, though you can ask locally to see it. Because of its remote location off the main highway, there aren't many visitors who make the trip out here.

El Petén, Guatemala

Tikal. Along with Copán in Honduras and Palenque in Mexico, Tikal is considered by many to be the most impressive of all Mayan sites. The Petén area is home to several other ruins, including **Nakúm, El Ceibal, Uaxactún, Yaxhá, Yaxchilán, El Zotz,** and **El Mirador.** Some, like El Mirador, are extremely remote, requiring a multiday jungle trek.

PLANNING YOUR ADVENTURE

These days more travelers than ever are seeking trips with an active or adventure component, and tour operators are responding with an ever-increasing selection of exciting itineraries. Belize, with its opportunities for many different kinds of activities, is at the leading edge of the adventure-travel trend.

In Belize you can select something easy, like cave tubing, snorkeling, fishing, horseback riding, hiking, birding, wildlife-spotting, and canoeing. Or you can go for jungle trekking, caving, windsurfing, sea kayaking, or mountain-biking expeditions that require higher degrees of physical endurance and, in some cases, considerable technical skill. You can rough it or opt for comfortable, sometimes even luxurious, accommodations; put adventure at the center of your trip or make it only a sideline; go for a multiweek package or only a day trip. Study multiple itineraries and packages to find the trip that's right for you.

Choosing a tour package carefully is always important, but it becomes even more critical when the focus is adventure or sports. When wisely chosen, special-interest vacations lead to distinctive, memorable experiences—just pack your curiosity along with the bug spray.

Belize Tourism Board. For information about a specific activity, destination, lodging, or transportation option within Belize, contact the Belize Tourism Board, a department of the Belize Ministry of Tourism. ✉ *64 Regent St., Belize City* ☎ *800/624–0686 toll-free from U.S. and Canada, 227/2420 in Belize* ⊕ *www.travelbelize.org.*

Choosing a Trip

With dozens of options for special-interest and adventure tours in Belize, including do-it-yourself or fully guided package trips, it's helpful to think about certain factors when deciding which company or package will be right for you.

■ **Are you interested in adventure travel on the sea or the mainland or both?** Belize offers two very different adventure environments: the sea and the mainland. The Caribbean, various bays and lagoons, the Barrier Reef that runs 185 miles (303 km) along the eastern coast of the country, and three South Pacific–style atolls are perfect for activities such as fishing, sailing, diving, snorkeling, and windsurfing. Inland, you can rappel hundreds of feet into a limestone sinkhole, explore an underworld labyrinth of caves full of Mayan artifacts, hike the rain forest, ride horses or bikes to remote waterfalls, or tube down underground rivers. Some travelers prefer to concentrate on either water or land activities, but you can combine the two. Just be sure to give yourself enough time.

■ **How strenuous a trip do you want?** Adventure vacations commonly are split into "soft" and "hard" adventures. Hard adventures, such as strenuous jungle treks and extended caving trips, usually require excellent physical conditioning and previous experience. Most hiking, biking, canoeing, kayaking, cave tubing, snorkeling, brief cave tours, and similar soft adventures can be enjoyed by persons of all ages who are in good health and are accustomed to a reasonable amount of exercise. A little honesty goes a long way—recognize your own level of physical fitness and discuss it with the tour operator before signing on. Keep in mind that for most of the year in Belize you'll face hot weather and high humidity, conditions that can take a lot out of you, even if you're in good shape.

■ **Would you like to pick up new skills?** Belize is a great place to pick up new skills, whether it's how to paddle a kayak, how to rappel down a cliff face, or how to dive. For example, you can take a quick resort diving course to see if you like scuba, or you can do a complete open-water certification course, usually in three to four days. Before committing to any program, do some research to confirm that the people running it are qualified. Check to see if the dive shop or resort is certified by one of the well-known international dive organizations, such as the Professional Association of Diving Instructors (PADI), the largest certification agency in the world, or National Association of Underwater Instructors (NAUI), the second largest. Among the other how-to programs or lessons offered in Belize are kayaking, horseback riding, snorkeling, kitesurfing, and windsurfing.

■ **Do you want an "off-the-shelf" tour package or do you prefer to build your own trip?** You can opt to buy a prepackaged adventure or special-interest trip, complete with full-time guides who will do everything from meeting your international flight to cooking your meals, or you can go the more independent route, arranging local guides or tour operators on a daily, or even hourly, basis. Because English is the official language in Belize and most tour operators have email and websites, it's easy to put together an adventure package à la carte. Many package tour operators also offer you the ability to combine two or more trips or to create a custom itinerary. It all comes down to whether you're happier doing it yourself or having someone else take care of all the logistics and details.

■ **How far off the beaten path do you want to go?** As one of the least densely populated countries in the hemisphere—more than two-fifths of the country is devoted to nature reserves and national parks—Belize offers many off-the-beaten-path experiences. Although many trips described here might seem to be headed into uncharted territory, tour operators carefully check each detail before an itinerary goes into a brochure. You won't usually be vying with busloads of tourists for photo ops, but you'll probably run into occasional small groups of like-minded travelers. Journeys into truly remote regions, such as Victoria Peak in the Maya Mountains, typically involve camping or the simplest of accommodations, but they reward with more abundant wildlife and locals who are less accustomed to the clicking of cameras.

■ **What sort of group is best for you?** At its best, group travel offers curious, like-minded companions with which to share the day's experiences. Do you enjoy mixing with people from similar backgrounds, or would you prefer to travel with people of different ages and backgrounds? Inquire about group size; many companies have a maximum of 10 to 16 members, but 30 or more is not unknown. The larger the group, the more time spent (or wasted) at rest stops, meals, and hotel arrivals and departures.

If groups aren't your thing, most companies will customize a trip for you. In fact, this has become a major part of many tour operators' businesses. Your itinerary can be as flexible or as rigid as you choose. Such travel offers all the conveniences of a package tour, but the "group" is composed of only you and those you've chosen as travel companions. Responding to a renewed interest in multigenerational travel, many tour operators also offer family trips, with itineraries carefully crafted to appeal both to children and adults.

Money Matters

■ **How much are you willing to spend?** Tours in Central America can be found at all price points, and Belize has an adventure for every budget. Local operators are usually the best deal. Tours that are run by as many local people and resources as possible are generally cheaper, and also give the greatest monetary benefit to the local economy. These types of tours are not always listed in guidebooks or on the Internet, so often they have to be found in person or by word of mouth. Safety and date specificity can fluctuate. Amenities such as lodging and transportation may be very basic in this category. Some agencies pay attention to the environment, whereas others do not. You really have to do your research on every operator, no matter the cost, to be sure you get what you need. When you find the right match, the payoff in terms of price and quality of experience will be worth it.

On the other end of the spectrum, the large (often international) tour agencies are generally the most expensive; however, they provide the greatest range of itinerary choices and highest quality of services. They use the best transportation, like private tour buses and boats, which rarely break down. First-rate equipment and safe, reliable guides are the norm. Dates and times are set in stone, so you can plan your trip down to the time you step in and out of the airport. Guides are certified, and well paid. When food and lodging is provided it is generally of high quality. If you are a traveler who likes to have every creature comfort provided for, look for tour operators more toward this end of the spectrum.

■ **Are there hidden costs?** Make sure you know what is and is not included in basic trip costs when comparing companies. International airfare is usually extra. Sometimes domestic flights in-country are, too. Is trip insurance required, and if so, is it included? Are airport transfers included? Visa fees, if any? Departure taxes? Gratuities? Although some travelers prefer the option of an excursion or free time, many, especially those visiting a destination for the first time, want to see as much as possible. Paying extra for a number of excursions can significantly increase the total cost of the trip. Many factors affect the price, and the trip that looks cheapest in the brochure could well turn out to be the most expensive. Don't assume that roughing it will save you money, as prices rise when limited access and a lack of essential supplies on-site require costly special arrangements.
■TIP→ **Tour prices operated by companies in Belize incur a 12.5% Goods and Services Tax. In some cases, the GST is not included in the tour prices shown (though technically it should be included).**

VOLUNTEERING IN BELIZE

Want to help others less fortunate than you? Want to make the world a better place? Then you may want to investigate volunteer opportunities in Belize. There are basically three kinds of volunteer opportunities available:

Church and mission trips. This typically involves a week to several weeks of volunteer work in a medical or dental clinic, or building churches or homes, or other hands-on assistance. Usually these volunteer groups are based outside Belize, often at a church or school or as a part of a local medical society. In most cases, volunteers pay for their own transportation to Belize, along with personal expenses in the country, but food and lodging may be provided by the mission. Your best bet is to contact your church, college, or local medical society and ask if they know of upcoming mission trips to Belize.

Independent volunteering. Find a worthwhile organization and volunteer your services. Conservation organizations, churches, libraries, medical clinics, humane societies, and schools are among those that may welcome volunteers. You typically won't receive any lodging or food in return for your volunteer activities. To arrange this kind of independent volunteer work, you usually need to be in Belize and make personal contact with the organization you are seeking to help.

Organized volunteer programs. These volunteer programs often revolve around conservation, such as working with wildlife or reef preservation. A few programs offer volunteer opportunities in education, animal care, or social work. Some programs require volunteers to pay a placement fee, which can be several hundred U.S. dollars or more, plus pay for room, board, and transportation to Belize. In other programs, volunteers do not pay a fee and they may receive food and lodging in exchange for their volunteer work, but they usually have to pay transportation and incidental expenses out of pocket. For longer-term volunteering, consider the U.S. Peace Corps, which currently has more than 30 volunteers here.

Some organizations that accept volunteers in Belize:

Belize Audubon Society (*BAS*). The Belize Audubon Society is the oldest and largest conservation group in Belize. It manages seven protected areas and parks in Belize and accepts qualified volunteers to assist in its park management, conservation, tourism development, and other programs. The BAS usually requires a minimum three-month commitment for its overseas volunteers working inland, and one month for volunteers in the marine program. Although the BAS prefers to partner with universities to get its interns, it does also accept individual volunteer applications. The BAS does not pay for lodging or living expenses. ⊠ *12 Fort St., Fort George* ☎ *223/5004 in Belize City* ⊕ *www.belizeaudubon.org* ✉ *Varies by location.*

Belize Botanic Gardens. Belize Botanic Gardens, 45 acres of tropical gardens at duPlooy's Lodge near San Ignacio, accepts occasional interns for field work in fields such as ethnobotany, botany, environmental science, environmental education, and tropical ecology, and also volunteers who have skills in horticulture, organic agriculture, landscape design and related fields. Volunteers pay a fee for food and lodging. ⊠ *Big Eddy, Chial Rd., duPlooy's Lodge, San Ignacio* ☎ *824/3101* ⊕ *www.belize-botanic.org.*

Belize Zoo and Tropical Education Center. The Belize Zoo, one of the great conservation organizations in Central America, and the associated Tropical Education Center have a wide range of education and outreach programs. A few motivated volunteers/interns are accepted to assist Belize Zoo and TEC programs. The zoo says it's looking for interns to help guide and teach Belizean students, to help manage the animals, and in certain professional and skill areas. Internships are usually two to four weeks in length. The zoo provides food and accommodations, but interns pay a weekly fee of US$300. To apply, at least eight weeks in advance send a letter of inquiry by mail, fax, or email indicating your reasons for applying, areas of interest, education, and experience, and a medical certificate from a physician with your health status. ⊠ *Mile 29, George Price Hwy., Belmopan* ☎ *822/8000* ⊕ *www. belizezoo.org.*

Cornerstone Foundation. This nonprofit's programs include cultural, community service, office work, HIV/AIDS outreach, construction, natural healing, and community volunteer programs in Cayo District. Volunteers commit for a minimum of one week and up to three months. For longer programs, individuals pay US$585 a month for bunk-style housing and food. Fees for one-week programs start at US$199. Volunteers at Cornerstone must have medical insurance. ⊠ *27 Far West St., San Ignacio* ☎ *667/0210* ⊕ *www.cornerstonefoundationbelize.org.*

Monkey Bay Wildlife Sanctuary. Monkey Bay is a private wildlife sanctuary and environmental education center on 1,060 acres near the Belize Zoo, with satellite campuses in the Mountain Pine Ridge and on Tobacco Caye. It has some volunteer intern opportunities in conservation and community service. Volunteers are expected to work about 30 hours a week. Monkey Bay also offers education programs on ecology, first aid, and natural history for students and others, ranging from a few days to more than a month. These education programs have various fees. In addition, Monkey Bay rents rustic accommodations to visitors. ⊠ *Mile 31.5 George Price Hwy., Belmopan* ☎ *822/8032* ⊕ *www. belizestudyabroad.net.*

Plenty Belize. Plenty Belize, an independent sister organization of Plenty International, has been working in Belize since 1990. It's currently helping the Maya and Garifuna communities in Toledo District with agriculture, school gardens, health, nutrition, solar energy, women's development, micro-enterprise, and education programs. Contact Plenty for current needs, as programs in Belize change from year to year. Volunteers have to pay their own expenses, including transportation to the project site and living expenses while in Belize. ⊠ *Plenty International, Punta Gorda* ☎ *931/964–4323 in U.S., 722/2198 Plenty contact in Belize* ⊕ *www. plenty.org.*

Ecotourism in Belize

Central America is one of the original ecotourism destinations; as a result, you'll see the term used liberally. For lodging it can be used to describe a deluxe private cabana on a well-tended beach or a hut in the middle of nowhere with pit toilets. It may also point to environmental conservation efforts by parks or tour companies that are conscious of natural resources and their role in not depleting them. Or it may mean just the opposite. Wildlife parks, butterfly farms, rain forests, and Mayan ruins are some of the incredible eco-destinations in Belize. Mountain biking, bird-watching, jungle hiking, scuba diving, cave tubing, fishing, and white-water rafting are just some of the eco-activities.

You can do your part to protect the natural heritage of Belize and the Tikal area of Guatemala by being an ecologically sensitive traveler. Where possible, choose green hotels, those that have taken care to protect the environment and that have energy-efficient cooking, lighting, and cooling systems, and that recycle and dispose of waste responsibly. Among these lodges and hotels are Hickatee Cottages near Punta Gorda; duPlooy's Lodge, Table Rock Jungle Lodge, and The Lodge at Chaa Creek near San Ignacio; Blancaneaux Lodge in the Mountain Pine Ridge; and Hamanasi on the beach in Hopkins. Be culturally sensitive, as both countries have highly diverse populations, each with different cultural attitudes and perspectives. Also, try to do business with companies that hire local people for positions at all levels, and where possible choose local restaurants and hotels over chain properties. When diving or snorkeling, avoid touching or breaking coral. Don't take part in swim-with-dolphins or swim-with-manatees tours, and don't touch nurse sharks or stingrays (even if your guide invites you to do so). Most naturalists say these programs disturb the animals. Also, use eco-friendly sunscreen. On caving or hiking trips, take nothing but photographs and leave nothing of yours behind. When visiting Mayan sites, never remove anything, not even a tiny shard of pottery.

For the most part, Belize has reaped the benefits of the growing tourism industry, drawing in much-needed capital to bolster national coffers. Without taxes and revenues from tourism, now the largest sector of the Belize economy, the government of Belize would be broke, unable to fund basic national services. The costs of tourism are less obvious, however. Among other effects, indigenous communities are undermined by increasingly tourist-oriented economies—cultivating a plot of land may no longer support a family, but selling knickknacks in the streets just might. Where tourists come, expats often follow, and land, especially beachfront land, is quickly priced out of the reach of locals. Mass cruise tourism is a particular problem; Belize gets three times as many day-trippers from cruise ships as it does overnight visitors, and cruise passengers outnumber Belize residents by three to one. On days when several large cruise ships are in port, thousands of cruise passengers overwhelm fragile environments in rivers, caves, reef areas, and at archeological sites. It is mostly only a handful of local businesses, mainly tender boat owners and well-connected tour operators, that benefit financially. The new NCL cruise port on Harvest Caye off Placencia poses a particular risk to the limited infrastructure and resources of southern Belize. There's no easy solution to this dilemma, and balancing the advantages of tourism against its drawbacks is, and will remain, a constant struggle for Belize. The long-term effects are as much dependent on the attitudes and behavior of visitors as they are on prudent national policies.

RETIRING IN BELIZE

So you fell in love with the Belize experience, outdoors and indoors, met some expats who bought their beachfront lot for a song, and want to do the same for your retirement years? Here's the scoop on what you can really expect if you decide to follow suit.

Belize can be enchanting for potential retirees. The climate is frost-free. Land and housing costs are still moderate, especially compared with already popular areas of the Caribbean. The official language is English, and the historical and legal background of the country is more comparable to that of the United States, Canada, and Great Britain than most other parts of Latin America and the Caribbean. Belize has a stable and democratic, if sometimes colorful and corrupt, political tradition. Recreational activities, on land and on the water, are almost limitless.

But there are drawbacks: high costs for imported food, fuel, and household items; high import duties (up to 70% of retail value or higher on imported vehicles); crime and drug problems; culture shock for those unaccustomed to the ways of a semitropical, developing country with a true multicultural society; some resentment of "wealthy" foreigners; plenty of red tape and petty corruption; increasing taxes such as the 12.5% Goods and Services Tax (GST) on everything from refrigerators to cars and restaurant meals; a 5% transfer tax on real estate purchases by foreigners, payable by the buyer (buyers of new or substantially renovated condos or houses also pay 12.5% sales tax, the latter usually built into the sales price); and, most important for many retirees, medical care that in many cases isn't up to first-world snuff.

If retirement or relocation in Belize still sounds like a good choice for you, there are three options to look into:

The Qualified Retired Persons Incentive Program. It's run by the Belize Tourism Board, and anyone at least 45 years old is eligible to participate in the program. It requires a pension, Social Security, or other provable, reliable income of at least US$2,000 a month. A QRP participant (an individual or couple) must deposit US$24,000 a year in a Belize bank. In return, you (and your spouse and minor children) have the right to import household goods, a car, boat, and even an airplane free of import duty. Income generated from outside Belize isn't taxed by Belize. Although as a QRP participant you can't work for pay in Belize, you can own a business or rental properties and have employees who work for you. Hundreds of QRP applications have been approved since the program was started in 2001. It's a wonder that more haven't applied: 75 million baby boomers in the United States alone are expected to retire over the next 20 years. Many of them will be looking for alternatives to cold winters and high prices up north. Contact the Belize Tourism Board for more information ⊕ *www.travelbelize.org.*

Official Permanent Residency. For those not ready to retire, it's still possible to move to Belize, although work permits usually are somewhat difficult to obtain and salaries are a fraction of those in the United States, Canada, or western Europe. The best option may be to invest in or start a business in Belize that employs Belizean workers, thus paving the way for a self-employment work permit and residency.

With official Permanent Residency, you can work in Belize or operate a business, just like any Belizean. You can bring in household goods duty-free. Before you can apply for residency, you need to live in Belize for a year leaving for no more than two weeks. Permanent Residency applications are handled by the Belize Immigration Department and may take a few months to a year for approval. Belize citizenship requires living in Belize for at least five years as a Permanent Resident.

Regular Tourist Permit. Many expats simply stay in Belize on a tourist permit (actually, it's a stamp in your passport). Upon entry, you receive a free visitor permit, good for up to 30 days. This permit can be renewed at any Immigration Office for BZ$50 a month per person for up to six months. After that, renewals cost BZ$100 a month. With a tourist permit, you can't work in Belize. If caught, you could be fined, jailed, and deported. Renewals are never guaranteed, and the rules could change at any time.

Ambergris Caye, the Corozal Town area, Placencia and Hopkins, and Cayo have attracted the largest number of foreign residents, some full time and others snowbirds. Ambergris Caye, the number one choice for expats, has an idyllic Caribbean island atmosphere, but real estate prices here are high. Corozal Town and its environs have among Belize's lowest living costs, and Mexico is right next door. The Cayo appeals to those who want land for growing fruit trees or keeping a few horses. Placencia and Hopkins have some of the best beaches in Belize. More off-the-beaten-path areas, such as Punta Gorda area in Toledo District and parts of northeast Corozal District on the Bay of Chetumal, such as Sarteneja, are beginning to generate interest from foreigners looking for lower stress and more affordable land prices.

The best advice for anyone contemplating retiring or relocating: Try before you buy. If possible, rent an apartment or house for a few months. Be cautious about buying property. Real-estate agents generally aren't licensed or regulated, and because the pool of qualified buyers in Belize is small, it's a lot harder to sell than to buy. Bottom line: Belize isn't for everyone. The country, as seen from the perspective of a resident, isn't the same as the Belize that's experienced by vacationers.

Easy Belize: How to Live, Retire, Work and Buy Property in Belize, the English Speaking, Frost Free Paradise on the Caribbean Coast by Lan Sluder (who authored the first six editions of *Fodor's Belize* and is co-author of the seventh edition), is a 460-page handbook for those considering retiring or relocation in Belize. The writer, with more than 25 years' experience in Belize, interviewed scores of expats and retirees in Belize to help provide readers with a realistic view of the pros and cons of living here.

FLAVORS OF BELIZE

The cuisine of Belize has three major influences: first, the spicy influence of its Latin neighbors and its own multicultural population; second, the influx of tourists with discerning palates who demanded, and eventually got, a higher standard of cooking at hotels and restaurants; and, third, the availability of fish, lobster, and conch fresh from the sea.

Rice and Beans

There is no single Belizean cuisine. Belize dining, like Belize itself, grew out of a gumbo of influences—Mexican, Guatemalan, African, Caribbean, Mayan, Garífuna, English, Chinese, East Indian, and American. The most Belizean of all dishes is rice and beans. Although originally considered a Creole dish, today it's eaten daily by just about everyone. Recipes vary, but most use kidney beans, garlic, coconut milk, onion, and seasonings like black pepper, *recado,* a paste made from annatto seeds and other spices, salt, and thyme. The kidney beans are boiled with seasonings and a little piece of meat—salt pork, pigtail, or pieces of bacon. Then the seasoned beans are cooked together with rice. A related but different dish is beans and rice, which is stewed beans served with white rice on the side, not cooked together as in its sister dish. In many restaurants you'll have a choice of rice and beans or beans and rice. Whatever and wherever you eat, you're likely to find a bottle of **Marie Sharp's** hot sauce on the table. This proud product of Belize—it's bottled near Dangriga—comes in a spectrum of heat, from Mild to Fiery Hot to No Wimps Allowed.

Regional Specialties

Among other Creole specialties are cow-foot soup (yes, made with real cows' hooves), "boil up" (a stew of fish, potatoes, plantains, cassava, and other vegetables, and eggs), and the ubiquitous "stew chicken." Many Creole dishes are cooked in coconut milk and seasoned with red or black *recado.* You'll also find many Mestizo or Latin favorites such as *escabeche* (onion soup, with lime, vinegar, and chicken), *salbutes* (fried corn tortillas with chicken and a topping of tomatoes, onions, and peppers), and the similar *garnaches* (fried tortillas with refried beans, cabbage, and cheese). Many of these homey dishes are sold at street stands, and it's usually very safe to eat at these stands. In Dangriga and Punta Gorda or other Garífuna areas, try dishes such as *sere lasus* (fish soup with plantain balls) or cassava dumplings.

Most local beef is grass-fed. Filets are generally the tenderest option. Belizean pork, however, is superb, and it's rare to get anything but a juicy, delicious pork chop in Belize. Chicken, the most popular meat in Belize, is also good. Most of Belize's chickens—and indeed much of other food, from eggs to cheese to vegetables—are provided by Mennonite farms in Spanish Lookout and elsewhere.

Seafood

On the coast and cayes, seafood is fresh, relatively inexpensive, and delicious. The Caribbean spiny lobster (*Panulirus argus*) is one of Belize's gourmet treats. Unlike its Maine cousin, it lacks claws, and the edible meat is in its tail. It's perfect lightly grilled and served with drawn butter, but you can also enjoy it in fritters, soups, bisques, salads, and even burgers. Lobster season runs from June 15 to February 15. Conch, in season all year except for the months of July, August, and September, also is widely served in Belize, as conch steak, fritters, ceviche, and soup.

On restaurant menus you're most likely to find snapper, snook, and grouper, each tasty without being too fishy. Belizeans themselves often favor barracuda. Farm-raised tilapia is also widely available. Most shrimp are also farm-raised, from one of the large shrimp farms near Placencia and elsewhere.

Belizeans love their ceviche—raw seafood marinated in lime juice. You'll find a variety of ceviche dishes on menus everywhere—conch, shrimp, lobster, fish, and even octopus and squid. Usually the seafood is mixed with onion, hot peppers, salt, and herbs such as cilantro or *culantro* (similar to cilantro but stronger in flavor), and then "cooked" with lime or other citrus juices. It's all delicious!

Fruits and Vegetables

Belize offers a cornucopia of delicious fresh tropical fruits, although unfortunately not too much of the fruit makes its way to restaurant tables. You may have to stop at fruit stands and buy your own. In season, fruits in markets are remarkably inexpensive. For example, you can buy 8 or 10 bananas for BZ$1 or a huge pineapple for BZ$2. Papayas, mangoes, bananas, oranges, cantalopes, and watermelons are the most common fruits served usually on breakfast plates. But the markets have many other kinds of fruit: one is *craboo* or *nance,* a small yellow fruit the size of a cherry, which ripens in July and August. They're excellent mashed and served with milk, or just eaten raw. Markets also have star fruit, soursop, breadfruit, dragon fruit, cashew fruit, and others. Among the best local markets in Belize are those in Corozal Town, Orange Walk Town, Belize City, Belmopan, San Ignacio, Dangriga, and Punta Gorda.

Most operate daily, with Saturday usually being the busiest.

Some uncommon vegetables include *cho cho,* a mild-flavored squash also known as *mirlton* or *chayote.* It's often served raw in salads and also baked, fried, boiled, and stuffed. *Chaya* is a green leafy plant that is sometimes called Mayan spinach. It's often served as cooked greens or in scrambled eggs. A similar, spinach-like green is *callaloo.*

Beer, Wines, and Spirits

The legal drinking age in Belize is 18. Nearly all restaurants serve local brew **Belikin,** lager and stout, and Belikin's sister ale, **Lighthouse.** Due to restrictive import laws, the fine beers of neighboring Mexico and Guatemala are rare, although due to Belize's membership in the Caribbean Community (CARICOM), Red Stripe, Presidente, and Heineken, all brewed in the Caribbean, can be imported into Belize. Many bars offer terrific tropical mixed drinks; a growing number offer wine. Imported liquor is expensive. Several Belize companies distill liquors, primarily rum, which is excellent, but also gin and vodka, which are virtually undrinkable. Also available are a variety of local fruit wines, such as cashew, nance, and soursop. **Travelers "One Barrel" Rum,** with a slight vanilla-caramel flavor, is a favorite. With tonic or cola, it goes for a bargain BZ$4 or BZ$5 in many bars. Imported wines are available in supermarkets and better restaurants, at about twice the price of the same wines in the United States. There are specialty wine stores in Belize City and San Pedro. Cashew, blackberry, and other local wines are available around the country. Beer, wine and liquor are sold in grocery stores in Belize.

BELIZE CITY

By Lan Sluder

Belize City is more of a town than a city—few of the ramshackle buildings here are taller than a palm tree, and the official population within the city limits is barely over 50,000, though the metro population is near 90,000. Not far beyond the city center, streets give way to two-lane country roads where animals outnumber people. Any restaurant downtown could leave the impression that everybody knows everybody else in this town, and certainly among the elite who can afford to dine out, that's probably true.

On a map Belize City appears to be an ideal base for exploring the central part of the country—it's two hours or less by car to San Ignacio, Corozal Town, Dangriga, and even less to Altun Ha, Belmopan, and the Belize Zoo. However, many old Belize hands will advise you to get out of Belize City as quickly as you can. They point to the high crime rate and to drugs and gang activity. They also note the relative lack of attractions in Belize City. There are no good beaches in or near the city, except for one man-made beach at the Old Belize facility west of town, built to attract cruise-ship visitors. Although you can sometimes spot manatees and porpoises in the harbor, and birding around the city is surprisingly good, this is not the wild rain forest visitors come to see.

All of that is true enough, and certainly any visitor to Belize City should take the usual precautions for travel in an impoverished urban area, which includes always taking a cab at night (and in rough parts of the city, anytime), but Belize City does have an energy and excitement to it. There are good restaurants, a vibrant arts community, and, outside some of the rougher parts of town on the South Side, nice residential areas and a number of pleasant hotels and B&Bs. Belize City offers the most varied shopping in the country, and it's the only place to find sizeable supermarkets, department stores, and the Belizean version of big-box stores. There is always some little treasure to be discovered in a shop with mostly junk. All in all, it's far more interesting than any modern mall.

Belize City also has an easygoing sociability. People meet on the street, talk, joke, laugh, and debate. Despite the Belize City streetscape's sometimes sketchy appearance, most people in the shops and on the street tend to be friendly, polite, and helpful.

If you haven't spent time in Belize City, you simply won't understand Belize. Belize City is the commercial, social, sports, and cultural hub of the country. It's even the political hub, despite the fact that the capital, Belmopan, is an hour west. The current prime minister, Dean Barrow, a lawyer who came to power in 2008, former prime ministers including Said Musa, many of the other ministers, and nearly all of the country's movers and shakers live in or near Belize City.

2

TOP REASONS TO GO

Great Photo Ops. Belize City is highly photogenic, full of interesting faces, streets full of color, and charming old colonial houses. In short, Belize City has character.

Colonial Architecture. Belize City rewards the intrepid traveler with a surprising number of interesting sights and memorable places, among them the everyday colonial-era buildings in the Fort George and Southern Foreshore sections, where people still live and work. For the most part, buildings are wood, with tin or zinc roofs. Many are in need of a bit of repair, but they still ooze Caribbean port-of-call atmosphere.

Because You Have To. As a visitor to Belize, you'll almost certainly have to spend a little time in Belize City, whether you like it or not. The international airport is in Ladyville, at the northern edge of the metropolitan area. Belize City is the transportation hub of the country, and most flights, buses, and car rentals originate here. If you're arriving late or leaving early, you'll probably have to overnight in or near the city. Make the best of it. Take care, but explore and enjoy the city.

One longtime Belize resident says that despite its problems she enjoys making day trips to the city and always encourages visitors to spend some time there: "Being a landlubber, I enjoy the boats, seabirds, and smell of the salt air, and of course the Swing Bridge, watching the fishermen on fishing boats sell their fish, and seeing what fish and sea creatures are for sale in the market. When I first came here I was amazed at the fish and meat stalls, at how they were out in the open, and weren't refrigerated like back home. I think it's good for tourists to see that there are other ways of living than what they are used to. Isn't that the point of traveling?"

Still—and we can't overemphasize this—you do have to be careful, as crime is not limited just to certain areas: When you're in Belize City, bring your street smarts and exercise caution at all times.

ORIENTATION AND PLANNING

GETTING ORIENTED

If you're prepared to go beyond a cursory excursion, Belize City will repay your curiosity. There's an infectious sociability on streets like Albert and Queen, the main shopping strips. The finest British colonial houses—graceful white buildings with wraparound verandas, painted shutters, and fussy Victorian woodwork—are in the Fort George area, near the Radisson Fort George, the most pleasant part of the city for a stroll.

Fort George. The "colonial" section of Belize City is notable for its grand, if sometimes dilapidated, old 19th- and early-20th-century homes and buildings.

Marine Parade Harbor Front. Along the water near the Ramada Princess Hotel & Casino and BTL Park, there is more open, public space than there are buildings, making this a pleasant escape from the bustle of the city center.

The Commercial District. On the South Side, mainly on Albert and Regent streets, this is the commercial center of the city. Be advised, however, that it is also near some of the worst slums in Belize.

King's Park. Upscale residences line the streets near Princess Margaret Drive, about 2 miles (3 km) north of the city center.

The Northern Suburbs. Along the Philip Goldson Highway (formerly the Northern Highway) between the city center and the international airport, this is the fastest-growing part of the metropolitan area, with middle-class residential sections such as Buttonwood Bay and Belama, some of the city's stores and supermarkets, and several hotels and B&Bs.

The Western Suburbs. A few tourist attractions have popped up here, such as the Old Belize complex. This multiuse commercial and residential area along the George Price Highway (until late 2012 called the Western Highway), beginning at a potentially confusing series of new roundabouts, is also on the way to the Belize Zoo, Belmopan, and Cayo.

> ### TOURING TIP
>
> If you're spending time in downtown Belize City, you may be better off without a car. Parking is limited, and leaving a car on the street overnight, especially with any valuables in it, is just asking for trouble. Streets are narrow, and many are closed for repairs, so you could find yourself lost in a maze of unmarked detours.

PLANNING

WHEN TO GO

As with the rest of Belize, the most pleasant time to visit Belize City is in the winter and early spring, December to March or April, when it's cooler and drier—similar to South Florida at that same time of year. The average high temperature in Belize City is 86.2°F, and the average low is 72.6°F. The coolest month is January, and the hottest is May. Hotel rates drop in the off-season, typically from just after Easter to U.S. Thanksgiving. September, a month marked by St. George's Caye Day (September 10) and Belize Independence Day (September 21), sees celebrations and parties; many expatriated Belizeans return home then for a visit to see family and friends. However, September is also peak time for tropical storms and hurricanes in the western Caribbean. September and October are the slowest months for tourism in Belize, and some hotels and restaurants close during this time for maintenance or to allow owners to take their own vacations.

GETTING HERE AND AROUND

AIR TRAVEL

Philip S. W. Goldson International Airport (BZE) is near Ladyville, 9 miles (14 km) north of the city. The international airport is served from U.S. gateways by American (some American flights from Miami operate as a codeshare with British Air), United, Delta, Avianca (formerly TACA, from its hub in San Salvador, El Salvador), Copa (from Panama City, Panama), Southwest, and Canada's WestJet. Tropic Air has flights between the international airport and Cancún and Mérida, Mexico; San Pedro Sula, Tegucigalpa, and Roatán, Honduras; and Flores, Guatemala, gateway to Tikal.

In addition to international flights, a domestic terminal at the international airport has flights on Maya Island Air and Tropic Air to Ambergris Caye and Caye Caulker and the coastal towns of Dangriga, Placencia, and Punta Gorda. Tropic Air also has flights from the international airport to Maya Flats airstrip near San Ignacio and to Belmopan. Maya Island flights go to Savannah airstrip at Independence across the lagoon from Placencia and Kantantik, between Hopkins and Placencia.

The Belize City municipal airport, on the seafront about 1 mile (2 km) north of the city center, has domestic flights only; Maya Island Air and Tropic Air serve most of the same domestic destinations from here as from the international airport. Fares from the municipal airport are about 10% to 40% cheaper, depending on the destination, than similar flights departing from the international airport.

Contacts Maya Island Air. ⊠ *Muncipal Airstrip* ☎ *223/1403 reservations countrywide* ⊕ *www.mayaislandair.com.* **Tropic Air.** ⊠ *San Pedro Airport, San Pedro Town* ☎ *226/2012 reservations in Belize countrywide, 800/422–3435 toll-free reservations in U.S. or Canada* ⊕ *www.tropicair.com.*

BOAT AND FERRY TRAVEL

You can travel from Belize City on fast boats that hold up to 50 to 100 passengers, or more, to San Pedro (Ambergris Caye) and Caye Caulker. The boats also connect San Pedro and Caye Caulker. From Belize City it's a 45-minute ride to Caye Caulker and a 90-minute trip to San Pedro, including a stop at Caye Caulker. Going between Caye Caulker and San Pedro takes about 30 minutes.

Belize Ocean Ferry boats depart from the Marine Terminal at 10 North Front Street near the Swing Bridge; San Pedro Belize Express boats (which also go to Caulker) leave from the nearby Brown Sugar dock at 111 North Front Street near the Tourism Village. Water taxis also will stop on demand at Caye Chapel and St. George's Caye. Each service has boats departing every couple of hours during daylight hours. Current schedules and prices are on the operators' websites but are subject to frequent change.

Currently, there is no scheduled daily water-taxi service from Belize City to Hopkins, Placencia, or other points on the coast, nor to remote cayes.

Contacts Ocean Ferry Belize. ⊠ *Marine Terminal, 10 N. Front St.* ✛ *Near Swing Bridge* ☎ *223/0033* ⊕ *www.oceanferrybelize.com.* **San Pedro Belize Express.** ⊠ *Brown Sugar Terminal, 111 N. Front St.* ☎ *223/2225 in Belize City* ⊕ *www.belizewatertaxi.com.*

BUS TRAVEL

Belize City is the hub of the country's fairly extensive bus network, so there's service to most regions of Belize and limited service by foreign bus companies to Mexico and Guatemala. The main bus terminal on

West Collet Canal Street in Belize City—still locally referred to as Novelo's, though the Novelo's bus company is no more—is used by most regional companies on the George Price Highway routes, the Goldson Highway routes, and the Hummingbird and Southern highways routes. From Belize City, service on the main routes north, west, and south is frequent and inexpensive. Most of these owner-operated buses are old Bluebird school buses from the United States, with cramped seating and no air-conditioning. ■ TIP→ **Take a cab to or from the Belize City bus terminal, especially after dark, as it is not in a safe area.**

There is limited bus service within Belize City on a number of small independent lines. Again, many of the buses are old U.S. school buses, but some are more modern minibuses. Ask locally about routes and times, as there are no published schedules. Also, local nonexpress regional buses will stop and drop off most anywhere in or near the city on the standard route. For example, if you're going from West Collet Canal terminal downtown to Brodie's supermarket on the Goldson Highway just north of downtown, you can take a nonexpress bus going to Orange Walk Town or Corozal Town and be dropped off at or near Brodie's.

Contacts Belize City Main Bus Terminal. ⊠ *W. Collet Canal St.*

CAR TRAVEL

There are only two highways to Belize City: the Philip Goldson Highway, which stretches to the Mexican border, 102 miles (165 km) away, and the George Price Highway, which runs 81 miles (131 km) to Guatemala. Both are paved two-lane roads, in fair to good condition. Signs guide you to nearby destinations such as the Belize Zoo.

Finding your way around the city itself can be confusing. With rare exceptions hotels in and near the city center offer mostly on-street parking, and you run the risk of a break-in if you leave the car overnight. Hotels in the suburbs north and west of the city usually have fenced or otherwise secured parking. Give your nerves a break and explore the city by taxi or on foot by day in safer sections like the Fort George area.

If you're driving between western and northern Belize, say from Belmopan to Orange Walk Town, you can take the Burrell Boom bypass around Belize City. The bypass runs between the roundabout on the George Price Highway at Hattieville at Mile 15.5 and and a roundabout at Mile 13 of the Philip Goldson Highway. The bypass, completely paved, is about 11½ miles (18½ km) in length; it saves you about 17 miles (28 km) and about a half hour of driving time.

If you are traveling from Belize City to one of the northern cayes and have a car, you won't be able to take your vehicle to the islands, so you'll need a safe place to park. Fenced and guarded parking is available at the international airport lot.

Contacts Edgar's Mini Storage. ⊠ *894 Vista del Mar, Ladyville* ☏ *602/4513* ⊕ *www.edgarsministorage.com.*

TAXI TRAVEL

Cabs cost BZ$7–BZ$10 for one person between any two points in the city, plus BZ$1 for each additional person. Outside the city, and from downtown to the suburbs, you'll be charged by distance traveled. Traveling between the international airport and any point in the city (including the businesses and hotels along the Goldson Highway north of the city center) is BZ$50 for two persons, with BZ$10 for each additional person. There are no meters, so agree on a price before you leave. Authorized taxis have green license plates. You can find taxis near the Swing Bridge and at the Novelo's bus terminal, or hotels will call them for you (this is preferred, because the hotel people know the dependable drivers). Otherwise, for pickup, call Cinderella Plaza Taxi Stand.

Contacts Cinderella Plaza Taxi Stand. ✉ *Freetown Rd., near Douglas Jones St.* ☎ *203/3340.*

TOURS

From Belize City you can take day trips to Crooked Tree Wildlife Sanctuary, the Community Baboon Sanctuary, the Belize Zoo, to Jaguar Paw for cave tubing, to Altun Ha, Lamanai, and Xunantunich Maya sites, and to nearby islands, including Caulker and Ambergris cayes. You can do most of these trips either on your own or with a local tour operator. Your hotel can also arrange day trips. Keep in mind that most Belize City tour operators focus more on the cruise-ship market than on individual travelers.

Fodor's Choice ★   **Belize Trips.** Belize Trips's Katie Valk, a transplanted New Yorker who has lived in Belize for more than 30 years, can organize a custom trip to almost any place in the country and also to Tikal in Guatemala. With her hotel connections she can even get you a room when everything seems booked, and being based in Belize City she is on hand should anything go wrong. She's also a warden for the U.S. Embassy. ✉ *Belize City* ☎ *223/0376, 561/210–7015 in U.S., 610/1923 mobile* ⊕ *www.belize-trips.com.*

CAVE TUBING

Several Belize City–based tour operators, including Butts Up and Cave Tubing with Vitalino Reyes, offer cave-tubing trips or cave-tubing and zip-lining combo tours, which usually include lunch. These inner tubes are usually bright yellow, custom-designed tubes with cup holders and head rests. Head lamps or other lights are provided for the dark caves.

Butts Up. Despite the risque name, the folks here get top marks from cruise passengers for their cave-tubing tours. You can choose from a basic cave-tubing outing (BZ$90 per person) or add a zip-line or ATV tour for a total of BZ$150. A separate zip-line tour with a visit to the ruins at Altun Ha is also available. Although most of the company's business is with cruise ship passengers, overnight visitors also can do the tours. ✉ *Near Terminal 1, Tourism Village, Fort George* ☎ *605/1575* ⊕ *www.cave-tubing.com* ⌚ *From BZ$90.*

Cave Tubing with Vitalino Reyes. Also known as Vital Nature and Mayan Tours, Cave Tubing with Vitalino Reyes is based in Corozal Town but does business primarily in Belize City. The company arranges to pick up customers at the cruise ship terminal, at hotels, at the water-taxi terminal or one of the airports, or elsewhere. Besides cave tubing at Jaguar Paw (Nohoch Che'en Caves Branch Archaeological Reserve), which costs from BZ$90 to BZ$150, the company also does zip-line tours and trips to most of the Maya sites in central and western Belize and even to Tikal. ⊠ *Tourism Village* ☏ *602/8975* ⌸ *From BZ$90.*

MAYAN RUINS

Tour operators based in Belize City including Butts Up, Cave Tubing with Vitalino Reyes and S&L Travel and Tours offer day trips by road, boat, or air to Lamanai and by road to Altun Ha, and also by road to Xunantunich and Cahal Pech near San Ignacio. The tours to western Belize may be combined with a stop at the Belize Zoo or cave tubing and zip-lining at Jaguar Paw.

Contacts Discovery Expeditions. ⊠ *5916 Manatee Dr., Buttonwood Bay, Northern Suburbs* ☏ *671/0748* ⊕ *www.discoverybelize.com.* **S&L Travel and Tours.** ⊠ *91 N. Front St.* ☏ *227/7593* ⊕ *www.sltravelbelize.com.*

VISITOR INFORMATION

Fodor's Choice ★ **Belize Tourism Board.** Belize Tourism Board, a department of the Ministry of Tourism, is the official tourism agency of the government of Belize. ⊠ *64 Regent St., Commercial District* ☏ *227/2420, 800/624–0686 toll-free in U.S. and Canada* ⊕ *www.travelbelize.org.*

EXPLORING BELIZE CITY

Belize City is defined by the water around it. The main part of the city is at the end of a small peninsula, jutting out into the Caribbean Sea. Haulover Creek, an extension of the Belize River, running roughly west to east, divides the city into the North Side and the South Side. The North Side is, to generalize, more affluent than the South Side. The venerable Swing Bridge connects the two sides, although in modern times other bridges over Haulover Creek, especially the Belcan Bridge northwest of the city center, carry more traffic. At the mouth of the river, just beyond Swing Bridge, is the Belize Harbor (or Harbour, as it's written locally, in the English style).

GETTING HERE AND AROUND

Coming from the north, follow the Goldson Highway through several roundabouts (traffic circles) to Freetown Road and Barracks Road to reach the center. Alternatively, you can swing west on Princess Margaret Drive to Barracks Road, along the seafront. This is the more scenic route. From the west, the George Price Highway, via a new roundabout intersection, takes you to the Goldson Highway, from which you approach the city as described above. The city center itself is a confusing warren of narrow streets, many of them one-way, and may be temporarily closed, with detours that are not well-marked or are not marked at all.

If you're staying in either the northern or western sprawling suburbs, a car is handy, as there's limited municipal bus service. There are many taxis, however, with affordable rates. It's not customary to tip taxi drivers, unless they help you with luggage or perform other services.

Most drivers are friendly and are happy to point out interesting sites to visitors. A few are licensed tour guides.

SAFETY AND PRECAUTIONS

Belize City has a reputation for street crime. The government has made some progress in cleaning up the problem, despite gang activity and drugs. Crimes against tourists in Belize City are relatively rare. Still, the crime rate in Belize City is comparable to that of a distressed inner-city area in the United States, and the homicide rate is among the highest in the world. Take the same precautions you'd take in any sketchy city—don't wear expensive jewelry or watches, avoid handling money in public, and leave valuables in a safe. Ignore offers to buy drugs. On buses and in crowded areas hold purses and backpacks close to your body. Check with the staff at your hotel before venturing into any unfamiliar areas, particularly at night. After dark you should always take a taxi rather than walk even a few blocks. Avoid leaving your rental car on the street overnight. Generally the Northern Suburbs are safer than downtown.

FORT GEORGE

This is the most pleasant and appealing section of the city, much of it cooled by prevailing breezes from the sea. It has stately if sometimes run-down colonial buildings that escaped the hurricanes of 1931 and 1961, several embassies (though the U.S. embassy was transplanted to Belmopan in 2006), upmarket restaurants that attract the city's elite, and the city's better hotels, including the Radisson Fort George and the Great House, plus the Museum of Belize, Fort George lighthouse, and the Tourism Village.

TOP ATTRACTIONS

FAMILY

Fodor'sChoice

★

Museum of Belize. This small but fascinating museum, under the aegis of the National Institute of Culture and History (NICH), was the Belize City jail from 1857 to 1993. Permanent displays include ancient jade and other Mayan artifacts; medicinal, ink, and alcoholic-beverage bottles dating from the 17th century; Belize and British Honduran coins and colorful postage stamps; and an actual prison cell. Temporary exhibitions change periodically. ⊠ *8 Gabourel La., Belize Central Bank Compound, Fort George* ☎ *223/4524, 822/3302 NICH administrative office in Belmopan City* ⊕ *www.nichbelize.org* ✆ *BZ$10* ☉ *Closed Sun. and Mon.*

WORTH NOTING

Fort George Lighthouse and Bliss Memorial. Towering 15 meters (49 feet) over the entrance to Belize Harbor, the lighthouse stands guard on the tip of Fort George Point. It was designed and funded by one of the country's greatest benefactors, Baron Henry Edward Ernest Victor Bliss. The English nobleman never actually set foot on the Belizean mainland, though in his yacht he visited the waters offshore. In his will he bequeathed most of his fortune to the people of Belize, and the date of his death, March 9, is celebrated as a national holiday, now officially called National Heroes and Benefactors Day. Bliss is buried here, in a small, low mausoleum perched on the seawall, up a short run

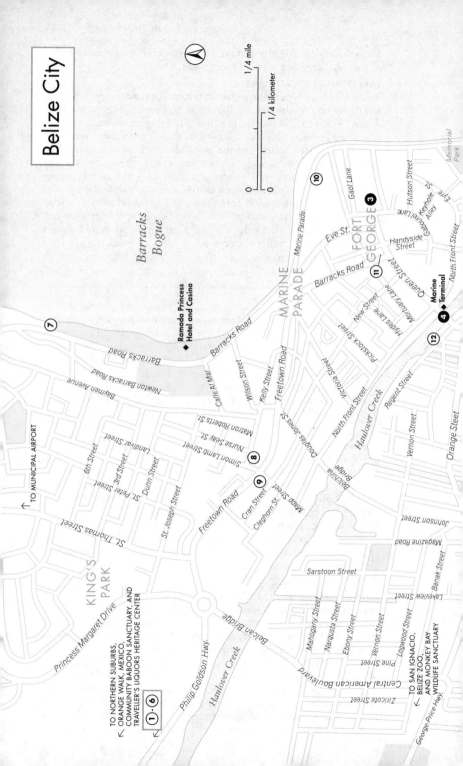

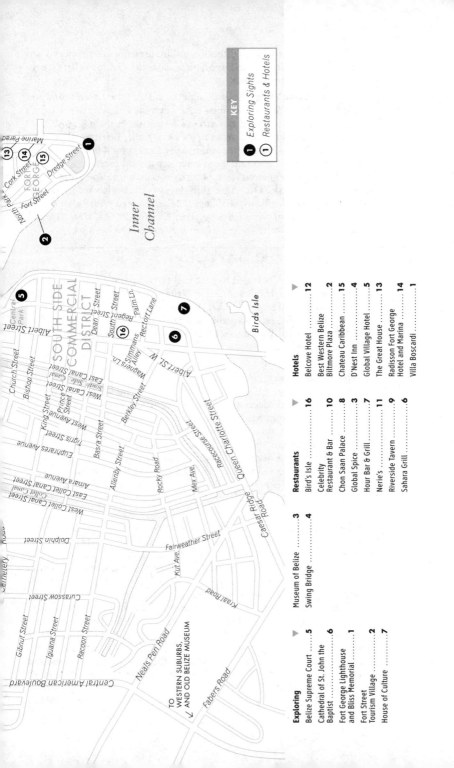

KEY

- ① Exploring Sights
- ① Restaurants & Hotels

Inner Channel

SOUTH SIDE COMMERCIAL DISTRICT

Birds Isle

TO WESTERN SUBURBS, AND OLD BELIZE MUSEUM

Exploring ▶

Belize Supreme Court	5
Cathedral of St. John the Baptist	6
Fort George Lighthouse and Bliss Memorial	1
Fort Street Tourism Village	2
House of Culture	7
Museum of Belize	3
Swing Bridge	4

Restaurants ▶

Bird's Isle	16
Celebrity Restaurant & Bar	10
Chon Saan Palace	8
Global Spice	3
Hour Bar & Grill	7
Nerie's	11
Riverside Tavern	9
Sahara Grill	6

Hotels ▶

Belcove Hotel	12
Best Western Belize Biltmore Plaza	2
Chateau Caribbean	15
D'Nest Inn	4
Global Village Hotel	5
The Great House	13
Radisson Fort George Hotel and Marina	14
Villa Boscardi	1

of limestone stairs. The lighthouse and mausoleum are for photo ops only—you can't enter. ⊠ *Marine Parade, near the Radisson Fort George Hotel, Fort George* 🖼 *Free.*

Fort Street Tourism Village. Even though the village (also called Fort Point Tourism Village & Mall) is open only when the cruise ships are in, it's a good place to stop, as it has around 30 gift shops including MOHO chocolate shop offering free samples or organic, Belize-made chocolates, plus the usual duty-free and jewelry stores you'll find all over the Caribbean. You'll also find clean restrooms, a cybercafe, tour kiosks, restaurants, and other services. Security is tight in the Tourism Village, and you'll feel safe. On cruise ship days, vendors also set up booths on streets near the Tourism Village. ⊠ *Fort George cruise-ship docks, 8 Fort St., east of Swing Bridge, Fort George* 🖀 *223/7789* ⊕ *www. tourismvillage.com* ⊘ *Closed when there are no cruise ships.*

SOUTH SIDE COMMERCIAL DISTRICT

This area, along Albert and Regent streets, two parallel streets running north–south from Haulover Creek, is the commercial heart of the city. It has many small stores, banks, and budget hotels, along with several places of interest, including the Supreme Court, St. John's Cathedral, and the House of Culture. A third parallel street, the Southern Foreshore, hugs the waterfront along the South Side.

TOP ATTRACTIONS

Belize Supreme Court. Not the oldest building in the city but one of the most striking, the 1926 Belize Supreme Court building is patterned after its wooden predecessor, which had burned in 1918. An 1820 court building had also burned down. The current building, painted white, has filigreed iron stair and balcony rails, similar to what you might see in New Orleans (the construction company came from Louisiana), between two arms of the structure, and above the balcony a four-sided clock. This being Belize, the clock faces all seem to show different times. You can't enter the building, but it's worth admiring from the outside. ⊠ *Regent St., opposite Battlefield Park, Commercial District* 🖀 *227/4387.*

FAMILY   **House of Culture.** Formerly called Government House, the city's finest
Fodor's Choice   colonial structure is said to have a design inspired by the illustrious
★   British architect Sir Christopher Wren. Built in 1814, it was once the residence of the governor-general, the British monarchy's representative in Belize. Following Hurricane Hattie in 1961, the decision was made to move the capital inland to Belmopan, and the house became a venue for social functions and a guesthouse for visiting VIPs. (Queen Elizabeth stayed here in 1985, Prince Philip in 1988.) Now it's open to the public. You can peruse its archival records, and art and artifacts from the colonial era, or mingle with the tropical birds that frequent the gardens. Renovations are in the works for the building and gardens. ⚠ **If going here after dark, take a cab, because it's close to some of the city's most crime-ridden areas.** ⊠ *Regent St. at Southern Foreshore, opposite Cathedral of St. John the Baptist, Commercial District* 🖀 *227/0518*

NICH office at House of Culture in Belize City ⊕ *www.nichbelize.org* ⊠ *BZ$10* ⊙ *Closed weekends.*

Swing Bridge. As its name suggests, the bridge spanning Haulover Creek in the middle of Belize City actually swings. When needed to allow a boat through or by special request of visiting dignitaries, four men hand-winch the bridge a quarter-revolution so waiting boats can continue upstream (when it was the only bridge in town, this snarled traffic for blocks). The bridge, made in England, opened in 1923; it was renovated and upgraded in 1999. Outsiders' recommendations to automate the swing mechanics or—heaven forbid—rebuild the bridge entirely are always immediately rejected. No one wants to eliminate the city's most unusual landmark. Before the Swing Bridge arrived, cattle were "hauled over" the creek in a barge. The bridge appears in a scene of the 1980 movie, *The Dogs of War*, set in a fictitious African country but mostly filmed in Belize. ⊠ *Haulover Creek, Queen and Albert Sts., Commercial District.*

WORTH NOTING

Cathedral of St. John the Baptist. On Albert Street's south end is the oldest Anglican church in Central America and the only one outside England where kings were crowned. From 1815 to 1845, four kings of the Mosquito Kingdom (a British protectorate along the coast of Honduras and Nicaragua) were crowned here. The cathedral, built of brick brought here to what once was British Honduras as ballast on English ships, is thought to be the oldest surviving building in Belize from the colonial era. Its foundation stone was laid in 1812. Inside, it has whitewashed walls and mahogany pews. The roof is constructed of local sapodilla wood, with mahogany beams. Residents of the city usually refer to the cathedral as simply "St. John's." ■TIP→ **You can combine a visit to the cathedral with a visit to the House of Culture, as they are just across the street from each other. Safe to visit during day; at night, take a taxi.** ⊠ *Albert St. at Regent St., opposite House of Culture, Commercial District* ☎ *227/3029* ⊠ *Free.*

WESTERN SUBURBS

For visitors, this part of the metropolitan area mostly is just a place to pass through on the way to the Cayo. However, local entrepreneurs have opened several businesses targeting cruise-ship passengers.

EXPLORING

FAMILY **Old Belize.** Many of the visitors here are tour groups from cruise ships, or boaters at the marina, but you can also visit the museum at Old Belize on your own (it's a BZ$20 taxi ride each way from downtown Belize City). In a large warehouse-style building, exhibits are devoted to the rain forest and the Maya, Garífuna, and Creoles in Belize City, with displays on logging, chicle harvesting, and sugar production. Some of the artifacts formerly housed at the Maritime Museum at the Marine Terminal are now on display here. Also at the site of the museum are a large marina; a restaurant where you can get a decent hamburger and other American-style dishes; a gift shop; and Cucumber Beach, a small man-made beach with a 600-foot zip line and a waterslide.

✉ *Mile 5, George Price Hwy., formerly Western Hwy., Western Suburbs* ☎ *222/4129* ⊕ *www.oldbelize.com* ✉ *BZ$10 for museum; BZ$20 for beach and waterslide; BZ$40 for beach, waterslide and zip line.*

NORTHERN SUBURBS

If you're arriving by air at the international airport, you'll pass through the Northern Suburbs on your way to the city, or (unless you take the Burrell Boom bypass) on your way to points south and west.

EXPLORING

Travellers Liquors Heritage Center. This museum, often just called the rum museum, celebrates Belize's love affair with rum and its oldest distillery, Travellers. Although it's small, the museum is fascinating, with displays of old rum bottles and distillery equipment and the history of rum making in Belize. You can also look through a window and see rum and other potables being made and bottled at the little factory behind the museum. Best of all, you can get samples of the various rums made by Travellers, including its best-selling One Barrel, along with samples of more exotic drinks such as cashew wine, Rumpope (rum with eggnog), Anise & Peppermint (called A&P, it may remind you of cough syrup and is usually mixed with milk), and Craboo Liquor. Initial samplings are free, with a small charge for further tastings. ✉ *Mile 2.5, Philip Goldson Hwy., formerly Northern Hwy., Northern Suburbs* ☎ *223/2855* ⊕ *www.onebarrelrum.com* ✉ *BZ$2* ☺ *Closed weekends.*

WHERE TO EAT

Though most restaurants here cater to locals, their number and quality rival those of tourist magnet San Pedro on Ambergris Caye. The city has inexpensive dives serving "dollah chicken" (fried chicken, a local favorite, though it no longer costs just a Belize dollar), Chinese joints of 1950s vintage specializing in chow mein, and lunch spots for downtown office workers seeking Creole dishes such as cow-foot soup and rice and beans. Belize City also has upmarket restaurants serving the city's affluent elite. Only a couple of these are "dressy" (by Belize standards, this means a nice collared shirt for men and perhaps a long tropical dress for women), and reservations are rarely necessary.

A few restaurants around the Tourism Village target cruise-ship passengers, typically for lunch and drinks, but the one thing you won't find here are chain restaurants.

WHAT IT COSTS IN BELIZE DOLLARS			
$	**$$**	**$$$**	**$$$$**
AT DINNER under BZ$15	BZ$15–BZ$30	BZ$31–BZ$50	over BZ$50

$$ ✕ **Bird's Isle.** This longtime local favorite is an open-air seaside bar and
SEAFOOD   restaurant on the little islet at the south end of Regent Street, also called
Bird's Isle. The thatched-roof spot is a great place to sip tropical drinks

and eat local seafood (the fried snapper is a favorite) or other dishes at lunch, away from the hustle of downtown. You'll like the prices, too. Take a taxi after dark, as the South Side area near Bird's Isle is not the best. $ *Average main: BZ$22 ⊠ 9 Albert St., at south end of Regent St., across bridge on Bird's Isle, on South Side, Commercial District ☎ 207/2179 ⊗ Closed Sun. dinner.*

$$$
LATIN AMERICAN
FAMILY
Fodor'sChoice
★

✕ **Celebrity Restaurant & Bar.** Visit at lunch or dinner almost any day and you'll see a cross-section of Belize City's movers and shakers— attorneys, businesspeople, politicians—enjoying the restaurant's large menu of U.S.-inspired seafood, steaks, pasta, and salads, along with Belizean comfort food. If you can get by the flamboyant wallpaper in the main dining room, and the fairly basic selection of drinks and wine, you'll enjoy it, too. There's a guarded parking lot. $ *Average main: BZ$38 ⊠ Volta Bldg., Marine Parade Blvd., Marine Parade Harbor Front ☎ 223/7272.*

$$
CHINESE

✕ **Chon Saan Palace.** Locally adored for four decades, Chon Saan Palace is the best Chinese restaurant in Belize City, which is otherwise full of bad Chinese eateries. It has some 200 dishes on the menu, most Cantonese-style, such as sweet-and-sour pork. We like the Chinese-style crab legs. There's a live-seafood tank with lobster and the catch of the day, kept alive until you're ready to eat it. On Sunday, the restaurant switches gears a bit and makes sushi and sashimi. $ *Average main: BZ$24 ⊠ 1 Kelly St., at Nurse Seay St., Commercial District ☎ 223/3008.*

$$
LATIN AMERICAN

✕ **Global Spice.** We don't often include airport restaurants, but Global Spice, a no-frills restaurant near the "waving gallery" on the second floor of the main terminal, will leave you with a nice taste of Belize. It's not a gourmet restaurant, just a good place to get that farewell plate of stew chicken with rice and beans and a cold Belikin. $ *Average main: BZ$18 ⊠ Philip S. W. Goldson International Airport, 2nd level of main terminal, Ladyville ☎ 225/3339.*

$$$
SEAFOOD

✕ **Hour Bar & Grill.** Created by a branch of the Bowen family (owner of Belize Brewing Company), Hour Bar & Grill has become a popular Belize City hangout. The food, mostly seafood, along with burgers, salads, and other standards like grilled chicken, is only mediocre. Its greater appeal is its breezy seaside location. There's plenty of safe, guarded parking, good drinks, and, naturally, plenty of cold Belikin. It's got a lively atmosphere with lots of locals. $ *Average main: BZ$34 ⊠ 1 Princess Margaret Dr., Marine Parade Harbor Front ☎ 223/3737 ⊕ www.hourbarbelize.com ⊗ Closed Mon.*

$
LATIN AMERICAN

✕ **Nerie's.** Often packed, Nerie's is the *vox populi* of dining in Belize City. The many traditional dishes on the menu include fry jacks for breakfast and cow-foot soup for lunch. Stew chicken with rice and beans and a soft drink is always an economical choice. There's another location on Douglas Jones St. $ *Average main: BZ$14 ⊠ Queen and Daly Sts., Commercial District ☎ 223/4028 ⊕ www.neries.bz ⊟ No credit cards ⊗ No dinner Sun.*

$$
AMERICAN
Fodor'sChoice
★

✕ **Riverside Tavern.** Owned and managed by the Bowen (of locally brewed Belikin-beer fame) family, Riverside Tavern is one of the city's most popular and agreeable restaurants, with dependably good food, friendly service, and safe parking. The signature hamburgers, which come in several sizes from 6 oz. to enormous, are arguably the best in Belize. Try one with the stacked onion rings. The Riverside has steak and prime rib dishes, from cattle from the Bowen farm at Gallon Jug. Sit inside in air-conditioned comfort, at tables set around a huge bar, or on the outside covered patio overlooking Haulover Creek. This is one of the few restaurants in Belize with a dress code—shorts aren't allowed at night (at least in theory). The fenced, guarded parking lot right in front of the restaurant makes it easy and safe to park for free. $ *Average main: BZ$28* ⌧ *2 Mapp St., off Freetown Rd., Commercial District* ☎ *223/5640* ☾ *Closed Sun.*

$$

MEDITERRANEAN

✕ **Sahara Grill.** This nondescript Mediterranean/Lebanese restaurant in the Northern Suburbs has good kabobs, kofta, falafel, and hummus, with many vegetarian options. Service isn't always perfect, but the food is consistently good. $ *Average main: BZ$20* ⌧ *Vista Plaza, Mile 3, Philip Goldson Hwy., across from Belize Biltmore Plaza, Northern Suburbs* ☎ *203/3031.*

WHERE TO STAY

For expanded hotel reviews, visit Fodors.com.

Belize City has the country's largest hotels, though size is relative in Belize. The Radisson, Ramada Princess Hotel and Casino, and Biltmore Plaza each have 75 or more rooms and strive, not always successfully, for an international standard. The city also has its share of small inns and B&Bs with character, such as the Great House, D'Nest Inn, and Villa Boscardi. Although easy on the pocketbook, the city's budget hotels frequently have thin, inexpensive mattresses and scratchy sheets, and amenities such as room phones may be scarce. In Belize City safety is an issue, especially at the cheaper hotels, so be sure to check that doors and windows securely lock and that the entrance is well lighted. In the downtown areas, don't walk around after dark, even in groups; always take a taxi.

Several of the city's best hotels are in the Fort George area, but there are also good choices in the Northern Suburbs between downtown and the international airport. The Commercial District on the South Side (south of Swing Bridge) has a number of budget hotels, but safety is always a concern.

WHAT IT COSTS IN BELIZE DOLLARS			
$	**$$**	**$$$**	**$$$$**
FOR TWO PEOPLE	under BZ$200	BZ$200–BZ$300	BZ$301–BZ$500	over BZ$500

Prices are for two people in a standard double room in high season, including tax and service.

$

HOTEL

▨ **Belcove Hotel.** Right in the middle of things, the Belcove is a popular budget hotel just south of Swing Bridge, literally at the edge of Haulover Creek. **Pros:** good value; friendly staff; central downtown location. **Cons:** slightly funky atmosphere; you need to be very careful downtown

CLOSE UP

Roots Belizean

If you spend time talking with Belizeans, sooner or later conversation will turn to "roots." It's not a vegetable, but a term referring to people born in Belize who share a certain set of values. Usually, but not always, it connotes ordinary folk, not wealthy Belizeans. These are Belizeans who ride the bus instead of driving a new Ford Explorer.

"Being roots Belizean is a way of life, a mind-set, and a unique set of values," says Wendy Auxillou, a Belizean who spent much of her life on Caye Caulker. Roots Belizeans enjoy the simple pleasures of life: talking with friends they run into on the streets of Belize City; skipping work or school to swim in the sea, river, or lagoon; sitting on a veranda on a hot afternoon; fishing in an old wooden skiff; raising chickens in the backyard for Sunday dinner.

Roots is also about community involvement. Children are often looked after by aunts and grannies, as well as neighbors. Misbehaving children might find themselves answering to a slew of adults in addition to their parents.

It's going to the market and eating boiled corn, *dukunu* (boiled cornbread), *garnaches* (crispy tortillas topped with beans and rice), and Belizean-style hot dogs, which are wrapped in bacon and grilled with onions. It's buying bananas 10 for a Belizean dollar. It's enjoying the smell and taste of all the local fruits, like tambran, grocea, a dozen different kinds of mangoes, sapodilla, mamie, jicama, watermelon, pineapple, guava, and papaya. It's about going to restaurants with local flavor, like Caladium in Belmopan, Nerie's or Dit's in Belize City, and Clarissa Falls in Cayo.

"It's about eating johnnycakes or plucking chickens with your neighbor, just because," says one Belizean.

Some claim that the original and perhaps only roots Belizeans are Creoles, descendents of the rough-and-ready Baymen and freed African slaves. Others argue that anybody can be a roots Belizean, that there are roots Mestizos, roots Maya, even roots Mennonites.

—Lan Sluder

after dark. Ⓢ *Rooms from: BZ$65* ⊠ *9 Regent St. West, just south of Swing Bridge, Commercial District* ☎ *227/3054* ⊕ *www.belcove.com* ↝ *12 rooms* ⃝l *No meals.*

$$$
HOTEL ⌂ **Best Western Belize Biltmore Plaza.** This suburban motel, which mostly gets guests who don't want to stay in the downtown area, has upgraded its pool, grounds, and rooms, though it's still a little shy of luxurious. **Pros:** comfortable, secure, motel-like suburban setting; bar has good happy hour deals; deluxe rooms worth extra cost. **Cons:** not much atmosphere; so-so restaurant; a few mosquitoes around pool. Ⓢ *Rooms from: BZ$320* ⊠ *Mile 3, Goldson Hwy., Northern Suburbs* ☎ *223/2302* ⊕ *www.belizebiltmore.com* ↝ *75 rooms* ⃝l *No meals.*

$
HOTEL ⌂ **Chateau Caribbean.** The breezy Fort George seaside location of this hotel is its strongest point, and some would say its only one. **Pros:** waterfront location; colonial atmosphere in public areas. **Cons:** shabby, worn rooms; you may see some bugs. Ⓢ *Rooms from: BZ$194* ⊠ *6*

Marine Parade, Fort George ☎ *223/0800* 🌐 *www.chateaucaribbean.com* 🛏 *20 rooms* 🍴 *Some meals.*

$ HOTEL Fodor's Choice ★ 🏨 **D'Nest Inn.** In Belama Phase 2, a safe, middle-class suburb between the international airport and downtown, D'Nest Inn is run by a charming couple, Gaby and Oty Ake. Gaby is a retired Belize City banker, and Oty is originally from Chetumal, Mexico. **Pros:** delightful B&B; delicious breakfasts included; charming and helpful hosts. **Cons:** only a few restaurant choices nearby; rooms need an update and upgrade. [$] *Rooms from: BZ$179* ✉ *475 Cedar St., Northern Suburbs* ✥ *From Goldson Hwy., turn west on Chetumal St. (newly resurfaced and now a divided boulevard), go about 300 yards, turn right at police station, go 1 short block and turn left, then turn right on Cedar St.* ☎ *223/5416* 🌐 *www.dnestinn.com* 🛏 *4 rooms* 🍴 *Breakfast.*

$ HOTEL 🏨 **Global Village Hotel.** This Chinese-owned motel has no atmosphere and no frills, but it's clean, with modern furniture and fixtures, and a good value at BZ$110 plus tax for a double. **Pros:** clean, bare-bones motel; free airport pickup and drop-off; secure parking. **Cons:** no atmosphere; mainly for an overnight en route to other locations. [$] *Rooms from: BZ$119* ✉ *Mile 8.5, Goldson Hwy., just south of turnoff to international airport, Ladyville* ☎ *225/2555* 🌐 *www.globalvillage-bz.com* 🛏 *40 rooms* 🍴 *Breakfast.*

$$$ B&B/INN 🏨 **The Great House.** Among Fort George's most appealing sights is the colonial facade of this large wooden house, across the street from the Radisson. **Pros:** lovely old inn; good location in the Fort George area. **Cons:** rooms are all upstairs on second and third floors with no elevator. [$] *Rooms from: BZ$399* ✉ *13 Cork St., Fort George* ☎ *223/3400* 🌐 *www.greathousebelize.com* 🛏 *16 rooms* 🍴 *Breakfast.*

$$$ HOTEL Fodor's Choice ★ 🏨 **Radisson Fort George Hotel and Marina.** Opened in 1953, the country's first modern hotel is now the city's best international-style large hotel, and it's located in the historic Fort George section with panoramic views of the sea from the more expensive rooms. **Pros:** Belize City's best large hotel; waterfront location in historic Fort George area. **Cons:** some rooms are small and could use updating. [$] *Rooms from: BZ$480* ✉ *2 Marine Parade, Fort George* ☎ *223/3333, 800/333–3333 toll-free in U.S. and Canada* 🌐 *www.radissonbelize.com* 🛏 *102 rooms* 🍴 *No meals.*

$$ B&B/INN Fodor's Choice ★ 🏨 **Villa Boscardi.** If you're anxious about downtown Belize City, this appealing B&B in the Northern Suburbs might be your cup of herbal tea. **Pros:** Belgian-born owner is very helpful; cheerful B&B in safe area; attractive rooms. **Cons:** only a few restaurants nearby. [$] *Rooms from: BZ$251* ✉ *6043 Manatee Dr., Northern Suburbs* ✥ *Turn toward sea off Goldson Hwy. at Golding Ave., then left on second lane to fifth house on right* ☎ *223/1691* 🌐 *www.villaboscardi.com* 🛏 *7 rooms* 🍴 *Breakfast.*

NIGHTLIFE AND PERFORMING ARTS

Travelers who like to use their vacations to catch up on their nightlife rather than sleep will find Belize City's scene limited at best. Although locals love to party, safety concerns keep visitors away from most nightspots except hotel bars, such as the bar at the Radisson Fort George.

After dark, take a taxi, or, if driving, park in a fenced and secured lot, such as at the Riverside Tavern.

Karaoke is a craze among many Belizeans. A hugely popular, locally produced karaoke television show, *Karaoke TV,* has been running on Channel 5 in Belize City since 2001. Most of the hotel bars have karaoke nights once or twice a week. Even in Belize you'll hear tried-and-true karaoke favorites such as "Crazy" by Patsy Cline and lots of Elvis and vintage Sonny and Cher, and you'll also hear songs like "Bidi Bidi Bam Bam" by Selena and "Greatest Love of All" by Whitney Houston. Singers may go from country to Motown and hip-hop to funk and R&B to reggae, ska, and Latin soca. Belizean taste in music is nothing if not eclectic. At live music shows and clubs in Belize City you can hear an equally diverse mix of music, although rap in all its variations is as popular in Belize City as in Los Angeles.

One uniquely Belizean style of music is punta rock. It's based on the traditional punta rhythms of the Garífuna, using drums, turtle shells, and rattles. In the late 1970s Pen Cayetano, a Garífuna artist in Dangriga, began writing punta songs, updating the music with an electric guitar, keyboard, and other electronic instruments. (Cayetano now lives in Germany, although he visits Belize regularly.) Punta rock, earthy and sexy, swept Belize and later became popular in other Central American countries, a result of the export of the music by the likes of Andy Palacio, "the ambassador of punta rock," who died unexpectedly at the peak of his career in early 2008.

BARS

The bars at the upmarket hotels, particularly those at the Princess Hotel & Casino and at the Radisson Fort George, are fairly popular—and safe—places to congregate for drinks. The Bowen (Belikin beer) family-owned Riverside Tavern is a popular place to have drinks, either indoors in air-conditioned comfort or on the outside patio next to the water, as is a bar owned by another branch of the Bowen family, Hour Bar & Grill *(see Where to Eat).*

Baymen's Tavern. This downtown bar at the Radisson Fort George is a comfortable, safe place to sip a rum and tonic, with live entertainment on weekends, usually a singer or a small band. There's also a more casual section of the bar, on an open-air deck, with views of a garden and the sea. On weekends, this bar jumps, with a mostly local crowd. ✉ *Radisson Fort George Hotel, 2 Marine Parade, Fort George* ☎ *223/3333* ⊕ *www.radissonbelize.com.*

Fodor's Choice   **Riverside Tavern.** At the Riverside Tavern you can have drinks before
★   dinner on the covered patio overlooking Haulover Creek or inside at the bar. Park your car safely in a fenced, guarded lot next to the tavern and restaurant. ✉ *2 Mapp St., off Freetown Rd., Commercial District* ☎ *223/5640.*

CASINOS

Ramada Princess Hotel and Casino. The only serious gambling in town is at the Princess Hotel and Casino, which has live tables for blackjack, roulette, and poker, along with about 400 slots. There are free drinks and a buffet for players, along with dance shows, two movie theaters, and a dance club. It's open 365 days a year from noon to 4 am. Gamble here if you like, but we don't recommend staying at the hotel. ⊠ *Newton Barracks, Marine Parade Harbor Front* ☎ *223/0638 casino, 223/2670 hotel* ⊕ *www.princessbelize.com.*

THEATERS

FAMILY **Bliss Center for the Performing Arts.** Overlooking the harbor from the Southern Foreshore near the Supreme Court, this building houses the Institute of Creative Arts and hosts cultural and arts events throughout the year—on a Saturday night you could hear a Mayan singer from Toledo or a marimba band from Benque Viejo del Carmen. Part of NICH, the National Institute of Culture and History, the center's 600-seat theater is headquarters for the Belize International Film Festival, usually held in July. Dramas, children's festivals, dance, art displays, and other cultural and musical performances take place at various times. It also houses a small art gallery with a George Gabb sculpture, *Sleeping Giant*, which appears as the watermark on Belize five-dollar bills. Most shows are in English, with Creole often mixed in. Ticket prices vary but typically range from BZ$10 to BZ$40. ⊠ *2 Southern Foreshore, between Church and Bishop Sts., Commercial District* ☎ *227/2110* ⊕ *www.nichbelize.org.*

SPORTS AND THE OUTDOORS

Belize City is a jumping-off spot for trips to the cayes and to inland and coastal areas, but the city itself offers little in the way of sports and outdoor activities. There are no golf courses, public tennis courts, or other sports facilities of note around Belize City, other than a sports stadium named after the now-disgraced Olympic track star Marion Jones, a Belizean-American. Unless you're on a cruise ship or otherwise have only a short time in Belize, you'll be better off going elsewhere for your sporting activities—to the cayes and Southern Coast for snorkeling, diving, and fishing, and inland to the Cayo or Toledo for caving, cave tubing, hiking, horseback riding, canoeing, and other activities. Most of the dive, snorkel, and tour operators in Belize City do cater to the cruise-ship crowd. *See chapters on The Cayo, Southern Coast, The Deep South, and The Cayes and Atolls, and also the Beyond Belize City section below.*

FISHING

If you're a serious angler, you'll likely end up in Placencia, Punta Gorda, or even San Pedro, but you can arrange fishing charters from Belize City. Both the Radisson Fort George and the Princess Hotel & Casino have marinas—the Radisson's marina is being rebuilt after Hurricane Earl destroyed it in 2016—and there is also the Cucumber Marina at Old Belize, the city's best. Local fishing-guide services and lodges operate near the city. The oldest continuously operating fishing lodge, Belize River Lodge, is located near Belize City. Fishing licenses are now required for all but pier and shore fishing. Your fishing charter company can arrange them for you.

Belize River Lodge. Owned by Mike Heusner and Marguerite Miles, Belize River Lodge is the oldest continuously operating fishing lodge in Belize. The original lodge, basic but with air-conditioning and good food, is on the Belize River near Belize City. It also has an outpost at Long Caye near Caye Chapel for closer access to tarpon, bonefish, jacks, and barracuda inside the reef. Three-night, two-day river fishing trips with lodging, meals, guides, skiff, and transfers start at BZ$3,100 per person, based on four people. Five-night, four-day fishing trips from the Long Caye outpost start at BZ$5,600 per person, based on four persons. ⊠ *Belize Old River* ☎ *225/2002, 888/275–4843 toll-free in U.S.* ⊕ *www.belizeriverlodge.com.*

HELICOPTER TOURS

Astrum Helicopters. Astrum offers customized aerial tours of the Blue Hole, Mayan sites, the Belize Barrier Reef, and others, using five-seat Bell helicopters. It also provides helicopter transfers to upscale resorts and lodges on the cayes and inland. ⊠ *Cisco Base, Mile 3.5, George Price Hwy.* ☎ *222/5100, 888/278–7864 toll-free in U.S.* ⊕ *www. astrumhelicopters.com.*

SCUBA DIVING AND SNORKELLING

Sea Sports Belize. Sea Sports, with an office downtown near the cruise ship tender docks, will take you to the Barrier Reef for diving (around BZ$250 to BZ$300). The dive shop also does trips to Turneffe and Lighthouse atolls. Most of their business is with cruise ships, but they also work with visitors staying in Belize City. ⊠ *83 N. Front St.* ☎ *223/5505* ⊕ *www.seasportsbelize.com.*

SHOPPING

Belize City has the most varied shopping in the country. Rather than catering to leisure shoppers, most stores in Belize City cater to the local market and those from other parts of the country who need to stock up on supplies at lumberyards, home-building stores, appliance outlets, and supermarkets. Gift shops and handicraft shops are concentrated in the downtown area in and near the Tourism Village.

About a dozen cruise ships per week call on Belize City, and each time the Tourism Village shops open their doors. Wednesday is usually the biggest day of the week for cruise ships in Belize City, often with three to five in port, and Saturday is another popular day. Rarely is there a ship in port on Sunday.

Most stores in the downtown area are open Monday through Saturday from around 8 am to 6 pm. On Sunday, nearly all stores downtown are dark, although some stores in the suburbs are open Sunday afternoon.

The Queen's Square Market, with fruit, vegetable, and other food vendors, just south of the Novelo's bus terminal on West Collet Canal Street, has been renovated and also goes by the name of Michael Finnegan's Market, after a local politician.

SHOPPING CENTERS AND MALLS

FodorsChoice **Brodies.** To stock up on picnic supplies or groceries, head to the
★ expanded, modern Brodies, a mini-department store and pharmacy as well as a supermarket, in a safe area on the Goldson Highway with plenty of free, safe parking. James Brodie & Co. has been in Belize since 1887. There's another location on Regent Street in downtown Belize City and also one in Belmopan City. ⊠ *Mile 2.5, Goldson Hwy., Northern Suburbs* ☎ *223/5587* ⊕ *www.brodiesbelize.com.*

Mirab's. Mirab's is a department store, worth a visit if you need to pick up something you forgot, like a flashlight or batteries. There also is a Mirab's furniture store at Mile 1.5 of the George Price Highway. ⊠ *2 Fort St. at N. Front St.* ☎ *223/2933.*

Save-U Supermarket. Save-U Supermarket is a good place for groceries, liquor, and sundries. ⊠ *San Cas Plaza, Goldson Hwy. at Central American Blvd.* ☎ *223/1291* ⊕ *www.santiagocastillo.com.*

SPECIALTY SHOPS

Image Factory. The cutting edge of Belize City's art and hipster scene is at the Image Factory. The Image Factory holds art and photography shows and publishes books. Its gallery and shop on North Front Street sells books, artwork, and CDs. There is free parking in a lot across North Front Street. ⊠ *91 N. Front St.* ☎ *223/4093* ⊕ *www.imagefactorybelize.com.*

BEYOND BELIZE CITY

If you're like most visitors to Belize, you'll spend at most only a night or two, if that, in Belize City before moving on. If you're heading west to the Cayo, plan to make a stop at the wonderful Belize Zoo, about 30 miles (49 km) west of Belize City. Going north or west, you can visit the Community Baboon Sanctuary, as there is road access to Bermudian Landing, where the sanctuary is located, via either the Goldson Highway or the Price Highway. For other areas of interest, including Crooked Tree Wildlife Sanctuary and the Altun Ha Mayan site to the north, and Belmopan to the west, within an hour or so of Belize City, *see the Northern Belize and Cayo chapters.*

ONE GUTSY AMERICAN WOMAN

The Belize Zoo owes its existence to the dedication and drive of one gutsy, American woman, Sharon Matola. Matola came to Belize as part of a film crew, but stayed on to care for some of the semi-tame animals used in the production. She opened the zoo in 1983, and in 1991 it moved to its present location. Matola's also an active environmentalist. Her story, and her crusade against the Chalillo Dam, is the subject of the 2008 book *The Last Flight of the Scarlet Macaw: One Woman's Fight To Save the World's Most Beautiful Bird* by Bruce Barcott.

BELIZE ZOO

One of the smallest, but arguably one of the best, zoos in the Americas, the Belize Zoo packs a lot into 29 acres. Home to some 200 animals, all native to Belize, the zoo has self-guided tours through several Belizean ecosystems—rain forest, lagoons, and riverine forest. Besides touring the zoo, you can stay overnight at the Belize Zoo Jungle Lodge or Belize Savanna Guest House nearby and hike or canoe the 84-acre Tropical Education Center. Tasty simple meals are offered at a nearby roadside restaurant, Cheers, about 1 mile (2 km) from the Zoo.

EXPLORING

FAMILY
Fodor'sChoice
★
Belize Zoo. Turn a sharp corner on the jungle trail, and suddenly you're face-to-face with a jaguar, the largest cat in the Western Hemisphere. The big cat growls a deep rumbling threat. You jump back, thankful that a strong but inconspicuous fence separates you and the jaguar. Along with jaguars, the zoo's nearly 50 species of native Belize mammals include the country's four other wild cats: the puma, margay, ocelot, and jaguarundi. The zoo also has a tapir, a relative of the horse and rhino known to locals as the mountain cow; it is Belize's national animal. You'll also see jabiru storks, a harpy eagle, scarlet macaws, howler monkeys, crocodiles, and many snakes, including the fer-de-lance. The zoo has an excellent gift shop. ■TIP→ **Come early in the day to avoid cruise ship groups and plan to stay for at least two hours; the Zoo opens at 8:30.** ⊠ *Mile 29, George Price Hwy.* ☎ *822/8000* ⊕ *www.belizezoo.org* ⊒ *BZ$30 adults.*

FAMILY
Tropical Education Center and Belize Zoo Jungle Lodge. Across the highway from the Belize Zoo is an 84-acre Tropical Education Center where you can hike or canoe. There are boardwalk trails through the savanna with wildlife viewing platforms and a deck for bird-watching. Rustic accommodations are available at the Tropical Education Center at the Belize Zoo Jungle Lodge, which include a 30-person dorm and four cabanas. Actress Cameron Diaz and the late TV animal expert Steve Irwin stayed here. Nighttime tours of the Belize Zoo are offered. ⊠ *Mile 29, George Price Hwy.* ☎ *822/8000* ⊕ *www.belizezoo.org.*

WHERE TO EAT AND STAY

A pleasant small B&B near the Belize Zoo, and officially endorse by it, is Belize Savanna Guest House. You could just stay at the Belize Zoo Jungle Lodge, part of the zoo's Tropical Education Center. Monkey Bay

Wildlife Sanctuary is also very near the zoo and has simple accommodations. A roadside restaurant and bar, Cheers, serves meals and also has several rental cabins. Otherwise, for a broader choice of accommodations and dining, if going west continue on about 25 miles (42 km) to the Belmopan area.

$ CAFÉ 🍴 **Cheers Restaurant and Cabañas.** Long a fixture on what is now the George Price Highway near the Belize Zoo, Cheers has a surprisingly good open-air restaurant that attracts local farmers and lots of zoo visitors. You won't go wrong with any of the local dishes, such as stew chicken with rice and beans, but it has good breakfasts and, for lunch, burgers, sandwiches, and daily specials. If you want to stay in the area longer, there are three simple cabins for rent on the property's 37 acres. Book ahead to get the lowest rates on lodging; walk-in rates are a little higher. [$] *Average main: BZ$14* ✉ *Mile 31.25, George Price Hwy.* ✥ *About 2 miles (4 km) west of Belize Zoo* ☎ *822/8014* 🌐 *www.cheersrestaurantbelize.com.*

$ B&B/INN 🏨 **Belize Savanna Guest House.** Officially endorsed by the Belize Zoo and Tropical Education Center, Belize Savanna Guest House is run by Carol and Richard Foster, nature photographers and videographers who helped get the zoo started in the early 1980s when they were filming a documentary in Belize. **Pros:** attractive but simple accommodations; run by noted nature photographers and documentary producers; affordable rates. **Cons:** nothing fancy. [$] *Rooms from: BZ$65* ✉ *Pine Savanna Nature Reserve, Mile 28.5, George Price Hwy.* ✥ *Approaching zoo from east, turn right at Mile 28.5. Go 0.5 mile (1 km) on dirt road in Pine Savanna Nature Reserve to guesthouse, which is third building on left* ☎ *822/8005* 🌐 *www.belizesavannaguesthouse.com* 🛏 *3 rooms* 🍽 *No meals* 💳 *No credit cards.*

MONKEY BAY WILDLIFE SANCTUARY

Located about 31 miles (51 km) northwest of Belize City, Monkey Bay is a privately owned wildlife reserve on 1,060 acres near the Belize Zoo.

FAMILY **Monkey Bay Wildlife Sanctuary.** At Monkey Bay you can canoe on the Sibun River, hike a 16-mile (31-km) nature trail along Indian Creek (only partly within Monkey Bay lands), or go bird-watching—some 250 bird species have been identified in the area. It has a natural history library with some 500 books and other reference materials, which visitors can use. The sanctuary also has educational and internship programs. Overnight accommodations for visitors are available if not occupied by students or interns, including tent camping (BZ$22 per person) and a bunkhouse (BZ$44 a person) with 38 beds and shared baths. The nine private cabins and rooms are around BZ$66 to BZ$220. Meals are also available at times, if an educational group is in residence. Otherwise you'll have to make your own meals. Monkey Bay accepts short-term volunteers (minimum stay one week). Internships also are available, usually with a minimum stay of one month. Most of the reserve's facilities demonstrate high ecological awareness. Most programs are geared for overnight or multinight visits, but you can come on a day visit. Call in advance to see what activities or facilities may be available when you want to come. ✉ *Mile 31, George Price Hwy., Belmopan* ✛ *A little over 3 miles (5 km) southeast of Belize Zoo, on opposite side of highway* ☎ *820/3032, 770/877–2648 U.S. number* ⊕ *www.belizestudyabroad.net.*

COMMUNITY BABOON SANCTUARY

One of Belize's most fascinating wildlife conservation projects is the Community Baboon Sanctuary, which is actually a haven for black howler monkeys (*baboon* is Kriol for the howler).

GETTING HERE

There are two routes to the sanctuary. If heading north on the Goldson Highway, turn west at Mile 13.2 onto the Burrell Boom Road. Go 3 miles (5 km) and turn right just beyond the new bridge over the Belize River. Signs to Bermudian Landing mark the turn. Stay on this road approximately 12 miles (20 km) to Bermudian Landing. If going west on the George Price Highway, turn north on the Burrell Boom Road at a roundabout at Mile 15.5 of the highway, and go 9 miles (15 km) to the new bridge over the Belize River. Just before the bridge, turn left. Signs to Bermudian Landing mark the turn. Stay on this road approximately 12 miles (20 km) to Bermudian Landing. You can also use the Burrell Boom Road as a shortcut between the Philip Goldson and George Price highways, avoiding Belize City. For this shortcut, stay on the Burrell Boom Road rather than turning toward Bermudian Landing. When on the Burrell Boom Road, you may want to stop at the **Central Prison Gift Shop** at the Central Prison, on the road to Burrell Boom about 3 miles (5 km) from the Price Highway. Prisoners at the "Hattieville Ramada" make small craft items and sell them at the gift shop.

FAMILY **Community Baboon Sanctuary.** Spanning a 20-mile (32-km) stretch of the Belize River, the reserve was established in 1985 by a group of local farmers. The black howler monkey (*Alouatta pigra*)—an agile bundle of black fur with a disturbing roar—was then zealously hunted throughout Central America and was facing extinction. Today the sanctuary is home, on some 200 private properties, to some 2,000 black howler monkeys, as well as numerous species of birds and mammals. Thanks to ongoing conservation efforts countrywide, you can see the howler monkeys in many other areas of Belize, including at Lamanai in northern Belize, along the Macal, Mopan, and Belize rivers in western Belize, near Monkey River and around Punta Gorda in southern Belize. You will also see howlers, along with spider monkeys, at Tikal. Exploring the Community Baboon Sanctuary is easy, thanks to about 3 miles (5 km) of trails that start near a small museum and visitor center. The admission fee includes a 45-minute guided nature tour during which you definitely will see howlers. Some guides may ask you to pay extra to hold or pet the howlers—this isn't appropriate, and don't encourage it. Other themed tours—birding, canoeing, crocodiles—are priced à la carte, although the admission per couple is little more than the per-person rate. ✉ *Bermudian Landing, 31 miles (50 km) northwest of Belize City, Bermudian Landing* ✛ *If heading north on Northern Hwy., turn west at Mile 13.2 onto Burrell Boom Rd. Go 3 miles (5 km) and* turn right just beyond new bridge over Belize River. Signs to Bermudian Landing mark the turn. Stay on this road approximately 12 miles (20 km) to Bermudian Landing. If going west on Western Hwy., turn north on Burrell Boom Rd. at roundabout at Mile 15.5 of Western Hwy., and go 9 miles (15 km) to new bridge over Belize River. Just before bridge, turn left. Signs to Bermudian Landing mark the turn. Stay on this road approximately 12 miles (20 km) to Bermudian Landing ☎ 660/3545 ⌨ BZ$14; tours from BZ$24.

WHERE TO STAY

$$$

RESORT

⌂ **Black Orchid Resort.** This Belizean-owned resort in a pleasant and safe rural setting northwest of Belize City perches at the edge of the Belize River, where you can launch a canoe or kayak from the hotel's dock, or just laze about the riverside swimming pool and thatch palapa bar. **Pros:** most upscale lodging near Baboon Sanctuary; lovely riverside setting; 15 minutes from international airport. **Cons:** not directly in Baboon Sanctuary. $ *Rooms from: BZ$357* ⊠ *2 Dawson La., 12 miles (20 km) from Baboon Sanctuary, Burrell Boom Village* ☎ *225/9158, 866/437–1301 toll-free in U.S. and Canada* ⊕ *www.blackorchidresort. com* ⇱ *16 rooms, 1 villa, 2 cabins* �‖ *No meals.*

$$

B&B/INN

⌂ **Howler Monkey Resort.** This family-run cottage colony is the closest lodging to the Community Baboon Sanctuary. **Pros:** close to Community Baboon Sanctuary; free pickup from international airport; family that runs this option is friendly and helpful. **Cons:** older accommodations. $ *Rooms from: BZ$250* ⊠ *Bermudian Landing, Bermudian Landing* ⊹ *Beside Belize River* ☎ *607/1571* ⊕ *www.howlermonkeyresort.bz* ⇱ *7 cabins* �‖ *Some meals* ⊟ *No credit cards.*

$$

HOTEL

⌂ **Orchid Garden Eco-Village.** A hardworking and promotion-minded couple from Taiwan runs this little hotel on the George Price Highway, heavily promoting all-inclusive packages that are handy but somewhat expensive given the location and the quality of the rooms. **Pros:** located outside Belize City en route to western destinations; clean rooms; tasty meals. **Cons:** not in a particularly scenic part of Belize; promotes pricey package options. $ *Rooms from: BZ$200* ⊠ *Mile 14.5, George Price Hwy.* ☎ *225/6991* ⊕ *www.trybelize.com* ⇱ *18 rooms* �‖ *Some meals.*

THE CAYES
AND ATOLLS

Updated
by Rose
Lambert-Sluder

Imagine heading back to shore after a day of snorkeling, the white prow of your boat pointing toward billowing clouds, the sky's base darkening to deep lilac, spray from the green water like warm rain. To the left, San Pedro's pastel buildings huddle among the palm trees like a detail from a Paul Klee canvas. To the right, the surf breaks in a white seam along the reef.

You can experience such adventures off the coast of Belize, where more than 400 cayes dot the Caribbean Sea like punctuation marks in a long, liquid sentence. A caye, sometimes spelled "cay" but in either case pronounced "key," is simply an island. It can be a small spit of sand, a tangled watery web of mangroves, or, as in the case of Ambergris Caye, a 25-mile-long (41-km-long) island about half the size of Barbados. (Ambergris is locally pronounced Am-BUR-griss.)

Besides being Belize's largest island, Ambergris Caye is also Belize's top visitor destination. Around half of all visitors to Belize make at least a stop at Ambergris, and many visit only this island.

Ambergris Caye is easy to get to from Belize City by water taxi or a quick commuter flight. It has the largest concentration of hotels, from budget to the ultradeluxe, and the most (and some of the best) restaurants in Belize. Although the island's beaches may not compare to classically beautiful sands of the Yucatán or the main Caribbean, Ambergris has miles and miles of beachfront on the east or Caribbean side, and the amazing Belize Barrier Reef is just a few hundred yards offshore.

San Pedro, the only real town on Ambergris Caye and growing in renown, is a place of paradox. It's mostly laid-back and low-rise, but traffic increases every day. It's traditionally a fishing town but now has resorts with ionic columns and combed sands. Rum is cheap but a taco salad can cost US$19. And a zinc-roof shack sits two doors down from a terra-cotta palace. These juxtapositions are what makes San Pedro a complicated product of modern economics; however, it remains a charming destination. In spite of the growth in tourism, most San Pedranos are authentically friendly and welcoming to visitors. Most main streets have concrete cobblestones, but side streets are hard-packed sand. Golf carts are still the prevalent vehicle, although the number of cars on the island continues to rise, and downtown the traffic on the narrow streets can be dangerous to pedestrians.

Since the paving of its single road, or "golf cart path," was completed in 2016, North Ambergris (above the Boca del Rio bridge) is more accessible and less remote than ever. A celebrated boost in infrastructure, the road means developers can almost be heard shouting "Land ho!" as they envision the area's potential. Currently, this 12-mile stretch has some of the most glamorous resorts in the country.

Caye Caulker is Ambergris Caye's sister island—smaller, less developed, and much cheaper. Caulker, whose name derives from the Spanish word for coco plum, *hicaco,* has the kind of sandy-street, no-rush, low-key Caribbean charm that some travelers pay thousands to experience. Here it can be had almost for peanuts. Less than 10 miles (16 km)—about 30 minutes by boat—from San Pedro, Caye Caulker, sometimes called Caye Corker, is definitely worth a day visit, and in our opinion, worth a week.

Most of Belize's cayes are inside the Barrier Reef, which allowed them to develop undisturbed by tides and winds that would otherwise have swept them away. The vast majority of them are uninhabited but for pelicans, brown- and red-footed boobies, and some creatures curiously named wish-willies (a kind of iguana). Island names are evocative and often humorous: Wee Caye, Laughing Bird Caye, and—why ask why?— Bread and Butter Caye. Names can suggest the company you should expect: Mosquito Caye, Sandfly Caye, and Crawl Caye, which is supposedly infested with boa constrictors. Several, like Cockney Range or Baker's Rendezvous, simply express the whimsy or nostalgia of early British settlers.

Some cayes have a population of one or two dozen, but also have exclusive villas and glamorous resorts. Cayo Espanto and Caye Chapel are slated for Four Seasons developments, among the first hotel chains in Belize.

Farther out to sea, between 30 miles and 45 miles (48 km and 74 km) off the coast, are Belize's atolls, Glovers (or Glover's), Lighthouse, and Turneffe, impossibly beautiful when viewed from the air. There are only four true Pacific-style atolls in the Americas, and Belize has three of them (the fourth is Chinchorro, off Mexico). At their center the water is mint green: the white sandy bottom reflects the light upward and is flecked with patches of mangrove and rust-color sediment. Around the atoll's fringe the surf breaks in a white circle before the color changes abruptly to ultramarine as the water plunges to 3,000 feet.

GETTING ORIENTED

Belize's two most important cayes, Ambergris and Caulker, are both off the northern end of the country, easily reached from Belize City. Other, smaller cayes dot the Caribbean Sea off the coast all the way south to Punta Gorda. The Belize Barrier Reef runs all along most of the coast of Belize. You're closest to the reef when you're on a beach on North Ambergris Caye. As you go south, the reef is farther from shore, 20 miles (12 km) or more off the Southern Coast. The three atolls are outside the reef, as much as 45 miles (74 km) offshore.

The Cayes. Ranging from tiny stretches of sand, mangrove, and palms to large islands like Ambergris and Caulker, Belize's cayes have excellent swimming, diving, fishing, and snorkeling.

The Atolls. Ovals of coral, majestic and remote, Belize's three atolls offer some of the best diving and snorkeling in the Western Hemisphere. The catch? They're difficult and time-consuming to get to, typically requiring a two-hour boat ride on open seas.

TOP REASONS TO GO

Scuba Diving. Dive destinations are often divided into reefs and atolls. Most reef diving is done on Belize's northern section, particularly off Ambergris Caye, but head to the atolls for some of the world's greatest diving opportunities.

No Shoes, No Shirt, No Problem. Unlike some parts of the mainland, the cayes are all about relaxing. "Go Slow" street signs dot the sandy roads, and you spend a lot of time lazing in hammocks or sipping beer in a beachside palapa alongside vacationing Belizeans.

Snorkeling. You don't have to don scuba gear to enjoy the colorful fish and psychedelic vistas under the surface of the sea. Some of the best snorkeling in the Caribbean is off

the coast of Belize. Jump in a boat for a short ride out to the reef or to patch coral.

Good Eats. Because they attract so many free-spending tourists, Ambergris Caye and Caye Caulker have more restaurants than anywhere else in Belize, and some of the best and most inventive, making the cayes an epicurean excursion.

Beaches. Although not your typical wide, sandy spreads, they're still classic postcard material, with windswept coco palms facing expanses of turquoise, green, and purple waters. You'll usually have a front-row seat, because most hotels in all price ranges are actually right on the beach.

PLANNING

WHEN TO GO

Island weather tends to be a little different from that on the mainland. The cayes are generally drier. Storm squalls come up suddenly, but just as quickly they're gone, leaving sunny skies behind. Late summer and early fall are prime tropical-storm season, a time when island residents keep a worried eye out for hurricanes; more than 8 out of 10 hurricanes that hit Belize arrive in either September or October. If a hurricane does threaten, the cayes are evacuated. The Christmas-to-Easter period, when the northern climes are cold and blustery, is the most popular time to visit the islands.

GETTING HERE AND AROUND

Island hopping in the northern cayes is simple, though getting to other cayes and the atolls can be more complicated. Water taxis connect Belize City, Ambergris Caye, and Caye Caulker. There is also frequent air service between Belize City and San Pedro and Caye Caulker. For the other cayes, you're generally stuck with whatever boat transport your hotel provides. Once on the islands, you'll get around by golf cart, bike, or on foot.

AIR TRAVEL

Maya Island Airways and Tropic Air operate flights between both the international and municipal airports in Belize City and Ambergris Caye and Caye Caulker. Each airline has roughly hourly service during daylight hours. Aircrafts are puddle-jumpers and people find them either dreadful or delightful, but regardless, aerial views are spectacular.

One-way fares on either Tropic and Maya Island to either San Pedro or Caye Caulker for the 15- to 20-minute flight are roughly BZ$100 (municipal) and BZ$175 (international). You save more than 40% by flying from the municipal airport in Belize City rather than the international airport north of the city. The catch is that if arriving or departing internationally you have to transfer by cab between the two airports—about a 25-minute ride—and a cab is BZ$50 (for the taxi, not per-person), so the extra hassle may not be worth the savings. ■TIP→ **Both airlines usually offer a 10% discount if you pay cash rather than use a credit card, and sometimes more. But you'll have to ask for the discount, which only applies in person, not online, and usually not on Saturday.**

Contacts Maya Island Airways. ⊠ *Belize City Municipal Airport, Belize City* ☎ *223/1140 for reservations* ⊕ *www.mayaislandair.com.* **Tropic Air.** ⊠ *San Pedro Airstrip, San Pedro Town* ☎ *226/2626, 800/422–3435 in U.S.* ⊕ *www. tropicair.com.*

BOAT, FERRY, AND WATER-TAXI TRAVEL

There are no scheduled water-taxi services up and down the coast of Belize, so for example you can't hop a boat in Belize City and go down the coast to Hopkins or Placencia or to one of the southern cayes. Between Belize City and busy Ambergris Caye and Caye Caulker, there's regular boat service; but there is no scheduled boat service to the smaller cayes. There is limited water-taxi service to these northern cayes from Corozal and from Chetumal, Mexico.

Several private boats do make the run from Dangriga to Tobacco Caye for around BZ$35–BZ$50 per person one-way. They leave Dangriga around 9:30 am and return from Tobacco Caye in late morning or the afternoon. Inquire with your hotel on Tobacco or at **Riverside Café** in Dangriga about its water-taxi service to Tobacco Caye.

Other than that, you're generally left to your own devices for private boat transportation. You can charter a small boat with driver—typically BZ$600 and up a day—or negotiate a one-way or round-trip price, up to BZ$800–BZ$1,500 or more one-way to the atolls. You'll have little luck renting a powerboat on your own, as boat owners are reluctant to risk their crafts, and new laws require that you need a captain's license before you can operate a boat in Belize waters (sailing charters are excepted).

BELIZE CITY TO SAN PEDRO AND CAYE CAULKER Your cheapest option for travel to the main cayes is by water taxi, really a buslike watercraft. There are two main water-taxi companies—San Pedro Belize Express and Ocean Ferry—with fast, cramped boats that hold 50 to 100 passengers (they've been likened to nautical saunas) connecting Belize City with San Pedro (Ambergris Caye) and Caye Caulker. They also connect San Pedro and Caulker. From Belize City it's a 45-minute ride to Caulker and 75 minutes to San Pedro. There's also a premium water-taxi service, Tropic Ferry, that meets you at the international airport and takes you from its dock near the airport to your resort on Ambergris.

Ocean Ferry Belize. This newer company competes with San Pedro Belize Express, but offers fewer trips (five daily) between Belize City, Caye Caulker and San Pedro. Ocean Ferry is the cheaper option. Amazingly, it also has free Wi-Fi on board. In Belize City, it departs from the Marine Terminal, then arrives at Caye Caulker's Front Street near Seaside Cabanas, then in San Pedro just north of Fido's. Once you arrive at your destination, it will be easy to find your way. ✉ *10 N. Front St., Belize City* ☎ *223/0033* ⊕ *www.oceanferrybelize.com/.*

Riverside Café. This local café on the river in Dangriga is a place to meet local boat owners and arrange transportation to Tobacco Caye. ✉ *Riverside and Oak Sts., west side of North Stann Creek River, Dangriga* ☎ *661/6390.*

Fodor'sChoice
★

San Pedro Belize Express Water Taxi. This company is quite dependable. San Pedro Belize Express water taxis depart from the Brown Sugar terminal on North Front Street. On Caye Caulker, the boats arrive at the pier near the basketball court on Front Street, and in San Pedro they arrive at the pier at Black Coral Street on the east (sea) side of the island. They also provide daily service between the Muelle Fiscal or municipal pier in Chetumal, Mexico, and San Pedro and Caye Caulker. ✉ *111 N. Front St., Brown Sugar Terminal, Belize City* ☎ *223/2225 in Belize City, 226/3535 in San Pedro* ⊕ *www.belizewatertaxi.com.*

Tropic Ferry. The Tropic Ferry provides a premium ferry service between the international airport near Belize City and most resorts on Ambergris Caye. A ferry representative meets you at the airport for a short ride to the dock in Ladyville. It's around a 75-minute trip to your destination on Ambergris Caye. You'll get a complimentary rum punch en route. Rates for this service are somewhat higher than a flight to San Pedro. (This water-taxi service is unrelated to Tropic Air, one of the domestic Belize airlines.) ✉ *1659 Yellowtail Snapper Dr., Vista del Mar, Ladyville* ☎ *631/9253* ⊕ *www.tropicferry.com.*

COROZAL
Thunderbolt Water Taxi. This small company has round-trip service between Corozal Town and San Pedro Friday–Monday, departing Corozal at 7 am and departing San Pedro at 3 pm. (Off-season service may be reduced or eliminated.) The trip takes 90 minutes to two hours, depending on weather, with stops in Sarteneja on-demand. In Corozal, the *Thunderbolt* arrives and leaves at the Reunion Pier in the center of town; in San Pedro it arrives and leaves at Black Coral Street on the back side of the island near the soccer field. ✉ *Reunion Pier, Corozal Town* ☎ *610/4475 boat captain's cell, 422/0026 landline in Corozal Town* ☉ *No service Tues.–Thurs.; service may be reduced off-season.*

UP AND DOWN
AMBERGRIS
CAYE
Coastal Xpress. This is a handy service and efficient, but it demands some preplanning. Coastal Xpress provides scheduled ferry service up and down the island—you stand on a dock and the cozy vessel picks you up at an appointed time. It offers about a dozen daily trips between the Amigos del Mar pier in town and La Beliza Resort in the north, with stops on demand at most hotel and restaurants docks. If you're staying in North Ambergris and want to head to town, have your hotel arrange the ferry and you'll pay when you arrive. At this writing, service starts at 5:30 am and ends around 11 pm. Coastal Xpress also offers charter boat service to other cayes and coastal locations. Ferry schedule and service is subject to change—check locally for updates. Arrive at your dock of departure 15 minutes early. Prices depend on how far you go,

starting at BZ$10. ⊠ *Amigos del Mar Pier, Beachfront, San Pedro Town* ☎ *226/2007* ⊕ *www.coastalxpress.com.*

GOLF CART TRAVEL

There are no car rentals on Ambergris and Caulker; instead, you can rent a golf cart, typically gas-powered and so mild they don't have a speedometer. The good news is they're novel, easy, safe, and fun (kids will love them). The bad news is golf cart rentals cost about as much as a car rental in the United States: around BZ$120 a day, or BZ$500–BZ$550 a week, plus 12.5% tax. These rental companies spring up like weeds, and many hotels have a few carts to rent. Compare prices and ask for discounts.

Contacts Cholo's Golf Cart Rentals. ⊠ *Jewfish St., behind police and fire stations, San Pedro Town* ☎ *226/2406* ⊕ *www.choloscartrentals.com.* **Island Adventures Golf Cart Rentals.** ⊠ *Coconut Dr., near airstrip, San Pedro Town* ☎ *226/4343* ⊕ *www.islandgolfcarts.com.* **Moncho's Cart Rentals.** ⊠ *11 Coconut Dr., near airstrip, San Pedro Town* ☎ *226/4490.*

TAXI TRAVEL

Regular taxicabs are available in San Pedro and in the developed area south of town on Ambergris Caye. Most trips in and close to town are BZ$10 for up to four persons (check the price before getting in). For trips north of the bridge over Boca del Rio, it's expensive: cabs charge BZ$25–BZ$50, including the BZ$12 vehicle bridge fee. Have your hotel arrange for a cab, or hail one of the cabs cruising the downtown area. On Caulker there are golf-cart taxis, which charge BZ$5–BZ$10 per person for most trips.

HEALTH AND SAFETY

In San Pedro Town and nearby, the water comes from a municipal water system and is safe to drink, although most people including local residents prefer to drink filtered water. On North Ambergris, water may come from cisterns or wells. On Caye Caulker the water, sometimes from brackish shallow wells, may smell of sulfur. A new village reverse osmosis system began operation in 2011, but not everyone is on it. If in doubt, drink bottled water. On other remote cayes, the water usually comes from cisterns; stick to the bottled stuff, unless you're assured that the water is potable. To be green, you can buy water in large one- or five-gallon bottles and refill your carry-around bottle; you'll save a little money, too.

In terms of crime risk, the cayes are among the safest areas of Belize. However, petty thefts—and sometimes worse—do happen. With some 20,000 people on Ambergris Caye, if you count tourists and itinerant workers, the island has the same crime problems, including rapes and murders, as any area of similar population. There are drugs, including crack cocaine, on both Caye Caulker and Ambergris Caye. Ignore any offers to buy drugs, even marijuana, which, while widely used in Belize, is still illegal, and police do make arrests for weed.

EMERGENCIES

The Ambergris Hope Clinic and the public San Pedro Dr. Otto Rodriquez Poly Clinic II on Ambergris Caye have services just short of a full-scale hospital. They are open weekdays 8–8 and Saturday 8–noon. Doctors and nurses are on 24-hour call. Three or four other clinics and private medical practices, four pharmacies, a chiropractic clinic, several dentists, and a hyperbaric chamber (affiliated with many Belize dive shops) are also on the island. For serious medical emergencies, patients are usually transferred to Karl Heusner Memorial Hospital, the nation's main public referral hospital, in Belize City, or to one of the private hospitals in Belize City, Belize Medical Associates or Belize Healthcare Partners.

On Caye Caulker the Caye Caulker Health Center is usually staffed by a volunteer doctor from Cuba. For dental care or serious ailments you need to go to Belize City. There are no medical facilities on any of the other cayes, but if you have an emergency, call your embassy or contact Karl Heusner Memorial Hospital, Belize Medical Associates, or Belize Healthcare Partners.

Astrum Helicopters provides emergency airlift services.

For police emergencies, call 911. On marine radios, channel 16 is the international distress channel.

Contacts Ambergris Hope Clinic. ⊠ *Pescador Dr., San Pedro Town* ☎ *226/2660.* **San Pedro Polyclinic II.** ⊠ *Manta Ray St., San Pedro Town* ☎ *226/2536.*

HOTELS

The more budget-oriented cayes, such as Tobacco and Caulker, have mostly small hotels and simple cabins, often built of wood and typically without any amenities beyond a fan or two, though this is changing on Caulker, which is growing more upscale. At the other end, notably on Ambergris Caye, are luxurious resorts and deluxe "condotels" (condo developments where individual owners rent their units on a daily basis through a management company) and an increasing number of vacation villas, usually rented by the week. Nearly all accommodations on Ambergris Caye have air-conditioning, and most also have swimming pools. Regardless of which caye you're staying on, lodgings have several things in common: they're small (usually fewer than 30 or 40 rooms), low-rise (nearly all have three stories or fewer), almost always are directly on the water. Most actual hotels are boutique, independently owned, or part of a small hotel group.

■ TIP→ **Off-season (typically May to around Thanksgiving), most island hotels, especially the luxurious kind, reduce rates by around 20% to 40%.**

HOTEL AND RESTAURANT PRICES

Prices in the restaurant reviews are the average cost of a main course at dinner or, if dinner is not served, at lunch. Prices in the hotel reviews are the lowest cost of a standard double room in high season, including taxes, service charges, but excluding meal plans (except at all-inclusives).

Prices for rentals are the lowest per-night cost for a one-bedroom unit in high season.

For expanded lodging reviews, visit Fodors.com.

WHAT IT COSTS IN BELIZE DOLLARS			
$	$$	$$$	$$$$
RESTAURANTS under BZ$15	BZ$15–BZ$30	BZ$31–BZ$50	over BZ$50
HOTELS under BZ$200	BZ$200–BZ$350	BZ$351–BZ$550	over BZ$550

Restaurant prices are per person for a main course at dinner. Hotel prices are for two people in a standard double room, including tax and service.

RESTAURANTS

Ambergris Caye has the biggest selection of restaurants in Belize. Restaurants range from barbecue and picnic tables to white linen and candlelight. At the latter type, you can spend BZ$100 a person or more, including a cocktail or wine. You have a wide choice of kinds of food on Ambergris: seafood, of course, but also steak, pizza, sushi, tapas, Chinese, Italian, Thai, and Mexican.

Caye Caulker has a number of small bistros where fish arrives at your table fresh from the ocean, and often you find yourself eating with your feet in the sand. On other islands you're limited to eating at your dive lodge or resort.

On both Caye Caulker and Ambergris Caye street vendors set up barbecue grills along Front Street and on the beachfront and cook chicken, fish, shrimp, and lobster. Use your own judgment, but we've found in almost all cases the food from these vendors is safe, tasty, and inexpensive.

TOURS

MAINLAND TOURS

From Ambergris and Caulker, and from smaller cayes with advance planning, you can do day trips to the mainland to see Mayan ruins, try cave tubing, visit the wonderful Belize Zoo, and do other activities. However, the cost will be significantly higher than if you did the tour from a closer point.

Tour operators on the Cayes run trips to Mayan sites such as **Lamanai** (usually a full-day trip by boat and road) and **Altun Ha** (normally a half-day trip, although it may be longer if it includes lunch and a spa visit at Maruba Spa). If you're up for a trek, you can visit **Tikal** on an overnight trip by air to Flores, Guatemala, with a change of planes in Belize City. It's also possible to see the small, unexcavated ruins on Ambergris Caye—including Marco Gonzalez on the south end of the island, reachable by golf cart or taxi, and **Chac Balam** at Bacalar, reachable by boat.

(See Ambergris Caye "Tour" section.)

SCUBA DIVING AND SNORKELING

Diving near the cayes is world-class and snorkeling is ubiquitous. Most dive-trip operators (who are usually also snorkel-boat operators) are on Ambergris Caye. Many operators also offer PADI courses. San Pedro has Belize's only hyperbaric chamber and an on-site doctor. Many dive shops are attached to hotels, where the quality of dive masters, equipment, and facilities can vary considerably. It's a short boat ride to the spur-and-groove formations along the Barrier Reef and to Hol Chan Marine Reserve. Several San Pedro operators with speedboats can take you to the Blue Hole, the largest ocean sinkhole in the world.

VISITOR INFORMATION

The best sources of information on the islands are online. Operated by Marty Casado, AmbergrisCaye.com (⊕ *www.ambergriscaye.com*) is the number one source, with thousands of pages of information on San Pedro, and to a lesser extent on Caye Caulker. For intimate insight that's very current, see American expat Rebecca Coutant's blog, the San Pedro Scoop (⊕ *www.sanpedroscoop.com*). The Belize Tourism Board has updated its website (⊕ *www.travelbelize.org*) with more information on the cayes and atolls. The Taco Girl blog (⊕ *www.tacogirl.com*) has timely info on island happenings, though some of it is a little commercial. Caye Caulker's official Belize Tourist Industry Association (BTIA) website is ⊕ *www.gocayecaulker.com*. Belize First (⊕ *www.belizefirst.com*) has information and extensive free downloads on the islands. The *San Pedro Sun* (⊕ *www.sanpedrosun.com*) newspaper publishes a free weekly tabloid-size visitor newspaper, the *San Pedro Sun Visitor Guide*. *Ambergris Today* (⊕ *www.ambergristoday.com*) is an online weekly newspaper for San Pedro.

THE CAYES

ST. GEORGE'S CAYE AND OTHER CAYES NEAR BELIZE CITY

9 miles (15 km) northeast of Belize City.

Just a stone's throw from Belize City, St. George's Caye is steeped in history. The country of Belize had its origins here, as St. George's Caye held the original British settlement's first capital. In 1798 the island was the site of a decisive battle with the Spanish. Islanders had only one sloop, while the Spanish had 31 ships. Their knowledge of the sea, however, helped them to defeat the invaders in two hours. Some affluent Belize City residents weekend in their private cottages here. Although St. George's Caye has great places to dive, many serious scuba enthusiasts choose to head out to the more pristine atolls or to private cayes farther south.

Another option about 9 miles (15 km) from Belize City is Royal Palm Island Resort on Little Frenchman Caye. This caye is indeed little, but it offers modern accommodations.

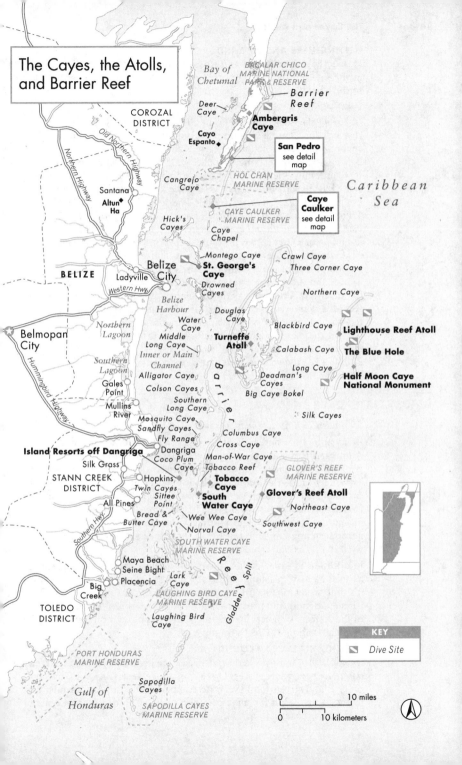

The Cayes, the Atolls, and Barrier Reef

COROZAL DISTRICT

Bay of Chetumal

BACALAR CHICO MARINE NATIONAL PARK & RESERVE

Barrier Reef

Deer Caye

Ambergris Caye

Cayo Espanto

San Pedro see detail map

Caribbean Sea

Cangrejo Caye

HOL CHAN MARINE RESERVE

CAYE CAULKER MARINE RESERVE

Caye Caulker see detail map

Santana

Altun Ha

Hick's Cayes

Caye Chapel

Montego Caye

Crawl Caye

Three Corner Caye

Belize City

Ladyville

BELIZE

Western Hwy.

St. George's Caye

Drowned Cayes

Northern Caye

Belize Harbour

Douglas Caye

Water Caye

Blackbird Caye

Lighthouse Reef Atoll

Northern Lagoon

Middle Long Caye

Turneffe Atoll

Calabash Caye

The Blue Hole

Belmopan City

Inner or Main Channel

Southern Lagoon

Alligator Caye

Long Caye

Deadman's Cayes

Half Moon Caye National Monument

Gales Point

Colson Cayes

Big Caye Bokel

Southern Long Caye

Mullins River

Mosquito Caye

Sandfly Cayes

Silk Cayes

Fly Range

Columbus Caye

Island Resorts off Dangriga

Cross Caye

Dangriga

Coco Plum Caye

Man-of-War Caye

Tobacco Reef

GLOVER'S REEF MARINE RESERVE

Silk Grass

Tobacco Caye

STANN CREEK DISTRICT

Hopkins

South Water Caye

Glover's Reef Atoll

Twin Cayes

Sittee Point

Northeast Caye

All Pines

Wee Wee Caye

Southwest Caye

Bread & Butter Caye

Norval Caye

SOUTH WATER CAYE MARINE RESERVE

Maya Beach

Seine Bight

Placencia

Lark Caye

Big Creek

LAUGHING BIRD CAYE MARINE RESERVE

TOLEDO DISTRICT

Laughing Bird Caye

Gladden Split

PORT HONDURAS MARINE RESERVE

Sapodilla Cayes

Gulf of Honduras

SAPODILLA CAYES MARINE RESERVE

Old Northern Highway

Northern Highway

Hummingbird Highway

Southern Hwy.

Reef

Barrier Reef

0   10 miles

0   10 kilometers

KEY

Dive Site

GETTING HERE AND AROUND

St. George's Caye Resort and Royal Palm Island Resort will meet you at the international airport and handle your 20-minute boat transfer to the islands.

WHERE TO STAY

$$$$
RESORT
FAMILY

Royal Palm Island Resort. For an all-inclusive, family-friendly option, Royal Palm Island is a good pick, with its giant inflatable toys, large swimming pool, welcoming service, and only 20 minutes by boat to Belize City. **Pros:** relaxing, intimate getaway near Belize City; friendly service; family-friendly. **Cons:** not directly on reef; tiny island; expensive. $ *Rooms from: BZ$1,708 ⊠ Little Frenchman Caye, 9 miles (15 km) east of Belize City* ☎ *223/4999, 888/969–7829 in U.S. and Canada* ⊕ *www.royalpalmisland.com* ⌇ *5 cottages* ⦿ *All-inclusive* ⌁ *Rate listed include meals and boat transfer.*

$$$$
RESORT

St. George's Caye Resort. In colonial days St. George's Caye was a British favorite because of its proximity to Belize City, about 20 minutes by boat; more recently wealthy Belize City families weekended on the island, and today visitors favor the adult-only resort as a rustic venue for adventure. **Pros:** good diving available, though not included in rates; secluded island resort atmosphere; free airport transfers. **Cons:** not easy to visit mainland or other islands; paradise comes unplugged (Wi-Fi only in the main lodge); mealtimes decided for you. $ *Rooms from: BZ$568 ⊠ St. George's Caye* ☎ *800/813–8498 in U.S. and Canada, 220/4444* ⊕ *www.belizeislandparadise.com* ⌇ *12 cabañas, 8 rooms* ⦿ *All-inclusive.*

AMBERGRIS CAYE AND SAN PEDRO

35 miles (56 km) northeast of Belize City.

At 25 miles (40 km) long and 4.5 miles (7 km) wide at its widest point, Ambergris is the queen of the cayes. Here the Northern Barrier Reef is just a few hundred yards from shore, making access to dive sites extremely easy—the journey by boat takes as little as 10 minutes. On early maps it was often referred to as Costa de Ambar, or the Amber Coast, a name supposedly derived from the blackish substance secreted by sperm whales—ambergris—that washes up on the beaches. Having never seen any ambergris in Belize, or a sperm whale, we're not sure we buy this explanation.

In addition to great diving, there's snorkeling, fishing, sailboarding, as well as just splashing in the sea or just lazing on the beach until it's time to sample one of the dozens of restaurants on the island. The island's friendly and prosperous population is around 16,000, has one of the country's highest literacy rates, and maintains admirable level of awareness about the reef's fragility.

GETTING HERE AND AROUND

In San Pedro, hard-packed sand streets are giving way to the concrete cobblestones of Barrier Reef Drive, Pescador Street, Coconut Drive and other island streets, and everyone complains about the worsening car traffic in town, but the most common forms of transportation remain golf cart, bike, and foot.

HISTORY

Because of their strategic locations on trade routes between the Yucatán in the north and Honduras in the south, the northern cayes, especially Ambergris Caye and Caye Caulker, were long occupied by the Maya. Then, as now, the reef and its abundance of fish provided a valuable source of seafood.

The origin of Belize's atolls remains a mystery, but evidence suggests they grew from the bottom up, as vast pagodas of coral accumulated over millions of years. The Maya were perhaps the first humans to discover the atolls, but by the time the first Spanish explorers arrived in 1508, the Mayan civilization had already mysteriously collapsed and few remained on the islands.

In the 17th century, English pirates used the cayes and atolls as a hideout, plotting their attacks on unwary ships. The most famous battle in Belize history happened on September 10, 1798, when a ragtag band of buccaneers defeated a Spanish armada at the Battle of St. George's Caye.

The economy on the islands has ebbed and flowed, as pirates were replaced by wealthy plantation owners, who were eventually usurped by lobster fishermen. The first hotel on Ambergris Caye, Holiday Hotel, opened in 1965 and soon began attracting divers. Jacques Cousteau visited the Blue Hole in 1971 and helped introduce Belize to the world. Today tourism is by far the top industry on the cayes and atolls.

North Ambergris is far more accessible by golf cart since the paving of the road. This has thinned the crowds in San Pedro and opened up possibility for more construction. When anticipating the future of Ambergris, look north.

For the far north, water-taxis remain the most common transportation to resorts and restaurants.

TIMING

Belize's most popular destination merits a significant chunk of your vacation time. Indeed, some visitors to Belize only experience Ambergris Caye. With its many restaurants, bars, and shops, plus myriad opportunities for water sports, you can easily spend a week or more on the island without beginning to run out of things to do.

SAFETY

With rapid growth and an influx of workers from other parts of Belize and Central America, Ambergris Caye has seen an increase in all types of crime. However, nearly all visitors to Ambergris Caye say they feel perfectly safe, and most of the larger hotels have full-time security. Use common sense and avoid walking on dark streets and deserted beaches after nightfall. Keep purses on the ground, not the back of your chair, at restaurants.

WATER ACTIVITIES

CHARTERS

El Gato. A 30-foot sailing catamaran, *El Gato* does day cruises to Caye Caulker, with stops for snorkeling, for BZ$130 per person (minimum three persons). Captain Geraldo Badillo is at the helm and will narrate the cruise. Half-day sails to Mexico Rocks or Hol Chan, are available. The sunset cruise is recommended; for a bit extra they'll host a beach barbecue with fresh-caught fish and lobster. *El Gato* can take up to 12 persons, but it's rarely fully booked; it's a less crowded experience than some snorkel tours. The boat will pick you up at your resort. ⊠ *San Pedro Town* 🕾 *226/2264* ✆ *elgatotours@yahoo.com* ⊕ *www. ambergriscaye.com/elgato.*

FISHING

Although southern Belize, especially Placencia, is the main sportfishing center in Belize, Ambergris Caye also has good opportunities for flats, reef, and deep-sea fishing. May to September is the best time for catching tarpon off Ambergris Caye; April to October is the best time for bonefish; and March through May is best for permit. Reef fishing for snapper, grouper, barracuda, and other reef fish is more expensive. Inquire about the cost of deep-sea fishing outside the reef for billfish, sailfish, wahoo, and tuna; sportfishing license (catch and release only) is now required for fishing in Belize waters, except for fishing off piers or from shore. You can buy a license online from the Belize Coastal Zone Management Authority and Institute (⊕ *www.coastalzonebelize.org*) or your fishing guide or hotel may be able to help you get it. El Pescador (⇨ *See full review in Where to Stay in San Pedro.*) is the leading fishing lodge on Ambergris Caye and one of the top in Belize.

For fishing that's easier on the pocketbook, you can fish for snapper, barracuda, and other fish from piers and docks on the island. No license is required. Bring your own gear or buy tackle at local hardware stores and ask local anglers about bait. Small sardines work well. For fly-fishing aficionados, there are multiple shops. You can also wade out in the flats near shore on North Ambergris, north of the river channel on the back (west) side, and try your luck with bonefish. Keep an eye out for the occasional crocodile. You'll catch more with a guide and boat, but fishing on your own is inexpensive fun.

FISHING **Fishing San Pedro.** A fishing service run by Steve DeMaio, Fishing San
GUIDES Pedro works with a number of guides on the island. Call and describe what you want and he'll arrange a guide and boat for spin or fly fishing. Rates for a half day of flats or reef fishing are around BZ$500 for up to four persons, including boat, guide, and tackle; full-day flats fishing runs around BZ$750 for up to two. A beach barbecue is BZ$100 per boat and tips to guides not included. ⊠ *San Pedro Town* 🕾 *607/9967, 860/966–3902 in U.S.* ⊕ *www.fishingsanpedro.com.*

George Bradley. Long-time local guide George Bradley specializes in fly-fishing for bonefish. ⊠ *San Pedro Town* 🕾 *226/2179.*

GoFish Belize. Local fishing guide Abbie Marin arranges flats, reef, and deep-sea fishing charters. A full day of fly or spin flats fishing is BZ$850 for one or two persons and beginners are welcome. ⊠ *Boca Del Rio Dr., San Pedro Town* ☎ *226/3121, 703/646–3474 in U.S.* ⊕ *www.gofishbelize.com.*

Lori-Ann Murphy. Lori-Ann Murphy is an extremely qualified guide and general resource on fishing in Belize. She also owns the Reel Women Fly Fishing Adventures. ⊠ *San Pedro Town* ⊕ *www.loriannmurphy.com.*

JET SKIS

FAMILY **Castaway Caye Water Sports.** A reputable outfit which lets you ride Jet Skis, waterski, parasail, and kayak, or ride banana boats and minipower catamarans. ⊠ *Beachfront, Boca del Rio Dr., at Wet Willy's, San Pedro Town* ☎ *671/3000* ⊕ *www.castawaycaye.com.*

FAMILY **Monkey Business Tour Shop.** Monkey Business Tour Shop at Banana Beach Resort has Jet Ski rentals for BZ$200 for one hour. ⊠ *Banana Beach Resort, Coconut Dr., San Pedro Town* ☎ *226/3890, 877/288–1011* ⊕ *www.monkeybusinesstours.com.*

SCUBA DIVING AND SNORKELING

Dives off Ambergris are usually single tank at depths of 50 to 80 feet, allowing about 35 minutes of bottom time. Diving trips run around BZ$90 for a single-tank dive, BZ$150 for a two-tank dive, BZ$90–BZ$110 for a one-tank night dive, BZ$500 for a three-tank full-day drive trip to Turneffe atoll, and BZ$750 for day trips with three dives to Lighthouse Reef. Dive gear rental is usually extra—a full package of gear including wet suit, buoyancy compensator, regulator, mask, and fins is around BZ$80. Snorkeling by boat around Ambergris generally costs BZ$80–BZ$100 per person for two or three hours or BZ$140–BZ$200 for a day trip, including lunch. If you go to Hol Chan Marine Reserve there's a BZ$20 park fee, but this fee is sometimes included in the quoted rate. A snorkel trip to the Blue Hole is around BZ$450–BZ$480, including the BZ$80 Marine Reserve fee. Snorkel gear rental may be additional. Prices also may not include 12.5% tax. (Businesses are supposed to include the 12.5% GST in their quoted prices, but not all do.) Most dive shops will pick you up at your hotel or at the nearest pier.

■TIP→ **Be careful when snorkeling off docks and piers on Ambergris Caye. There's heavy boat traffic between the reef and shore, and boat captains may not be able to see snorkelers in the water. Several snorkelers near shore have been killed or seriously injured by boats.**

DIVE AND SNORKEL SITES

Fodor's Choice ★

Bacalar Chico Marine National Park & Reserve. Development on Ambergris continues relentlessly, but most of the far north of the island remains pristine, or close to it. At the top of the caye, butting up against Mexico, Bacalar Chico National Park and Marine Reserve spans 41 square miles (105 square km) of land, reef, and sea. Here, on 11 miles (18 km) of trails you may cross paths with whitetail deer, ocelots, saltwater crocodiles, and, according to some reports, pumas and jaguars. There are beautiful diving, snorkeling, and fishing opportunities, especially off Rocky Point, and a small visitor center and museum will get you oriented. You'll need a boat and a guide to take you here, where there are at least nine ancient Mayan sites. Walk carefully, as loggerhead and green sea turtles nest here. Be sure to bring insect repellent. An all-day snorkel trip to Bacalar Chico from San Pedro will be unforgettable. ⊠ *North end of Ambergris Caye, Ambergris Caye* ☎ *226/2833* 🎫 *BZ$10 day pass or BZ$30 week pass.*

Fodor's Choice   **Belize Barrier Reef.** From the island shore, or from the air, you see the
★   coral reef as an almost unbroken chain of white surf. Get closer and
the water is clear and shallow; the reef itself is a beautiful living wall
formed by billions of small coral polyps. The Belize Barrier Reef runs
along the eastern shore of Ambergris Caye and is one of the most wor-
thy attractions in Belize, accessible by boat and kayak. Just outside the
reef, the seabed drops sharply, and gives the water the blue and amethyst
tones that astonish. The reef is closest to shore on the far-north end
of Ambergris Caye. In and around San Pedro Town, the barrier reef is
a few hundred yards off the beach. It's a widely accepted rumor that
this UNESCO World Heritage site is the second-longest barrier reef
in the world, after the Great Barrier Reef in Australia and it's no less
spectacular. ⊠ *Ambergris Caye.*

Fodor's Choice   **Hol Chan Marine Reserve.** The reef's focal point for diving and snor-
★   keling near Ambergris Caye and Caye Caulker is the spectacular Hol
Chan Marine Reserve (Maya for "little channel"). It's a 20-minute
boat ride from San Pedro, and about 30 minutes from Caye Caulker.
Hol Chan is a break in the reef about 100 feet wide and 20 to 35 feet
deep, through which tremendous volumes of water pass with the tides.
Shark-Ray Alley, now a part of Hol Chan, is famous as a place to
swim, snorkel, and dive with sharks (nearly all are nurse sharks) and
Southern stingrays.

■TIP→ **During peak visitor periods to the cayes or when several cruise
ships are docked off Belize City, snorkel tour boats can stack up at Hol
Chan. Check locally to see when Hol Chan may be less busy, and consider visiting in early morning before most of the tours arrive.**

The expanded 21-square-mile (55-square-km) park has a miniature Blue
Hole and a 12-foot-deep cave whose entrance often attracts the fairy
basslet, an iridescent purple-and-yellow fish frequently seen here. The
reserve is also home to a large moray eel population.

Varying in depth from 50 feet to 100 feet, Hol Chan's canyons lie
between buttresses of coral running perpendicular to the reef, separated
by white, sandy channels. You may find tunnel-like passageways from
one canyon to the next. It's exciting to explore because as you come over
each hill you don't know what you'll see in the "valley." Because fishing generally is off-limits here, divers and snorkelers can see abundant
marine life. There are throngs of squirrelfish, butterfly fish, parrotfish,
and queen angelfish, as well as Nassau groupers, barracuda, and large
shoals of yellowtail snappers. Unfortunately, also here are lionfish, an
invasive Indo-Pacific species that is eating its way—destroying small
native fish—from Venezuela to the North Carolina coast. Altogether,
more than 160 species of fish have been identified in the marine reserve,
along with 40 species of coral, and five kinds of sponges. Hawksbill,
loggerhead, and green turtles have also been found here, along with
spotted and common dolphins, West Indian manatees, stingrays and
several species of sharks.

⚠ **The currents through the reef can be strong here at times, so tell
your guide if you're not a strong swimmer and ask for a snorkel vest
or float. Also, although the nurse sharks are normally docile and very**

used to humans, they are wild creatures that on rare occasions have bitten snorkelers or divers who disturbed them. ⊠ *Off southern tip of Ambergris Caye, Ambergris Caye* ☎ *526–2247 in San Pedro* ⊕ *www. holchanbelize.org* ⊠ *BZ$20, normally included in snorkel or dive tour charge.*

Shark-Ray Alley. Shark-Ray Alley is a sandbar within Hol Chan Marine Reserve where you can snorkel alongside nurse sharks (which can bite but rarely do) and stingrays (which gather here to be fed) and near even larger numbers of day-trippers from San Pedro and from cruise ships. Sliding into the water is a small feat of personal bravery—the sight of sharks and rays brushing past is spectacular yet daunting. Although they shouldn't, guides touch and hold sharks and rays, and sometimes encourage visitors to pet these sea creatures (which you shouldn't do, either). The Hol Chan Marine Reserve office is on Caribena Street in San Pedro. ■ TIP➔ **A night dive at Shark-Ray Alley is a special treat: bioluminescence causes the water to light up, and many nocturnal animals emerge, such as octopus and spider crab. Because of the strong current you'll need above-average swimming skills.** ⊠ *Southern tip of Ambergris Caye in Hol Chan Marine Reserve, Ambergris Caye* ☎ *226/2247 Hol Chan office on Caribena St. in San Pedro* ⊕ *www.holchanbelize. org* ⊠ *BZ$20 marine reserve fee included as a part of Hol Chan fee.*

DIVE SHOPS AND OPERATORS Many dive shops and resorts have diving courses. A half-day basic familiarization course or "resort course" costs around BZ$350. A complete four-day PADI open-water certification course costs BZ$900–BZ$1,100. One popular variant is a referral course, where the academic and pool training is done at home, or online, but not the required dives. The cost for two days in Belize is about BZ$550–BZ$650. Prices for dive courses vary a little from island to island, generally being least expensive on Caye Caulker. However, even prices on Ambergris Caye, which tends to have higher costs for most activities, are a little lower than on the mainland.

If you're staying on Ambergris Caye, Glover's Reef is out of the question for a day trip by boat. Even with perfect weather—which it often isn't—a trip to Lighthouse Reef takes between two and three hours. Most trips to Lighthouse and the Blue Hole depart at 6 am and return at 5:30 or 6 pm, making for a long day in the sun and water. Turneffe is more accessible, though it's still a long and costly day trip, and you're unlikely to reach the atoll's southern tip, which has the best diving. Consult your hotel or a dive shop for your best options for your time and budget. Most companies include refreshments like soda and fresh fruit to fortify you during the resurface interval.

Amigos del Mar. Amigos del Mar, established in 1987, is perhaps the island's most consistently recommended dive operation. The SSI/SDI facility has a dozen dive boats, 16 contracted divemasters, and a range of local dives as well as trips to Turneffe Atoll and Lighthouse Reef in a fast 56-foot dive boat. You can choose from a local two-tank dive or a 12-hour trip to the Blue Hole, including the park entry fee and lunch. An open-water certification course is also offered. Amigos also offers snorkel and fishing trips. ✉ *On pier off Barrier Reef Dr., near Mayan Princess Hotel, San Pedro Town* ☎ *226–2706, 800/882–6159* ⊕ *www.amigosdivebelize.com.*

Fodor's Choice
★

Chuck and Robbie's Scuba Diving and Instruction. Playful, considerate, and professional, these guides can safely accommodating every skill level. With four boats of varying lengths for different water conditions, dive trips depart at 9 am and 2 pm daily. They also do snorkel and fishing tours. Two-tank dives begin at BZ$100 before equipment and other fees. ✉ *Boca del Rio Dr., Beachfront, San Pedro Town* ☎ *226/4425* ⊕ *www.ambergriscayediving.com.*

Ecologic Divers. This PADI shop has won a good reputation for safety, service, and ecologically sound practices. Local two-tank dives go out daily at 9 and 2 and cost BZ$160, not including any equipment rental or 12.5% tax. Full-day Turneffe trips are BZ$500 including breakfast and lunch, but not 12.5% tax. ✉ *On pier at north end of San Pedro, just south of The Phoenix resort, San Pedro Town* ☎ *226/4118, 800/244–7774 in U.S. and Canada* ⊕ *www.ecologicdivers.com.*

Lil' Alphonse Tours. Specializing in snorkeling, Lil' Alphonse himself usually captains the tours, doing a fabulous job making snorkelers feel comfortable in the water. ✉ *Coconut Dr., across street from Changes in Latitudes B&B, San Pedro Town* ☎ *226/3136* ✎ *lilalphonsetours@ yahoo.com* ⊕ *www.ambergriscaye.com/alfonso.*

SEAduced by Belize. This locally run, reputable snorkeling, sailing, and inland tour company does full-day snorkeling trips to Bacalar Chico, Hol Chan, Mexico Rocks, and Robles Point, as well as mainland trips to Mayan sites and cave tubing. They offer sailing cruises as well. Their website is dated so communication is sometimes slow. ✉ *Vilma Linda Plaza, Tarpon St., San Pedro Town* ☎ *226/2254* ⊕ *www.seaducedby-belize.com.*

SEArious Adventures. This long-established snorkeling and sailing shop does day snorkel trips to Caye Caulker (BZ$100 plus park fees and equipment rental), along with a variety of other snorkel and sail trips. It also offers day sails and mainland tours. ✉ *Beachfront, on dock, Between Tarpon and Black Coral St., San Pedro Town* ☎ *226/4202* ⊕ *www.seariousadventures.com.*

Fodor's Choice
★

White Sands Dive Shop. White Sands Dive Shop isn't at White Sands Resort but at Las Terrazas. Never mind, this PADI dive center is run by Elbert Greer, a noted diver and birder who has taught scuba in San Pedro for more than 20 years, getting some 2,500 divers certified. ✉ *Beachfront at Las Terrazas, Ambergris Caye* ☎ *226/2405* ⊕ *www. whitesandsdiveshop.com.*

DIVE BOATS

If you want to hit the best dive spots in Belize and dive a lot—up to five or six dives a day—live-aboard dive boats may be your best bet. The *Aggressor* Fleet concentrates on dives around Lighthouse Reef atoll and the Blue Hole. The boats are based at the Radisson Fort George Hotel in Belize City.

Aggressor Fleet. The *Aggressor* Fleet operates two luxurious live-aboard yachts, the *Belize Aggressor III* and Belize *Aggressor IV*. Boats leave on Saturday evening from Belize City for Lighthouse Reef, Half Moon

HOW TO CHOOSE A DIVE MASTER

Many dive masters in Belize are former anglers who began diving on the side and ended up doing it full time. The best have an intimate knowledge of the reef and a superb eye for coral and marine life.

When choosing a dive master or dive shop, first check the Web. Participants on forums and newsgroups such as ⊕ www.ambergriscaye.com and ⊕ www.scubaboard.com field many questions on diving and dive shops in Belize. On islands where there are multiple dive shops, spend some time talking to dive masters to see which ones make you feel most comfortable. Find out about their backgrounds and experience, as well as the actual crew that would be going out with you. Are they dive masters, instructors, or just crew? Get a sense of how the dive master feels about reef and sea life conservation.

Besides questions about costs and equipment, ask:

■ How many people, maximum, go out on your dive trips?

■ Is there a minimum number of divers before you'll make the trip?

■ What dive sites are your favorites, and why?

■ What kind of boats do you have, and how long does it take to get where we're going?

■ Who is actually in the water with the divers?

■ What kind of safety and communications equipment is on the boat?

■ What's the procedure for cancellation in case of bad weather?

■ How do you decide if you're going out or not?

If you're not comfortable with the answers, or if the dive shop just doesn't pass your sniff test, move on.

Caye, and the Blue Hole, with as many as five or six dives each day available. They return to port the next Friday. The *Aggressor IV*, a 138-foot cruiser, can accommodate up to 20 passengers in 10 staterooms. The *Aggressor III* is slightly smaller. All staterooms have private bathroomss, TVs, and DVDs, plus individual climate controls. Both all-inclusive yachts are about US$3,000 per person for the week, exclusive of port fees, equipment and other fine print matters. Guests are met at the international airport near Belize City and are taken to the dock at the Radisson Fort George. ⊠ *Lighthouse Reef* ☎ *706/993–2531 U.S. office, 800/348–2628 in U.S. and Canada* ⊕ *www.aggressor.com.*

WINDSURFING AND KITESURFING

Caye Caulker is actually better known as a windsurfing destination, perhaps because it attracts a younger crowd than Ambergris Caye, but the winds are equally good and consistent off Ambergris Caye. February through July sees the windiest conditions, with winds 12 to 20 knots most days. Kitesurfing, combining a windsurfing-type board pulled by a large kite, is also available on Ambergris.

FAMILY   **ConTour Ocean Ventures.** This locally owned company pledges low-impact water explorations that include windsurfing trips, paddleboard tours of mangrove areas, snorkeling, and volunteering with conservation efforts.

You'll learn much from the excellent guides about everything from sea horses to crocodiles (you may encounter both). ✉ *Playa Ascunción, Caye Caulker* ☎ *635/8757* 🌐 *www.contourbelize.com.*

KiteXplorer. This company has an office in San Pedro as well as Caye Caulker. The cost is slightly more on San Pedro, but the difference isn't worth an extra trip to Caulker. These folks know kites, and you can trust them to coordinate a good experience whether you're seasoned or just learned the word *kitesurfing*. A three-hour intro to kitesurfing costs BZ$380 including equipment and insurance; basic course over three or four days is BZ$1,150; and supervised equipment rental is BZ$120 an hour. ✉ *San Pedro Town* ☎ *635/4769, 632/4101* 🌐 *www.kitexplorer.com.*

MAINLAND TOURS

Mainland tours are pricier from here. If tour prices from San Pedro seem too high, you can take a water taxi to Belize City and rent a car or take a cab for your own DIY tour, though the hassle factor might not make it worth it.

Tanisha Eco Tours. One of the best San Pedro tour operators for mainland trips, Tanisha specializes in full-day Lamanai trips where you'll boat up the New River past cohune palms en route to the Mayan ruins. This includes a light breakfast, lunch, beer, rum punch, and soft drinks, and costs around BZ$240. Tanisha also offers cave tubing, zip-lining, trips to Altun Ha, and other tours. ✉ *Beachfront, Coconut Dr., at Hurricane's Ceviche Bar, San Pedro Town* ☎ *226/4124* 🌐 *www.tanishatoursbelize.com.*

WILDLIFE TOURS

FAMILY Fodor's Choice ★ **American Crocodile Education Sanctuary** (*ACES*). A remarkable tour that puts you on a small skiff to witness a croc wrangler tag and release these primordial creatures for environmental research. If you can, try to do a night tour, where you'll help look for those wily red eyes breaking the water. ✉ *Elliot Subdivision, San Pedro Town* ✣ *On lagoon side, at Office Bar and Grill* ☎ *623/7920* 🌐 *www.americancrocodilesanctuary.org.*

WHERE TO EAT

Ambergris Caye has the largest and most diverse selection of restaurants in the country. Buy cheap tacos, papusas, or grilled chicken from a street vendor, eat barbecued fish on the beach, or, at the other end, dine on lobster, crab claws, and steak at upscale eateries. Even the most upmarket spots have a casual atmosphere, some with sand floors and screenless windows open to catch the breezes from the sea.

The largest concentration of restaurants is in town, but many, including some of the best on the island, are opening on the South End and especially on North Ambergris.

SAN PEDRO TOWN

$ BAKERY Fodor's Choice ★ ✕ **Annie's Pastries.** Snug as a pink box of pastries, Annie's is open only in the late afternoon and evening, and offers empanadas, sandwiches, and mini loaves of banana bread at local prices. Or you can select from the unlabeled display in the window and see what you bite into. [$] *Average main: BZ$4* ✉ *Laguna Dr., San Pedro Town* ✣ *Across street from high school* ☎ *226/2032* 💳 *No credit cards.*

$$$ CARIBBEAN FAMILY

🍴 **Caliente.** The red pepper logo and "Eat Love Margarita" signs may remind you of a hokey chain restaurant, and frankly parts of the menu might, too, but the food—Mexican with a Caribbean and Belizean spin—hits all the right notes. The ginger-rum shrimp is brightly flavored, the waterfront patio is airy, and the attitude is unpretentious. The same seasoned owners also operate Red Ginger and Blue Water Grill. [$] *Average main: BZ$34* ✉ *Barrier Reef Dr., in Spindrift Hotel, San Pedro Town* ☎ *226/2170* 🌐 *www.calientebelize.com* 🕒 *Closed Mon.*

$ CAFÉ FAMILY Fodor's Choice ★

🍴 **DandE's Frozen Custard & Sorbet.** You'll know from the patchy wallpaper of kids' (and adults') drawings that this parlor is beloved. American expats Dan and Eileen (DandE) Jamison, who used to run the *San Pedro Sun*, have been serving creamy custards and cooling sorbets—so dense they resist quick melting—for more than 10 years. For an island flavor, try the mango sorbet or the soursop frozen custard. [$] *Average main: BZ$7* ✉ *Pescador Dr., next to Cocina Caramba, San Pedro Town* ☎ *660/5966* 🌐 *www.dande.bz* 💳 *No credit cards* 🕒 *Closed Mon. and Tues.*

$$ CARIBBEAN Fodor's Choice ★

🍴 **El Fogon.** Named for the open wood-fire cooking method, El Fogon serves authentic down-home Belizean cooking like *chaya* tamales, gibnut, and stew chicken, in a quaint thatch building with dirt floor. But this is no hole-in-the-wall secret gem. It embodies island-casual but with the niceness dial turned up: you sit at picnic tables, but the picnic tables have cloth runners. Food is prepared in cast-iron pots in a traditional fogon, a wood-burning stove. Though it's in town just two blocks north of the Tropic Air terminal at the airstrip, it's a little hard to find. Ask any local where it is. [$] *Average main: BZ$28* ✉ *North of Tropic Air terminal, 2 Trigger Fish St., near airport, between Esmeralda and Tarpon St., San Pedro Town* ☎ *206/2121* 💳 *No credit cards* 🕒 *Closed Sun.*

$$$ CARIBBEAN FAMILY

🍴 **Elvi's Kitchen.** Here is an island institution. In the old days, in 1974, Elvi Staines sold burgers from the window of her house. Soon she added a few tables on the sand under a flamboyant tree. Today, the floors are still sand, and the tree remains (lifeless now and cut back to fit inside the roof), but most else is changed. Enter through massive mahogany doors and you'll be tended to by a large and gracious staff. The Mayan pulled pork and other sandwiches are popular midday, and for dinner Elvi's now features upmarket dishes such as shrimp flambeéd in tequila or grilled pork with sorrel barbecue sauce. For dessert, don't pass on the coconut pie. The Mayan Feast every Friday should be on your weekend list. It's a bit touristy, but we always enjoy Elvi's. [$] *Average main: BZ$37* ✉ *Pescador Dr., near Ambergris St., San Pedro Town* ☎ *226/2404* 🌐 *www.elviskitchen.com* 🕒 *Closed Sun.*

$$ AMERICAN FAMILY

🍴 **Estel's Dine by the Sea.** Build your ideal breakfast from a mix-and-match chalkboard menu at San Pedro's most classic breakfast spot, famous for its fry jacks served with honey and mango jam. Estel's even has grits. Though a visitor favorite, the breakfast has become a bit pricey and overhyped. But the white-and-aqua building is right on the beach, as you might infer from the sandy floor and porthole-shaped windows. Best seats in the morning are on the porch where you can watch pelicans from plastic chairs. Later in the day you'll find burgers,

3

Mexican meals, and good seafood dishes here. Ⓢ *Average main: BZ$22* ✉ *Beachfront, Buccaneer St., San Pedro Town* ☎ *226/2019.*

$$ ✕ **Fido's Courtyard and Pier.** Sooner or later you're sure to end up at Fido's
AMERICAN (pronounced Fee-dough's), sipping something cold and contemplating
FAMILY the sea views, under what the owners claim is the largest thatch palapa
in Belize. If not the largest in Belize, it may at least be the largest on
Ambergris Caye. This casual joint serves mediocre burgers, fish-and-
chips, seafood tacos, and other bar food, but it's a good place to get a
cold beer and enjoy the near-nightly live music. It can also accommodate
large groups. Ⓢ *Average main: BZ$24* ✉ *Barrier Reef Dr., Beachfront,
just north of Catholic church, San Pedro Town* ☎ *226/3176* ⊕ *www.
fidosbelize.com.*

$$$ ✕ **Finn and Martini.** A chic, festive favorite with innovative cocktails like
ECLECTIC the horchaitini (rice cream, cinnamon, vanilla-infused vodka). Small
Fodor's Choice plates, think lobster pupusa with goat cheese, are generous and change
★ often. Belizean creator Finley Khalipa describes running the restaurant
as hosting a birthday party every day of the week. You'll drop a pretty
penny but it's worth the experience. The molten chocolate cake is a cal-
dera of decadence. Ⓢ *Average main: BZ$44* ✉ *Laguna Dr., San Pedro
Town* ☎ *627/4789* ☾ *Closed Tues. No lunch.*

$ ✕ **Manelly's Ice Cream.** There's nothing glossy about Manelly's, aside
CAFÉ from the ice cream melting in the cone, and that's what makes this spot
FAMILY so charming. Have a cheap coconut ice cream or sugarcorn *paleta* (pop-
sicle). The supersweet ice cream isn't quite delicate, but it's handmade
on-site with some local ingredients. Ⓢ *Average main: BZ$4* ✉ *Barrier
Reef Dr., San Pedro Town* ☎ *206/2285* ⊟ *No credit cards.*

$$$$ ✕ **Red Ginger.** With its minimalist décor and ice-cold air-conditioning,
SEAFOOD this restaurant could be in L.A., but it's actually at The Phoenix resort
Fodor's Choice at the north end of San Pedro. No sea views here—you gaze at deep
★ red and mocha cream walls and tropical wild ginger plants in glass
vases. After a ginger or basil mojito, start with ceviche, your choice of
grouper, or mixed shrimp and lobster. Try the grilled snook with guava
tamarind glaze and salsa, or the blackened snapper. Breakfast and lunch
are superb, cheaper, and less stuffy. Over the years, Red Ginger has
only gotten better. Ⓢ *Average main: BZ$50* ✉ *The Phoenix, Barrier
Reef Dr., at north end of town, San Pedro Town* ☎ *226/4623* ⊕ *www.
redgingerbelize.com.*

$$ ✕ **Waruguma.** A local joint and open-air favorite that's geared towards
CARIBBEAN gringos (note the giant lobster photo prop), but the pupusas are no less
FAMILY succulent nor the portions of ceviche no less fresh. Fair-sized pupusas,
Fodor's Choice from spinach to "crazy," make a cheap and filling meal. For tropical
★ decadence try the coconut cream burritos with seafood or chicken and
enjoy the town's bustle just feet away. Credit cards are only accepted
for purchases of more than US$50. Ⓢ *Average main: BZ$28* ✉ *Almond
St., San Pedro Town* ☎ *206/2893* ⊟ *No credit cards.*

$$$ ✕ **Wild Mango's.** Noted local chef Amy Knox made Wild Mango's one
FUSION of the most interesting dining choices on the island. Many of the dishes
have a Mexican base but with Knox's sophisticated twist. She calls her
cooking New Wave Latin—Caribbean food infused with spicy Latin
flavors from Cuba, Argentina, and Mexico. Her trio of shrimp and fish

ceviche is the most creative you'll find on the island, and alone worth the visit. Snazzy specials include pineapple-glazed burger with chili onion rings, and the vegetarian menu is expanding. Seating is beach casual, with stools at tables on a covered, open-air veranda. We especially like Wild Mango's for a casual lunch. [$] *Average main: BZ$32* ✉ *Beachfront, 42 Barrier Reef Dr., south end of town just south of Ruby's Hotel, San Pedro Town* ☎ *226/2859* ⏲ *Closed Sun.*

NORTH OF SAN PEDRO

The newly paved golf cart path makes the more local dining options accessible but some still are a mild trek from town. Fancy spots usually ferry you to them in their own water taxi (ask your hotel to arrange this). Unless you're staying near one of the North Ambergris restaurants listed *below,* you may want to take a water taxi—the Coastal Xpress—especially after dark. Cabs from town will drive farther north, but the cost is steep (BZ$30–BZ$50 for most destinations, including the BZ$12 vehicle bridge fee).

$$$$ ECLECTIC Fodor's Choice ★

🍴 **Mambo.** Upscale Mambo designs dishes that are no less artful than the restaurant's elegant atmosphere. Bringing an Italian sensibility to local ingredients, it specializes in seafood such as the slow-roasted lime grouper with garlic, olive oil, and paprika. Despite the Continental influence, the chef resists innovation over quality, so the dishes are sophisticated but simple. Lunch is also lovely, and less expensive. Matachica resort will provide complimentary boat service. [$] *Average main: BZ$56* ✉ *Beachfront, 5 miles (8 km) north of bridge, at Matachica, Ambergris Caye* ☎ *223/0002* 🌐 *www.matachica.com/eat/.*

$ CAFÉ

🍴 **Marbucks Coffee House.** You'll recognize the circular logo from the monolithic coffee chain it references, but vibrant-tiled Marbucks is worlds better. The coffee beats Belize's Maxwell House standard and the bagel sandwiches are thick with whichever fillings you please. Sit outside on stools or tables. Marbucks hosts the groovy Wine Down Thursdays gathering from 4:30 to 7:30. [$] *Average main: BZ$12* ✉ *1.5 miles (2.4 km) north of bridge, Ambergris Caye* ✣ *Right of main road* ☎ *601/3306 (Daydreamin' B&B's number)* 🌐 *www.marbuckscoffeehouse.com.*

$$$$ FUSION

🍴 **Rain Restaurant and Rooftop.** Minimalist decor and few walls make space for this rooftop's real ambience: the Caribbean horizon and watery sunsets. The menu is expensive but well worth it; pineapple ginger coulis is a sunny sauce on many dishes, and the bleu cheese–crusted filet mignon brings ingredients the island seldom sees. Housemade pastas are reasonably priced, appetizers are generous, and there's a fair selection of vegetarian dishes. It's possible to pop in for just a cocktail and watch the sunset. [$] *Average main: BZ$60* ✉ *2 miles (3 km) north of bridge, at Grande Caribe, San Pedro Town* ☎ *226/4000* 🌐 *www.rainbelize.com* 💳 *No credit cards.*

$$$ FUSION Fodor's Choice ★

🍴 **Rojo Beach Bar.** This red-hot bar and bistro, both stylish and whimsical, has an infinity pool with submerged table where you can rest your drink, a Jenga game so giant you could build a log cabin from the pieces, and beer pong. All make this a fun park for adults, but kids are also welcome, too. Known for killer frozen mojitos and other fascinating, boozy inventions, there's also a good food menu with imaginative plates, like snapper ramen and lobster pizza. $ *Average main: BZ$45* ✉ *Beachfront, 5 miles (8 km) north of bridge, at Azul Resort, Ambergris Caye* ☎ *226/4012* ⊕ *www.rojolounge.com* ☺ *Closed Sun. and Mon.* ⌆ *Reservations not accepted.*

$$
ECLECTIC
FAMILY
Fodor'sChoice
★

✕ **The Truck Stop Food Park and Beer Garden.** Created by American Ben Popik, The Truck Stop is five stationary food trucks that dish up Malaysian, "Nuevo Latino," pizza by Casa Picasso, and ice cream, plus a bar. The ice-cream truck has inventive flavors like bacon maple syrup, and some of the best ice cream on the island. Out back is a deck over the lagoon (the "Warning: Crocodiles" signs are not just decorative) where folks gather for the sunset. You can play corn hole with your kids or sunbathe with a Belikin. This isn't just for tourists; San Pedranos love this spot, too. Wednesday a film is shown over the lagoon, and every Sunday is a pig roast. $ *Average main: BZ$22* ✉ *1 mile (1.6 km) north of bridge, Ambergris Caye.*

SOUTH OF SAN PEDRO

$
LATIN AMERICAN
FAMILY

✕ **Antojito's San Telmo.** A no-frills restaurant known for its tasty Belizean fare and friendly service. Step off the tourist trail and have a lunch of stew chicken, stew beans, and coconut rice peppered in Marie Sharp's. Breakfast is a good bet, too, with tacos priced as cheap as gumballs in the States. $ *Average main: BZ$14* ✉ *Coconut Dr., San Pedro Town* ⌖ *Across from The Baker* ☎ *226/4575* ▭ *No credit cards.*

$
BAKERY
FAMILY

✕ **The Baker.** Warm cinnamon rolls are a favorite at this Irish-owned bakery. You'll also find a cheering bounty of croissants, cookies, and coconut tarts, plus made-to-order egg sandwiches and, at lunch, tuna or ham sandwiches. Coffee is better than the run-of-the-mill, but the cups are dainty compared with big American mugs. $ *Average main: BZ$10* ✉ *Coconut Dr. (aka Seagrape Dr.), San Pedro Town* ⌖ *Near Marina's grocery* ☎ *206/2036* ▭ *No credit cards* ☺ *Closed Sun.*

$$$
FUSION

✕ **Black Orchid.** The restaurant is named for the spidery, delicate national flower of Belize, but the cuisine is global fusion in an island-elegant atmosphere, with some thatch accents, a fountain tiered like a Mayan temple, and real cloth napkins. A nice happy hour starts at 3 pm and reservations are recommended for dinner. Vibrant dishes include ginger pork egg rolls and rib eye charbroiled on lava rocks. $ *Average main: BZ$44* ✉ *S. Coconut Dr., about 2.5 miles (4 km) south of town, San Pedro Town* ☎ *206/2441* ⊕ *www.blackorchidrestaurant.com* ☺ *Closed Sun and Mon. No lunch.*

$$$$
CONTEMPORARY

✕ **Casa Picasso.** A testament to San Pedro's epicurean vitality, dishes at Casa Picasso, like chocolate and vanilla pork short ribs (chocolate dusting, vanilla risotto) and culture-crossing tapas, give the restaurant renown. They're happy to work around dietary restrictions and can accommodate groups, making it a good choice for a special occasion. It's tucked away in a yellow house with a white picket fence; call and they'll pay for a taxi from your hotel. $ *Average main: BZ$52* ✉ *Sting Ray St., San Pedro Town* ☎ *226/4443* ⊕ *www.casapicassobelize.com* ☺ *No lunch. Closed Sun. and Mon. Closed Sept. and Oct.*

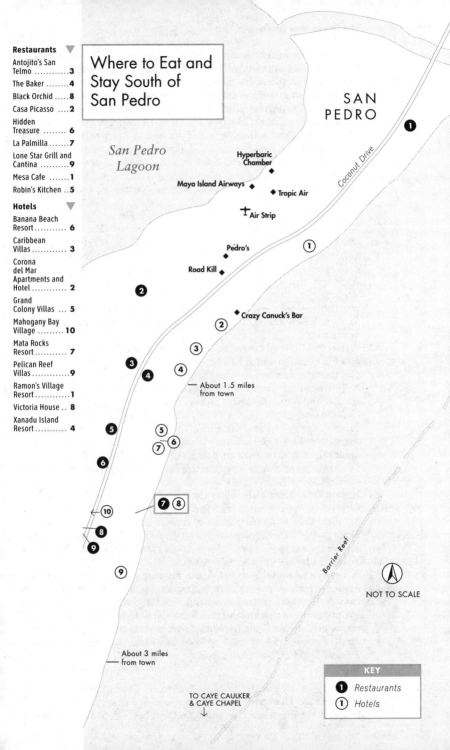

Where to Eat and Stay South of San Pedro

Restaurants ▼

Antojito's San Telmo 3
The Baker 4
Black Orchid 8
Casa Picasso 2
Hidden Treasure 6
La Palmilla 7
Lone Star Grill and Cantina 9
Mesa Cafe 1
Robin's Kitchen ..5

Hotels ▼

Banana Beach Resort 6
Caribbean Villas 3
Corona del Mar Apartments and Hotel 2
Grand Colony Villas ... 5
Mahogany Bay Village 10
Mata Rocks Resort 7
Pelican Reef Villas 9
Ramon's Village Resort 1
Victoria House .. 8
Xanadu Island Resort 4

SAN PEDRO

San Pedro Lagoon

Coconut Drive

Hyperbaric Chamber

Maya Island Airways

Tropic Air

✝ Air Strip

Pedro's

Road Kill

Crazy Canuck's Bar

— About 1.5 miles from town

— About 3 miles from town

Barrier Reef

NOT TO SCALE

TO CAYE CAULKER & CAYE CHAPEL
↓

KEY

❶ *Restaurants*

① *Hotels*

$$$$
CARIBBEAN
Fodor's Choice
★

✕ **Hidden Treasure.** Hidden away on a back street in a residential neighborhood south of town, at Hidden Treasure you dine romantically by candlelight, in the sultry tropical air under a pitched roof set off by bamboo, mahogany, and cabbage-bark wood. The signature barbecue ribs are seasoned with traditional Garífuna spices and glazed with pineapple or papaya sauce. *Mojarro à la Lamanai* is snapper seasoned with Mayan spices and cooked in a banana leaf. $ *Average main: BZ$64* ✉ *Escalante Residential Area, 2715 Flamboyant Dr., San Pedro Town* ✛ *About 1.5 miles (2.4 km) south of town; go south on Coconut Dr. past Royal Palm Villas and watch for signs* ☎ *226/4111* ⊕ *www.hiddentreasurebelize.com* ⊘ *Closed Tues. No lunch* ☞ *Complimentary transportation to your hotel.*

$$$$
ECLECTIC

✕ **La Palmilla.** La Palmilla restaurant at Victoria House is classy without being stuffy and romantic without being precious. The setting, near one of the Victoria House pools with views of the sea, in manicured grounds, is among the most attractive in San Pedro. The restaurant does an especially fine job with local seafood, especially grilled lobster. Although there's a lovely indoor dining room, in good weather you might prefer dining on the patio in the open air, with sea views and a nice breeze from the water. $ *Average main: BZ$58* ✉ *Coconut Dr., at Victoria House resort, San Pedro Town* ☎ *226/2067* ⊕ *www.victoria-house.com.*

$$
AMERICAN
FAMILY

✕ **Lone Star Grill and Cantina.** If you're in need of a fried steak sandwich or a big screen to watch baseball, here you'll find both. Lone Star Grill and Cantina, run by a couple from the Lone Star State, is an outpost of Texas cooking on the south end of the island. Enjoy cold beer, margaritas, and some piled-high fajitas. $ *Average main: BZ$25* ✉ *South end of island, about 3 miles (5 km) south of town, Mosquito Dr., near south police substation, San Pedro Town* ✛ *Go south on Coconut Dr. to end of cobblestones and then continue on dirt road past water treatment plant. Follow road to police substation. Bear right, and Lone Star is on right side of road* ☎ *226/4666* ⊕ *www.lonestargrillbelize.com* ⊘ *Closed Tues.*

$$
ECLECTIC
FAMILY
Fodor's Choice
★
.

✕ **Mesa Cafe.** Mesa Cafe serves the island equivalent of fast food in a surprisingly quiet setting. It's a great spot for an inexpensive breakfast or lunch. Uncommon breakfasts of chorizo or lobster scramble and for lunch try the shrimp burger or fish tacos. Finish with craboo ice cream. $ *Average main: BZ$18* ✉ *Vilma Linda Plaza, Tarpon St., San Pedro Town* ☎ *226/3444* ⊘ *Closed weekends. No dinner.*

$
CARIBBEAN

✕ **Robin's Kitchen.** Line up beside the smoking grill for a delicious, no-nonsense plate of jerk chicken with sides. Homemade sauce is dished from a big plastic mixing bowl and Fanta and juices are in the back. Eat under the thatch and chat with the lovely Jamaican-Belizean owners, or get it to go. Bring napkins. $ *Average main: BZ$14* ✉ *Coconut Dr., 1.5 miles (2.5 km) south of town, San Pedro Town* ✛ *Across from Banana Beach* ▭ *No credit cards.*

WHERE TO STAY

One of your biggest decisions in Ambergris Caye will be choosing a place to stay. There are three basic options: in or near the town of San Pedro, in the South Beach or South End area beyond town, or on North

Ambergris, beyond the river channel. Access to restaurants, bars, and other activities is easiest in and around San Pedro. Accommodations in and near town are generally simple and reasonably priced (BZ$50–BZ$300), with a few notable upscale exceptions such as the deluxe Phoenix; but rooms on the main streets can be noisy from late-night revelers and traffic.

For silence and sand, head out of town for resort-style accommodations. To get more privacy, consider the South End. Though it, too, is developing rapidly, it's still less hectic than in town, and it's only a golf cart or taxi ride away.

If you really want to get away, choose the more remote North Ambergris, which is reached mainly by water taxis, golf carts, and sometimes by regular land cabs.

With the exception of a few budget places, nearly all the resorts on the island are on the sea. Most are small, under 30 or 40 rooms, and nearly all are four stories or less. Some are owner-managed. The newer resorts and hotels are on North Ambergris Caye, the farthest around 12 miles from the bridge.

■TIP➡ **During the off-season (May–November), lodging properties often have walk-in rates that are up to a third less than advertised rates. But you'll usually have to ask for them, as otherwise you'll pay the regular rate.**

Besides full-service hotels and resorts, the island has condotels, which are individually owned condos managed by an on-site management company. The condo units usually are offered on a nightly basis, and in most cases the properties have full kitchens and most of the amenities of a regular hotel, except perhaps a restaurant.

Ambergris Caye has dozens of homes that can be rented on a weekly basis. These range from simple two-bedroom cottages to luxurious four- or five-bedroom villas. In some cases credit cards are not accepted. Vacation Rentals By Owner (⊕ *www.vrbo.com*). VRBO lists more rentals than any local management company, and Airbnb (⊕ *www.airbnb. com*) is a dependable resource for a range of rentals.

Also on the island are clusters of upscale homes or villas offered for weekly, and sometimes nightly, rental and function much like a resort. These luxury homes, often with 4,000–5,000 square feet of space or more, typically have a shared pool and concierge service. Although they usually have no restaurant, they may offer food service prepared by a chef and delivered to guests in the homes.

Caye Management. This is the island's oldest rental management company, with 30 years experience, and typically has around 16 vacation homes for rent. ⊠ *Beachfront, Boca del Rio Dr., San Pedro Town* ✛ *At north end of town near high school* ☎ *226/3077* ⊕ *www.cayemanagement.com.*

Time-shares have been on the island for years. Captain Morgan's is one of them. It opened a small casino at its property in mid-2011. Reef Village, on North Ambergris just beyond the bridge, was known for its aggressive time-share touts, but in 2011 it ran into financial and

Restaurants
- Annie's Pastries **2**
- Caliente **11**
- DandE's Frozen Custard & Sorbet **8**
- El Fogon **14**
- Elvi's Kitchen ... **9**
- Estel's Dine by the Sea **10**
- Fido's Courtyard and Pier **7**
- Finn and Martini **3**
- Manelly's Ice Cream **5**
- Mesa Café **13**
- Red Ginger **6**
- Sand Bar **4**
- Warugama **1**
- Wild Mango's . **12**

Hotels
- Blue Tang Inn **2**
- Holiday Hotel **5**
- Mayan Princess **4**
- Ocean Tides Beach Resort ... **1**
- The Phoenix **3**
- SunBreeze Hotel **6**

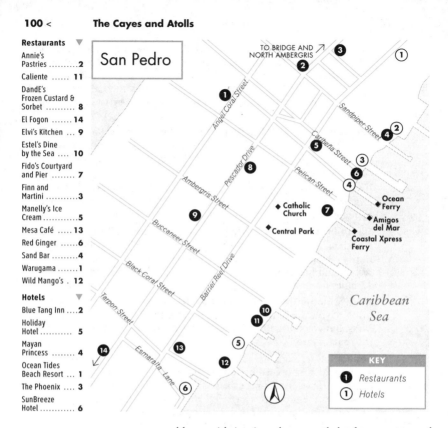

San Pedro
TO BRIDGE AND NORTH AMBERGRIS
Angel Coral Street
Sandpiper Street
Caribeña Street
Pescador Drive
Pelican Street
Ambergris Street
Catholic Church
Ocean Ferry
Amigos del Mar
Central Park
Coastal Xpress Ferry
Buccaneer Street
Barrier Reef Drive
Black Coral Street
Caribbean Sea
Tarpon Street
Esmaralta Lane
KEY
Restaurants
Hotels

management problems with its time-shares, and the future course of this development is up in the air. Fairly new to the island are upscale "fractional ownership" or "residential club" resorts, which sell longer-term memberships and rights to use the property, typically for two, four, or six months a year. One of these, Sueño del Mar, opened on North Ambergris in 2006 but shut down in 2010, leaving more than 100 owners at least temporarily out in the cold, before reopening in 2011. The moral? Think twice before putting any money in a time-share or fractional ownership scheme.

SAN PEDRO TOWN

$$ B&B/INN FAMILY 🏨 **Blue Tang Inn.** Intimate beachfront suites that are less fancy but more wallet-friendly and still within walking distance to town. **Pros:** an affordable option; colorful rooms; well-managed. **Cons:** tiny swimming pool; sometimes hear noise from town. [$] *Rooms from: US$340* ✉ *Sand Piper St., San Pedro Town* ☎ *226/2326* 🌐 *www.bluetanginn.com* 🛏 *14 units* 🍴 *Breakfast.*

$$ HOTEL FAMILY 🏨 **Holiday Hotel.** Flat teardrop spindles and icing-like trim give this heart-of-town hotel a modest colonial style; and indeed, it's San Pedro's first inn, now a dependable place to sleep in between the water and the bustle. **Pros:** central location; affordable and clean; island's first hotel. **Cons:** no pool; in-town beach isn't very good for swimming; busy

town area can be noisy. $ *Rooms from: BZ$308* ✉ *Beachfront, Barrier Reef Dr., San Pedro Town* ☎ *226/2014, 713/893–3825 in U.S.* ⊕ *www.sanpedroholiday.com* ↝ *16 rooms* ⭘ *No meals.*

$$ ⬚ **Mayan Princess.** Sitting pretty and pink in the middle of town, this
HOTEL long-established seafront three-story condo hotel has basic but pleasant
FAMILY efficiencies lacking only a pool to make it a perfect mid-level choice.
Pros: central in-town location; all apartments have lovely sea views
and verandas; near good dive shop. **Cons:** no swimming pool; beach
area has heavy boat and pedestrian traffic; not fancy. $ *Rooms from:*
BZ$320 ✉ *Beachfront, Barrier Reef Dr., in center of town, San Pedro*
Town ☎ *226/2778, 800/850–4101* ⊕ *www.mayanprincesshotel.com*
↝ *23 1-bedroom suites* ⭘ *No meals.*

$$ ⬚ **Ocean Tides Beach Resort.** If diving is your reason for being in Belize,
HOTEL and you don't want to spend a ton of money, you couldn't do bet-
FAMILY ter than this beachfront hotel at the north end of town, owned by
Patojo Paz, one of the island's most experienced dive masters, and
his wife. **Pros:** locally owned beachfront hotel; respected dive shop,
Patojo's, on-site; good value. **Cons:** rooms aren't huge and can be a bit
crusty; beds and furnishings in some rooms need upgrading. $ *Rooms*
from: BZ$253 ✉ *Beachfront, Boca del Rio Dr., north end of town,*
San Pedro Town ☎ *226/2283* ⊕ *www.ambergriscaye.com/tides* ↝ *15*
rooms ⭘ *Breakfast.*

$$$$ ⬚ **The Phoenix.** Hard right angles of concrete make this luxury resort
RESORT a striking study in geometry, though suites are softer: expect cabinets
Fodor's Choice and doors of silky tropical hardwood, greetings lettered in palm leaves
★ on your bed, and covetable kitchenware. **Pros:** deluxe, stylish condo
suites; in-town's most luxurious hotel; first-rate service. **Cons:** for some
it lacks a get-away-from-it-all feel; the ultrastylish exterior can be visually harsh. $ *Rooms from: BZ$872* ✉ *Beachfront, Barrier Reef Dr., at*
north end of town, San Pedro Town ☎ *226/2083, 877/822–5512 in*
U.S. and Canada ⊕ *www.thephoenixbelize.com* ↝ *30 suites (not all in*
rental pool) ⭘ *No meals.*

$$$ ⬚ **SunBreeze Hotel.** A Spanish arcade makes a pleasant passageway
HOTEL between the rooms and the courtyard of this waterfront hotel, on the
FAMILY busy southern side of town. **Pros:** comfortable and well-run; great res-
taurant on-site (under separate management); some rooms handicap-
accessible. **Cons:** not much of a beach; not much local flavor. $ *Rooms*
from: BZ$458 ✉ *Coconut Dr., San Pedro Town* ⊹ *Across from Tropic*
Air terminal and airstrip ☎ *226/2191, 800/688–0191 in U.S. and Can-*
ada ⊕ *www.sunbreeze.net* ↝ *43 rooms* ⭘ *Some meals.*

NORTH OF SAN PEDRO

$$ ⬚ **Ak'bol Yoga Retreat & Eco-Resort.** This hip little beach resort on North
RESORT Ambergris has seven simple thatch cabañas, some with sea views,
around a natural stone swimming pool. **Pros:** cool, small, laid-back
resort; good value; spectacular setting for yoga studio. **Cons:** you may
feel out of your element if you can't do downward dog; outdoor showers
are the cabañas' only showers. $ *Rooms from: BZ$336* ✉ *Beachfront,*
1.75 mile (3 km) north of center of town, Ambergris Caye ☎ *226/2073*
⊕ *www.akbol.com* ↝ *7 units* ⭘ *No meals* ☞ *Daily yoga class at 9 am*
included. Complimentary use of yoga mats.

$$
B&B/INN
Fodor's Choice
★

Cayo Frances Farm and Fly. Lodging is rustic at this out-of-the-way fishing camp, with simple, functional clapboard cabins that recall an earlier time, an outdoor shared bathroom with all the standard plumbing, and, of course, outstanding flats fishing. **Pros:** great fishing conditions; earnest and uncommercial operation; delicious food. **Cons:** very niche and not for everyone; ultra remote and best for short stays; utilitarian digs. $ *Rooms from: BZ$350* ⊠ *Leeward side of island, 12 miles (19 km) north of bridge, Ambergris Caye* ☎ *610/3841* ⊕ *www.belizeflyfishcamp. com* �Θ *Closed Sept. and Oct.* ᗒ *2 units* ⦿ *All meals.*

$$$$
RESORT
FAMILY

Coco Beach Resort. Coco Beach Resort is one of the top-end condotels on the island, with spacious one- and two-bedroom suites and large rooms on an attractive stretch of beach about 3.5 miles (6 km) north of San Pedro. **Pros:** big, well-appointed suites; gorgeous swimming pools perfect for play; nice beach; frequent rate specials. **Cons:** high prices; decor can be more cheesy than tasteful; no elevators, and upper level suites require walking a lot of steps. $ *Rooms from: BZ$833* ⊠ *Beachfront, 4 miles (7 km) north of San Pedro, Ambergris Caye* ☎ *844/360–1553 in U.S. and Canada, 226/4840* ⊕ *www.cocobeach-belize.com* ᗒ *62 rooms* ⦿ *No meals.*

$$
RESORT
FAMILY

Cocotal Inn & Cabanas. If you're looking for a small, homey spot on the beach, Cocotal could be it. **Pros:** friendly, small resort on the beach; pool; affordable rates. **Cons:** no restaurant on-site; nothing deluxe; some cottages set back from the breeze and beach. $ *Rooms from: BZ$345* ⊠ *2.5 miles (4 km) north of center of town, San Pedro Town* ☎ *226/2097* ⊕ *www.cocotalbelize.com* ᗒ *8 rooms* ⦿ *No meals.*

$$$$
RESORT
FAMILY

Costa Blu Dive and Beach Resort. With tropical colors and aqua accents, this new resort invokes the ocean at every turn and makes a great resting place between your marine tours. **Pros:** geared to divers but lots of stuff for nondivers, too; discounts make rates lower than they look; kid-friendly, with complimentary kayaks, paddleboards, and bikes. **Cons:** not deluxe but not a huge bargain; hard to find a cheap dinner at the restaurant. $ *Rooms from: US$702* ⊠ *Beachfront, 6.5 miles (10.5 km) north of town, Ambergris Caye* ☎ *844/360–1553 U.S. reservations* ⊕ *www.costablubelize.com* ᗒ *36 rooms* ⦿ *No meals.*

$$$
B&B/INN
Fodor's Choice
★

Daydreamin' Bed & Breakfast. Four elegant cabañas ring a glittering plunge pool at this bed-and-breakfast just north of the bridge. **Pros:** intimate; charming hosts; not far north of town. **Cons:** rooms are quite compact; a block from the waterfront; might expect a cheaper rate. $ *Rooms from: BZ$400* ⊠ *Tropicana Dr., Tres Cocos, San Pedro Town* ☎ *226/4449* ⊕ *www.daydreaminbelize.com* ᗒ *4 units* ⦿ *Breakfast.*

$$$$
RESORT
FAMILY
Fodor's Choice
★

El Pescador. Nearly every hotel on Ambergris Caye claims that it can arrange fishing trips, but this resort really has the best angling resources, plus plenty to do for companions with other passions (half the guests are snorkelers and divers). **Pros:** the place for saltwater anglers, but inviting even if you don't fish; top-notch service; beloved spot for more than 40 years. **Cons:** rooms in original lodge are not too spacious; not inexpensive. $ *Rooms from: BZ$600* ⊠ *2.5 miles (4 km) north of San Pedro, Ambergris Caye* ☎ *226/2398, 804/661–2259 in U.S.* ⊕ *www. elpescador.com* ᗒ *13 rooms, 8 villas* ⦿ *Some meals* ☞ *Complimentary bikes and kayaks.*

$$$$
RESORT
Fodor'sChoice
★

El Secreto. Billed as "barefoot luxury," El Secreto is on a sandy strip 11 miles north of San Pedro and offers a secluded beach and 13 private villas kitted out with Egyptian cotton sheets, outdoor Jacuzzis, and private decks with hammocks. **Pros:** quiet beach and exotic villas; honeymooners' paradise; great spa. **Cons:** expect sticker shock (except off-season); nearly locked into spending loads at the subpar restaurant; bugs are notorious; not recommended for kids. $ *Rooms from: BZ$1,145* ✉ *11 miles (7.7 km) north of town, Ambergris Caye* ☎ *501/236–5111* ⊕ *www.elsecretobelize.com* ⤦ *13 rooms* ⦿ *No meals.*

$$$$
RENTAL
FAMILY
Fodor'sChoice
★

Grand Caribe Resort and Condominiums. Set in an arc on a 5-acre beachfront site, Grand Caribe's 72 superluxury condos, in eight four-story, red-tiled-roof clusters, face the sea and a 500-foot stretch of sandy beach. **Pros:** luxury condos, all with sea views; short bike, golf cart ride, or taxi ride to restaurants and to town; complimentary laundry service; 650 feet of beachfront. **Cons:** expensive but worth it if you want the best; taxi to town is BZ$35; behemoth condos that some may find gratuitous. $ *Rooms from: BZ$1,069* ✉ *Tres Cocos area of North Ambergris, 1.25 miles (2 km) north of bridge, Ambergris Caye* ☎ *226/4726, 800/488–5903 in U.S. or Canada* ⊕ *www.grandcaribe. com* ⤦ *72 condominium suites* ⦿ *No meals.*

$$$$
RENTAL
FAMILY

La Perla del Caribe. Clusters of two- to five-bedroom villas command the beachfront, all named after precious jewels such as Sapphire, Opal, and Emerald—and they really do dazzle. **Pros:** bold and textured villas with every amenity; lovely beach; peaceful. **Cons:** somewhat remote; no on-site restaurant; expensive unless divided in a group. $ *Rooms from: BZ$1,150* ✉ *North Ambergris, 6 miles (10 km) north of San Pedro, Beachfront, Ambergris Caye* ☎ *226/5888* ⊕ *www.laperladelcaribe.com* ⤦ *8 rooms* ⦿ *No meals.*

$$$$
RENTAL
FAMILY

Las Terrazas Resort and Residences. Las Terrazas luxury condos have nine-foot ceilings, travertine tile floors, fully equipped kitchens with Brazilian granite countertops, cable TV, and high-speed Internet. **Pros:** elegant interior design; romantic but also kid-friendly; good on-site dive shop. **Cons:** not inexpensive, especially for larger units; farther from town than some would like. $ *Rooms from: BZ$690* ✉ *Beachfront, 4 miles (6.5 km) north of town, Ambergris Caye* ☎ *226/4249, 800/447–1553 in U.S. and Canada* ⊕ *www.lasterrazasresort.com* ⤦ *39 units* ⦿ *Some meals.*

$$$$
RESORT
Fodor'sChoice
★

Matachica Resort & Spa. Thatch casitas in shades of mango, banana, and blueberry offset by brilliant white sand give this deluxe beachfront resort a Gauguin-like quality. **Pros:** charming collection of casitas on the beach; friendly staff and good management; postcard-pretty beach. **Cons:** no kids under 14 allowed; expensive. $ *Rooms from: BZ$663* ✉ *Beachfront, 5 miles (8 km) north of San Pedro, Ambergris Caye* ☎ *226/5010, 223/0002 reversations line* ⊕ *www.matachica.com* ⤦ *31 rooms* ⦿ *Some meals* ⌕ *Complimentary boat transfers upon arrival and departure.*

$$$$
RESORT
FAMILY

Portofino Beach Resort. This luxury-meets-adventure resort embodies much of Belize's character: cabañas with ragged crowns of thatch, wonderful staff, imperfect beaches, and exquisite water. **Pros:** beloved by many return guests; romantic rooms; plenty of services. **Cons:**

run-down buildings given the cost; faraway from San Pedro's culinary scene; expensive on-site restaurant. $ *Rooms from: BZ$738* ⊠ *6 miles (9.5 km) north of bridge, Ambergris Caye* ☎ *226/5096, 305/848–1980 in U.S.* ⊕ *www.portofinobelize.com* ⇥ *17 units* †◎| *Breakfast.*

$$$$
RENTAL
FAMILY
Fodor'sChoice
★

⌂ **Seascape Villas.** Organic forms characterize these six gorgeous villas, with curved outer walls echoing curved couches and slate floors that sweep under cathedral ceilings, all encircling an estuary-like pool. **Pros:** truly inspired design and amenities; beautiful pool and Jacuzzis; stunning sea views. **Cons:** no restaurant on-site; very expensive if not split among a group. $ *Rooms from: BZ$2,645* ⊠ *Beachfront, 3.5 miles (6 km) north of San Pedro, Ambergris Caye* ☎ *226/2119, 888/753–5164* ⊕ *www.seascapebelize.com* ⇥ *6 rooms* †◎| *No meals.*

SOUTH OF SAN PEDRO

$$
RESORT
FAMILY

⌂ **Banana Beach Resort.** A throwback to days before pillow menus and baffling body scrubs, laid-back Banana Beach is a friendly, casual, though time-worn hotel that's much cheaper than some spots on the island. **Pros:** unpretentious and beachy; good value; friendly staff; hot breakfast included. **Cons:** some furnishings are dated; beach has a sea-wall. $ *Rooms from: BZ$292* ⊠ *Coconut Dr., 1.5 miles (2.5 km) south of San Pedro, San Pedro Town* ☎ *226/3890, 877/288–1011 in U.S. and Canada* ⊕ *www.bananabeach.com* ⇥ *66 rooms* †◎| *Breakfast.*

$$
RESORT
FAMILY

⌂ **Caribbean Villas.** It may not be as modern as some of the island's newer resorts, but Caribbean Villas, with its gardens, pleasant quiet beachfront, and fun two-story waterslide, is an affordable and low-key alternative to the glitzier developments. **Pros:** reliable hotel with high return rate; good beach; waterslide and water trampoline are a hit. **Cons:** some units could use updating; not crazy cheap. $ *Rooms from: BZ$294* ⊠ *Seagrape Dr., 1 mile (1.5 km) south of town, San Pedro Town* ☎ *226/2715, 800/213–8347 in U.S. and Canada* ⊕ *www.caribbeanvillashotel.com* ⇥ *5 rooms, 9 suites* †◎| *No meals.*

$$
HOTEL
FAMILY

⌂ **Corona del Mar Apartments and Hotel.** An older seaside hotel, the Corona del Mar has cracked and grayed with age, and some of the comforters show a 1990s color sensibility, but the well-equipped suites are a stellar value for Amergris. **Pros:** fair value; breakfast included; renovated seafront penthouses. **Cons:** weather-worn and outdated. $ *Rooms from: BZ$253* ⊠ *Coconut Dr., 1 mile (1.5 km) south of town, Ambergris Caye* ☎ *226/2055, 800/520–8110 in U.S. and Canada* ⊕ *www.coronadelmarhotel.com* ⇥ *43 rooms* †◎| *Breakfast.*

$$$$
RENTAL
FAMILY

⌂ **Grand Colony Villas.** Rose-color buildings hold upscale condos spacious enough for the whole family, with soft-toned walls that complement granite counters, mahogany features, and luxurious furnishings. **Pros:** deluxe condo villas; beautifully finished and furnished; on a lovely beach; lots of privacy. **Cons:** expensive; no restaurant on-site. $ *Rooms from: BZ$1,365* ⊠ *Coconut Dr., 1.5 miles (3 km) south of town, San Pedro Town* ☎ *226/3739, 866/352–1163 in U.S. and Canada* ⊕ *www.grandcolonyvillas.com* ⇥ *16 units* †◎| *No meals.*

$$$
RESORT
FAMILY

⌂ **Mahogany Bay Village.** The pulse of south Ambergris is changing with this 60-acre village of white, colonial-nostaglic villas by Hilton's Curio brand, with boutique shopping, a spa, a clubhouse, a taco truck, and all the trappings of a planned community in the States. **Pros:** stylish and airy rooms; a recognizable brand. **Cons:** on the lagoon and more than a walk to town; accused of environmental irresponsibility. $ *Rooms from: BZ$436* ⊠ *2.5 miles (4 km) south of town, San Pedro Town* ⊕ *www.mahoganybayvillage.com* ↝ *195 rooms* ⊙| *No meals.*

$$$

HOTEL

FAMILY

⊡ **Mata Rocks Resort.** The squeaky-clean rooms at this intimate, mid-level hotel right on a nice stretch of beach, about a 30-minute walk or 10-minute bike ride from town, have sea views and breezes. **Pros:** quiet beachside resort; good value; friendly staff. **Cons:** no restaurant on-site; "resort" may be a misnomer. $ *Rooms from: BZ$340* ⊠ *Coconut Dr., 1.5 miles (2.5 km) south of town, San Pedro Town* ☎ *226/2336, 888/628–2757 in U.S. and Canada* ⊕ *www.matarocks.com* ↝ *17 rooms* ⊙| *Breakfast* ↷ *Bikes complimentary.*

$$$$

RENTAL

FAMILY

⊡ **Pelican Reef Villas.** While watching the pool's turquoise waterfall, it's easy to believe you've stumbled upon a hidden tropical treasure; however, the faux cave is a swim-up bar, and Pelican Reef is only a couple miles south of San Pedro's bustle. **Pros:** well-run condo colony in quiet south-end location; luxurious digs; lovely breakfast selections included; good beach area. **Cons:** golf cart rental nearly necessary; a lot of steps to climb to upper-level units; no dinner on-site. $ *Rooms from: BZ$910* ⊠ *Coconut Dr., 2.5 miles (4 km) south of town, San Pedro Town* ☎ *226/4352, 281/394–3739 in U.S.* ⊕ *www.pelicanreefvillas.com* ↝ *24 rooms* ⊙| *Breakfast.*

$$

RESORT

FAMILY

⊡ **Ramon's Village Resort.** One of the first and most famous resorts on the island, Ramon's really is a village, with its many buildings paneled in furry palmetto and canopied footpaths that you can get lost in. **Pros:** good in-town beach; has island atmosphere many are looking for. **Cons:** busy location across from the airstrip, in an area that's increasingly congested; no sale of liquor means no rum punches; two restaurants are convenient but not high quality. $ *Rooms from: BZ$338* ⊠ *Coconut Dr., across from airstrip just south of town, Ambergris Caye* ☎ *226/2071, 800/624–4215 in U.S. and Canada* ⊕ *www.ramons.com* ↝ *71 rooms* ⊙| *No meals.*

$$$

RESORT

Fodor'sChoice

★

⊡ **Victoria House.** With its bougainvillea-filled gardens, this resort south of San Pedro is stately and secluded. **Pros:** quiet and lovely; variety of gorgeous beachside accommodations; idyllic spot for meals overlooking the pool and beach. **Cons:** not a budget place; some will object to the imperialism nostalgia (i.e., "Plantation Suites") and exclusive air. $ *Rooms from: BZ$488* ⊠ *Coconut Dr., 2 miles (3 km) south of town, Ambergris Caye* ☎ *226/2067, 800/247–5159 in U.S. and Canada* ⊕ *www.victoria-house.com* ↝ *29 units* ⊙| *Breakfast.*

$$$

RESORT

FAMILY

Fodor'sChoice

★

⊡ **Xanadu Island Resort.** A lovely resort that's eco-minded, relaxed, just a short walk to town, and without the pageantry of some upscale resorts. **Pros:** friendly folks; tropically perfect pool; convenient location. **Cons:** seawall at beach; furnishings not deluxe. $ *Rooms from: BZ$480* ⊠ *Sea Grape Dr., 1 mile (1.66 km) south of town, San Pedro Town* ☎ *226/2814, 866/351–4752* ⊕ *www.xanaduislandresort.com* ↝ *19 rooms* ⊙| *No meals.*

CAYO ESPANTO

$$$$
RESORT

⌂ **Cayo Espanto.** On this tiny private island just off Ambergris Caye, you'll find nothing more than seven deluxe beachfront villas and a team dedicated to giving you a memorable experience. **Pros:** outrageous luxury and service; beautiful views; catered to your wishes. **Cons:** wildly expensive; island is on the back side of Ambergris Caye, not on the main Caribbean Sea; privacy can sometimes be oppressive. $ *Rooms from: BZ$3,707* ⊠ *3 miles (5 km) west of Ambergris Caye, Cayo Espanto* ☎ *910/323–8355 in U.S.* ⊕ *www.aprivateisland.com* ⟳ *7 units* ⦿ *All-inclusive.*

NIGHTLIFE

San Pedro has the most active nightlife scene in Belize, but, still, don't expect Miami's South Beach. A few in-town spots such as Fido's have live music. At Jaguar's Temple nightclub, the action starts after 10 or 11 and often goes until almost daybreak. (Be careful going back to your hotel in the middle of the night after sampling rums—take a taxi if possible.) There are plenty of spots just to have a cold one, including some classic beach and pier bars like BC's, Tackle Box, Wet Willy's, and Palapa Bar, or tonier spots like Rojo Bar. There's a small casino at Captain Morgan's on North Ambergris. Many hotels have bars that mostly draw their own guests, but anyone, staying there or not, is welcome. Among the better resort bars are those at Victoria House, Banana Beach Resort, Spindrift, Pedro's Hotel, Mata Rocks, Matachica, and Ramon's Village. Karaoke is big in Belize, and some bars and clubs in San Pedro have karaoke nights, which are as much for locals as visitors. In late January and early February, singer Jerry Jeff Walker holds "Camp Belize," two weeklong events in San Pedro during which Walker puts on shows for his loyal fans. ⚠ **Don't let your taxi driver pick up an extra passenger at night, a common practice that is unsafe. Don't walk on the beach alone at night—it's unlit and can be dangerous.**

BARS AND CLUBS

Crazy Canuck's Beach Bar. A lively beachside bar that rocks out until midnight. Tuesday they host hermit crab races (ethically questionable) that support local charities, and Funday Sunday draws crowds. Live music here can be thunderous. ⊠ *On the beach, South Coconut Dr., at Exotic Beach Hotel, San Pedro Town* ☎ *670/8001.*

Fido's Courtyard and Pier. Under a giant seaside thatch palapa, Fido's is usually jumping and has live music most nights. The bar food is so-so, and service can be spotty, but the beer is cold and the setting is fun. ⊠ *Barrier Reef Dr., San Pedro Town* ☎ *226/2056* ⊕ *www.fidosbelize.com.*

Jaguar's Temple. San Pedro's largest dance club is slightly seedy, mostly male, and you can party here on weekends until the wee hours. ⊠ *Barrier Reef Dr. and Pelican St., across from Central Park, San Pedro Town* ☎ *226/4077* ⊕ *www.jaguarstempleclub.com.*

Pedro's Sports Bar & Pizzeria. A veritable cave of floor-to-ceiling Jägermeister bottles, Pedro's is your spot for pizza, sports watching and cold Belikins. It attracts mostly expats and visitors. There are poker games some nights, a popular ladies' night on Wednesday, and karaoke on Thursday. ⊠ *Seagrape Dr., south of town, San Pedro Town* ☎ *226/3825* ⊕ *www.pedroshotel.com.*

Road Kill Bar. Find a BZ$5 "panti rippa" at this grimy and happening roadside bar, which also serves a wide variety of beers (for Belize) and, despite the name, grills a good hamburger. Karaoke on Wednesday night. ⊠ *Coconut Dr., about 0.25 mile (0.5 km) from south edge of town, San Pedro Town.*

Fodor'sChoice ★ **Rojo Beach Bar.** This stunning beachfront bar on North Ambergris is a sophisticated, yet casual, romantic place to sip a Shark Bite (light rum, coconut rum, Meyer's rum, mango, and pineapple) or knock back some flavored shots until late evening. Delicious shared plates are generous. ⊠ *Beachfront, 5 miles (8 km) north of town, at Azul Resort, Ambergris Caye* ☎ *226/4012* ⊕ *www.rojolounge.com.*

Fodor'sChoice ★ **Sandbar Beachfront Restaurant.** In daytime you can read under expansive umbrellas and sip something blended, while at night you can join the (sometimes rowdy) crowds and board and drinking play games. Fritters and brick-oven pizza make tasty snacks to share. Fun lasts until midnight, but it's island-flexible. ⊠ *7 Boca del Rio Dr., San Pedro Town* ☎ *226/2008.*

Wahoo's Lounge. On the odd side of the nightlife spectrum is the Chicken Drop, held on Thursday night at the beachfront Wahoo's Lounge. Bet on a numbered square on a sort of giant bingo board, and if the chicken poops on your square, you win the pot. It's hugely popular. ⊠ *At Spindrift Hotel, Beachfront, Barrier Reef Dr., San Pedro Town* ⌖ *Near Buccaneer St.* ☎ *226/2002* ☞ *Chicken drop starts around 6 pm Thurs.*

CASINO

Captain Morgan's Retreat Casino. The small casino at Captain Morgan's Retreat, a time-share resort, with about 40 slot and video poker machines, plus live table games, poker tournaments, and a full bar with tapas and courtesy drinks. Some nights there's poolside blackjack. There's free evening boat transfer from Fido's dock. ⊠ *3 miles (5 km) north of bridge, at Captain Morgan's Retreat, Ambergris Caye* ☎ *226/2207* ⊕ *www.captainmorgans.com.*

MOVIE THEATER

FAMILY **Paradise Theater.** Here is a Belizean take on an American-style cinema, where you can watch first-run or near-first-run movies in air-conditioned comfort and with Dolby 5.1 sound. It's cheap though usually only open on weekends. The theater, which has 300- and 150-seat rooms, is also used for live shows and is a favorite among San Pedranos. If you're thirsty, there's a bar. ■TIP→ **If you're staying in town or south and don't want to pay the BZ$10 fee to take your golf cart across the bridge, you can park it on the south side of the bridge and walk over (no toll for pedestrians), as the theater is a just a few hundred feet from the bridge.** ⊠ *Golf cart path, North Ambergris, just across bridge near Reef Village development, San Pedro Town* ☎ *636/8123* ▧ *BZ$10.*

SHOPPING

Barrier Reef Drive, formerly sandy Front Street, and sadly now paved with concrete cobblestones, is San Pedro's Street of Shopping Dreams—it's lined with souvenir shops complemented by restaurants, small hotels, banks, and other anchors of tourist life on the island. Stores with more local appeal are on Pescador Drive (Middle Street) and Angel

Coral Street (Back Street), especially at the north end of town. Barrier Reef Drive is closed to golf carts and vehicles on weekends, starting around 6 pm Friday, and local vendors set up shop selling locally made jewelry and wood carvings (they're also out during the week in high season). Except for these items, few are made on the island. Most of the souvenir shops sell crafts from Guatemala and Mexico, along with carved wood and slate from the mainland.

Belizean hot sauces, such as Marie Sharp's and Gallon Jug's Lissette Sauce, along with local rums, make good souvenirs; they're cheaper in grocery stores than in gift shops. To avoid worsening the plight of endangered sea life, avoid buying souvenirs made from black coral or turtle shell.

Vendors on the beach occasionally try to sell you carvings, jewelry, Guatemalan fabrics, and sometimes drugs. Do not buy drugs as the consequences can be higher for foreigners.

Belizean Arts. The country's first art gallery, established more than 20 years ago by Londoner Lyndsey Hackston, Belizean Arts today has the largest selection of art by Belizeans and Belize residents, including paintings by Walter Castillo, Pen Cayetano, Nelson Young, Leo Vasquez, Piva, and others. The gallery also carries art by Cuban and other Caribbean artists, along with ceramics, jewelry, and other crafts. Even if you don't intend to buy, it's worth a look. ⊠ *Fido's Courtyard, Barrier Reef Dr., San Pedro Town* ☎ *226/3019* ⊕ *www.belizeanarts.com.*

D & G Fine Jewelry and Art. This long-established shop crafts locally made jewelry. If you don't see a design you like, the artist will work with you to create one. We encourage you not to buy items made of black coral, because it is highly endangered. ⊠ *Boca del Rio, San Pedro Town* ✛ *1 block north of high school* ☎ *226/2069* ⊕ *ambergriscaye.com/DandG.*

Fodor's Choice
★ **Graniel's Dreamland Construction & Cabinet Shop.** At Graniel's Dreamland, the showroom for Armando Graniel's beautiful carpentry, you can find the high-quality woodwork, like clam chairs or checkered cuttingboards made from tropical hardwoods. Some pieces the shop will break down and package for shipping, or for carrying back on the airplane. ⊠ *South end of Pescador Dr., San Pedro Town* ☎ *226/2632* ⊕ *www.graniels-dreamlandbelize.com.*

The Greenhouse. A trove of good ingredients, that may rival Whole Foods for pricey-ness. ⊠ *Pescador St., San Pedro Town* ☎ *226/2084.*

Man O' War Men's Supplies. What are men's supplies? Apparently they include Sperry's topsiders and Star Wars Lego sets. If you forgot anything from an extension cord to anti-chafing powder, this variety store might carry it. ⊠ *Caribena St., San Pedro Town.*

Marina's Store. Marina's Store south of town has good prices for groceries but only a small selection. ⊠ *Seagrape Dr., about 1 mile (1.5 km) south of town, San Pedro Town* ☎ *226/3647.*

Mata Grande Grocery. This dependable little store serves residents and condo guests on North Ambergris. You can even order and pay online, and Mata Grande will deliver groceries to your vacation rental or condo north of the Boca del Rio bridge. ⊠ *4.5 miles (7.5 km) north of bridge, Ambergris Caye* ☎ *226/4290* ⊕ *www.matagrandegrocery.com.*

Super Buy. Many local residents buy their groceries at Super Buy, because of lower prices. ⊠ *Angel Coral St., San Pedro Town* ☎ *226/4667.*

Toucan Gift Shops. For gaudy geegaws and unabashedly touristy souvenirs, the Toucan Gift Shops, including Toucan Too, all sporting the bright green, yellow, and red Toucan logo, are hard to miss. ⊠ *Barrier Reef Dr., San Pedro Town* ☎ *226/2499.*

Fodor's Choice **12 Belize.** Shop for chic clutches and totes handmade in southern Belize
★ with Mayan fabric, as well as plumeria scrubbing butter, candles, and other fashionable gifts. A percentage of proceeds go to community causes. ⊠ *Tarpon St., in Vilma Linda Plaza, San Pedro Town* ⚑ *Look for signs that point to little alley* ☎ *670/5272* ⊕ *www.12belize.com.*

Wine De Vine. Wine De Vine has a good selection of wines and imported cheeses, at prices (due to import taxes) roughly double the cost in the United States. ⊠ *Coconut Dr., San Pedro Town* ☎ *226/3430* ⊕ *www. winedevine.com* ⊗ *Closed Sun.*

SPORTS AND THE OUTDOORS

The San Pedro Family Fitness Club. The San Pedro Family Fitness Club has two hard-surfaced outdoor tennis courts, along with a large swimming pool and a fully equipped air-conditioned gym open to the public. Day, weekly, and monthly passes available. ⊠ *0.5 mile (1 km) south of town, Hurricane St., San Pedro Town* ⚑ *From town, go south on Coconut Dr. until you reach Road Kill Bar. Turn on Hurricane St. west toward lagoon. Go three blocks* ☎ *226/4749* ⊕ *www.sanpedrofitness.com.*

W.O.D. Zone. An equipped warehouse where for BZ$30 a day you can use the open gym or join the morning and evening Workout of the Day, with professional instructors. ⊠ *Sea Star St., near airport, San Pedro Town* ☎ *670/5575* ⊕ *www.wodzonebz.com.*

CAYE CAULKER

5 miles (8 km) south of Ambergris Caye, 18 miles (29 km) northeast of Belize City.

A half-hour away from San Pedro by water taxi and sharing essentially the same reef and sea ecosystems, Caye Caulker is very different from its big sister island, Ambergris Caye. It's smaller (with a population of around 1,500), less developed, cheaper, and deliciously slow. Flowers outnumber cars 1,000 to 1 (golf carts, bicycles, and bare feet are the preferred means of transportation).

As you might guess from all the "no shirt, no shoes, no problem" signs at the bars, the living is relatively easy here. This is the kind of place where many of the listings in the telephone directory give addresses like "near football field." Caye Caulker has long been a stop on the Central America backpacker trail, and it remains Belize's most popular budget destination, with an eternal high season. However, it isn't immune to change. Most hotels have added air-conditioning, and the island now has several upmarket restaurants. Still, it remains the epitome of laid-back, and as development continues at a fevered pace on neighboring Ambergris Caye, Caulker's simpler charms exercise even more appeal to those who seek an affordable island experience.

For those used to researching and booking everything online, here's a caution about Caye Caulker: Some of the tour operators and cheaper lodging choices on Caulker don't have websites. In fact, some tour operators work from a spot on the beach and have only a cell phone, if that. Those that are online often have websites that are done on the cheap, with poor graphics and servers that are down intermittently.

GETTING HERE AND AROUND

Other than a few emergency vehicles and several private cars, there are few cars on Caye Caulker. Most locals and visitors get around the island's sand streets on foot, although you can rent a golf cart or bike. (Golf-cart taxis charge around BZ$5–BZ$10 per person to most destinations in the village.)

Like Ambergris Caye, Caye Caulker can be used as a base for exploring part of the mainland. It's only about 45 minutes by water taxi, or 15 minutes by air, to Belize City. Two water-taxi companies now offer daily service between Caye Caulker and Chetumal, Mexico. Tours run from Caulker to the Mayan ruins at Lamanai and Altun Ha, and other tours go to the Belize Zoo and to the Caves Branch River for cave tubing.

Caye Caulker is a fairly small island, only 5 miles (8 km) long and a little more than 1 mile (2 km) wide at the widest point—most of the island is only a few hundred feet wide. All the streets on the island are hard-packed sand. On the east side you can also walk along the beachfront. Generally, the north end of the village bustles more than the south end, which is primarily residential, and is home to the airstrip. The island itself is divided by "the Split," a small channel of water separating the north area and the south area. The area north of the Split is mostly mangroves and lagoons, accessible only by boat, while the only village occupies most of the area south of the Split. From the Split to the airstrip, which is at the south end of the island, is about a mile (1.6 km). When you're told directions, things are either north or south of the main public pier.

TIMING

Caye Caulker's low-key charms take a while to fully appreciate. Stay here a day, and you'll complain that there's nothing to do. Stay a week, and you'll probably tell everyone how much you hate overdeveloped islands like Ambergris.

SAFETY

Several high-profile muggings, rapes, and stabbing of visitors have brought Caulker unwanted attention. Despite these crimes, and the general disreputable vibe of some Rasta-phonians who hang out at bars or call out to passing tourists, Caye Caulker remains one of the safest places in Belize. Just don't bring the barfly back to your room or wander around dark alleys at night. Also, keep your camera, wallet, and other possessions close to you, especially in cheaper hotels.

WATER ACTIVITIES AND TOURS

When you see the waves whiten at the Barrier Reef just a few hundred yards from the shore, boats full of eager snorkelers and divers, and striped sails of windsurfers dashing back and forth, you know you've come to the right place for water play. You can dive, snorkel, and fish the same areas that you can from San Pedro, but usually for a little less dough. However, one area where Caulker suffers by comparison with its neighboring island is in the quality of its beaches. Caulker's beaches, though periodically nourished by dredging to replenish the sand, are modest at best, mostly narrow ribbons of sand with shallow water near the shore and, in places, a mucky sea bottom and lots of sea grass. You'll also glimpse the reality of plastic-ridden oceans, getting more and more dire, in the speckles of plastic that appear like seashells in the sand.

You can, however, have a wonderful swim at the Split, a channel originally cut through the island by Hurricane Hattie in 1961 and expanded over the years, at the north end of the village, or from the end of piers. The water remains tepid and inviting.

FISHING

Caye Caulker was a fishing village before it was a visitor destination. From Caulker you can fly-fish for bonefish or permit in the grass flats behind the island, troll for barracuda or grouper inside the reef, or charter a boat to take you to blue water outside the reef for deep-sea fishing. Ambergris Caye offers more options for chartering boats for deep-sea fishing than Caye Caulker. If you're a do-it-yourself type, you can fish off the piers or in the flats. Anglers Abroad has a small fly-fishing and tackle shop where you can rent fishing gear, if you didn't bring your own. Blue marlin weighing more than 400 pounds have been caught beyond the reef off Caye Caulker, along with big sailfish, pompano, and kingfish. Remember, you now need a fishing license to fish in Belize waters, except from shore or piers. Your guide or hotel can help you get a license.

Fodor's Choice
★

Anglers Abroad. Haywood Curry, a transplanted Texan, and his crew run all types of fishing trips, starting with half-day trips at around BZ$500 for two persons and "for the adventurous" two- or three-day camping and fishing expeditions, with camping on a remote caye. Anglers Abroad, associated with Seadreams Hotel, also has a fly-fishing and tackle shop. ⊠ *At Seadreams Hotel near the Split, Hattie St.* ☎ *226/0602* ⊕ *www.anglersabroad.com.*

Tsunami Adventures. Tsunami Adventures offers reef and flats fishing trips starting at BZ$500 for a half day for up to four persons, including boat and guide inclusive of tax. ⊠ *Front St.* ☎ *226/0462* ⊕ *www.tsunamiadventures.com.*

MANATEE SPOTTING

Several operators do boat trips to see West Indian manatees. The 9,000-acre Swallow Caye Wildlife Sanctuary, established in 2002 in great part due to the efforts of Chocolate Heredia, who sadly passed away in 2013, and his wife Annie Seashore, is home to many of these endangered mammals. It's just 10 minutes by boat from Caye Caulker. It's illegal in Belize to get into the water with the gentle sea cows, but a few tour operators unfortunately do permit it. Half-day tours typically cost around BZ$100 per person, including the BZ$10 sanctuary admission fee. Some stop at Goff's Caye, which has excellent snorkeling.

FAMILY

Fodor'sChoice

★

Caveman Snorkeling Tours. Caveman and staff are known for sensitivity to the marine ecosystem, playful attitudes, and vigilance in giving you the best experience. A daylong manatee-watching tour, combined with snorkeling spots, is about BZ$180 per person, including lunch, gear, and park fees. Very navigable website and booking options. ⊠ *Av. Hicaco* ✛ *On water across from Dirty McNasty's.*

SAILING

A few small sailboats offer sailing and snorkeling trips to nearby areas. One company, Raggamuffin Tours, also offers multiday combination sailing, snorkeling, and camping trips to Placencia.

FAMILY

Fodor'sChoice

★

Blackhawk Sailing. Captain "Big Steve" offers snorkeling, overnight camping, and charter trips on a 32-foot vintage sailboat, made in the fishing village of Sarteneja, Belize. Touring the aquatic world is made more special by the elegance of sails. ⊠ *Av. Hicaco* ✛ *Next to De Real Macaw* ☎ 607/0323 ⊕ *www.blackhawksailingtours.com.*

Raggamuffin Tours. With a fleet of four beautiful sailboats, Raggamuffin offers sunset, moonlight, and day sails, but the winner is a two-night/three-day camping and sailing trip to Dangriga, with nights at Rendezvous Caye and Raffa Caye, at BZ$800 per person, including meals, reserve fees, gear, and taxes. These normally depart Caulker twice a week, on Tuesday and Friday, weather permitting. Raggamuffin also offers standard all-day snorkeling tours. ⊠ *Av. Hicaco* ✛ *North of main public pier, near the Split* ☎ 226/0348 ⊕ *www.raggamuffintours.com.*

SCUBA DIVING AND SNORKELING

Hol Chan Marine Reserve at the southern tip of Ambergris Caye *(see Ambergris Caye section, above)* is a popular destination for snorkel and dive trips from Caye Caulker. At Hol Chan you can swim with nurse sharks and stingrays and see hundreds of tropical fish, some quite large due to the no-fishing restrictions in the reserve. On the way, your boat may be followed by a pod of frolicking dolphins, and you may spot sea turtles or even a manatee. Larger boats from Caulker also go to Lighthouse Reef, including the Blue Hole, and Turneffe atolls.

The Caye Caulker Marine Reserve north and east of Caye Caulker, with its coral canyons, is a favorite of divers, especially for night dives. Caulker has its own mini version of San Pedro's Shark-Ray Alley, called Shark-Ray Village.

CHARTERS,

LESSONS, AND

EQUIPMENT

A plethora of dive and snorkel operators offer reef tours (some of them are "cowboys"—unaffiliated and unreliable—so make sure you use a reputable company). Plan on spending about BZ$70 for a snorkel trip around the island or BZ$130–BZ$140 for a five-hour snorkel trip to Hol Chan Marine Reserve.

Local two-tank reef dives typically begin at BZ$180, and those to Hol Chan or other nearby areas cost more. If you stop at Half Moon Caye, there's an additional BZ$80 park fee. At Hol Chan, the park fee is BZ$20, and at Caye Caulker Marine Reserve, BZ$10. These park fees, which apply for divers and snorkelers, are sometimes not included in the quoted prices for dive and snorkel trips. The 12.5% Goods and Services Tax (GST) may—or may not—be included in the price you're quoted. There are sometimes fine print costs. Ask, to be sure.

FAMILY **Anwar Tours.** Anwar Tours, run by brothers Erico and Javier Novelo, offers a variety of snorkel trips starting at BZ$80. A night snorkel trip is BZ$100. Anwar also provides manatee-watching, and a slew of mainland tours. Stops and length of trips vary depending on weather and sea conditions. You can use their underwater camera and record your sights. ⊠ *Av. Hicaco, at Pasero St.* ☎ 226/0327 ⊕ *www.anwar-tours.com.*

FAMILY
Fodor's Choice
★
Belize Diving Services. Established in 1978, the reputable Belize Diving Services trains around 500 divers every year, with a full open-water course for around BZ$1,000. BDS excels at organization, and they have a complete diving schedule. A two-tank local reef dive is BZ$190, not including gear, tax, and BZ$10 reserve fee. A two-tank Turneffe North (not Elbow) trip is BZ$280 plus all the fixings. You may pay a slight premium for the service, but their reputation is well-deserved. ⊠ *Chapoose St.* ✚ *Near soccer field and Iguana Reef Inn* ☎ 226/0143 ⊕ *www.belizedivingservices.com.*

Frenchie's Diving Services. Frenchie's, a respected local operator, leaves early to try to be the first boat to the Blue Hole. The three-dive, full-day trip, including gear, breakfast, lunch, BZ$80 park fee, and tax is BZ$520 per person for divers, and BZ$290 for snorkelers. Four-day open-water certifications courses run BZ$800. They also offer an overnight at Half Moon Caye, plus a menu of other fantastic sites with professional divemasters. If visiting in high season, book ahead because Frenchie's is popular. ⊠ *Beachfront, Av. Hicaco* ✚ *On dock north of main public pier* ☎ 226/0234 ⊕ *www.frenchiesdivingbelize.com.*

FAMILY **Raggamuffin Tours.** Take a great three-stop, full-day snorkeling trip off a sailboat to Hol Chan for around BZ$140 including park entrance fee, gear and tax, lunch, and rum and ceviche on the way home. ⊠ *Av. Hicaco* ☎ 226/0348 ⊕ *www.raggamuffintours.com.*

WINDSURFING AND KITESURFING

With brisk easterly winds most of the year, Caye Caulker is one of Belize's premier centers for windsurfing. The island gets winds over 12 knots most days from November to July. The best windsurfing is in the morning and afternoon, with lulls around midday. In the late winter and spring, winds frequently hit 20 knots or more.

CHARTERS, LESSONS, AND EQUIPMENT
KiteXplorer. KiteXplorer offers beginning and advanced kitesurfing lessons. A three-hour introduction to kitesurfing costs BZ$360 including equipment and insurance. A basic course over three or four days is BZ$980. If you already are an experienced kitesurfer, supervised equipment rental is BZ$120 an hour. KiteXplorer also sells equipment. ⊠ *Beachfront, Playa Asunción* ☎ 632/6355 ⊕ *www.kitexplorer.com.*

WHERE TO EAT

Once your dining choice on Caulker was fish, fish, or fish, but now you can also enjoy Italian, Mexican, and Chinese, as well as wonderful fresh conch and lobster and, of course, fish. Several restaurants serve

Restaurants

- Amor y Café 9
- Ana's Aladdin's Cuisine 1
- Bambooze 5
- Caribbean Colors Arts Café 6
- Errolyn's House of Fry Jacks 4
- Glenda's Café ... 11
- Habaneros 8
- Il Pelicano 3
- Rose's Grill and Bar 7
- Syd's 10
- Wish Willy's 2

Hotels

- Caye Caulker Condos 2
- CayeReef Condos .. 3
- Colinda's Cabañas 10
- De Real Macaw ... 4
- Iguana Reef Inn .. 5
- Island Magic Beach Resort 7
- Maxhapan Cabañas 8
- OASI 11
- Seadreams Hotel .. 1
- Seaside Cabañas .. 6
- Treetops Guesthouse 9

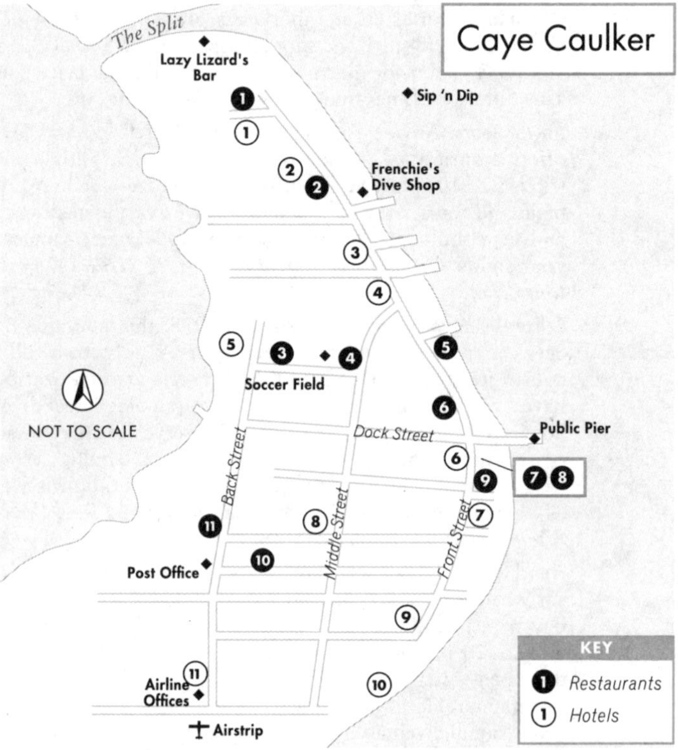

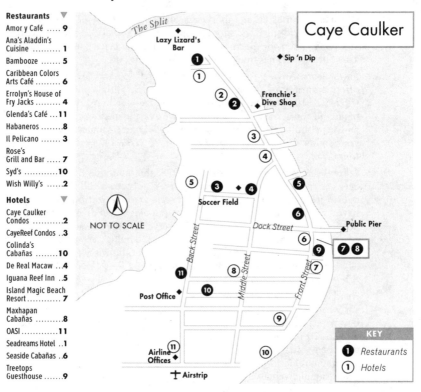

wholesome natural foods and vegetarian dishes. Prices for meals here are generally lower than on other islands, and even a lobster dinner is usually less than BZ$45. The cheapest way to eat on the island is to buy grilled fish, chicken, lobster, and other items from the folks with barbecue grills who set up along Front Street and elsewhere. Though you should use good judgment, the food is almost always well prepared and safe to eat. Locals also sell meat pies, tacos, tamales, cakes, and other homemade items at very low prices. Do what local people do and buy your snacks and some of your meals from these street vendors.

$ CAFÉ FAMILY ✕ **Amor y Café.** This is a classic spot on this island for a warm smile, coffee (including espresso and lattes), and breakfast. Sit on the front porch, do some people-watching on Front Street, and try the fruit with granola and homemade yogurt, or the yummy house-made breads. [$] *Average main: BZ$10* ✉ *15 Av. Hicaco* ⊕ *1 block south of main pier* ☎ *610/2397* 💳 *No credit cards* ⏰ *No dinner.*

$$ MIDDLE EASTERN FAMILY Fodor's Choice ★ ✕ **Ana's Aladdin's Cuisine.** Enjoy stove-fresh pita bread, skewers of shrimp with onions and parsley grilled in a boat of foil, and creamy hummus, made by the charming chef Ana. These deep-flavored dishes are a wonderful surprise. It's not fast food, so have a smoothie while you wait. Vegetarians will appreciate the superior options here. [$] *Average main: BZ$16* ✉ *Av. Hicaco* ⊕ *By the Split* ☎ *605/3305* ⏰ *Closed Mon.* 💳 *No credit cards.*

3

$
ECLECTIC
✕**Bambooze.** Grab a seat on one of the swinging benches near the water, and order a fresh pineapple juice and One Barrel on your walk to the Split. A choose-your-protein, choose-your-sauce kind of menu, it's nothing to write home about, but it's hard to go wrong with fish in garlic butter. $ *Average main: BZ$20* ⊠ *Av. Hicaco, Beachfront* ☉ *Closed Fri.*

$
CAFÉ
FAMILY
✕**Caribbean Colors Arts Café.** For a good cup of coffee, a really good cup of coffee, this little café cum art gallery and gift shop in the heart of Front Street is the place to go. It's owned by an expat artist, Lee Vanderwalker, who has lived on the island for many years. The café, called Coco Loco, also serves a few breakfast items such as bagels (rare in Belize) and pancakes, but coffee is the thing. $ *Average main: BZ$14* ⊠ *Av. Hicaco* ✛ *Across from basketball court* ☎ *605/9242* ⊕ *www. caribbean-colors.com* ☉ *Closed Thurs. No dinner.*

$
LATIN AMERICAN
Fodor'sChoice
★
✕**Errolyn's House of Fry Jacks.** Fry jacks are those puffy pillows of fried dough restaurants serve at breakfast; here they come stuffed with a slew of options, from egg and ham to chicken and beans, all for a buck or two. Just one makes a good meal, and at the stand next door you can get a liter of fresh orange juice (in a repurposed Crystal bottle) for BZ$5. Another example of a Belizean female cook's entrepreneurial act of ingenuity, Errolyn does it right. She also holds a barbecue every Saturday. $ *Average main: BZ$4* ⊠ *Pasero St., at Av. Langosta* ☉ *Closed Mon. No dinner* ⊟ *No credit cards.*

$
CAFÉ
FAMILY
✕**Glenda's Café.** Glenda's menu is on a chalkboard, short and sweet, and you place your order at the window of a clapboard house. At breakfast, when this café is most popular, for a pittance you can get a hearty breakfast of eggs, bacon, beans, johnnycakes and fresh O.J. Dine under the solemn eyes of a print of "The Last Supper," or take it to go. It opens at 7 am; get there early to get a cinnamon bun. $ *Average main: BZ$8* ⊠ *Av. Mangle* ✛ *North of post office* ☎ *226/0148* ⊟ *No credit cards* ☉ *Closed Sun. and sometimes on other days. No dinner.*

$$$
FUSION
Fodor'sChoice
★
✕**Habaneros.** The most expensive dining spot on Caye Caulker, Haberneros is also a place that tends to generate mixed reactions: One diner goes ga-ga over the coconut encrusted snapper with "fruit compound butter" and loves the dramatic lighting, while another guest sniffs at the pork topped with crab and thinks the restaurant is too dark. Chef-owner Darren Casson hits for the fences with some of his dishes, and he doesn't always connect, with too many competing flavors and over-the-top presentations, but for a splurge on Caye Caulker this is your most interesting, if conflicted, choice. Know that with drinks, appetizers, dessert, tip, and taxes (Haberneros doesn't include the 12.5% GST in the menu price), you'll face a hefty check, at least for Caye Caulker. And you could be one of those who just don't care for Habaneros. $ *Average main: BZ$46* ⊠ *Calle del Sol at Av. Hicaco* ✛ *East of Rose's* ☎ *626/4911* ☉ *No lunch. Closed Thurs. Closed Sept. and Oct.*

$$$
ITALIAN
Fodor'sChoice
★
✕**Il Pellicano.** Theatrical flowers, hanging lanterns of colored glass, and fabric draped across the ceiling all make a seductive ambience on an island where you expect picnic tables and sand. The menu features classics like risotto, gnocchi, and margherita pizza, with imported rarities like capers and porcini mushrooms. The menu changes frequently and the desserts change daily. Good for a special occasion or romantic

evening. [$] *Average main: BZ$35* ⊠ *Back side of island, Pasero St.* ⊹ *Past Atlantic Bank on right—enter around corner* ☎ *226/0660* ⊕ *www.ilpellicano.bz* ⊘ *Closed Mon. No lunch.*

$$$
SEAFOOD

✕ **Rose's Grill & Bar.** The tables on the porch and inside are often packed at this fresh seafood palapa restaurant. There's an iced display of the catch of the day; choose from snapper, grouper, barracuda, or lobster and have it grilled on the spot. It's a bit more expensive than other area restaurants but well worth the mark up. [$] *Average main: BZ$35* ⊠ *Calle del Sol* ⊹ *Behind Habaneros* ☎ *226/0407* ⊘ *No lunch May–Oct.*

$
LATIN AMERICAN
FAMILY
Fodor's Choice
★

✕ **Syd's.** If you ask a local resident for a restaurant recommendation, chances are you'll get a vote for Syd's, in an old white frame house on Middle Street. It serves Belizean favorites like beans and rice, stew chicken, *garnaches,* and tostadas, along with (in-season) lobster and conch at prices lower than you'll pay at most other eateries. The fried chicken here is the absolute best on the island. [$] *Average main: BZ$14* ⊠ *Av. Langosta at Aventurera St.* ☎ *226/0294* ⊘ *Closed Sun.*

$$
CARIBBEAN

✕ **Wish Willy's.** At Wish Willie's you eat on picnic tables in the sandy backyard of the owner, Maurice Moore, and he will tell you what's on the menu for the day. It may be fresh fish, lobster, or chicken. In most cases, the prices are very low, and the rum drinks cost less than almost anywhere else on the island. You may have to share a table with other guests, and the service is sometimes slow, but keep in mind the money you're saving and the good time you're having! [$] *Average main: BZ$20* ⊠ *Park St., off Av. Hicaco* ⊹ *Due west of Frenchies* ☎ *660/7194* ▭ *No credit cards* ⊘ *Hrs inconsistent. Usually closed Sept. and Oct.*

WHERE TO STAY

Caye Caulker has more than 50 hotels, mostly small places with just a few rooms. The older budget hotels are mostly clapboard, with fans but no air-conditioning, and usually without TV or room phones. If they're not on the water where they can catch the prevailing sea breezes, they are often burning hot during the day. Hotels built in the last decade or so are generally constructed of concrete, and most newer properties have air-conditioning. There are only a handful of swimming pools on the island, though the number is growing. ■ TIP→ **Many hotels on the island offer your 7th night free, so be sure to check before you book.**

$$
RENTAL
FAMILY

⌂ **Caye Caulker Condos.** If you want a full kitchen to prepare some of your own meals, these moderately priced condos with all the mod-cons including a pool are a good choice. **Pros:** pleasant small apartments with kitchens; good location near water and most restaurants; swimming pool; good value. **Cons:** units don't led you spread out much; rowdiness near the Split can make itself known. [$] *Rooms from: BZ$216* ⊠ *Av. Hicaco at Calle Almendro* ⊹ *Near Split* ☎ *226/0072* ⊕ *www. cayecaulkercondos.com* ↰ *8 apartments* ⧫ *No meals* ↻ *Complimentary bikes.*

$$$$
RENTAL
FAMILY

⌂ **CayeReef Condos.** CayeReef Condos are among the most upmarket and spacious digs on the island, especially for families or couples traveling together. **Pros:** upscale condo apartments; lots of space; pool; convenient location. **Cons:** some furnishings are looking a bit worn; prices are high for Caulker; pool feels towered over by concrete. [$] *Rooms* *from: BZ$589 ✉ Av. Hicaco at Park St., near Split ☎ 226/0382 🌐 www.cayereef.com 🛏 6 units 🍴 No meals.*

$ B&B/INN FAMILY Fodor's Choice ★ 🏨 **Colinda's Cabañas.** Quaint cabañas with the blue-meets-yellow coloring of a pastel angelfish and various rooms, most raised on stilts, that suit a range of budgets—all have a refrigerator, covered porch, ample drinking water, two bicycles, and a communal grill. **Pros:** the hammocked, Caribbean paradise; affable managers and staff; very clean. **Cons:** you might miss having a pool; bugs seem to like it; not all rooms have a/c; often fully booked. [$] *Rooms from: BZ$130 ✉ On beach south of town, ✥ Near Anchorage Resort ☎ 226/0383 🌐 www.colindacabanas.com 🛏 13 rooms 🍴 No meals.*

$ HOTEL 🏨 **De Real Macaw.** These gently priced, dim rooms are showing the wear and tear of the years, but it's a friendly island experience in the heart of Front Street, just a short walk to the Split. **Pros:** clean and well-run; good location near water and most restaurants. **Cons:** no frills; no a/c in some units. [$] *Rooms from: BZ$109 ✉ Av. Hicaco, at Crocodile St. ✥ North of main public pier ☎ 226/0459 🌐 www.derealmacaw.biz 🛏 10 units 🍴 No meals.*

$$ HOTEL FAMILY Fodor's Choice ★ 🏨 **Iguana Reef Inn.** A collection of sturdy, sand-color buildings fanned by mature palms, this is one of Caye Caulker's most upscale lodgings. **Pros:** attractive, well-designed lodging, with pool; manicured grounds; attentive staff; away from the youthful hubbub of Front Street. **Cons:** on back side of island; expensive for Caulker. [$] *Rooms from: BZ$347 ✉ Near north end of Av. Langosta ✥ Next to soccer field ☎ 226/0213 🌐 www.iguanareefinn.com 🛏 15 rooms 🍴 Breakfast ☞ Complimentary canoes, kayaks, and bikes.*

$$ HOTEL FAMILY 🏨 **Island Magic Beach Resort.** With seafoam or teal tones, these rooms are dependable and equipped but the more seductive places to spend time are the swinging deck chairs, the polished bar, your private balcony, or the pineapple-yellow loungers next to one of the nicest pools on the island. **Pros:** pleasant rooms; close to everything; great pool. **Cons:** reasonable but not mega bargain rates; uninspired decor. [$] *Rooms from: BZ$240 ✉ Av. Hicaco ☎ 604/3658 🌐 www.islandmagicbelize.com 🛏 12 rooms 🍴 No meals.*

$ HOTEL FAMILY Fodor's Choice ★ 🏨 **Maxhapan Cabañas.** This little spot is in the center of the village and not on the water, but it makes up for it by being neat and clean and a fine value, and set in a small, shady, sandy garden. **Pros:** Belizean-owned; darling cabañas have all the amenities you need; such a bargain. **Cons:** not on the water; bugs can happen. [$] *Rooms from: BZ$142 ✉ 55 Av. Pueblo Nuevo ✥ In center of village south of main public pier ☎ 226/0118 🛏 3 units 🍴 No meals ☞ Complimentary bikes and snorkel gear.*

$$ B&B/INN FAMILY Fodor's Choice ★ 🏨 **OASI.** Four excellent efficiency apartments have accents of driftwood or bamboo, petite kitchens, and a shady garden; each uniquely decorated with intimacy and privacy in mind. **Pros:** excellent price for the experience; leafy, hibiscus-filled grounds; low-key bar in the evening. **Cons:** not on the water and no sea views; kitchens are small. [$] *Rooms from: BZ$207 ✉ 9 Av. Mangle ☎ 226/0384 🌐 www.oasi-holidaysbelize.com 🛏 4 units 🍴 No meals; Breakfast.*

3

$$ B&B/INN FAMILY Fodor's Choice ★ 🏨 **Seadreams Hotel.** Seadreams is ideal for those who like to fish or enjoy taking in beautiful sunsets from a private pier on the lagoon. **Pros:** convenient location near the Split; ideal for anglers; private pier on lagoon; warm owners. **Cons:** a small walk to the beach; fewer views than beachside hotels. [$] *Rooms from: BZ$250* ✉ *Hattie St.* ✣ *Near the Split* ☎ *226/0602* 🌐 *www.seadreamsbelize.com* 🛏 *11 units* 🍴 *Breakfast.*

$$ B&B/INN FAMILY Fodor's Choice ★ 🏨 **Seaside Cabanas.** Warm in ambience and in attitude, these orange cabañas are arranged snugly in a U-shape around a blue pool. **Pros:** a top choice on the island; sunny decor; pool; feels private despite prime location. **Cons:** beach swimming in front of hotel is not good; not dirt cheap; not actually cabañas but rooms. [$] *Rooms from: BZ$294* ✉ *Av. Hicaco , at main public pier* ☎ *226/0498* 🌐 *www.seasidecabanas.com* 🛏 *17 units* 🍴 *Breakfast.*

$$ B&B/INN FAMILY 🏨 **Treetops Guesthouse.** Austrian-born owner Doris Creasey brings an eccentric flair and Teutonic cleanliness to this three-story colonial-style guesthouse, set back a ways from the sea. **Pros:** meticulously clean and well run; quiet location near the water. **Cons:** some guests complain about fairly strict rules; prices have increased. [$] *Rooms from: BZ$202* ✉ *Beachfront, Playa Asunción* ✣ *South of main public pier* ☎ *226/0240* 🌐 *www.treetopsbelize.com* 🛏 *6 units* 🍴 *No meals.*

VACATION HOME RENTALS

A handful of privately owned homes are available for rent on the island, either daily or by the week. Expect to pay around BZ$100–BZ$200 a night or BZ$800–BZ$2,000 a week. In most cases, credit cards are not accepted.

Caye Caulker Rentals (🌐 *www.cayecaulkerrentals.com 630–1008*) is the largest vacation home rental source on the island. It manages a number of cottages from BZ$130 a night, plus 9% tax. Small beachfront houses start at around BZ$1,300 a week. Airbnb has a growing number of options for room and home rentals (🌐 *www.airbnb.com).*

NIGHTLIFE

You don't come to Caye Caulker for the hot nightlife, but the island does have its share of laid-back bars. The most famous is the Lazy Lizard, while a newer complement is the nearby Sip n Dip. There are also a couple joints away from the water to hang out postsunset.

FAMILY **Bondi Bar & Bistro.** All kinds of hip, this bar pops with texture, from stamped-tin paneling to cushioned benches and a suspended bicycle. Cocktails like mango mojitos and habanero margaritas are perfectly exececuted but come at mixologist prices. The dinner menu is as eclectic as the ambience, with Taco Tuesdays and popular Sushi Fridays, plus a smattering of other bar food. Monday and Wednesday is movie night in their little outdoor cinema. On DJ nights the scene gets groovy. ✉ *Av. Hicaco* ✣ *Next to Habaneros* ☎ *226/0610* 🎟 *Movies BZ$12 for adults, BZ$6 for kids.*

I&I Reggae Bar. Knock back a Belikin or two to the beat of reggae jams at this three-story, red-green-yellow venue. Swings hang from the ceiling, replacing bar stools, on the first floor, and the top floor has hammocks and a thatch roof. The second floor is for dancing, often with a live DJ. This is the kind of place that gives prizes of thongs and nail polish on

Ladies' Night. ⊠ *Av. Langosta at Luciano Reyes St.* ✛ *South of public pier. Go south on Front St. to dead end, then turn right* ☎ *633/3126* 🖭 *BZ$3 on some nights.*

Lazy Lizard. "Sunny place for shady people" is the slogan of the Lazy Lizard, which sits right at the edge of the water at the northernmost tip of the village. During the day you can swim at the Split and cool off with some Belikins. Sunsets are amazing and after dark there's a spotlight pointed into the water so you can see fish, small sharks, and occasionally even a crocodile swimming around. Don't expect clean bathrooms, seating or delicious bar snacks, but because of the location this is by far the most popular hangout on the island. ⊠ *At the Split* ☎ *634/9714.*

FAMILY **Sip n Dip Beach Bar.** The new, less hip, less loud competitor of Lazy Lizard, Sip n Dip is a great place to kick it with your feet in the water, drink in hand. The swimming here is not as good or deep as at the Lizard, but you're a stone's throw from that area. It's more family-friendly, with a playground and a little upcycled waterslide into the sea. There's a basic lunch menu but it's only open until 6 pm, so it's a good spot to beat the daytime heat. ⊠ *On water just south of the Split* ☎ *600/0080.*

SHOPPING

You won't find nearly as many shops here as in San Pedro, but there are a few standout stores to poke around in for some interesting souvenirs. Every day vendors set up on a section of Front Street north of the main public pier, selling crafts and souvenirs. A few vendors along Front Street can be pretty aggressive—ignore them and buy from someone else.

Caribbean Colors. This gallery sells watercolors, handpainted silk, and other works by Lee Vanderwalker, as well as handmade jewelry and scarves by local artists. The small café serves tasty coffee and eclectic breakfast and lunch dishes. ⊠ *Av. Hicaco* ✛ *Just south of main public pier* ☎ *226/0208, 877/809–1659* ⊕ *www.cafepress.com/ caribbeancolors.*

Chan's Mini Mart. Chan's is a popular grocery in the village. Pick up your basic groceries and Marie Sharp's hot sauce here. ⊠ *Av. Langosta at Calle del Sol* ☎ *226/0165.*

Cooper's Art Gallery. Cooper's Art Gallery has dynamic paintings and prints by Walter Castillo, Nelson Young, and other Belizean artists, along with beautiful pieces by owner Debbie Cooper. ⊠ *Av. Hicaco* ✛ *North of main public pier* ☎ *226/0420* ⊕ *www.debbiecooper.artspan.com.*

SOUTHERN CAYES

GETTING HERE AND AROUND

The southern cayes are specks of land spread out over hundreds of square miles of sea, and they are spectacular. With their sense of depth-lessness, the vistas here make you feel you might fall into the sky. There is no scheduled air or boat service to any of these islands. In the case of Tobacco Caye, private boats leave Dangriga daily around 9 to 9:30 am. If you're lodging at the other cayes and atolls, your resort will help you arrange your boat transfer (usually it is included); if not you can charter your own boat at high cost.

TIMING

Because of the difficulty and expense of getting to the islands, most resorts have minimum-stay requirements, sometimes as little as three days but often a week. Bring several beach novels, and be prepared to enjoy a quiet vacation filled with salty adventures on and under the sea.

TOBACCO CAYE

11 miles (18 km) southeast of Dangriga.

Tobacco Caye is at the northern tip of the South Water Caye Marine Reserve, a 62-square-mile (160-square-km) reserve that's popular for diving and fishing and has some of the most beautiful islands in Belize. Visitors to the South Water Caye Marine Reserve pay BZ$10 a day for up to three days, or BZ$30 a week, park fee. Rangers come around and collect it from guests at the Tobacco Caye hotels.

The island has no shops or restaurants, except those at the hotels, and just a couple of bars, but there is one small dive shop. Boats leave from the Riverside Café in Dangriga for the 40-minute, roughly BZ$50 trip to Tobacco Caye. Get to the Riverside by 9 am; most boats leave around 9:30 (though at busy times such as Easter they come and go all day long). You can get information on the boats, as well as breakfast, at the Riverside Café. ⇨ *See Southern Coast chapter.*

If you don't want to pay a lot for your place in the sun, Tobacco Caye may be for you. It's a tiny island—barely 4 acres, and a walk around the entire caye takes 10 minutes—but it's right on the reef, so you can wade in and snorkel all you want. Though the snorkeling off the caye is not as good as in some other areas of Belize (some of the coral is dead and most of the fish are small), you can see spotted eagle rays, moray eels, octopi, and other sea life.

WHERE TO STAY

All the accommodations are budget places, basically simple wood cabins, some not much larger than sheds. Because four hotels vie for space, the islet seems even smaller than it is. Periodically the hotels get blown away by storms but are rebuilt, usually a little better than they were before. Unfortunately, garbage tends to pile up on the island, and the hotels don't always use the most ecologically sound methods for disposing of it.

Though rates have increased, most prices remain affordably low.

$$ HOTEL FAMILY **Tobacco Caye Lodge.** This cluster of pastel blue cabins is a few feet from the turquoise sea. **Pros:** the Caribbean made affordable; great price considering all meals are included; friendly staff. **Cons:** basic living, just slightly above backpacker level; trash can wash ashore. [$] *Rooms from: BZ$220* ✉ *Tobacco Caye Lodge, Tobacco Caye* ☎ *532/2033* 🌐 *www.tclodgebelize.com* 🛏 *6 units* 🍴 *All meals.*

$$ B&B/INN Fodor's Choice ★ **Tobacco Caye Paradise Cabins.** Whether it's paradise or not depends on your expectations, but if what you're seeking is a gently priced little shack built partly over the water, backed by coco palms, with snorkeling and swimming right out your door, this could be it. **Pros:** huts on the beach at a great value; snorkeling is 15 feet away; friendly staff. **Cons:** very basic

rooms; past time for repairs; charge for snorkel gear and kayaks. $ *Rooms from: BZ$304* ✉ *Tobacco Caye Paradise, Tobacco Caye* ☎ *532/2101, 800 /667–1630* ⊕ *www.tobaccocaye.com* ➷ *6 units* ¡○¡ *No meals.*

ISLAND RESORTS OFF DANGRIGA
WHERE TO STAY

$$$$
RESORT
FAMILY
Fodor's Choice
★

Coco Plum Island Resort. It all comes down to this: relax in a hammock on the veranda of your cottage, sip a cold drink, and gaze at the Caribbean at this all-inclusive private island resort off Dangriga. **Pros:** delivers even more than it promises; you'll miss the lovely staff when you leave; package discounts. **Cons:** only fair snorkeling off beach; not on reef. $ *Rooms from: BZ$1,990* ✉ *Coco Plum Caye, 8 miles (13 km) from Dangriga, Coco Plum* ☎ *522/2200, 800/763–7360 in U.S.* ⊕ *www.cocoplumcay.com* ➷ *15 units* ¡○¡ *All-inclusive.*

$$$$
RESORT
FAMILY

Thatch Caye. Thatch Caye is all about you and your private island vacation, so you can head out for a day of fishing, diving, sea kayaking, or snorkeling and return to supremely comfortable accommodations. **Pros:** beautiful private island with congenial hosts; plenty of marine activities; attractive cabañas directly on the water. **Cons:** limited snorkeling off beach; not on reef; no pool. $ *Rooms from: BZ$747* ✉ *9 miles (15 km) or about 25 minutes by boat from Dangriga, Thatch Caye* ☎ *800/435–3145 in U.S. and Canada* ⊕ *www. thatchcayebelize.com* ➷ *12 units* ¡○¡ *No meals* ⌕ *Boat transfer from Dangriga included.*

SOUTH WATER CAYE
14 miles (23 km) southeast of Dangriga.

This is one of our favorite underrated spots in Belize. The 15-acre South Water Caye has good off-the-beaten-reef diving and snorkeling in a stunning tropical setting, and the beach at the southern end of the island is one of Belize's sandy beauties. The reef is only a short swim from shore. The downside of the small caye? The sand flies here can be a nuisance, and there aren't any facilities other than those at the island's two resorts and the International Zoological Expeditions' student dorm.

WHERE TO STAY

$$$$
RESORT
FAMILY

Pelican Beach Resort South Water Caye. Steps from one of Belize's best beaches, where you can swim, snorkel, and dive from shore, and fish to your heart's content, is this former convent turned peaceful island retreat on 3½ seaside acres. **Pros:** on great little beach, with snorkeling from shore; tasty Belizean food; comfortable, eco-friendly no-frills accommodations. **Cons:** you have to make your own entertainment; remember: no-frills accommodations. $ *Rooms from: BZ$750* ✉ *South Water Caye* ☎ *522/2044* ⊕ *www.pelicanbeachbelize.com* ➷ *13 units* ¡○¡ *All meals.*

SOUTHERN CAYES OFF PLACENCIA AND SOUTHERN COAST

8–18 miles (13–30 km) east of Placencia.

A few miles off the coast of southern Stann Creek District are several small islands with equally small tourism operations. If Placencia and Hopkins aren't far enough away from civilization for you, consider an overnight or longer visit to one of these quiet little paradises surrounded by fish.

WHERE TO STAY

$$$$
RENTAL
FAMILY

Bird Island. A patch of coral, the shape of a perfect pancake and not much bigger, is a self-catering, real-life private island where the solitude and starry skies are exquisite. **Pros:** atoll to yourself; spectacular sunsets and starry nights; extremely private. **Cons:** can get lonely; three-night minimum. $ *Rooms from: BZ$763* ⊠ *Placencia Village* ☎ *634/3997* ⊕ *www.birdislandplacenciabz.com* ⊘ *Closed mid-June to mid-July* ➶ *1 unit* �‖ *No meals.*

$$$$
RESORT
FAMILY
Fodor'sChoice
★

Hatchet Caye. On a private island about 17 miles (28 km) east of Placencia, Hatchet Caye offers an unspoiled, remote getaway for honeymooners, divers, or just anyone wanting a complete escape. **Pros:** modern, upscale resort in remote setting; on-site PADI shop offers good diving and snorkeling nearby; island open to mariners. **Cons:** small island with no shops or choice of restaurants; the suite unit doesn't have much of a sea view. $ *Rooms from: BZ$833* ⊠ *Hatchet Caye, Hatchet Caye* ⊹ *17 miles (28 km) east of Placencia* ☎ *533/4446* ⊕ *www.hatchetcaye.com* ⊘ *Closed Oct.* ➶ *9 rooms* �‖ *No meals.*

THE ATOLLS

There are only four atolls in the Western Hemisphere, and three of them are off Belize (the fourth is Chinchorro Reef, off Mexico's Yucatán). Belize's atolls—Turneffe, Lighthouse, and Glover's—are oval-shape masses of coral. A few small islands, some sandy and others mostly mangrove, rise up along the atolls' encircling coral arms. Within the coral walls are central lagoons, with shallow water 10 to 30 feet deep. Outside the walls, the ocean falls off sharply to 1,000 feet or more, deeper than any diver can go.

Unlike the more common Pacific atolls, which were formed from underwater volcanoes, the Caribbean atolls began forming millions of years ago, atop giant tectonic faults. As giant limestone blocks slowly settled, they provided platforms for coral growth.

Because of their remoteness (they're 25 miles [40 km] to 50 miles [80 km] from the mainland) and because most of the islands at the atolls are small, the atolls have remained nearly pristine. Only a few small dive and fishing resorts are here, and the serious divers and anglers who favor the area know that they have some of the best diving and fishing in the Caribbean, if not the world. The atolls are also wonderful for beachcombing, relaxing, and snorkeling—just bring plenty of books, as there are no shops or restaurants other than at the hotels. Of course, paradise has its price: most of the atoll resorts are very, very expensive and have minimum-stay requirements. You can buy a basic new compact car for the cost of bringing your family for a week to most of these atoll lodges. Although there are good reasons why remote fishing and diving lodges on the cayes must charge a small fortune just to break even, the high rates are one prominent reason Belize is considered a high-cost vacation destination.

Getting to the atolls usually requires a long boat ride, sometimes rough enough to bring on *mal de mer.* You'll need to take one of the scheduled boats provided by your lodge or ride out on a dive or snorkel boat with a group; otherwise, you'll likely pay BZ$800–BZ$2,000 or more to charter a boat one-way. Remember, there are no commercial services at the atolls, except those associated with an island dive or fishing lodge. To charter a boat, check with a lodge on the atoll where you wish to go, or ask locally at docks in Belize City, San Pedro, Dangriga, Hopkins, or Placencia.

Dive shops and sailing charters in San Pedro, Caye Caulker, Placencia, and Hopkins make regular trips to the atolls, and may take additional passengers, for a fee, if space is available. *See Scuba Diving and Snorkeling sections of the pertinent destination chapter for contact information on dive shops.*

TIMING

Because of the difficulty and expense of getting to the atolls, most resorts have minimum-stay requirements of at least three days. There's little to do on the atolls except dive, snorkel, fish, eat, sleep, and drink. If you don't like sea sports, or if you do but hit consecutive days of bad weather, you may be bored out of your gourd. Of course, that remote shelter from daily noise may be just what you seek.

TURNEFFE ATOLL

25 miles (40 km) east of Belize City.

The largest of the three atolls, Turneffe, is the closest to Belize City. It's one of the best spots for diving, thanks to several steep drop-offs. Only an hour from Lighthouse Reef and 45 minutes from the northern edge of Glover's Reef, Turneffe is a good base for exploring all the atolls.

The best-known attraction, and probably Belize's most exciting wall dive, is the **Elbow,** at Turneffe's southernmost tip. You may encounter ethereal eagle rays—as many as 50 might flutter together, forming a rippling herd. Elbow is generally considered an advanced dive because of the strong currents, which sweep you toward the deep water beyond the reef.

Though it's most famous for its spectacular wall dives, the atoll has dives for every level. The leeward side, where the reef is wide and gently sloping, is good for shallower dives and snorkeling; you'll see large concentrations of tube sponges, soft corals such as forked sea feathers and sea fans, and plenty of fish. Also on the atoll's western side is the wreck of the *Sayonara.* No doubloons to scoop up here—it was a small passenger and cargo boat that sank in 1985—but it's good for wreck dive practice.

Fishing here, as at all of the atolls, is world-class. You can fly-fish for bonefish and permit in the grassy flats, or go after migratory tarpon from May to September in the channels and lagoons of the atoll. Jack, barracuda, and snappers lurk in the mangrove-lined bays and shorelines. Billfish, sailfish, and other big creatures are in the blue water around the atoll.

WHERE TO STAY

$$$$
RESORT
Fodor'sChoice
★

Turneffe Flats. The sound of the surf is the only night noise at this smart, red-roofed resort, where you'll commune with others who love fishing and other water activities as much as you do. **Pros:** quality fishing lodge with flats you dream of; special atoll scenery; diving and just plain relaxing available. **Cons:** comes at a price; sand fleas are friendly. $ *Rooms from: BZ$1,507 ✉ Turneffe Flats Lodge, Turneffe Atoll* ☎ *232/9022, 888/512–8812* ⊕ *www.tflats.com* ⇥ *10 units* ¶◯¶ *All-inclusive.*

$$$$
RESORT
Fodor'sChoice
★

Turneffe Island Resort. The white-uniformed staff all lined up for your boat's arrival, the preserved colonial-era buildings, and the oxidized anchor of an 18th-century British warship all set the tone at this upscale, legend-filled resort. **Pros:** breathtaking atoll setting near great diving and snorkeling; delicious and varied meals; you're sure to be pampered. **Cons:** may need to dive for a treasure chest to pay for this vacation; no other restaurant options. $ *Rooms from: BZ$2,010 ✉ Coco Tree Caye* ☎ *532/2990, 800/874–0118* ⊕ *www.turnefferesort.com* � *Closed Sept. and Oct.* ⇥ *22 units* ¶◯¶ *All-inclusive.*

LIGHTHOUSE REEF ATOLL, THE BLUE HOLE, AND HALF MOON CAYE

50 miles (80 km) east of Belize City.

If Robinson Crusoe had been a man of means, he would have repaired here for a break from his desert island.

Lighthouse Reef is about 18 miles (29 km) long and less than 1 mile (2 km) wide and is surrounded by a seemingly endless stretch of coral. Here you'll find two of the country's best dives.

At this writing, visiting Lighthouse Reef is best done as a side trip from Ambergris Caye, Caye Caulker, or another location in northern Belize. The marine reserve fee here is a pricey BZ$80 per person.

TOP ATTRACTIONS

Fodor'sChoice
★

Blue Hole. From the air, the Blue Hole, a breathtaking vertical chute that drops several hundred feet through the reef, is a dark blue eye in the center of the shallow lagoon. The Blue Hole was first dived by Jacques Cousteau in 1970 and has since become a diver's pilgrimage site. Just over 1,000 feet wide at the surface and dropping almost vertically to a depth of 412 feet, the Blue Hole is like swimming down a mineshaft, but a mineshaft with hammerhead sharks. This excitement is reflected in the thousands of stickers and T-shirts reading, "I Dived the Blue Hole." ✉ *Lighthouse Reef, Blue Hole.*

Half Moon Caye Wall. The best diving on Lighthouse Reef is at Half Moon Caye Wall, a classic wall dive. Half Moon Caye begins at 35 feet and drops almost vertically to blue infinity. Floating out over the edge is a bit like free-fall parachuting. Magnificent spurs of coral jut out to the seaward side, looking like small tunnels; they're fascinating to explore and invariably full of fish. An exceptionally varied marine life hovers around this caye. On the gently sloping sand flats behind the coral spurs, a vast colony of garden eels stirs, their heads protruding from the sand-like periscopes. Spotted eagle rays, sea turtles, and other underwater wonders frequent the drop-off. ⊠ *Lighthouse Reef, Half Moon Caye* ⊕ *www.belizeaudubon.org* ✉ *BZ$80.*

Half Moon Caye National Monument. Belize's easternmost island offers one of Belize's greatest wildlife encounters, although it's difficult to reach and lacks accommodations other than camping. Part of the Lighthouse Reef system, Half Moon Caye owes its protected status to the presence of the red-footed booby. The bird is here in such numbers that it's hard to believe it has only one other nesting ground in the entire Caribbean (on Tobago Island, off the coast of Venezuela). Some 4,000 of these birds hang their hats on Half Moon Caye, along with iguanas, lizards, and loggerhead turtles. The entire 40-acre island is a nature reserve, so you can explore the beaches or head into the bush on the narrow nature trail. Above the trees at the island's center is a small viewing platform—at the top you're suddenly in a sea of birds that will doubtless remind you of a certain Alfred Hitchcock movie. Several dive operators and resorts arrange day trips and overnight camping trips to Half Moon Caye. Managed by the Belize Audubon Society, the park fee here is a steep BZ$80 per person. ⊠ *Half Moon Caye National Monument* ⊕ *www.belizeaudubon.org* ✉ *BZ$80.*

GLOVER'S REEF ATOLL

70 miles (113 km) southeast of Belize City.

Fodor's Choice ★ Named after the pirate John Glover, this coral necklace strung around an 80-square-mile (208-square-km) lagoon is the southernmost of Belize's three atolls. There are five islands at the atoll. Visitors to Glover's Reef are charged a BZ$20 park fee (BZ$25 for fly-fishing).

WORTH NOTING

Emerald Forest Reef. Although most of the best dive sites are along the Glover's Atoll's southeastern side, this is the exception. It's named for its masses of huge green elkhorn coral. Because the reef's most exciting part is only 25 feet down, it's excellent for novice divers. ⊠ *Glover's Reef Atoll.*

Long Caye Wall. This is an exciting wall at Glover's Atoll, and between its bright coral and dramatic drop-off hundreds of feet down, diving it truly feels like extraterrestrial exploration. It's a good place to spot turtles, rays, and barracuda.

Southwest Caye Wall. Southwest Caye Wall is an underwater cliff that falls quickly to 130 feet. It's briefly interrupted by a narrow shelf, then continues its near-vertical descent to 350 feet. This dive gives you the exhilaration of flying in blue space, so it's easy to lose track of how deep you are going. Both ascent and descent require careful monitoring.

Kayaking is another popular sport here; you can paddle out to the atoll's many patch reefs for snorkeling. Most hotels rent kayaks.

WHERE TO STAY

$$$$ RESORT
Isla Marisol. Spend your days here snorkeling off the dock, doing acrobatics on one of the water trampolines, and, most dramatically, diving at "The Pinnacles," where coral heads rise 40 feet from the ocean floor. **Pros:** Belizean-owned and run; great diving in an unbeatable setting; barracuda and nurse sharks hang around the dock. **Cons:** prices aren't budget; sandflies sometimes troublesome; basic accommodations. [$] *Rooms from: BZ$1,066* ✉ *Southwest Caye, Isla Marisol* ☎ *610/4204* 🌐 *www.islamarisolresort.com* 🛏 *11 units* 🍴 *All meals.*

$$$$ RESORT
Off the Wall Dive Center & Resort. The name doesn't do justice to this lodge on Glover's Atoll, which focuses on diving (sites are a four-minute boat ride away), but snorkeling, fishing, bird-watching and stargazing are also excellent, and with only five cabañas, you may feel the coral island was conjured all for you. **Pros:** competitive price (for an atoll lodge in Belize); easy access to great diving; very knowledgeable dive staff. **Cons:** modest accommodations; bugs can be a nuisance. [$] *Rooms from: BZ$965* ✉ *Off the Wall Dive Center, Long Caye, Glover's Reef Atoll* ☎ *532/2929* 🌐 *www.offthewallbelize.com* 🛏 *5 cabañas* 🍴 *All meals.*

NORTHERN
BELIZE

By Lan Sluder   Razzmatazz and bling are in short supply in northern Belize. Here you'll find more orange groves than beach bars, more sugarcane than sugary sand, and more farms than restaurants. Yet if you're willing to give in to the area's easygoing terms and slow down to explore back roads and poke around small towns and villages, this northern country will win a place in your traveler's heart. You'll discover some of Belize's most interesting Mayan sites, several outstanding jungle lodges, and a sprinkling of small, inexpensive inns with big personalities.

Northern Belize includes the northern part of Belize District and all of Orange Walk and Corozal districts. Altogether, this area covers about 2,800 square miles (7,250 square km) and has a population of more than 90,000. The landscape is mostly flat, with mangrove swamps on the coast giving way to savanna inland. Scrub bush is much more common than broadleaf jungle, although to the northwest near the Guatemala border are large, wild tracts of land with some of the world's few remaining old-growth mahogany trees. The region has many cattle ranches, citrus groves, sugarcane fields, and, in a few areas, marijuana fields.

The only sizable towns in the region are Orange Walk, about 53 miles (87 km) north of Belize City, with about 14,000 residents, and Corozal Town, which is 85 miles (139 km) north of Belize City, and has a population of around 15,000. Both are on the Philip Goldson Highway, formerly the Northern Highway, a paved two-lane road that runs 95 miles (156 km) from Belize City up the center of the region, ending at the Mexican border.

Northern Belize gets less rain than anywhere else in the country (roughly 50 inches annually in Corozal), a fact that's reflected in the sunny disposition of the local population, mostly Maya and Mestizos. Both Orange Walk and Corozal towns have a Mexican ambience, with central plazas serving as the focus of the downtown areas. Many locals speak Spanish as a first language, although most also know some English, and many speak both Spanish and English fluently. While several new hotels and restaurants have opened here, Orange Walk Town is mostly a jumping-off point for trips to Lamanai and other Mayan ruins, to Mennonite farmlands, and to several well-regarded jungle lodges in wild, remote areas. Corozal Town, next door to Chetumal, Mexico, is a place to slow down, relax, and enjoy the laid-back atmosphere of a charming small town on the beautiful Corozal Bay (or, as Mexico calls it, Chetumal Bay).

TOP REASONS TO GO

Mayan Sites: Several of the most interesting Mayan sites in the region are in northern Belize. These include Altun Ha, Lamanai, Santa Rita, and Cerros. Altun Ha gets the most visitors of any Mayan site in Belize, and Lamanai, on the New River Lagoon, and Cerros, on Corozal Bay, are notable because of their beautiful locations. Santa Rita at the edge of Corozal Town, is newly opened to visitors.

Wild, Open Spaces: This part of Belize has some of the country's wildest tracts of land. The quarter-million acres of Río Bravo Conservation & Management Area attract only a few thousand visitors each year. Although people are scarce, Río Bravo teems with wildlife. Other large tracts of land include the Gallon Jug lands, 130,000 privately owned acres around Chan Chich Lodge. The Shipstern Reserve is a 22,000-acre expanse of swamps, lagoons, and forests on the Sarteneja peninsula. Huge numbers of birds nest at the Crooked Tree Wildlife Sanctuary.

Jungle Lodges: Northern Belize is home to several first-rate lodges, including Chan Chich Lodge, a paradise for birders and the place where you're most likely to spot the jaguar in the wild. Lamanai Outpost, on the New River Lagoon, is a center for crocodile research.

If you tire of small-town pleasures, the Belize side of the Mexican border has three casinos, including one called Las Vegas that claims to be the largest casino in Central America, and a duty-free zone (though the shopping here is mostly for cheap clothing and appliances, with little of interest to international visitors). Corozal has begun to draw foreign expats looking for inexpensive real estate and proximity to Chetumal, the Quintana Roo Mexican state capital, whose metropolitan population is nearly as large as that of the entire country of Belize. Chetumal offers urban conveniences that Belize doesn't, including a modern shopping mall, fast food, a multiplex cinema, and big-box stores including Walmart and Sam's Club. Sarteneja Village, in the far northeastern part of Corozal District, about 35 miles (57 km) from Corozal Town, is a still-undiscovered fishing village at the edge of the sea, near the Shipstern Wildlife Reserve. On the way are several pristine lagoons, including the lovely Progresso Lagoon.

ORIENTATION AND PLANNING

GETTING ORIENTED

The Philip Goldson Highway, a paved two-lane road, renamed in 2012 for a prominent politician (the international airport is also named for him), is the transportation spine of the region, running about 95 miles (156 km) from Belize City to the Mexican border at Chetumal, passing the two main towns in northern Belize, Orange Walk and Corozal. A bypass around Orange Walk provides a way to avoid the congested downtown.

Branching off the Goldson Highway are a number of tertiary roads, mostly unpaved, including the road to Crooked Tree Wildlife Sanctuary; the Old Northern Highway that leads to the Altun Ha ruins and Maruba Lodge and Spa; a road to Shipyard, a Mennonite settlement, which also connects with roads to the Lamanai ruins and to La Milpa ruins and Chan Chich Lodge at Gallon Jug; the San Estevan Road that is a route to Progresso, Copper Bank, and the Cerros Maya ruins, or, via a different branch, to Sarteneja. Another route, unpaved, to Sarteneja runs from Corozal Town and requires crossing the New River and the mouth of Laguna Seca on hand-pulled auto ferries.

Crooked Tree Wildlife Sanctuary. A paradise for birders, this wildlife sanctuary is an "inland island" surrounded by a chain of lagoons, in total covering about 3,000 acres. Traveling by canoe among countless birds, you're likely to see iguanas, crocodiles, coatis, and turtles.

Altun Ha. Easy to get to from the Northern Cayes or Belize City, Altun Ha is the most visited Mayan ruin in Belize. Cruise ship tours bring hundreds of visitors here daily. After the ruins, treat yourself to a cold drink or mud bath at nearby Maruba Resort Jungle Spa.

Northwest Orange Walk District. A fascinating combination of Mennonite farm country, wild jungle, and Mayan sites including Lamanai, La Milpa, and Chan Chich, this remote part of Belize is anchored by two remarkable jungle lodges, Chan Chich Lodge and Lamanai Outpost. Sadly, and almost unbelievably, one of the largest Mayan temples in Belize, Nohmul on private lands near Orange Walk Town, in mid-2013 was bulldozed by a contractor for use as roadfill.

Corozal Bay. It's so low-key you may doze off occasionally, but for relaxation at modest cost you can't find a better spot than the shores of Corozal Bay (also known as the Bay of Chetumal). Copper Bank and Sarteneja are especially laid-back. Corozal Town is an expat magnet.

PLANNING

WHEN TO GO
Corozal Town and the rest of northern Belize get about the same amount of rain as Atlanta, Georgia, so even the "rainy season"—generally June to November—here is not to be feared. It's hot and humid for much of the year, except in waterfront areas where prevailing breezes mitigate the heat. December to April is usually the most pleasant time, with weather similar to that of southern Florida. In winter, cold fronts from the north occasionally bring rain and chilly weather, and when the temperature drops to the low 60s, locals wear sweaters and sleep under extra blankets.

GETTING HERE AND AROUND
AIR TRAVEL
Corozal Town has flights only to and from San Pedro (Ambergris Caye). Tropic Air and Maya Island Air each fly four to six times daily between Ambergris Caye and the airstrip at Corozal, about 2 miles (3 km) south of town off the Goldson Highway. The journey takes 20 minutes. From Corozal, there's no direct air service to Belize City or other destinations

in Belize. Charter service is available to Chan Chich Lodge and the Indian Church/Lamanai area.

Contacts Maya Island Air. ✉ *Corozal Air Strip, Ranchito* ☎ *422/0711 Corozal Airstrip, Ranchito, 223/1403 Belize City* ⊕ *www.mayaislandair.com.* **Tropic Air.** ✉ *Corozal Air Strip, Ranchito* ☎ *226/2626 reservations in Belize, 800/422–3435 in U.S.* ⊕ *www.tropicair.com.*

BOAT AND WATER-TAXI TRAVEL

Ferry from Corozal. An old, hand-pulled sugar barge ferries passengers and cars across the New River from just south of Corozal Town to the road to Copper Bank, Cerros, and the Shipstern peninsula. The ferry is free from 6 am to 9 pm daily. To get to the ferry from Corozal, take the Philip Goldson Highway south toward Orange Walk Town and look for the ferry sign just south of town. Turn left and follow the unpaved road to the ferry landing.

Ferry between Copper Bank and Sarteneja. A second, hand-pulled auto ferry is between Copper Bank and Sarteneja, at the mouth of Laguna Seca. From Copper Bank, follow the ferry signs. Near Chunox, at a T-intersection, turn left and follow the unpaved road 20 miles (32 km) to Sarteneja.

Water Taxi between Corozal Town and Ambergris Caye. A daily water taxi operates between Corozal Town and Ambergris Caye, with a stop on demand at Sarteneja. The *Thunderbolt* departs from Corozal at the pier near Reunion Park behind Corozal House of Culture at 7 am and also goes from a pier on the back side of San Pedro near the soccer field to Corozal at 3 pm. The trip usually takes nearly two hours but may be longer if there's a stop at Sarteneja, or if the weather is bad. Off-season, service is sometimes reduced and occasionally is discontinued altogether.

Chetumal to San Pedro and Caye Caulker. Two Belize-based water-taxi companies, San Pedro Belize Express and Water Jets International, provide service direct from Chetumal, Mexico, to San Pedro and Caye Caulker. The two companies alternate days of service, so there's only one boat each way daily.

Contacts San Pedro Belize Express. ☎ *223/223–2225 in Belize City, 983/832–1648 in Mexico* ⊕ *www.belizewatertaxi.com.* **Thunderbolt.** ✉ *Municipal Pier, 1st Ave., Corozal Town* ⚓ *Municipal pier is next to Corozal House of Culture on 1st Ave.* ☎ *422/0026 in Corozal Town, 610/4475 cell phone* ⊕ *www. ambergriscaye.com/thunderbolt/.* **Water Jets International.** ✉ *Water Jets International, San Pedro Town* ☎ *226/2194 in San Pedro* ⊕ *www.sanpedrowatertaxi.com.*

BUS TRAVEL AND SHUTTLE SERVICE

Buses between Belize City and Corozal run about every half hour during daylight hours in both directions, and some of these continue on to Chetumal, Mexico. Several small bus lines make the 3- to 3½-hour journey between Belize City and Corozal Town/Chetumal. Northbound buses depart from the Novelo's bus station on West Collet Canal St. in Belzie City beginning at 5:30 am, with the last departure around 7:30 pm. Southbound buses begin around 3:45 am, with the last departure at 7:30 pm. Any nonexpress bus will stop and pick up almost anywhere along the highway.

■ TIP → **Bus service to the villages and other sites off the Goldson Highway is limited, so to reach them you're best off with a rental car or a guided tour.** There is some bus service on the Old Northern Highway and from Orange Walk to Sarteneja. Ask locally for updates on bus lines, routes, and fares.

Two shuttle services based in Corozal Town, Belize VIP Transfers and GetTransfers, and also known as George and Esther Moralez Travel, provide inexpensive and handy transportation across the border between Corozal and Chetumal. These services make crossing the border easy and hassle free. The transfer services also provide shuttles to and from Cancún and other destinations in the Yucatán and in Belize.

Contacts Belize VIP Transfers. ⊠ *Caribbean Village, South End, Corozal Town* ☎ *422/2725* ⊕ *www.belizetransfers.com.* **Get Transfers.** ⊠ *3 Blue Bird St., Corozal Town* ☎ *422/2485 in Belize* ⊕ *www.gettransfers.com.*

CAR TRAVEL

Corozal is the last stop on the Goldson Highway before you hit Mexico. The 95-mile (153-km) journey from Belize City will probably take about two hours, unless you're slowed by sugarcane trucks. The Goldson Highway is a two-lane paved road in fairly good condition. Other roads, including roads to Lamanai, Río Bravo, and Gallon Jug, and the road to Sarteneja are mostly unpaved. The Old Northern Highway, the route to Altun Ha, has been repaved for the first 12 miles (20 km), with the remaining 9 miles (15 km) a mixture of old broken pavement and dirt. Because tour and long-distance taxi prices are high, especially if you're traveling with family or in a group, you likely will save money by renting a car.

Car-rental agencies in Belize City will usually deliver vehicles to Corozal and Orange Walk, but there will be a drop fee, starting at around BZ$150. Two small local car-rental agencies, Corozal Cars and Belize VIP Service, have a few cars to rent, at rates starting around BZ$140 a day, plus tax.

Contacts Belize VIP Transfers. ⊠ *Caribbean Village, South End, Corozal Town* ☎ *422/2725* ⊕ *www.belizetransfers.com.* **Corozal Car Rental.** ⊠ *Mile 85, Philip Goldson Hwy., formerly Northern Hwy., Corozal Town* ☎ *422/3339* ⊕ *www.corozalcarrental.com.*

TAXI TRAVEL

It's usually easiest to have your hotel arrange taxi service for you, but if you want to do it yourself, both Corozal and Orange Walk have a Taxi Association. Fares to most destinations in town are low, at BZ$10 or less, but rates to points outside town can be expensive; agree on a price beforehand.

Contacts Taxi Association in Corozal. ⊠ *1st. St. South, Corozal Town* ☎ *422/2035.* **Taxi Association in Orange Walk.** ⊠ *Queen Victoria Ave., Orange Walk Town* ✛ *Across from main plaza* ☎ *322/2560.*

EMERGENCIES

For dental and medical care, many of Corozal's residents go to Chetumal, Mexico. In Corozal, visit Bethesda Medical Centre if you need medical care. The Corozal Hospital, with only limited facilities, is on the Goldson Highway. In Orange Walk, the Northern Regional Hospital doesn't look very appealing, but it provides emergency and other services. Your hotel can provide a list of local doctors and dentists. Consider going to Belize City or Chetumal for medical and dental care, if possible. For police and emergencies, dial 911.

ABOUT THE HOTELS

Most hotels in northern Belize are small, family-run spots. In Corozal and Orange Walk towns, hotels are modest affairs costing a fraction of the hotel rates in San Pedro or other more popular parts of Belize. Generally, the hotels are clean, well maintained, and offer a homey atmosphere. They have private baths and plenty of hot and cold water, and most also have air-conditioning. Hotels and lodges in Crooked Tree, Sarteneja, and Copper Bank are also small and inexpensive; some have air-conditioning. The jungle lodges near Lamanai, Gallon Jug, and Altun Ha, however, are a different story. Several of these, including Chan Chich Lodge, Maruba Jungle Lodge and Spa, and Lamanai Outpost Lodge, are upscale accommodations, with gorgeous settings in the jungle or on a lagoon and prices to match; meals and tours are extra. These lodges also offer all-inclusive and other package options.

HOTEL AND RESTAURANT PRICES

For expanded lodging reviews, visit Fodors.com.

WHAT IT COSTS IN BELIZE DOLLARS			
$	$$	$$$	$$$$
RESTAURANTS under BZ$15	BZ$15–BZ$30	BZ$31–BZ$50	over BZ$50
HOTELS under BZ$200	BZ$200–BZ$300	BZ$301–BZ$500	over BZ$500

Restaurant prices are per person for a main course at dinner. Hotel prices are for two people in a standard double room, including tax and service, in high season.

ABOUT THE RESTAURANTS

With the exception of dining rooms at upscale jungle lodges, restaurants are almost invariably small, inexpensive, family-run places, serving simple meals such as stew chicken with rice and beans. Here, you'll rarely pay more than BZ$25 for dinner, and frequently much less. If there's a predominant culinary influence, it's Mexican, and many restaurants serve tacos, tamales, *garnaches* (small, fried corn tortillas with beans, cabbage, and cheese piled on them), and soups such as *escabeche* (onion soup with chicken). A few places, mostly in Corozal Town, cater to tourists and expats with burgers, pizza, and steaks. For a quick snack, restaurants on the second floor of the Corozal market sell inexpensive breakfast and lunch items (usually closed Sunday). Likewise, the stalls at the central plaza in the heart of Orange Walk Town sell cheap snacks and food. You can also buy delicious local fruits and vegetables at the Corozal Town market—a huge papaya, two lovely mangoes, and a bunch of bananas cost as little as BZ$2.50 or BZ$3. There is also a fruit and vegetable market in the center of Orange Walk Town.

SAFETY

Corozal is one of Belize's safer areas, but petty theft and burglaries aren't uncommon, so use common sense when traveling through the area. Both Corozal Town and Orange Walk Town have some crack cocaine users. Often, they stand on the street with a pigtail bucket (a 5-gallon bucket) of water and try to earn money by washing car windshields—ignore them if you can.

TOURS

SEEING THE RUINS

Your hotel in Orange Walk Town or Corozal Town can arrange tours to Lamanai, Cerros, and other sites, starting at around BZ$80 per person. In Orange Walk, Reyes & Sons River Tours, Lamanai Eco-Adventures, and J. Avila & Sons run boat trips up the New River to Lamanai. In Corozal Town, Belize VIP Transfers *(see Bus Travel)* can arrange tours of Cerros, Santa Rita, and elsewhere. In Sarteneja, members of the Sarteneja Tour Guide Association can arrange tours to Shipstern, Cerros, and Bacalar Chica on North Ambergris Caye.

Contacts J. Avila & Sons River Tours. ⊠ *42 Riverside St., Orange Walk Town* ☎ *322/0419.* **Lamanai Eco Adventures.** ⊠ *Tower Hill, Philip Goldson Hwy., Orange Walk Town* ✚ *On west side of Goldson Hwy. just south of Tower Hill bridge* ☎ *610/2020* ⊕ *www.lamanaiecoadventures.com.* **Reyes & Sons River Tours.** ⊠ *Tower Hill, Philip Goldson Hwy., Orange Walk Town* ☎ *322/3327.*

SNORKELING

From Sarteneja, Sarteneja Adventure Tours can take you to Bacalar Chico Marine Reserve and National Park off North Ambergris Caye. Full-day rates include guide, park admission, snorkeling gear, and lunch.

Contact Sarteneja Tour Guide Association. ⊠ *N. Front St., Sarteneja* ☎ *633/0067, 621/6465 Sarteneja Tour Guide Association.*

VISITOR INFORMATION

An excellent source of general information on northern Belize is the website Northern Belize.

Contact Corozal. ⊕ *corozal.com.* **Northern Belize.** ⊕ *northernbelize.com.*

CROOKED TREE WILDLIFE SANCTUARY

33 miles (54 km) northwest of Belize City.

Crooked Tree Wildlife Sanctuary is one of Belize's top birding spots. The 16,400-acre sanctuary includes more than 3,000 acres of lagoons, swamp, and marsh, surrounding what is essentially an inland island. Traveling by canoe, you're likely to see iguanas, crocodiles, coatis, and turtles. The sanctuary's most prestigious visitors, however, are the jabiru storks, which usually visit between November and May. With a wingspan up to 12 feet, the jabiru is the largest flying bird in the Americas.

■ TIP→ **For birders the best time to come is in the dry season, roughly from February to late May, when lowered water levels cause birds to**

GREAT ITINERARIES

IF YOU HAVE 3 TO 5 DAYS IN NORTHERN BELIZE

If you are starting in Belize City, rent a car and drive to Crooked Tree Wildlife Sanctuary, which has great birding and offers the chance to see the jabiru stork, the largest flying bird in the Americas. Spend a few hours here, canoeing on the lagoon and hiking trails. If you have an interest in birding, you'll want to overnight here at one of the simple lagoon-side lodges, such as Bird's Eye View Lodge or Crooked Tree Lodge. Otherwise, you could drive on to Maruba, an upscale jungle lodge and spa. The drive from Crooked Tree takes about 45 minutes. While you're at Maruba, visit the Altun Ha Mayan site, which you can see in a couple of hours. On the second day, drive to Corozal Town, about 1½ hours from Maruba or Crooked Tree. Base here in Corozal Town for two days, at one of the small hotels on Corozal Bay such as Almond Tree Hotel Resort or Tony's Inn and Beach Resort, making day trips by boat to Lamanai and Cerros ruins (or you can drive). If you have additional days in the north, you can add a visit to Sarteneja or cross the border into Chetumal, Mexico. Alternatively, after the first night in Crooked Tree or at Maruba, drive to the Lamanai Mayan site and spend the night there at Lamanai Outpost Lodge on the New River Lagoon, or, for a different experience, proceed to Blue Creek Village, a Mennonite area, and spend the night at Hillside B&B, or at La Milpa Field Station. Then, continue on through Programme for Belize lands to Chan Chich Lodge and spend the rest of your time in northern Belize at this amazing jungle lodge. If money isn't much of an object and you want one of the best jungle lodge experiences in Central America, then ditch the car and fly from Belize City to Chan Chich, where you can spend all your time looking for jaguars and listening to the howler monkeys.

group together to find water and food, making them easy to spot. Birding is good year-round, however, and the area is more scenic when the lagoons are full. Snowy egrets, snail kites, ospreys, and black-collared hawks, as well as two types of duck—Muscovy and black-bellied whistling—and all five species of kingfishers native to Belize can be spotted. Even on a short, one- to three-hour tour, you're likely to see up to 40 species of birds. South of Crooked Tree, on Sapodilla Lagoon and accessible by boat, is a small Mayan site, Chau Hiix.

GETTING HERE AND AROUND

An easy 30-minute drive north from the international airport takes you to the entrance road to Crooked Tree Wildlife Sanctuary at Mile 30.8 of the Goldson Highway. From there it's another 2 miles (3 km) on an unpaved causeway to the sanctuary visitor center and Crooked Tree village. If you don't have a rental car, any of the frequent nonexpress buses going north to Orange Walk or Corozal will drop you at the entrance road, but you'll have to hike across the causeway to the village (or arrange a pickup by your Crooked Tree hotel). Jex buses leave at 10:50 am from the corner of Regent Street West and West Canal Street in Belize City and go directly to the village, and another leaves from

LOCAL FOOD FESTIVALS

Belizeans love to party, and festivals celebrating lobster, chocolate, cashews, and other local foods give them—and you—the chance to join in the fun. Here are some of the food festivals in Belize. Note that dates can change from year to year.

Cashew Festival, Crooked Tree in early May. Crooked Tree village is named for the cashew tree that often grows in a serpentine fashion, curling and growing sideways as well as up. The yellow cashew fruit, which tastes a little like mango and smells like grapes, ripens in late spring, and the Crooked Tree Festival celebrates the cashew in all its forms: fruit, nut, juice, jam, and wine.

Chocolate Festival of Belize, Toledo in late May. Toledo's increasingly popular tribute to local cacao celebrates the home of chocolate in Belize, with tours of small chocolate factories in Punta Gorda and nearby, visits to organic cacao farms, and local music and dances. Belikin beer even brews a special chocolate stout for the occasion.

Hopkins Mango Festival and Cultural Jam in late May or early June. The Hopkins Mango Fest is devoted to the sweet, juicy mango, spiced by local Garifuna culture. Events include a Garifuna drumming competition, along with bicycle and canoe races.

Placencia LobsterFest in late June. Belize's biggest and best salute to the spiny lobster is held in Placencia village, usually on the last weekend in June. Booths sell local lobster grilled, fried, curried, and in fritters, and there's music, dancing, and lots of Belikin. LobsterFests also are held, typically in late June or early July, in San Pedro and Caye Caulker.

the Save-U Plaza at the corner of the Goldson Highway and Central American Boulevard at 5:15 pm. Both currently operate daily except Sunday. Another option is a transfer by your Crooked Tree hotel from the international airport in Ladyville or from other points in or near Belize City.

TIMING

One full day is enough to do a canoe trip on the lagoon, hike local trails, and see the small Creole village. But if you're a birder you'll want at least another day.

Bus Information Jex and Sons Bus Service. ☎ 225/7017.

EXPLORING

Fodor'sChoice ★ **Crooked Tree Village.** One of Belize's oldest inland villages, established some 300 years ago, Crooked Tree is at the center of the Crooked Tree Wildlife Sanctuary. With a population of about 900, most of Creole origin, the community has a church, school, and one of the surest signs of a former British territory: a cricket pitch. There are many large cashew trees around the village, the serpentine growth pattern of which gave the village its name. The cashews are highly fragrant when in bloom in January and February, and when the cashew fruit ripen to a golden yellow color in May and June, they taste something like mango and smell like sweet grapes. The cashew nuts require roasting to make them edible. Villagers make and sell cashew wine. A Cashew Festival is held annually in early May. ✉ *Off Philip Goldson Hwy. (formerly Northern Hwy.), Crooked Tree Village* ☎ *223/5004* 🌐 *www.belizeaudubon.org* ☞ *Visits to Crooked Tree village are free, but hiking, boating, and bird-watching in Crooked Tree Sanctuary are BZ$8 per person.*

> **CROOKED TREE GUIDES**
>
> For an introduction to the sanctuary, and for a guide, visit the Crooked Tree Wildlife Sanctuary's Visitor Center at the end of the causeway. The visitor center can put you in touch with all the best local guides. Expect to pay about BZ$20–BZ$30 an hour for guide services, more if you're going by boat or horseback.

Fodor's Choice ★ **Crooked Tree Wildlife Sanctuary.** The sanctuary's visitor center is at the end of the causeway. Stop here to pay your sanctuary admission fee or arrange a guided tour of the sanctuary or rent a canoe for a do-it-yourself trip. The sanctuary, one of the country's top bird-watching spots, is managed by the Belize Audubon Society. You can also walk through the village and hike birding trails around the area. If you'd prefer to go by horseback, you pay by the hour. The visitor center has a free village and trail map. If you're staying overnight, your hotel can arrange canoe or bike rentals and set up tours and trips. Although tours can run at any time, the best time is early in the morning, when birds are most active. ✉ *Crooked Tree Village* ☎ *223/5004 Belize Audubon Society in Belize City* 🌐 *www.belizeaudubon.org* 🎫 *BZ$8.*

WHERE TO STAY

$ B&B/INN FAMILY 🏨 **Bird's Eye View Lodge.** Many of the 20 spic-and-span rooms, all with air-conditioning and all recently refurbished, at this modern concrete hotel have expansive views of the lagoon. **Pros:** on shores of Crooked Tree Lagoon; good meals made with local ingredients; breezy second-floor patio with great lagoon views. **Cons:** undistinguished, blocky buildings; no-frills guestrooms. [$] *Rooms from: BZ$155* ✉ *Bird's Eye View Lodge, on lagoon, Crooked Tree Village* ☎ *203/2040 at main office, 235/7333 at lodge* 🌐 *birdseyeviewbelize.com* 🛏 *20 rooms* 🍴 *No meals.*

$ B&B/INN FAMILY Fodor's Choice ★ 🏨 **Crooked Tree Lodge.** Owned by a Belizean-British couple, this small lodge has six comfy hardwood cottages, five with one bedroom and one with two bedrooms, on a gorgeous 11-acre site on the shores of the Crooked Tree Lagoon. **Pros:** perfect lagoon-side location; friendly hosts; good food. **Cons:** no a/c. [$] *Rooms from: BZ$150* ✉ *Crooked Tree Lodge, on Crooked Tree Lagoon, Crooked Tree Village* ☎ *626/3820* 🌐 *www.crookedtreelodgebelize.com* 🛏 *6 rooms* 🍴 *No meals.*

ALTUN HA

28 miles (45 km) north of Belize City.

If you've never experienced an ancient Mayan city, make a trip to Altun Ha, which is a modern translation of the Mayan name "Rockstone

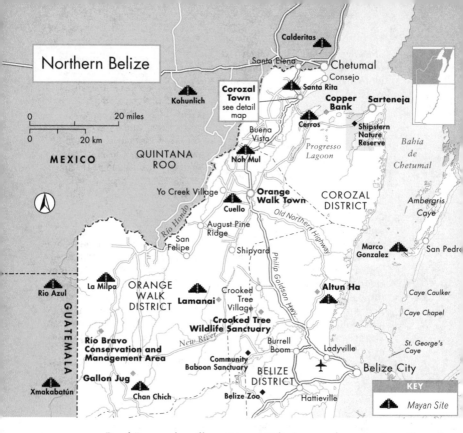

Northern Belize

Calderitas

Santa Elena · Chetumal

Consejo

Corozal Town
see detail map

Santa Rita

Kohunlich

Copper Bank

Sarteneja

Cerros

Shipstern Nature Reserve

MEXICO

QUINTANA ROO

Buena Vista

Progresso Lagoon

Bahía de Chetumal

Noh Mul

0 —— 20 miles
0 —— 20 km

Yo Creek Village

Orange Walk Town

COROZAL DISTRICT

Ambergris Caye

Cuello

Old Northern Highway

Río Hondo

August Pine Ridge

Marco Gonzalez

San Pedro

San Felipe

Shipyard

Philip Goldson Hwy

Rio Azul

La Milpa

ORANGE WALK DISTRICT

Crooked Tree Village

Altun Ha

Caye Caulker

GUATEMALA

Lamanai

Crooked Tree Wildlife Sanctuary

Caye Chapel

Río Bravo Conservation and Management Area

New River

Burrell Boom

Ladyville

St. George's Caye

Xmakabatún

Gallon Jug

Community Baboon Sanctuary

BELIZE DISTRICT

Belize City

Chan Chich

Belize Zoo

Hattieville

KEY

▲ *Mayan Site*

Pond," a nearby village. It's not Belize's most dramatic site—Caracol and Lamanai vie for that award—but it's one of the most accessible and most thoroughly excavated. The first inhabitants settled before 300 BC, and their descendants finally abandoned the site after AD 1000. At its height during the Classic period the city was home to 10,000 people.

GETTING HERE AND AROUND

Altun Ha is easily visited on your own—if you have a car. From Belize City, drive north on the Goldson Highway to Mile 18.9; turn right on the *Old* Northern Highway and go 10.5 miles (17 km). Coming from the south, the first 12 miles (20 km) of the Old Northern Highway is a good paved road, but the rest is a mix of gravel areas and broken pavement. The turnoff from the Old Northern Highway to Altun Ha, on the left, is well marked and the entrance road to Altun Ha is paved. If coming from Corozal or Orange Walk, you can also enter the Old Northern Highway at Mile 49 of the Goldson Highway, but that takes you over the worst section of the Old Northern Highway. There's limited bus service from Belize City to Maskall Village near Altun Ha. Tour operators in Belize City, mostly catering to the cruise crowd, also offer tours to Altun Ha.

TIMING

You can see Altun Ha in a couple of hours. If you add lunch and a spa treatment at the nearby Maruba Resort Jungle Spa, you'll spend most of the day in the area.

SAFETY AND PRECAUTIONS

Marijuana is illegally grown in remote areas off the Old Northern Highway. Avoid hiking off trail, where you might accidentally stumble on someone's weed plantation.

EXPLORING

FAMILY **Altun Ha.** A team from the Royal Ontario Museum first excavated the site in the early 1960s and found 250 structures spread over more than 1,000 square yards. At Plaza B, in the Temple of the Masonry Altars, archaeologists unearthed the grandest and most valuable piece of Mayan art ever discovered—the head of the sun god Kinich Ahau. Weighing nearly 10 pounds, it was carved from a solid block of green jade. The head is kept in a solid steel vault in the Central Bank of Belize, though it is occasionally displayed at the Museum of Belize. The jade head appears on all denominations of Belize currency. If the Masonry Altars temple looks familiar to you, it's because an illustration of the Masonry Altars structure appears on Belikin beer bottles. Because the Altun Ha site is small, it's not necessary to have a tour guide, but licensed guides may offer their services when you arrive.

Tours from Belize City, Orange Walk, and Crooked Tree also are options. Altun Ha is a regular stop on cruise ship excursions, and on days when several ships are in port in Belize City (typically midweek) Altun Ha may be crowded. Several tour operators in San Pedro and Caye Caulker also offer day trips to Altun Ha, often combined with lunch at the nearby Maruba Resort Jungle Spa. Most of these tours from the cayes are by boat, landing at Bomba Village. From here, a van makes the short ride to Altun Ha. If traveling independently or on a tour that includes it, you can stop at Maruba Resort Jungle Spa for a drink, lunch, or a spa treatment. ⊠ *Rockstone Pond Rd., off Old Northern Hwy., Maskall Village ⊹ From Belize City, take Northern Hwy. north to Mile 18.9. Turn right (east) on Old Northern Hwy., which is only partly paved, and go 14 miles (23 km) to signed entrance road at Rockstone Pond Rd. to Altun Ha on left. Follow this paved road 2 miles (3 km) to visitor center* ☎ *822/2106 NICH/Belize Institute of Archeology* ⊕ *www.nichbelize.org* ⊠ *BZ$10.*

WHERE TO STAY

$$$$ ⚏ **Maruba Resort Jungle Spa.** Maruba delivers an exotic experience in a
RESORT jungle setting, complete with 24-hour electricity, air-conditioned cabañas, fresh flowers in the rooms, high-thread-count sheets, and, in some suites, hot tubs. **Pros:** remote jungle location near Altun Ha Maya site; some find it hip and sexy. **Cons:** some find it outlandish; can be buggy. Ⓢ *Rooms from: BZ$610* ⊠ *Mile 40.5 Old Northern Hwy., 10 miles (17 km) north of Altun Ha, Maskall Village* ☎ *225/5555, 800/627–8227 reservations in U.S. and Canada* ⊕ *www.maruba-belize.com* ⇥ *21 rooms* ⚏ *Some meals.*

NORTHERN BELIZE HISTORY

The Maya settled this area thousands of years before the time of Christ. Cuello, near Orange Walk Town, dates from 2500 BC, making it one of the earliest known Mayan sites in all of Mesoamerica (the region between central Mexico and northwest Costa Rica). In the Pre-Classic period (2500 BC–AD 300) the Maya expanded across northern Belize, establishing important communities and trading posts at Santa Rita, Cerros, Lamanai, and elsewhere.

During the Classic period (AD 300–AD 900), Santa Rita, Lamanai, Altun Ha, and other cities flourished. To feed large populations perhaps totaling several hundred thousand, the Maya developed sophisticated agricultural systems, with raised, irrigated fields along the New River and other river bottoms. After the mysterious collapse of the Mayan civilization by the 10th century AD, the region's cities went into decline, but the Maya continued to live in smaller communities and rural areas around the many lagoons in northern Belize, trading with other settlements in Belize and in Mexico. Lamanai, perched at the edge of the New River Lagoon, was continuously occupied for almost three millennia, until late in the 17th century.

The Spanish first set foot in these parts in the early 1500s, and Spanish missionaries made their way up the New River to establish churches in Mayan settlements in the 16th and 17th centuries. You can see the remains of a Spanish church at the entrance of Lamanai near Indian Church Village. About this same time, small groups of shipwrecked British sailors established settlements in Belize but the Battle of St. George's Caye in 1789 effectively put an end to Spanish control in Belize.

In the second half of the 19th century, the so-called Caste Wars (1847–1904), pitting Mayan insurgents against Mestizo and European settlers in Mexico's Yucatán, had an important impact on northern Belize. Refugees from the bloody wars moved south from Mexico, settling in Corozal Town, Orange Walk Town, Sarteneja, and also on Ambergris Caye and Caye Caulker.

Today more than 40,000 acres of sugarcane are harvested by some 4,000 small farmers in northern Belize. Mennonites, who came to the Blue Creek, Shipyard, and Little Belize areas in the late 1950s, have contributed greatly to agriculture in the region, producing rice, corn, chickens, milk, cheese, and beans. And tourism, foreign retirement communities, and casino gaming are becoming important, especially in northern Corozal District.

NORTHWEST ORANGE WALK DISTRICT

This district borders both Mexico and Guatemala, and holds four areas well worth the time it takes to visit them: Lamanai Archeological Reserve, at the edge of the New River Lagoon; the Mennonite communities of Blue Creek and Shipyard; the 260,000-plus acres of the Río Bravo Conservation Area; and Gallon Jug lands, 130,000 acres in which the remarkable Chan Chich Lodge nestles.

These areas, especially Río Bravo and Gallon Jug, are best visited on an overnight or multinight stay. You can visit Lamanai on a day trip by boat or road from Orange Walk Town (and guided day tours are also available from Belize City, San Pedro, and Caye Caulker), though it's well worth at least an overnight stay. If you're staying in Blue Creek, you can go to Río Bravo, Lamanai, and even Gallon Jug and Chan Chich on a day trip, but the poor roads will slow you down, and you'll have little time to explore. Both the Gallon Jug and Programme for Belize (Río Bravo) lands are private, with gated entrances, so you'll need advance permission to visit.

ORANGE WALK TOWN

52 miles (85 km) north of Belize City.

Orange Walk Town is barely on the radar of most visitors, except as a jumping-off point for boat trips to Lamanai, road trips to Gallon Jug and Río Bravo, or as a place to gas up en route from Corozal to Belize City. Though its population of around 14,000, mostly Mestizos, makes it the sixth-largest urban center in Belize (after Belize City, San Pedro, Belmopan City, San Ignacio, and Corozal Town), it's more like a "county seat" in an agricultural area than a city. In this case, it's county seat of Belize's sugarcane region, and you'll see big tractors and trucks hauling sugarcane to the Tower Hill refinery. Happily, a bypass around Orange Walk Town has reduced through traffic.

The town's atmosphere will remind you a little of Mexico, with signs in Spanish, a central plaza, and sun-baked stores set close to the streets. The plaza, near the Orange Walk Town Hall, has a small market (daily except Sunday and holidays) with fruits, vegetables, and inexpensive local foods for sale. This was once the site of Fort Cairns, which dates to the Caste Wars of the 19th century, when Mayan attacks drove Mestizo residents of Mexico down into northern Belize.

GETTING HERE AND AROUND

Orange Walk Town is about midway between Belize City and Corozal Town, a drive of an hour or so from either one. Most buses on the busy Goldson Highway route will drop you in Orange Walk Town. Tropic Air provides air service most days between San Pedro and Caye Caulker and the Tower Hill airstrip just south of Orange Walk. One-way fares start at around BZ$70.

TIMING

The reason most visitors stop at Orange Walk Town is to take a day trip to Lamanai, up the New River. Several excellent local restaurants make a stopover in Orange Walk more pleasant.

SAFETY AND PRECAUTIONS

While generally safe, Orange Walk Town does have its share of drug problems, and the cheap bars can get rough on weekend nights.

EXPLORING

FAMILY **Las Banquitas House of Culture.** This small museum—the name refers to the little benches in a nearby riverside park—presents changing exhibitions on Orange Walk District history and culture. Among the permanent displays are artifacts from Lamanai and Cuello. A restaurant, Paniscea, is located under the House of Culture. Las Banquitas is one of four

CLOSE UP

What's in a Name?

The name *Belize* is a conundrum. According to *Encyclopaedia Britannica,* it derives from *belix,* an ancient Mayan word meaning "muddy water." Anyone who's seen the Belize River swollen by heavy rains can vouch for this description. Others trace the name's origin to the French word *balise* (beacon), but no one can explain why a French word would have caught on in a region once dominated by the English (Belize was known as British Honduras). Perhaps nothing more than a drinker's tale, another theory connects Belize to the Mayan word *belikin* (road to the east), which also happens to be the name of the national beer. A few even think the name may have come from Angola in West Africa, where some of the slaves who were brought to the West Indies and then to Belize originated, and where today there is a town called Belize. Some say Belize is a corruption of Wallace, the name of a Scottish buccaneer who founded a colony in 1620; still others say the pirate wasn't Wallace but Willis, that he wasn't Scottish but English, and that he founded a colony not in 1620, but in 1638.

There was indeed a pirate named Wallace, a onetime lieutenant of Sir Walter Raleigh's who later served as Tortuga's governor. Perhaps it was liquor or lucre that turned him into a pirate, but at some point in the early-to-mid-1600s he and 80 fellow renegades washed up near St. George's Caye. They settled in and lived for years off the illicit booty of cloak-and-dagger raids on passing ships. In 1798 a fleet of 31 Spanish ships came to exterminate what had now blossomed into an upstart little colony. Residents had a total of one sloop, some fishing boats, and seven rafts, but their maritime knowledge enabled them to defeat the invaders in two hours. That was the last Spanish attempt to forcibly dislodge the settlement, though bitter wrangles over British Honduras's right to exist continued for nearly a century.

We may never know whether Wallace and Willis were one and the same, but what's in a name, anyway? Grab a Belikin and come up with a few theories of your own.

House of Culture museums; the other three are in Belize City, Corozal Town, and Benque Viejo. These museums are operated by NICH, the National Institute of Culture and History. ✉ *Main and Bautista Sts.* ☎ *822/3302 NICH* 🌐 *www.nichbelize.org* 🎫 *Free, some exhibits have small fees* ⏲ *Closed weekends.*

WHERE TO EAT

$$ LATIN AMERICAN FAMILY Fodor's Choice ★

🍴 **Cocina Sabor.** Succulents populate the restaurant's patio, as do Orange Walk residents and a smattering of tourists who know a good food joint when they find it. The reasonably priced menu is a mix of Mestizo and other Belizean favorites, and include flavors such as coconut rum salsa and ginger-citrus glaze that give Belizean classics an energetic twist. Come on Thursday for popular Dollah Wing Day or any night for dreamy frozen mojitos. Simply put, this is one of the best and most pleasant places to eat in town. [$] *Average main: BZ$25* ✉ *South*

Belize-Corozal Rd., aka Philip Goldson Hwy. ✛ *South end of town on west side of street near L&R Liquor* ☎ *322/3482* ⊘ *Closed Tues.*

$$ ⨯ **Maracas Bar and Grill.** A well-run new option in Orange Walk Town,
LATIN AMERICAN Maracas Bar and Grill has one of the town's most scenic settings over-
FAMILY looking the New River—you might even spot a crocodile. Sit in the
covered riverside patio or in the air-conditioned dining room and start
your meal with an appetizer of shrimp, conch, or lobster ceviche (lobster
is available mid-June to mid-February and conch is usually October
to late April). Indulge your comfort food cravings with pizza, fajitas,
tacos, quesadillas, or a beef or fish burger. *Escabeche* (a tangy chicken
and onion soup) is offered Sunday only. Occasionally local parties here
get loud, but you'll probably be welcome to join the festivities. $ *Aver-*
age main: BZ$20 ⊠ *El Gran Mestizo hotel, Naranjal St.* ☎ *600/9143*
⊘ *Closed Mon.–Wed.*

$$ ⨯ **Nahil Mayab.** Orange Walk Town may be the last place you'd expect to
LATIN AMERICAN find an upscale restaurant like this, with its Maya-inspired decor, well-
Fodor'sChoice prepared food, and extra-friendly servers. Nonetheless, it opened here,
★ on a corner behind the Shell station to rave reviews and has enjoyed
steady business since opening in 2008. Sit in the tropical gardens in
the back, or in air-conditioned comfort in the main dining room, and
enjoy a cold drink and a delicious shrimp or conch (in season) ceviche
appetizer. For a main course try the lobster fajitas (in season) or one
of the Yucatán-inspired dishes such as *hor'och,* corn balls cooked in
black beans and served with stew chicken. $ *Average main: BZ$26*
⊠ *Guadeloupe and Santa Ana Sts.* ✛ *Two blocks behind Shell station on*
Belize-Corozal Rd. (Goldson Hwy.) ☎ *322/0831* ⊕ *www.nahilmayab.*
com ⊘ *Closed Sun., no dinner Mon.*

WHERE TO STAY

$ ⊡ **El Gran Mestizo Riverside Cabins.** Operated by the same couple who
RESORT own Hotel de la Fuente, the new El Gran Mestizo is now the top place
Fodor'sChoice to stay in the Orange Walk area. **Pros:** new cabin colony is top place to
★ stay in Orange Walk Town; pleasant setting on the New River; range of
rates and accommodations from hostel dorm to premium cabins. **Cons:**
breakfast is not included; restaurant only open Thursday–Sunday; riverside location means mosquitos. $ *Rooms from: BZ$160* ⊠ *Naranjal*
St. ☎ *322/2290* ⊕ *www.elgranmestizo.com* ⤵ *18 rooms* ⧀ *Breakfast.*

$ ⊡ **Hotel de la Fuente.** Orlando and Cindy de la Fuente's place is a step
HOTEL up from other hotels in central Orange Walk Town, and the low rates
Fodor'sChoice (starting at BZ$87 including tax) for the standard rooms with air-con-
★ ditioning, free Wi-Fi, cable TV, and Continental breakfast, put it among
the best values in northern Belize. **Pros:** excellent value for attractive,
modern rooms; central location; variety of tours offered. **Cons:** no pool.
$ *Rooms from: BZ$87* ⊠ *14 Main St.* ☎ *322/2290* ⊕ *www.hoteldela-*
fuente.com ⤵ *22 rooms* ⧀ *Breakfast.*

$$ ⊡ **Lamanai Landings Resort and Marina.** With balconies perched above the
RESORT New River, this Belizean-owned resort gives guests the feeling of being
FAMILY in the jungle—keep your eyes out for the river crocs that often spend
the night under the hotel—while conveniently located just south of
Orange Walk Town. **Pros:** new in late 2015; each room has a balcony
overlooking the river; easy river access to Lamanai ruins. **Cons:** room

decor lacks flair; no swimming pool; so-so restaurant. $ *Rooms from: BZ$283* ✉ *Tower Hill, Philip Goldson Hwy.* ☎ *670/7846* ⊕ *www.lamanailandingsresortandmarina.com* ⇆ *24 rooms* ⚭ *Breakfast.*

LAMANAI

About 2½ hrs northwest of Belize City, or 24 miles (39 km) south of Orange Walk Town.

Lamanai ("submerged crocodile" in Yucatec Maya) is Belize's longest-occupied Mayan site, inhabited until well after Christopher Columbus "discovered" the New World in 1492. In fact archaeologists have found signs of continuous occupation from 1500 BC until AD 1700.

GETTING HERE AND AROUND

There are several ways to get here. One option is to drive on the mostly unpaved road from Orange Walk Town. Turn west off the Goldson Highway (also known in Orange Walk Town as Queen Victoria Avenue or Belize-Corozal Road) at the Orange Walk fire station. From here go to Yo Creek, then southwest to San Felipe Village, a total of 24 miles (39 km). In San Felipe, go straight for another 12 miles (19 km) to reach the ruins. Another route by road is via Shipyard—the unpaved road to Shipyard is just south of Orange Walk. The best way to approach the ruins, however, is by boat, which takes about an hour and a half from Orange Walk. Boats leave around 9 am from the Tower Hill bridge over the New River on the Goldson Highway, about 6 miles (10 km) south of Orange Walk, and from a dock in town. If you are staying at Lamanai Outpost Lodge, the lodge has its own boats to take you up the river, departing from a dock just southwest of the dock where other Lamanai boats depart. Some hotels in Orange Walk Town arrange Lamanai tours, with pickup and drop-off at the hotel. You can also take a 15-minute charter plane trip from Belize City.

TIMING

Most people visit Lamanai as a day trip, but to see the ruins and explore the New River Lagoon, you'll want to overnight at least, and preferably stay two to three nights.

EXPLORING

FAMILY

Fodor'sChoice

★

Lamanai (*"submerged crocodile"*). What makes Lamanai so special is its setting on the west bank of a beautiful 28-mile-long (45-km) lagoon, one of only two waterside Mayan sites in Belize (the other is Cerros, near Corozal Town). Nearly 400 species of birds have been spotted in the area and a troop of howler monkeys visits the archaeological site regularly.

For nearly 3,000 years Lamanai's residents carried on a lifestyle that passed from one generation to the next, until the Spanish missionaries arrived. You can still see the ruins of the missionaries' church near the village of Indian Church. The same village also has an abandoned 19th-century sugar mill. With its immense drive wheel and steam engine—on which you can still read the name of the manufacturer, Leeds Foundry of New Orleans—swathed in strangler vines and creepers, it's a haunting sight. In all, 50 to 60 Mayan structures are spread over this 950-acre

CLOSE UP

The Mennonites in Belize

About 12,000 Mennonites live in a dozen different communities in Belize. Some communities, such as Blue Creek in Northern Belize and Spanish Lookout in Cayo District, are "progressive." Modern vehicles and agricultural methods are used and the community even gets involved in the government. Others, such as Little Belize and Shipyard in Northern Belize, are conservative—traditional, inward-looking, and shunning modern conveniences, opting for horses and buggies instead. Most Mennonites in Belize speak a Low German dialect among themselves. Although not unfriendly to visitors, they do not seek tourism, and there are few visitor facilities in Mennonite areas. However, Mennonites, known in Belize as hard-working and savvy about business, provide much of the food produced in Belize and dominate a good part of the construction business in the country.

archaeological reserve. The most impressive is the largest Pre-Classic structure in Belize—a massive, stepped temple built into the hillside overlooking the New River Lagoon. Many structures at Lamanai have been partially excavated. Trees and vines grow from the tops of some temples, and the sides of one pyramid are covered with vegetation. On the grounds you'll find a visitor center with educational displays on the site, and pottery, carvings, and small statues, some dating back 2,500 years. Local villagers from the Indian Church Village Artisans Center set up small stands on the grounds to sell handmade carvings, jewelry, and other crafts, along with T-shirts and snacks. Many visitors enjoy Lamanai not only for the stunning setting on the New River Lagoon, but also for the boat ride up the New River, where you are likely to see many birds, along with howler monkeys and crocodiles. ■ TIP→ **Lamanai is a popular destination for cruise ship excursions; some days there can be large number of day visitors from cruise ships.** ✉ *Near Indian Church Village* 🌐 *www.nichbelize.org* 🎟 *BZ$10.*

WHERE TO STAY

$$$$ B&B/INN FAMILY Fodor's Choice ★ 🏨 **Lamanai Outpost Lodge.** Perched on a low hillside on the New River Lagoon within walking distance of the Lamanai ruins, this eco-lodge's well-designed thatch cabañas sit amid lovely gardens and have porches with lagoon views. **Pros:** gorgeous setting on the New River Lagoon; easy access to Lamanai ruins; good tours. **Cons:** high rates; no a/c; no swimming pool. [$] *Rooms from: BZ$1,000* ✉ *Near Indian Church Village* ☎ *235/2441, 954/636–1107 in U.S.* 🌐 *www.lamanai.com* 🛏 *17 rooms* 🍴 *Some meals.*

RÍO BRAVO CONSERVATION AND MANAGEMENT AREA

2½ hrs west of Belize City.

Created with the help of distinguished British naturalist Gerald Durrell, the Río Bravo Conservation & Management Area spans 260,000 acres near where Belize, Guatemala, and Mexico meet. The four-hour drive from Belize City takes you through wildlands where you may encounter a troupe of spider monkeys, wildcats, flocks of ocellated turkeys, a dense shower of butterflies—anything but another vehicle.

GETTING HERE AND AROUND

By car from Belize City or Corozal Town, drive to Orange Walk Town, going into town rather than taking the bypass. Turn west at the crossroads near the Orange Walk fire station toward Yo Creek. Continue on through Yo Creek, following the road that turns sharply south and goes through San Lazaro, Trinidad, and August Pine Ridge villages. At San Felipe, 24 miles (40 km) from Orange Walk Town, the road turns sharply to the west (right) at a soccer field. Follow this road for about 7 miles (12 km) to the Río Bravo bridge and into Programme for Belize lands. If you don't have your own car, contact Programme for Belize and ask if they can arrange transportation for you from Orange Walk Town, Belize City, or elsewhere.

Contact Programme for Belize. ☎ 277/5616 *Programme for Belize* ⊕ *www. pfbelize.org.*

TIMING

If you decide to visit this remote part of Belize, you'll want to spend a minimum of two days, and preferably longer, so you can explore the jungle, La Milpa, and nearby Mestizo villages.

SAFETY AND PRECAUTIONS

Once away from the Field Station grounds, you're in the bush. Keep a wary eye out for poisonous snakes, scorpions, stinging insects, and other denizens of the wild.

EXPLORING

FAMILY **Río Bravo Conservation & Management Area.** Managed by Belize City–based Programme for Belize, a not-for-profit organization whose mission is the wise use and conservation of Belize's natural resources, the Río Bravo Conservation Area contains nearly 400 species of birds, 70 species of mammals, and 200 types of trees. About one-half of Río Bravo is managed as a nature reserve, and the rest is managed to generate income, from forestry and other activities, including tourism. Programme for Belize is actively involved in research and conservation programs to protect endangered species including the Yellow Headed Parrot.

Within the reserve's borders are more than 60 Mayan sites; many have yet to be explored. The most important is **La Milpa**, Belize's largest site beside Caracol and Lamanai. At its height between AD 400 and 830, La Milpa was home to almost 50,000 people. The suburbs of this city spread out some 3 miles (5 km) from the city center, and the entire city encompassed some 30 square miles (78 square km) in area. So far, archaeologists have discovered 20 large courtyards and 19 stelae.

Visiting Río Bravo, like the other areas of northwestern Orange Walk, is best done in a four-wheel-drive vehicle. You must make arrangements to visit in advance with **Programme for Belize**, as the entire Río Bravo Conservation Area is managed by this private, nonprofit organization, and the main road through its lands is gated. You also need advance reservations to stay at La Milpa Field Station. Staying overnight or longer at this field station is the best way to see Río Bravo, but you can visit it briefly on a day trip. Another field station, at Hill Bank, primarily serves as a research base for sustainable forest management but visitors with an interest in forest research can be accommodated in two cabañas and a dorm that sleeps six. Contact Programme for Belize for information.

Guides and information are available at La Milpa Field Station. Chan Chich Lodge, Lamanai Outpost Lodge, and other hotels also can arrange visits with guides to La Milpa and the Río Bravo Conservation & Management Area. ✉ *Río Bravo Conservation & Management Area, Orange Walk Town* ☎ *227/5616 Programme for Belize* 🌐 *www.pfbelize.org.*

WHERE TO STAY

$$$$ B&B/INN FAMILY 🏨 **La Milpa Field Station.** About 3 miles (5 km) from La Milpa Mayan site, this field station is a combination lodge and summer camp. **Pros:** you'll feel like an archaeologist or naturalist here; quiet and remote setting surrounded by nature; dining room serves filling Belizean dishes. **Cons:** accommodations are very basic; not easy to get to. [$] *Rooms from: BZ$610* ✉ *Programme for Belize, 1 Eyre St., Belize City* ☎ *227/5616* 🌐 *www.pfbelize.org* 🛏 *9 rooms* 🍴 *All meals.*

GALLON JUG

3½ hrs west of Belize City.

The 130,000 acres of Gallon Jug Estates, owned by the family of the late Sir Barry Bowen, is home to old-growth mahogany trees and many other tropical hardwoods along with more than 350 species of birds and many mammals and reptiles. The name Gallon Jug is said to come from the fact that an employee of Belize Estates Company, which formerly owned the property, discovered many discarded items from an old Spanish camp, including a number of ceramic gallon jugs.

GETTING HERE AND AROUND

The easiest and fastest way to get here is by charter airplane (about BZ$800 for two people to Gallon Jug Estates' own 3,000-foot airstrip). Javier Flying Service in Cayo District has three- and five-passenger Cessna airplanes, and charter flights are also available through Tropic Air. Chan Chich Lodge will arrange the flights for you. With advance permission, you can also drive to Chan Chich, about 3½ hours from Belize City. Follow the route to Río Bravo and continue on through Programme for Belize lands to the Cedar Crossing gatehouse and into Gallon Jug lands. It's a long but beautiful drive, and you're almost certain to see a considerable amount of wildlife along the dirt road. Chan Chich offers a transfer by road from Belize City.

Contacts **Javier Flying Service.** ✉ *Central Farm, George Price Hwy., Central Farm Airstrip, San Ignacio* ☎ *824/0460* 🌐 *www.javiersflyingservice.com.*

TIMING

You'll want to spend at least two to three days at Chan Chich Lodge, longer if you have a keen interest in birding or wildlife spotting.

SAFETY AND PRECAUTIONS
Despite its remote location, Chan Chich is one of the safest places in Belize.

EXPLORING

Fodor's Choice ★ **Gallon Jug Estates.** Once part of the venerable Belize Estates & Produce Company that owned one-fifth of all the land in Belize, Gallon Jug Estates is now 130,000 private acres that straddle Orange Walk and Cayo districts. There's a 3,000-acre working farm that produces coffee, grows cacao and corn, and raises cattle; it's the only truly commercial coffee operation in Belize. Gallon Jug also produces hot sauces and delicious mango and other jams, which sell in Belize and elsewhere. Tours of the coffee plantings and the production facility, along with other farm and jungle tours, can be arranged through Chan Chich Lodge. Jaguar sightings are fairly common around the Chan Chich Lodge, averaging around one a week. You're likely to see toucans, many different hummingbirds, flocks of parrots and oscellated turkeys, as well as deer. Chan Chich, one of the best jungle lodges in Central America, is the only place to stay in the area. It's possible to visit on a day trip from La Milpa Field Station, Blue Creek Village, or even Lamanai or Orange Walk Town, but you need your own transportation and advance permission to come on the gated, private Gallon Jug lands. Gallon Jug has its own private landing strip. ⊠ *Gallon Jug Estates* ⊕ *www.chanchich.com.*

WHERE TO STAY

$$$$
B&B/INN
FAMILY
Fodor's Choice ★
Chan Chich Lodge. Arguably the most memorable lodge in Belize and one of the top lodges in all of Central America, Chan Chich is set in a remote, beautiful area literally on top of a Mayan ruin, with 12 rustic yet comfortable cabañas—the price of a vacation here is similar to a five-star hotel in New York, yet the high cost is worth it for a once-in-a-lifetime experience. **Pros:** some of the best birding and wildlife spotting in Belize; so safe you don't lock your cabaña's door; magnificent setting within a Mayan site; understated but eminently comfortable accommodations. **Cons:** somewhat difficult and expensive to get to; pricey, but worth it; no air-conditioning except in two-bedroom villas. $ *Rooms from: BZ$1,085* ⊠ *Gallon Jug Estates* ☎ *223/4419 in Belize City, 877/279–5726 toll-free in U.S. and Canada* ⊕ *www.chanchich. com* ⇗ *13 rooms* ⧉ *All-inclusive.*

COROZAL BAY

Corozal Bay, or Chetumal Bay as it's called on most maps, has tropically green and turquoise waters. It provides a beautiful waterside setting for Corozal Town and a number of villages along the north side of Corozal District. Tarpon, bonefish, permit, and other game fish are not hard to find. The drawback is that there are few natural beaches in Corozal District, although some hotels have trucked in sand to build human-assisted beach areas. Also, there's no good snorkeling or diving locally, and the Belize Barrier Reef is several long hours away by boat. However, the Mexican border and the outskirts of the city of Chetumal are only 9 miles (14.5 km) away. Chetumal, capital of Quintana Roo state, with a modern mall, big-box stores such as Walmart and Sam's

Warehouse, and air-conditioned multiplex movie theaters, provides a bustling counterpoint to small, easygoing Corozal.

At the border, the Commercial Free Zone (usually called the Corozal Free Zone, though that's not its official name) promises duty-free goods and cheap gas. The reality is a little less appealing. Most of the duty-free items are cheap trinkets from China and elsewhere in Asia, and the gasoline, while one-third cheaper than in Belize, is more expensive than in Mexico. Plus, to sample the questionable enticements of the Free Zone, visitors have to formally exit Belize, paying exit taxes and fees.

Casinos have sprung up on the Belize side of the border, at the edge of the Commercial Free Zone. There are three casinos: the Princess Casino, the larger Royal Princess Casino (both associated with the Princess Hotel & Casino in Belize City), and the largest of the three, Las Vegas Casino. Las Vegas casino has 54,000 square feet of gaming area, making it, according to management, the largest in Central America. In addition to more than 300 slot machines, plus blackjack, roulette, and poker, the casino has gaming areas designed to appeal to visitors from Asia, with Pai Gow, mah-jongg, and other games. There's also a private club area for high rollers, and a large hotel, which opened in 2015. The casinos are busy on weekends, but the crowds thin out during the week.

COROZAL TOWN

95 miles (153 km) north of Belize City.

Settled by refugees from the Yucatán during the 19th-century Caste Wars, Corozal is the last town before Río Hondo, the river separating Belize from Mexico. Though thoroughly ignored by today's travelers, this friendly town is great for a few days of easy living. It's hard not to fall into the laid-back lifestyle here—a sign at the entrance of a local grocery used to advertise "Strong rum, 55 Belize dollars a gallon."

English is the official language in Corozal, but Spanish is just as common here. The town was largely rebuilt after Hurricane Janet nearly destroyed it in 1955. Many houses are clapboard, built on wooden piles, and other houses are simple concrete-block structures, though the growing clan of expats is putting up new houses that wouldn't look out of place in Florida. One of the few remaining 19th-century colonial-era buildings is a portion of the old fort in the center of town, now the Corozal House of Culture.

GETTING HERE AND AROUND

Corozal Town is the last stop on the Goldson Highway before the Mexico border. There's frequent bus service from early morning to early evening on the Goldson Highway from Belize City. Maya Island Air and Tropic Air have about four or five daily flights between the Corozal airstrip and San Pedro Aiport. A daily water taxi, the *Thunderbolt,* runs between Corozal Town and San Pedro with a stop on demand at Sarteneja.

TIMING

Although from your base in Corozal Town you can make day trips to the ruins at Cerros and Lamanai, the main activity for visitors in Corozal is simply relaxing and hanging out.

SAFETY AND PRECAUTIONS

Corozal Town and the rural parts of the district are among the safer places in Belize, but crack cocaine has made its ugly appearance here (police seem oddly unable to find and close down the crack houses), which is one reason petty thefts are an issue.

Contacts ADO Bus Line. ✉ *ADO Bus Terminal, Av. Insurgentes and Av. Belice, Chetumal* ☎ *800/369–4652, 998/887–9533 in Cancún* ⊕ *www.ado.com.mx.*

> **HOT PROPERTY**
>
> Corozal District has become a hot spot for U.S., Canadian, and European retirees and snowbirds. Several hundred expats live full-time in Corozal District, and the numbers are growing. They're attracted by the home prices—a two-bedroom, modern home in a nice area near the water can go for less than US$150,000. Two-bedroom rental apartments and small houses are available starting at US$250 to US$400 a month. An expat "friendship luncheon" is held monthly in Corozal Town. Newcomers and wannabes welcome.

EXPLORING

FAMILY **Commercial Free Zone.** About 600 wholesale and retail companies are located in the Corozal Commercial Free Zone/Zona Libre Belice on the Belize side of the Belize-Mexico border. Visitors may find some bargains on clothing and household items imported from Asia, along with discounted gasoline and liquor, though the retail stores target Mexicans rather than Belizeans or U.S. or other international tourists. Three casinos also target the Mexican market, especially on weekends. Visitors going from Belize to the Free Zone must pay the Belize BZ$40 exit fee, which cuts into any savings on gas or merchandise, and pay duties on goods (especially liquor) brought back into Belize. ✉ *1 Freedom Ave., Belize-Mexico Border* ☎ *423/7010* ⊕ *www.belizecorozalfreezone.com.*

Corozal House of Culture. The architecturally elegant old Corozal Cultural Center, for many years the main Corozal market, was completely renovated and reopened in 2012 as the Corozal House of Culture. Located in one of the oldest buildings in northern Belize (other than ancient Mayan structures), the House of Culture was built in 1886. It's operated by the National Institute of History and Culture (NICH) as an art gallery and museum devoted to the history of Corozal Town and northern Belize. NICH operates other museums including ones in Belize City, Orange Walk Town, San Pedro, San Ignacio, and Benque Viejo, along with many Maya archaeological sites. ✉ *1st Ave., near Corozal Bay* ☎ *422/0071* ⊕ *www.nichbelize.org* ✆ *Free* ☾ *Closed weekends.*

FAMILY **Corozal Museum.** This tiny one-room museum is the work of Lydia Ramcharam Pollard, a third-generation Indian-Belizean, whose grandparents came to Belize as indentured servants in the mid-19th century and worked in the sugarcane and rice fields. Pollard has collected a variety of Corozal historical artifacts, including old domestic household items, sugarcane tools, tortilla-making equipment, and other Mestizo pieces, along with some items that represent her family's history. ⊠ *129 South End, aka Goldson Hwy.* ✛ *0.5 mile south of Corozal Town, in house on east side of highway* ☎ *402/3314* 🖥 *By donation* ☉ *Closed Sun.*

FAMILY **Gabrielle Hoare Market.** This market on 6th Avenue has stalls selling a good selection of local fruits and vegetables, along with clothes and miscellaneous household items. Local fruit—bananas, mangos, papayas, pineapples, and large, in-season watermelons—are cheap. ⊠ *6th Ave.*

Santa Rita. Not far from Corozal are several Mayan sites. The closest, Santa Rita, is a short walk or drive from the town center. It's on a low hill across from the Coca-Cola plant near Corozal Hospital at the north end of town. Only one large temple building has been excavated. The government of Belize in 2012 designated Santa Rita as an official "Wedding Gardens of Belize," and a number of mostly Belizean weddings have been held there. Usually in December a reenactment of the wedding of Tzazil-Ha, a Mayan princess, and Gonzalo Guerrero, a Spanish conquistador, is held here. Although there isn't a visitor center yet, a caretaker/guide will show you around and collect the admission fee. ⊠ *Santa Rita, near Corozal Hospital and Coca-Cola plant* ⊕ *www.nichbelize.org* 🖥 *BZ$10.*

WHERE TO EAT

$$ ✕ **Corozo Blue's.** This popular eatery in a stone building on the bay at
PIZZA the South End serves excellent wood-fired pizza, burgers, sandwiches,
FAMILY and ceviche, plus a few traditional Belizean dishes like rice and beans. By Corozal standards, prices are on the high side, but the atmosphere, bay-side setting, and friendly staff make it well worth a visit. Ⓢ *Average main: BZ$27* ⊠ *South End* ☎ *422/0090* ⊕ *corozoblues.com.*

$ ✕ **June's Kitchen.** The best breakfast in Corozal is served by Miss June
LATIN AMERICAN at her home, but there's only seating for about a dozen guests on the
FAMILY open-air patio. Everything is homemade, freshly prepared, and served
Fodor'sChoice by Miss June and her family. For example, you can have a delicious
★ breakfast of an omelet, pepper sausage, fried potatoes, warm bread, and freshly squeezed orange juice for about BZ$10. Lunch is delicious, and the entire menu can (and will) be spoken in a few words: likely stew chicken, stew beef, or stew pork, plus a daily special. Delivery is available, brought to you by Miss June's husband on his bike. Ⓢ *Average main: BZ$12* ⊠ *3rd St. S* ☎ *422/2559* ☉ *Closed Sun. No dinner.*

$$ ✕ **Patty's Bistro.** Patty's Bistro (sometimes spelled Patti's) serves some of
LATIN AMERICAN the best food in town, the service is sprightly and friendly, the atmo-
FAMILY sphere is no-frills, and prices are low. For a local treat, try the hearty
Fodor'sChoice conch soup (in season, usually October to late April). Ⓢ *Average main:*
★ *BZ$19* ⊠ *2nd St. N* ☎ *402/0174* ☉ *Closed Sun.*

WHERE TO STAY

$$ 🏨 **Almond Tree Hotel Resort.** Directly on the bay just south of town, Almond
RESORT Tree Hotel Resort raises the bar on Corozal Town lodging. **Pros:** nicest
Fodor'sChoice accommodations in town; attractively designed rooms; swimming pool;
★ bay-side setting with views. **Cons:** on the South End, a bit away from the main part of town; limited dining options at resort but good restaurants nearby. Ⓢ *Rooms from: BZ$214* ⊠ *425 Bayshore Dr., South End* ☎ *628/9224* ⊕ *www.almondtreeresort.com* ⤴ *8 rooms* ◉| *No meals.*

Restaurants ▼

Corozo Blue's ... 1
June's Kitchen 3
Patty's Bistro 2

Hotels ▼

Almond Tree Hotel Resort 1
George Hardie's Las Vegas Hotel & Casino ... 5
Hok'ol K'in Guest House 3
Las Palmas 4
Serenity Sands B&B 6
Tony's Inn and Beach Resort ... 2

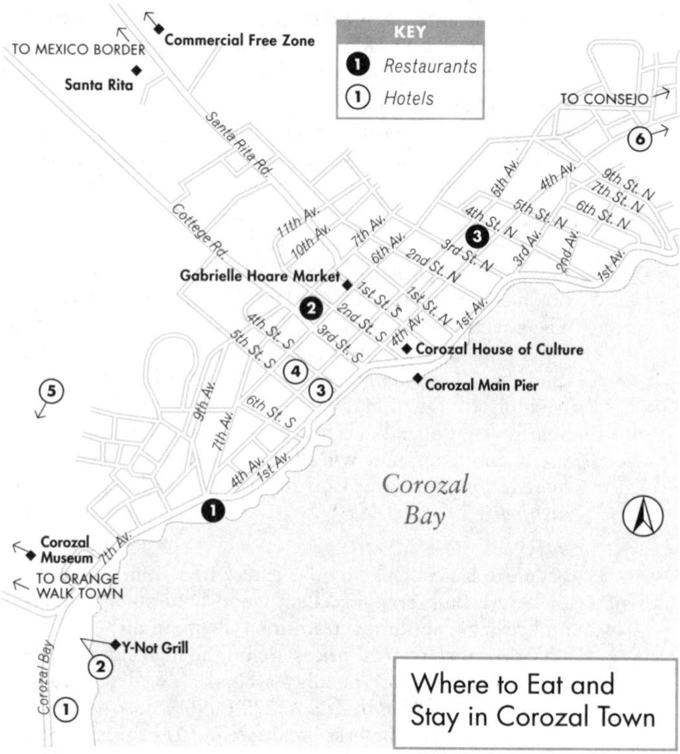

Where to Eat and Stay in Corozal Town

$$ HOTEL 🏨 **George Hardie's Las Vegas Hotel & Casino.** Opened in late 2015, George Hardie's Las Vegas Hotel & Casino is northern Belize's largest and most upscale hotel. **Pros:** built in 2015; large, full-service hotel with pool and restaurant; friendly staff. **Cons:** located in Free Zone, not in Corozal Town; visitors to Free Zone must pay US$20/BZ$40 Belize exit fee; caters mainly to gamblers. [$] *Rooms from: BZ$280* ✉ *Mile 91.5, Philip Goldson Hwy.* ✥ *In Corozal Commercial Zone aka Corozal Free Zone, on Belize territory but requiring official exit from Belize (Mexican visitors do not need to go through Belize customs and immigration)* ☎ *423/7000 in Belize* 🌐 *www.lvbelize.com* 🛏 *106 rooms* 🍴 *No meals.*

$ HOTEL FAMILY 🏨 **Hok'ol K'in Guest House.** Yucatec Maya for "coming of the rising sun," Hok'ol K'in, founded by an American Peace Corps veteran and now operated by Belizeans, is a friendly small budget hotel on the Corozal bayfront. **Pros:** breezy bayfront location within walking distance of most shops and restaurants; friendly management; some handicap-accessible rooms. **Cons:** no-frills rooms; only have the guest rooms have a/c. [$] *Rooms from: BZ$150* ✉ *89 4th Ave.* ☎ *422/3329* 🌐 *www.corozal.net* 🛏 *11 rooms* 🍴 *No meals.*

$ HOTEL FAMILY 🏨 **Las Palmas.** Totally renovated and rebuilt, this whole property has gone somewhat upmarket, while remaining a good value. **Pros:** convenient central location in town; good value. **Cons:** not on the water; limited secure parking. $ *Rooms from: BZ$126* ✉ *123 5th Ave.* ☎ *422/0196* ⊕ *www.laspalmashotelbelize.com* ↩ *20 rooms* ⦿ *No meals.*

$$ ⛺ **Serenity Sands B&B.** This upscale, eco-oriented B&B is hidden away
B&B/INN off the Consejo Road north of Corozal Town, with four tastefully
FAMILY decorated rooms on the second floor with private balconies overlook-
Fodor's Choice ing gardens, Belizean art, and locally made hardwood furniture. **Pros:**
★ immaculately maintained grounds; family-friendly; eco-oriented management. **Cons:** out-of-the-way location warrants a rental car; a short
walk through lovely grounds to bay. $ *Rooms from: BZ$218* ✉ *Mile 3,*
Consejo Rd. ⚓ *From Corozal Town, take 4th Ave. N, which becomes*
unpaved Consejo Rd. Stay on Consejo Rd. 3 miles (5 km). Turn right
at Serenity Sands sign. Follow Serenity Rd. 0.75 mile (1.2 km); turn at
first right and follow this road turning left, then right until you reach
Serenity Sands B&B ☎ *669/2394* ⊕ *www.serenitysands.com* ↩ *5 rooms*
⦿ *Breakfast.*

$$ ⛺ **Tony's Inn and Beach Resort.** One of the oldest hotels and restaurants in
HOTEL northern Belize, Tony's Inn is still going strong, with spacious, recently
FAMILY refurbished rooms and a popular bay-side restaurant and bar, all on
beautifully landscaped grounds. **Pros:** attractive, recently renovated
rooms; breezy bayside setting with landscaped grounds; open-air res-
taurant; safe guarded parking. **Cons:** no swimming pool. $ *Rooms*
from: BZ$207 ✉ *South End* ☎ *422/2055* ⊕ *www.tonysinn.com* ↩ *24*
rooms ⦿ *No meals.*

COPPER BANK

12 miles (20 km) southeast of Corozal Town.

Copper Bank is a tidy and small (population around 500) Mestizo fish-
ing village on Corozal Bay. The village is something of a footnote to the
nearby Mayan site, Cerros.

GETTING HERE AND AROUND

One way to get here is by boat from Corozal. You can also drive from
Corozal Town, crossing the New River on the hand-pulled ferry. To get
to the ferry from Corozal, take the Northern Highway south toward
Orange Walk Town (watch for ferry sign). Turn left and follow this
unpaved road for 2.5 miles (4 km) to the ferry landing. After crossing
the river, drive on to a T-intersection and turn left for Copper Bank. The
trip from Corozal Town to Copper Bank takes about a half hour, but
longer after heavy rains, as the dirt road can become very bad. As you
enter Copper Bank, watch for signs directing you to "Cerros Maya."

TIMING

Most visitors do only a day trip to see the Cerros ruins, although if you
want a quiet, off-the-main-path place to finish writing that novel, you
won't find a better place than Cerros Beach Resort.

EXPLORING

Cerros. Like the Tulum site in Mexico, Cerros (also referred to as Cerro
Maya, or Mayan Hill in Spanish) is unusual in that it's directly on the
water. Unlike Tulum, however, there is little development around it, and
at times you can have the place all to yourself. With a beautiful setting

on a peninsula jutting into Corozal Bay, near the mouth of the New River, the late Pre-Classic center dates to 2000 BC and includes a ball court, several tombs, and a large temple. Altogether, there are some 170 structures, many just mounds of stone and earth, on 52 acres. There's also a small visitor center. Bring plenty of bug spray—mosquitoes can be fierce here. TIP→ **The easiest way to get to Cerros is to charter a boat in Corozal Town, for a 15-minute ride across the bay.** ✉ *2.5 miles (4 km) north of Copper Bank* ✥ *Follow signs from south end of Corozal Town and cross New River on Pueblo Nuevo hand-cranked ferry. At T-intersection, go left to Copper Bank Village and follow signs west on unpaved roads to Cerros* ☎ *822/2106 NICH Institute of Archeology* 🌐 *www.nichbelize.org* 🎫 *BZ$10.*

WHERE TO EAT AND STAY

$$ AMERICAN FAMILY 🍴 **Tradewinds Restaurant.** The "house restaurant" for the Orchid Bay real estate development, Tradewinds is run by David and Demaris, an American-Belizean couple. The menu features adequate American pub food such as burgers and wings, along with ceviche and other seafood and some traditional Belizean dishes such as rice and beans with stew chicken. Once a week there is a soup night, which attracts locals for an inexpensive night out and a chance to benefit the local community—one half of the evening's proceeds go to support various good works in the community. [$] *Average main: BZ$20* ✉ *Orchid Bay Club* ☎ *650/1925* 🌐 *www.orchidbaybeachclub.com.*

$ B&B/INN 🏨 **Cerros Beach Resort.** Cerros Beach Resort is an off-the-grid option for good food and simple lodging on Corozal Bay, near the Cerros ruins. **Pros:** low-key, crowd-free small resort on the bay; tasty food and home-brewed beer; good value. **Cons:** mosquitoes sometimes can be pesky; cabins are basic. [$] *Rooms from: BZ$131* ✉ *Cerros Beach Resort* ✥ *Near Cerros Mayan site on north side of Cerros peninsula; entering Copper Bank village, watch for signs to Cerros Beach Resort. The resort will arrange for pickup by boat from Consejo or Corozal Town for parties of five or more* ☎ *623/9530, 518/872–3052 in U.S.* 🌐 *www.cerrosbeachresort.com* 🕓 *Restaurant closed Mon.* 🛏 *4 rooms* 🍽 *No meals.*

$$ B&B/INN 🏨 **Crimson Orchid B&B.** An unexpected addition to Orchid Bay real estate development is this stylish three-level, nine-room B&B, which opened in 2012. **Pros:** newest and nicest accommodations in the Cerros-Sarteneja area; reasonable prices; full English breakfast included. **Cons:** out-of-the-way location in Orchid Bay development that gets few tourists; no pool. [$] *Rooms from: BZ$218* ✉ *Pescadores Park, off Sarteneja Rd., at Orchid Bay development* ☎ *669/5076* 🛏 *9 rooms* 🍽 *Breakfast.*

SARTENEJA

40 miles (67 km) from Corozal Town.

The bay setting of the Mestizo and Creole community of Sarteneja makes it one of the most relaxed and appealing destinations in Belize. It's also the largest fishing village in Belize. You can swim in the bay here, though in many places the bottom is gunky.

Lobster fishing and pineapple farming are the town's two main industries, and Sarteneja is also a center for building wooden boats. Most residents speak Spanish as a first language, but many also speak English. Visitors and real-estate buyers are beginning to discover Sarteneja, and while tourism services are still minimalist, several small guesthouses are now open, and there are a few places to get a simple, inexpensive bite to eat.

GETTING HERE AND AROUND

Driving to Sarteneja from Corozal Town takes about 1½ hours via the New River ferry and a second, bay-side ferry across Laguna Seca. The road is unpaved and can be very muddy after heavy rains. You also can drive to Sarteneja from Orange Walk Town, a trip of about 40 miles (67 km) and 1½ hours. There are several Sarteneja Bus Line buses a day, except Sunday, from Belize City via Orange Walk Town. The trip from Belize City takes 3½ to 4 hours.

The daily water taxi, *Thunderbolt*, which sails between Corozal Town and San Pedro, will drop you at Sarteneja on request. You also can hire a private boat in Corozal to take you and your party to Sarteneja.

Sarteneja has an airstrip, with flights on Tropic Air from San Pedro to Corozal Town stopping at Sarteneja on demand.

TIMING

Once you visit Shipstern and take a splash in the sea, you've just about exhausted all there is to do in Sarteneja. So bring several good books and enjoy the slow-paced village life.

EXPLORING

Shipstern Nature Reserve. About 3½ miles (6 km) west of Sarteneja on the road to Orange Walk or Corozal is the Shipstern Nature Reserve; this is the driest place in Belize and best visited January through April. You pass the entrance and visitor center as you come into Sarteneja. The 31 square miles (81 square km) of tropical forest forming the reserve are, like the Crooked Tree Wildlife Sanctuary, a paradise for birders. Shipstern is managed by the Corozal Sustainable Future Initiative (CSFI), an NGO. More than 300 species of birds have been identified here. Look for egrets (there are 13 species), American coots, keel-billed toucans, flycatchers, warblers, and several species of parrots. Mammals are in healthy supply as well, including tapirs, pumas, and jaguars. The former butterfly farm next to the visitor center is now a small education area, and butterflies are being repopulated; don't apply bug spray if you are entering the butterfly enclosure. Nearby, a small museum at Mahogany Park focuses on the history and uses of this beautiful tropical hardwood. There is a botanical trail leading from the visitor center, with the names of many plants and trees identified on small signs. Admission, a visit to the butterfly center, and a guided tour of the botanical trail is BZ$10 per person. Other tours are available, including one to the lagoon at Xo-Pol (BZ$70 per person) to see birds and crocodiles; stop at the Shipstern visitor center for more information. Bring plenty of bug juice. ■TIP→ **Although you can stay and eat in Sarteneja village, Shipstern offers basic cabin accommodations or a budget; meals are an added daily cost.** ☒*Shipstern Nature Reserve, Chunox-Sarteneja Rd., near*

Sarteneja village ☎ 660/1807 *Corozal Sustainable Future Initiative in Corozal Town* ⊕ *www.visitshipstern.com* 🖅 *BZ$10 per person, with minimum charge of BZ$20; birding tours BZ$50 per person, with a minimum charge of BZ$100.*

WHERE TO EAT AND STAY

$

LATIN AMERICAN

FAMILY

✕ **Liz's Fast Food.** You can get a sack full of tacos, *sabutes* (corn tortillas topped with refried beans, shredded stewed chicken, lettuce, onions, tomatoes and cilantro), empananda, *garnaches* (fried corn tortillas with refried beans, grated cheese, onions, habanero pepper, and cilantro) and other Mestizo dishes here for almost nothing. Most items, though small as a sand dollar, are extremely tasty and cost only a Belize dollar for two or three. Daily specials may include fish, beans and rice, stew chicken or other Belizean dishes, all extremely inexpensive. Place your order at a takeout window in the flaking green, streetside stall. Ⓢ *Average main: BZ$2* ⊠ *Av. Primitivo Aragon* ✛ *Near center of town* 🚭 *No credit cards.*

$

SEAFOOD

FAMILY

✕ **Ritchie's Place.** This no-frills, family-run restaurant serves the freshest seafood in Sarteneja, from a whole fried snapper to fish empanadas to conch and lobster in season. Owner Ritchie Cruz lives next door to his restaurant, which used to be just a few tables on a screened porch. Even a hungry family of four will find it difficult to spend more than BZ$75 for dinner unless you buy specials such as lobster. Ⓢ *Average main: BZ$15* ⊠ *Ritchie's Place, Front St., near public pier* ☎ *423/2031* 🚭 *No credit cards.*

$

B&B/INN

🖭 **Fernando's Seaside Guesthouse.** Lounge on the second-floor veranda of this small waterfront guesthouse and watch the fishing boats anchored just a few hundred feet away. **Pros:** across Front St. from the sea; water views from the second-floor porch. **Cons:** rooms at back lack a sea view. Ⓢ *Rooms from: BZ$109* ⊠ *64 N. Front St.* ☎ *423/2085* 🛏 *4 rooms* ⑩ *No meals.*

THE CAYO

By Ian Sluder   When the first jungle lodges opened in the early 1980s in the Cayo, few thought this wild area would become a tourist magnet. The mountainous region was too remote. Roads were bad. Restaurants were few. What would visitors do, besides visit cattle ranches and orange groves? After three decades of development, and remarkable growth in lodging, restaurants, and other infrastructure, more than half of those touring Belize visit the Cayo during their trip, making this the country's second most popular destination after Ambergris Caye.

You'll be lured by the rugged beauty of the region, with its jagged limestone hills, low green mountains where tapirs, peccaries, and jaguars still roam free, and its boulder-strewn rivers and creeks. You'll also appreciate its diversity, in a compact and accessible package. Even on a short stay, you can canoe or kayak rivers, hike remote mountain trails, visit a Mayan ruin, explore underground cave systems, go birding or wildlife-spotting, shop at a busy local market, chill out at a sidewalk café, and dine in style at a good restaurant or by lamplight at a jungle lodge.

You'll know when you've entered the Cayo a few miles east of Belmopan. Running along the Belize River for miles (though it's usually not visible from the road), the George Price Highway (formerly the Western Highway) then winds out of the valley and heads into a series of sharp bends. In a few minutes you'll see cattle grazing on steep hillsides and horses flicking their tails. The Creole people who live along the coast give way to Maya and Mestizos; English is replaced by Spanish as the predominant language (though English is also widely spoken). The lost world of the Maya comes alive through majestic, haunting ruins. And the Indiana Jones in you can hike through the jungle, ride horseback, canoe down the Macal or Mopan River, and explore incredible caves such as Actun Tunichil Muknal, which some call the highlight of their entire Central American experience.

The best of Cayo is mostly found in its scenic outdoors—nearly two-thirds of the district is in national parks and forest reserves. But you should also take time to appreciate its towns and villages. Belmopan, once just a sleepy village, is in the middle of a boom, with new government and residential construction fueled by real-estate speculation. These days, it's officially known as Belmopan City, one of only two such official government city destinations, the other, of course, being Belize City. San Ignacio is a thriving little town, its downtown area usually busy with locals buying supplies and backpackers looking to book tours or grab a bite and a Belikin at one of San Ignacio's many inexpensive eateries. Santa Elena, just to the east of San Ignacio, merges seamlessly

TOP REASONS TO GO

National Parks and Reserves.
About 60% of the Cayo District is national parks and reserves. That's good news if you like hiking, birding, wildlife-spotting, canoeing, or engaging in other outdoor activities.

Caves. Although there are caves in Toledo and elsewhere in Belize, Cayo has the biggest and most exciting ones. Actun Tunichil Muknal is the top caving experience in Belize.

Mayan Sites. The Cayo is home to the largest and most important Mayan site in Belize; Caracol has more than 35,000 buildings, though so far only a handful have been excavated. Cayo also has the most easily accessible Mayan sites in the country, Cahal Pech and

Xunantunich, along with dozens of smaller ones.

Jungle Lodges. With more than 30 jungle lodges, the Cayo has far more than all the other districts of Belize combined. There's a lodge for every budget, from bare-bones cabins along the Mopan River to ultradeluxe villas on the Macal River and in the Mountain Pine Ridge.

Mountains. The Mountain Pine Ridge's 2,000–3,600 foot mountains, with their waterfalls, caves, and rivers, provide a welcome respite from the heat and humidity of lowland Belize, though most of it is not broad-leaf jungle but piney woods not too different from the Southern Appalachians in Alabama or Georgia.

to turn the so-called Twin Towns into one. The village of San Antonio on the Cristo Rey Road is predominantly Mayan. Benque Viejo del Carmen, 2 miles (3 km) from the border, feels more Guatemalan than Belizean, and Spanish Lookout, the Mennonite center, with its well-kept farms and no-nonsense farm-supply and general stores, could as well be in the U.S. Midwest.

El Cayo is Spanish for "the caye" or key. Local residents still call San Ignacio Town "El Cayo," or just "Cayo," which can potentially create some confusion for outsiders. The name is thought to have originally referred to the small island formed where the Macal and Mopan rivers meet at San Ignacio.

ORIENTATION AND PLANNING

GETTING ORIENTED

The Cayo's main connection to the coast is the George Price Highway (formerly the Western Highway), a paved two-lane road running 78 miles (128 km) between Belize City and the Guatemala border. The highway is in generally good condition, but shoulders are narrow, and parts of the highway can be extremely slick after rain. Scores of people have died in traffic accidents on the highway in recent years. Secondary roads, mostly unpaved and sometimes difficult to drive on, branch off the Western Highway, leading to small villages and to the Mountain Pine Ridge, the Spanish Lookout Mennonite area, and various jungle lodges. The Mountain Pine Ridge is crisscrossed by an extensive network of gravel and dirt roads, some formerly logging trails.

At Belmopan the paved Hummingbird Highway is one of Belize's most scenic roads (its rival is the newer San Antonio Road towards the Guatemalan border in Toledo District), cutting 54 miles (90 km) southeast through the Maya Mountains to Dangriga, passing Blue Hole National Park. Mile markers on the Hummingbird start in Dangriga and increase as they go to Belmopan.

Belmopan City. Although hardly a tourism hot spot, Belmopan is Belize's newest city (in Belize the government designates urban areas as cities, towns, or villages) with a growing number of restaurants and hotels. The U.S. Embassy has a US$50 million compound here, and around Belmopan are several excellent jungle lodges.

San Ignacio. The hub of western Belize, San Ignacio is a bustling little town. Here you can arrange tours (often at lower prices than from jungle lodges), shop at the local market, and get a good meal, whether you're hungry for Indian, Italian, Chinese, Belizean, or even Sri Lankan.

Benque Viejo. The last town in Belize before you reach Guatamala, Benque Viejo has modest art and cultural attractions worth checking out, as well as a Mayan burial cave.

Mountain Pine Ridge. The largest forest reserve in Belize, the Mountain Pine Ridge covers almost 300 square miles (777 square km). Crisscrossed by old logging roads and small rivers, and dotted with waterfalls, the Mountain Pine Ridge—at elevations up to almost 3,400 feet, and noticeably cooler than other parts of the Cayo—is the gateway to the Chiquibul wilderness and to Caracol. It's also home to three top-notch jungle lodges.

Caracol. The largest and most important Mayan site in Belize, Caracol rivals Tikal in Guatemala in historical importance and archaeological interest.

PLANNING

WHEN TO GO

The best time to visit the Cayo is late fall and winter, when temperatures generally are moderate. During the peak of the dry season, March to May or early June, at the lower elevations around San Ignacio and Belmopan daytime temperatures can reach 100°F, though it does cool off a bit at night. Seasonal rains usually reach the Cayo in early June. In summer, after the rains begin, temperatures moderate a little, but humidity increases. Year-round the Mountain Pine Ridge is noticeably cooler and less humid than anywhere else in Belize, and at times in winter it can be downright chilly, but lodges in the Pine Ridge do have fireplaces.

GETTING HERE AND AROUND
AIR TRAVEL

Most people bound for the Cayo fly into Belize City. Tropic Air has flights to Maya Flats airstrip on the Chial Road between San Ignacio and Benque Viejo. For charter flights, there also is an airstrip near San

Ignacio at Central Farm. Blancaneaux Lodge and Hidden Valley Inn in the Mountain Pine Ridge have their own private airstrips and helipads.

Fodor's Choice ★ **Maya Flats Airstrip.** The small Maya Flats Airstrip (MYF) is on the Chial Road off the Benque Viejo Road (aka George Price Highway) about midway between San Ignacio and Benque Viejo del Carmen. Currently it is served only by **Tropic Air** and a few private aircraft. Tropic has three 30-minute flights daily between San Ignacio and the international airport in Ladyville (near Belize City), plus four flights daily from the municipal airport in Belize City. Some of the municipal airport flights stop at either the international airport or Belmopan. ✉ *Chial Rd., San Ignacio* ☎ *226/2626 in Belize, 800/422–3435 toll-free number in U.S. and Canada* ⊕ *www.tropicair.com.*

BUS TRAVEL

A number of bus lines provide frequent service—about once every half hour during daylight and early evening hours—between Belize City and Cayo, with a stop in Belmopan. Among small bus companies authorized to operate on the George Price Highway are BBOC, D and E, Guerra's Bus Service, Middleton's, Shaw Bus, and Westline. James Line runs from Belize City to Belmopan, and then down the Hummingbird and Southern highways to Dangriga and Punta Gorda. Westbound buses depart from Belize City about every half hour beginning at around 5 am, with the last departures at 9 or 9:30 pm.

The cost between Belize City and San Ignacio is BZ$7 on a local, and BZ$9 on an express if you can find one. From Belize City regular buses are about BZ$5 to Belmopan and BZ$8 to Benque Viejo. Buses are typically old U.S. school buses and are not air-conditioned. Most buses from Belize City leave from what is still called the Novelo's terminal on West Collet Canal Street, even though the Novelo's bus line is defunct. Look for any bus with "Cayo" or "Benque" on the front. There is a bus station in the center Belmopan, while buses stop at a parking area next to the Cayo Welcome Center on Savannah Avenue in the center of San Ignacio. The Belize Bus Blog (⊕ *www.belizebus.wordpress.com*) has helpful information on bus travel.

FAMILY **Welcome Center Bus Area.** ✉ *Savannah St., next to Cayo Welcome Center, San Ignacio.*

CAR TRAVEL

Other than the two-lane George Price Highway most roads in the Cayo are unpaved and dusty in the dry season, muddy in the rainy season. To get to the Cayo, simply follow the Price Highway west from Belize City. Watch out for "sleeping policemen" (speed bumps) near villages along the route. ■TIP➔ **Be especially careful when driving the Price Highway. Most of the road lacks shoulders, and the surface can be extremely slick when wet. Horrific auto accidents occur frequently on this highway, which is long overdue for major upgrading.** If you didn't rent a car in Belize City, you can rent one in San Ignacio.

In August 2016, Hurricane Earl flooded much of the low-lying areas of San Ignacio. The lower bridge over the Macal River, which was the route for all traffic coming from the east into San Ignacio and points west, was seriously damaged. It is currently still closed, and it's expected

5

to remain closed until a new bridge, presently under construction, is completed nearby, likely in 2017. Until then, the one-lane Hawksworth Bridge over the Macal is used for traffic going east and west, with flag-persons alternating traffic over the bridge. This results in some traffic delays in both directions.

Rental Information Cayo Auto Rentals. ✉ *81 Benque Viejo Rd., aka George Price Hwy., San Ignacio* ☎ *824/2222* ⊕ *www.cayoautorentals.com.* **Matus Car Rental.** ✉ *18 Benque Viejo Rd., George Price Hwy., San Ignacio* ☎ *824/2005* ⊕ *www.matuscarrental.com.*

TAXI TRAVEL AND SHUTTLES

Taxis are plentiful in and around San Ignacio, but they're expensive if you're going to a remote lodge. For example, a taxi from San Ignacio to one of the Mountain Pine Ridge lodges is likely to be BZ$100–BZ$150, and to one of the lodges west of San Ignacio on the Macal River, about BZ$50–BZ$80 (rates are negotiable). Taxis within San Ignacio shouldn't be more than BZ$6 to most points and around BZ$15 to Bullet Tree. Collective taxis (they pick up as many passengers as possible) run to the Guatemala border from San Ignacio for BZ$5 (ask a local to show you where they pick up). Colectivos to Bullet Tree are BZ$2 to BZ$4. You can find taxis at Market Square in the middle of town, near Burns Avenue, or call **Cayo Taxi Association** (*824/2196*) or **Savannah Taxi** Association (*824/2155*), or, easiest of all, have your hotel call a taxi.

Many Cayo hotels and lodges provide van transportation from the international airport and other points in Belize City for about BZ$200–BZ$300 for up to four people one way. Several operators run shuttle vans between Belize City and San Ignacio for around BZ$70–BZ$100 per person. Among those currently offering shuttles are **William's Shuttle, Belize Shuttles and Transfers, and Discounted Belize Shuttles and Tours.** William's Shuttle is run by Dutch expat William Hofman, who is reliable, friendly, and knowledgeable; he charges around BZ$90 per person for two between Belize City and San Ignacio, or BZ$70 per person for three or more. Belize Shuttles and Transfers has both on-demand and fixed-time shuttle trips, the fixed-time shuttles to San Ignacio from either Belize City airport costing BZ$70 per person, plus 12.5% tax. Discounted Shuttles charges BZ$70 per person for two people from the international airport to Belmopan and BZ$90 per person to San Ignacio; these rates include tax. **Mayan World** and **PACZ Tours** also offer shuttles, including to Flores or Tikal in Guatemala (BZ$70 per person with a minimum of two people). Shuttles to Guatemala do not include the BZ$40 per person Belize exit fee. *For more information on these shuttles, please visit the Shuttle section in the Travel Smart chapter.*

A taxi from the international airport near Belize City to San Ignacio will cost around BZ$180–BZ$250 (for the cab, not per person), depending on your bargaining ability.

SAFETY IN THE CAYO

Although most visitors report feeling completely safe in the Cayo, in recent years occasional carjackings and robberies have occurred in bor-der areas and in the Mountain Pine Ridge and Chiquibul areas. Belize

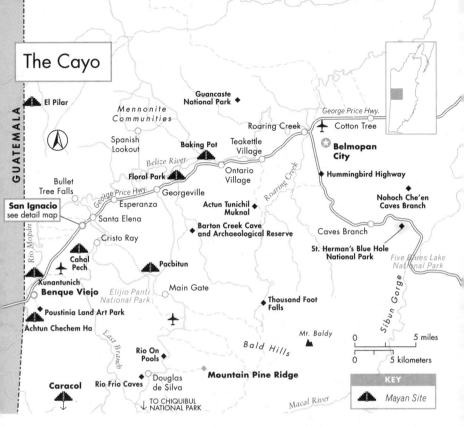

The Cayo

El Pilar

Mennonite Communities

Guancaste National Park

George Price Hwy.

Roaring Creek — Cotton Tree

Spanish Lookout

Baking Pot

Teakettle Village

Belmopan City

Belize River

Floral Park

Ontario Village

Bullet Tree Falls

George Price Hwy.

Georgeville

Hummingbird Highway

San Ignacio
see detail map

Esperanza

Rio Mopán

Santa Elena

Cristo Ray

Cahal Pech

Xunantunich

Benque Viejo

Actun Tunichil Muknal

Barton Creek Cave and Archaeological Reserve

Nohoch Che'en Caves Branch

Caves Branch

St. Herman's Blue Hole National Park

Five Blues Lake National Park

Pacbitun

Main Gate

Elijio Panti National Park

Poustinia Land Art Park

Achtun Chechem Ha

Last Branch

Thousand Foot Falls

Mt. Baldy

Bald Hills

Sibun Gorge

0   5 miles

0   5 kilometers

Rio On Pools

Douglas de Silva

Mountain Pine Ridge

Caracol   Rio Frio Caves

↓ TO CHIQUIBUL NATIONAL PARK

Macal River

KEY

△ Mayan Site

GUATEMALA

Defence Forces soldiers usually accompany vehicles going to Caracol. Ask locally about any recent incidents before starting road trips to remote areas.

Being close to Guatemala's El Petén region, thousands of Cayo visitors take short trips across the border to view the fantastic ruins of Tikal. Its proximity to this tourist attraction is a boon for the Cayo but also a burden, as the poverty-stricken population of northern Guatemala spills over into relatively affluent Belize. On several occasions armed gangs from Guatemala have robbed tourists around San Ignacio, especially near the El Pilar Mayan site and in the Mountain Pine Ridge. Incidents also have occurred in Guatemala near Tikal and towns in the Petén. However, most visitors to the Cayo say they feel quite safe and as a visitor, you're unlikely to encounter any problems.

A silent killer in Cayo is the George Price Highway, formerly the Western Highway. The two-lane road is paved, but it's narrow and most sections have no shoulders on the side of the highway. Worse, the surfacing material on parts of the road is extremely slick when wet. More people die in traffic accidents on this highway than on any other road in Belize, so exercise extreme caution if you find yourself traveling this road.

HEALTH

While the Cayo normally has relatively few mosquitoes, thanks to the porous limestone terrain that doesn't allow water to stand in puddles, there are occasional outbreaks of dengue fever. Dengue, which causes flulike symptoms, and, in more serious cases, death from internal bleeding, is transmitted by the bite of *Aedes aegypti* and *Aedes albopictus* mosquitoes. The Zika virus is also present in mosquitoes in Belize; Zika causes a rash and flulike symptoms as well as microcephaly in newborn babies when infected during pregnancy. These species of mosquitoes that carry Zika are most active in the early morning and late afternoon. Travelers, especially during the rainy season, should consider using insect repellent with DEET. There is as yet no preventative medicine for dengue or for Zika, although vaccines for both are currently under development. Pay close attention to travel warnings, and avoid travel to this region if you are pregnant or are thinking of becoming pregnant.

Health standards in the Cayo are high. The water in San Ignacio and Santa Elena comes from a treated municipal system, so it's safe to drink, though many people prefer the taste of bottled water. Resorts in the region have their own safe water systems.

ABOUT THE HOTELS

In the Cayo you have two very different choices in accommodations: jungle lodges and regular hotels. Jungle lodges, regardless of price or amenities, offer a close-to-nature experience, typically next to a river or in a remote mountain setting. Many lodges house their guests in thatch cabanas patterned after traditional Mayan houses. At the top end, lodges such as Blancaneaux Lodge and The Lodge at Chaa Creek deliver a truly deluxe experience, with designer toiletries, imported mattresses, and decor that wouldn't be out of place in *Architectural Digest*. At the other end, some budget lodges have outdoor bathrooms and thin foam mattresses. In between are a number of mid-level lodges providing an off-the-beaten-path experience at moderate prices.

Whereas the district's lodges are back-a-bush (a Belizean expression for "out in the jungle"), the Cayo's hotels are in towns or along the George Price Highway. The area's least expensive hotels are clustered in downtown San Ignacio, one of the backpacker centers of Belize. Hotels in and around Belmopan are a little more expensive because they cater to people in the capital on government business. Whether hotel or jungle lodge, most properties in the Cayo are small, typically run by the owners.

Generally, inexpensive hotels and lodges maintain the same rate year-round, though some may discount a little in the off-season (generally mid-April to early December). More expensive places usually have off-season rates 20% to 40% less than high season.

ABOUT THE RESTAURANTS

San Ignacio is the culinary center of the Cayo, with some two-dozen restaurants. Most are small spots with only a few tables. Restaurants offer Indian, French, German, and even Sri Lankan fare as well as burritos and beans. Prices, designed to appeal to the budget and mid-level travelers who stay in town, rarely rise above the moderate level. At the jungle lodges outside San Ignacio prices are much higher. Some lodges charge BZ$70–BZ$80, or more, for dinner.

WHAT IT COSTS IN BELIZE DOLLARS				
	$	$$	$$$	$$$$
RESTAURANTS	under BZ$15	BZ$15–BZ$30	BZ$31–BZ$50	over BZ$50
HOTELS	under BZ$200	BZ$200–BZ$300	BZ$301–BZ$500	over BZ$500

Restaurant prices are per person for a main course at dinner. Hotel prices are for two people in a standard double room in high season, including tax and service.

TOURS

ADVENTURE

San Ignacio and, to a lesser extent, Belmopan are Belize's centers for outdoor adventure, including hiking, river canoeing, rafting, birding, caving, cave tubing, mountain biking, horseback riding, and other activities. Most lodges offer extensive tour options, either using their own guides or guides they know and trust. Jungle lodges and hotels often provide complimentary kayaks, canoes, and bikes, or rent them for a modest charge.

FAMILY **Green Dragon Adventure Travel.** Associated with the Belize Jungle Dome Lodge near Belmopan, Green Dragon Adventure Travel offers 3- to 14-day tours of Belize. Among them are four- and five-day adventure tours of the Cayo, incorporating visits to Mayan ruins and caves with activities including hiking, river kayaking, and horseback riding. Rates for these Cayo tours are BZ$2,200 to BZ$3,300 per person, not including airfare to Belize, alcohol, or gratuities. ⊠ *Banana Bank, Mile 47, George Price Hwy., Belmopan* ☎ *822/2124* ⊕ *www.greendragonbelize. com.*

MOUNTAIN BIKING

Backroads. Pedal your way through Cayo and Tikal with a seven-day, six-night tour from Backroads. The tour takes you biking through the Mountain Pine Ridge and Tikal National Park, with a stay at the luxurious Blancaneaux Lodge. You also get to fly to southern Belize and snorkel on the Belize Barrier Reef. Packages start at around BZ$8,000 per person. ⊠ *801 Cedar St., Berkeley* ☎ *800/462–2848 toll-free in U.S. and Canada, 510/527–1555* ⊕ *www.backroads.com.*

SEEING THE RUINS

San Ignacio makes a good jumping-off spot to see Tikal, either on a day trip or overnight. It's also a good base for visiting Mayan sites in the Cayo, including **Caracol, Xunantunich, Cahal Pech,** and **El Pilar.** It's also a base for visiting Actun Tunichil Muknal, the amazing caves that introduce you to the Mayan underworld.

Belize Magnificent Mayan Tours. Run by local tour guide Albert Williams, Belize Magnificent Mayan Tours (or BZM Tours for short) does tours to Caracol, Tikal, Xunantunich, and elsewhere. Day tours to Mayan sites range from around BZ$440 per person for Caracol to BZ$850 for an overnight trip to Tikal. BZM Tours also has tours to Xunantunich,

Cahal Pech, and Chechem Ha Cave, with extras such as a visit to the Belize Zoo and cave tubing. ✉ *3 Burns Ave., San Ignacio* ☎ *621/0312* ⊕ *www.bzmtours.com.*

Fodor's Choice   **PACZ Tours.** A long-established San Ignacio tour operator, PACZ spe-
★   cializes in tours to the spooky, wonderful Actun Tunichil Muknal near Belmopan (BZ$220 per person for a guided full-day tour). They also offer other Mayan tours, including ones to Tikal and Caracol. The day tour to Tikal is BZ$290 and includes transportation from downtown San Ignacio, lunch, and admission to Tikal. The full-day Caracol tour is BZ$220 and includes transportation from downtown San Ignacio, admission fees, lunch, and stops at some sites in the Mountain Pine Ridge including Rio On and Rio Frio Cave. ✉ *30 Burns Ave., San Ignacio* ☎ *824/0536, 604/6921* ⊕ *www.pacztours.net.*

VISITOR INFORMATION

The Cayo Welcome Center has a visitor information center and displays of Mayan artifacts. The Belize Tourism Board website, ⊕ *www. travelbelize.org*, has some information on visiting the Cayo. San Ignacio Town (⊕ *www.sanignaciotown.com*), though a commercial site, has considerable information on the Cayo. Belmopan City Online (⊕ *www. belmopancityonline.com*) has tourism information on the Belmopan area, along with local news of the capital city. For information on how Belize is governed, visit the National Assembly of Belize website (⊕ *www.nationalassembly.gov.bz*)—the site also explains how you can request a visit to the legislative assembly

BELMOPAN CITY

50 miles (80 km) southwest of Belize City.

It used to be said that the best way to see Belize's capital, which was moved here from Belize City in 1970, was through the rearview mirror as you head toward San Ignacio or south down the Hummingbird. It's still mostly a dreary cluster of concrete office buildings plunked in the middle of nowhere, surrounded by residential areas that may remind you of a central Florida town, proving that cities can't be created overnight. However, with the opening of the main campus of the University of Belize in Belmopan in 2002, the relocation of several embassies (including the U.S. embassy) from Belize City to Belmopan, and new commercial activity around the capital, Belmopan—finally—is showing signs of life. The population has grown to more than 18,000. Commercial and retail activities are booming, and there's a minor real-estate gold rush going on.

GETTING HERE AND AROUND

Belmopan is about 48 miles (79 km) on the George Price Highway from Belize City. By car, it takes about an hour. As you approach the roundabout to Belmopan from the east, Guanacaste National Park is on your right. Turn south at Mile 47.4 on the Hummingbird Highway. In about 1.25 miles (2 km) you'll come to the main entrance road to Belmopan City. Turn left and soon you come to the Ring Road, a two-lane road that circles the city and provides access to the streets inside

GREAT ITINERARIES

IF YOU HAVE 3 DAYS IN THE CAYO

Upon arrival at the international airport, immediately head to the Cayo by rental car, bus, or shuttle van. If you have time, stop en route at the Belize Zoo. Stay at one of the jungle lodges around San Ignacio if it's within your budget. On your first full day in the Cayo, explore the area around San Ignacio, visiting the Xunantunich and Cahal Pech Mayan ruins, the Belize Botanic Gardens on the grounds of duPlooy's Lodge, and Green Hills Butterfly Farm. Assuming you have the energy, walk the Rainforest Medicine Trail and spend a few minutes at the Natural History Center, both at The Lodge at Chaa Creek. On the second day, if you're not planning to move on to Tikal in Guatemala after your stay in the Cayo, at least take a day tour there. Guided tours from San Ignacio usually include van transportation to the Tikal park, a local guide at the site, and lunch. Alternatively, if you're heading to Tikal later, take a day trip to Caracol in the Mountain Pine Ridge. Bring a picnic lunch and make stops at Río On pools, the Río Frio cave, and a waterfall, such as Five Sisters on the grounds of Gaia Lodge, or Big Rock Waterfall nearby. On your final day, take a full-day guided tour of Actun Tunichil Muknal. Have dinner at a restaurant in San Ignacio.

IF YOU HAVE 5 DAYS IN THE CAYO

Rent a car at the international airport and drive to a jungle lodge near Belmopan. If you have time, stop en route at the Belize Zoo and do a quick driving tour of the capital. On your first full day, go cave tubing and take a zip-line canopy tour at Nohoch Che'en Caves Branch Archeological Reserve, also called Jaguar Paw after a now-closed jungle lodge at the site. Alternatively, for a more strenuous day, take a trip with Caves Branch Adventure Camp, or do its cave-tubing trip. End your day with dinner at your lodge and a night wildlife-spotting tour. On your second day, drive down the Hummingbird Highway and take a dip in the inland Blue Hole. Also, visit St. Herman's Cave, or go horseback riding at Banana Bank Lodge near Belmopan. On the third day, move on to a jungle lodge near San Ignacio or in the Mountain Pine Ridge and follow the three-day itinerary above.

the ring. The jungle lodges near Belmopan are located either off the Price or Hummingbird highways.

TIMING

The highlights of Belmopan City itself can easily be seen in a couple of hours. If you're staying at a jungle lodge nearby, you can easily spend two to three days exploring the wider area, or longer, if you want to see the San Ignacio area while basing here.

EXPLORING

At the edge of Belmopan City is **Guanacaste,** Belize's smallest national park. **Actun Tunichil Muknal,** the cave that many view as one of the top sights and experiences in the region, is not far from Belmopan, off Mile

BUTTERFLY MIGRATIONS

Belize is on the flyway for Sulphur and other butterfly migrations from the United States and Canada to and through Central America. The summer migration usually starts in June and can last for several weeks. Among the species of butterflies migrating at this time are Cloudless Sulphur (*Phoebis sennae*), Orange Banded Sulphur (*Phoebis philea*), Ruddy Daggerwing (*Phoebis philea*), Great Southern White (*Ascia monuste*), and Giant Swallowtail (*Heraclides cresphontes*), among many others. Monarchs (*Danaus plexippus*) usually migrate south to and through Belize in the late fall, and northward in the early spring. (Monarchs are believed to be the only species that migrate both north and south.) Butterfly and moth expert Jan Meerman at **Green Hills Butterfly Farm** estimates that as many as two million butterflies and moths migrate through Belize in a single day during migration season.

52.5 of the Price Highway. Neither is the **Nohoch Che'en Caves Branch** archaeological park far, accessible on a paved road off the Price Highway at Mile 37, with its exhilarating cave tubing. Belmopan is also the gateway to the **Hummingbird Highway,** one of Belize's most scenic roadways and home to the inland **Blue Hole** and what remains of **Five Blues Lake.** If you have an interest in Belizean history and politics, the **George Price Centre for Peace and Development** is a museum, library, and cultural center focused on Belize's founding father and first prime minister.

TOP ATTRACTIONS

Fodor's Choice
★

Hummingbird Highway. One of the most scenic roadways in Belize, the Hummingbird Highway, a paved two-lane road, runs 54.5 miles (91 km) from the junction of the George Price Highway (formerly Western Highway) at Belmopan to Dangriga. Technically, only the first 32 miles (53 km) is the Hummingbird—the rest is the Stann Creek District Highway, but most people ignore that distinction and call it all the Hummingbird. As measured from Belmopan at the junction of the George Price Highway, the Hummingbird first winds through limestone hill country, passing St. Herman's Cave (Mile 12.2) and the inland Blue Hole (Mile 13.1). It then starts rising steeply, with the Maya Mountains on the west or right side, past St. Margaret's village and Five Blues Lake (Mile 23). The views, of green mountains studded with cohune palms and tropical hardwoods, are incredible. At the Hummingbird Gap (Mile 26, elevation near 1,000 feet, with mountains nearby over 3,000 feet), you're at the crest of the highway and now begin to drop down toward the Caribbean Sea. At Middlesex village (Mile 32), technically the road becomes the Stann Creek District Highway and you're in Stann Creek District. Now you're in citrus country, with groves of grapefruit and Valencia oranges. Near Steadfast village (watch for signs around Mile 37) there's the 1,600-acre Billy Barquedier National Park, where you can hike to waterfalls. At Mile 48.7 you pass the turn-off to the Southern Highway and at Mile 54.5 you enter Dangriga, with the sea just ahead. ■TIP→ **If driving, keep a watch for "sleeping policemen," speed bumps to slow traffic**

near villages. Most are signed, but a few are not. Also, gas up in Belmopan, as there are few service stations until you approach Dangriga. ⊠ *Belmopan to Dangriga, Hummingbird Hwy., Belmopan.*

FAMILY **St. Herman's Blue Hole National Park.** Less than a half hour south of Belmopan, the 575-acre St. Herman's Blue Hole National Park has a natural turquoise pool surrounded by mosses and lush vegetation, wonderful for a cool dip. The "inland Blue Hole" is actually part of an underground river system. On the other side of the hill is St. Herman's Cave, once inhabited by the Maya. There's a separate entrance to St. Herman's. A path leads up from the highway, but it's quite steep and difficult to climb unless the ground is dry. To explore St. Herman's cave beyond the first 300 yards or so, you must be accompanied by a guide (available at the park), and no more than five people can enter the cave at one time. With a guide, you also can explore part of another cave system here, the Crystal Cave (sometimes called the Crystalline Cave), which stretches for miles; the additional cost is BZ$20 per person for a two-hour guided tour. The main park visitor center is 12.5 miles (20.5 km) from Belmopan. The park is managed by the Belize Audubon Society, which administers a network of seven protected areas around the country. ⊠ *Mile 42.5, Hummingbird Hwy., Belmopan* ☎ *223/5004 Belize Audubon Society in Belize City* ⊕ *www. belizeaudubon.org* 🖅 *BZ$8.*

WORTH NOTING

Belize Bird Rescue. Focusing on the rescue of parrots, Belize Bird Rescue rehabilitates the birds and, when possible, releases them back in the wild. At any one time, the avian rehabilitation center and bird sanctuary may have up to 200 birds on their farm near Belmopan, including as many as 9 of the country's 10 species of parrots, along with some owls and other raptor birds. The center is especially involved in protecting the endangered yellow-head parrot, a subspecies unique to Belize. Tours of the center can be arranged by phoning or emailing in advance; the tours are free, but donations are welcome. The owners of the center also operate the on-site Rock Farm Inn B&B to help generate funds to support the program. ⊠ *3 miles (5 km) from Belmopan, Roaring River Dr., Belmopan* ☎ *610/0400* ⊕ *www.belizebirdrescue.org.*

FAMILY **George Price Centre for Peace and Development.** A permanent exhibit at this cultural center, library, and museum follows the life story of the Right Honorable George Price as he led the British colony to independence. Born in 1919 in Belize City, George Price was Belize's first and longest-serving prime minister. The "George Washington of Belize" is widely respected for his incorruptible dedication to the welfare of Belize and Belizeans. There's a sizeable library of books on human rights, peace, and national development, and the center hosts art shows, concerts, and film screenings. George Price passed away September 19, 2011, at age 92, just two days short of the 30th anniversary of Belize's independence. ⊠ *Price Centre Rd., Belmopan* ☎ *822/1054* ⊕ *www.gpcbelize. com* ☉ *Closed Sat.*

FAMILY **Guanacaste National Park.** Worth a quick visit on the way in or out of Belmopan is Belize's smallest national park, Guanacaste National

Park, named for the huge guanacaste trees that grow here. Also called monkey's ear trees because of their oddly shaped seedpods, the trees tower more than 100 feet. (Unfortunately, the park's tallest guanacaste tree had to be cut down in 2006, due to safety concerns that it might fall.) The 50-acre park, managed by the Belize Audubon Society, has a rich population of tropical birds, including smoky brown woodpeckers, black-headed trogons, red-lored parrots, and white-breasted wood wrens. You can take one of the eight daily hourly tours, or you can wander around on your own. After, cool off with a refreshing plunge in the Belize River; there's also a small picnic area. ✉ *Mile 47.7, George Price Hwy., formerly Western Hwy., Belmopan* ☎ *223/5004 Belize Audubon Society in Belize City* 🌐 *www.belizeaudubon.org* 🎟 *BZ$5.*

A WACKY TALE

Five Blues Lake National Park. At the 4,000-acre Five Blues Lake National Park, until 2006 you were able to hike 3 miles (5 km) of trails, explore several caves, and canoe and swim in a 10-acre lake with five shades of blue. The lake was a cenote, a collapsed cave in the limestone. In July 2006, despite heavy rains, the water level in the lake began to recede. On July 20, 2006, local residents heard a strange noise "as if the lake were moaning." A giant whirlpool formed, and most of the water in the lake was sucked into the ground. Many of the fish died, and the lake looked like a dry pit. Researchers believe that a sediment "plug" dissolved and the lake drained, like water from a bathtub, into underground sinkholes and caves. The lake has since refilled with water, but the park isn't what it was before 2006. The park entrance is about 3.5 miles (5.75 km) from the Hummingbird Highway, via a narrow and very rough dirt road. Bikes can be rented in St. Margaret's village, from which village volunteers manage the park, and homestays and overnight camping in the village also can be arranged. ✉ ***At end of Lagoon Rd., off Mile 32, Hummingbird Hwy., St. Margaret's Village.***

WHERE TO EAT

In addition to the restaurants listed here, the food and produce stalls at the Belmopan market (**Market Square,** open Monday–Saturday, off Bliss Parade next to the bus terminal on Constitution Drive) are good places to buy tasty Belizean produce, snacks, and fruit at inexpensive prices—for example, you can get 8 or 10 bananas for BZ$1. If you can't wait to get to Belmopan to eat, near the Belize Zoo is a well-known roadside eatery where you can grab a good burger and a cold beer, **Cheers** (*Mile 31, Western Hwy. 822–8014*).

$$ LATIN AMERICAN

🍴 **Caladium.** In business since 1984, the Caladium is one of the oldest businesses in this young capital. Most Belizeans know it, since it's next to the bus station at Market Square. Here you'll find many of the country's favorites on the menu, including fried chicken, tender barbecued pork ribs, traditional rice and beans with chicken, beef, or pork, and conch soup. It's authentic, clean, affordable, well-run, and air-conditioned. [$] *Average main: BZ$18* ✉ *Market Sq., Belmopan* ☎ *822/2754* 🕒 *Closed Sun.*

CAYO HISTORY

The Maya began settling the Belize River Valley of the Cayo some 5,000 years ago. At the height of the Maya civilization, AD 300 to 900, Caracol, El Pilar, Xunantunich, Cahal Pech, and other cities and ceremonial centers in what is now the Cayo were likely home to several hundred thousand people, several times the population of the district today.

Spanish missionaries first arrived in the area in the early 17th century, but they had a difficult time converting the independent-minded Maya, some of whom were forcibly removed to the Petén in Guatemala. The first significant Spanish and British settlements were logwood and mahogany logging camps. The town of San Ignacio and its adjoining sister town, Santa Elena, were established later in the 1860s. Though only about 70 miles (115 km) from Belize City, San Ignacio remained fairly isolated until recent times, because getting to the coast by horseback through the bush or by boat could take three days or longer. What was then the Western Highway was paved in the 1980s, making it easier to get here. The first jungle lodges began operation, and tourism now vies with agriculture as the main industry.

5

$$ ✕ **Corkers Restaurant and Bar.** Next door to the Hibiscus Hotel, Corkers
ECLECTIC   is run by the husband-and-wife team of Geoff Hatto-Hembling and Sam
FAMILY   Buxton from the United Kingdom. To catch any breezes, sit in the cov-
Fodor's Choice   ered, open-air patio, or you can dine inside in the cozy air-conditioned
★   dining room. The menu is eclectic, ranging from classic English fish-and-chips to a grilled American cheeseburger with fries to Indian curries, plus pasta, steak, pork ribs, fried chicken, and a nice variety of salads. Drink prices are reasonable, with half-price cocktails at extended happy hour 4–10 pm Thursday–Saturday. $ *Average main: BZ$22* ⊠ *Corkers, Hibiscus Plaza, Belmopan* ☏ *822/0400* ⊕ *www.corkersbelize.com* ⊙ *Closed Sun.*

WHERE TO STAY

$$ ⬚ **Banana Bank Lodge.** Set on the banks of the Belize River, this lodge
B&B/INN   is a good spot for families, especially those who like to ride horses, as
FAMILY   equestrians of all skill levels have a choice of horses from their herd of about 100. **Pros:** swimming pool and bar; very friendly atmosphere. **Cons:** some object to the lodge's caged birds and animals. $ *Rooms from: BZ$283* ⊠ *Banana Bank Ranch, Belmopan* ✛ *By boat: across Belize River, turn north at Mile 47 of George Price Hwy. Continue to split in road and keep right. At next sharp turn, keep right and continue 0.5 mile (1 km) to end of road, park, and bang gong to summon a boat from Banana Bank. By road: from Price Hwy., turn north at Mile 46.9 and cross bridge over Belize River. Follow gravel/dirt road 3 miles (5 km) to Banana Bank sign. Turn right and follow dirt road for 2 miles (3 km) to lodge* ☏ *832/2020* ⊕ *www.bananabank.com* ⤳ *18 rooms* ⦿*Breakfast.*

$$ RESORT **Belize Jungle Dome.** This well-appointed small inn near the Belize River has four attractively furnished small suites, with tile floors, lots of windows, and an uncluttered look. **Pros:** intimate and upscale accommodations in a lovely setting; large selection of tours; a/c. **Cons:** stairs may be a problem for guests with mobility limitations. [$] *Rooms from: BZ$207* ✉ *Banana Bank, off Mile 47, George Price Hwy., Belmopan* ✣ *From George Price Hwy. turn north at Mile 46.9 and cross bridge over Belize River. Follow gravel/dirt road 3 miles (5 km) until you see Banana Bank sign. Turn right and follow dirt road 2 miles (3 km). Belize Jungle Lodge is on right just before Banana Bank Lodge* ☎ *822/2124* 🌐 *www.belizejungledome.com* 🛏 *5 rooms, 1 3-bedroom house* 🍴 *No meals.*

$$ RESORT **Dream Valley Jungle Lodge.** With somewhat eccentric decor and televisions in every room, Dream Valley is not quite luxurious and not quite rustic, but guests enjoy its intimacy and quiet location right at the jungle's edge. **Pros:** beautiful views of Belize River; good value. **Cons:** not as polished as some more established lodges; not that many dining options. [$] *Rooms from: BZ$286* ✉ *Young Gyal Rd., Teakettle Village* ☎ *665/1000, 888/969–7829 toll-free in U.S. and Canada* 🌐 *www.dreamvalleybelize.com* 🛏 *15 rooms* 🍴 *No meals.*

$$$ RESORT FAMILY **Ian Anderson's Caves Branch Adventure Co. & Jungle Camp.** This adventure lodge has gone upscale, adding hillside "treehouse suites" 20 feet above the ground, a multilevel swimming pool with whirlpool, and a botanical garden featuring orchids and bromeliads. **Pros:** some of the best adventure tours in Belize; lush jungle setting; nice swimming pool and botanical garden. **Cons:** no a/c; now rather pricey. [$] *Rooms from: BZ$368* ✉ *Mile 42.5, Hummingbird Hwy., 12 miles (19.5 km) south of Belmopan, Belmopan* ☎ *610/3451* 🌐 *www.cavesbranch.com* 🛏 *29 rooms* 🍴 *No meals.*

$ HOTEL **Hibiscus Hotel.** If you want to sleep well literally and figuratively, try the Hibiscus Hotel, where one-half of the profit from your stay goes to the bird rescue and rehab program at Belize Bird Rescue near Belmopan. **Pros:** central location; good value; a/c and free Wi-Fi. **Cons:** no pool; basic rooms. [$] *Rooms from: BZ$131* ✉ *Hibiscus Plaza, Melhado Parade, Belmopan* ☎ *822/0400* 🌐 *www.hibiscusbelize.com* 🛏 *6 rooms.*

$$$ B&B/INN FAMILY Fodor's Choice ★ **Pook's Hill.** When the lamps are lit each night on the polished rosewood veranda, this low-key, remote jungle lodge is one of the most pleasant places in the Cayo. **Pros:** well-managed jungle lodge in true jungle setting; on doorstep of Actun Tunichil Muknal; bar and dining room are conducive to guest interaction. **Cons:** insects can be a nuisance; with meals and tours lodge is pretty expensive. [$] *Rooms from: BZ$476* ✉ *Pook's Hill, off Mile 52.5, George Price Hwy., Belmopan* ✣ *At Mile 52.5 of George Price Hwy., at Teakettle village, head south on unpaved track for 5 miles (8 km)* ☎ *832/2017* 🌐 *www.pookshillbelize.com* 🛏 *11 cabañas* 🍴 *No meals.*

$ B&B/INN FAMILY Fodor's Choice ★ **Rock Farm Guest House.** British expats opened their large, comfortable home on a 52-acre farm to guests as a way of supporting Belize Bird Rescue, their bird sanctuary and rehab center located on the same grounds. **Pros:** large, comfortable rooms at modest prices; interesting and friendly hosts; proceeds go to bird sanctuary. **Cons:** no a/c; noise from birds not to

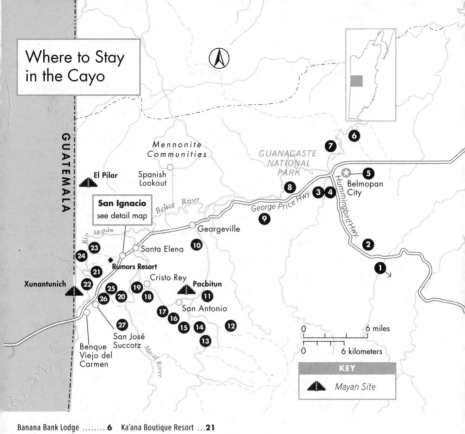

Where to Stay in the Cayo

GUATEMALA

Mennonite Communities

El Pilar

Spanish Lookout

San Ignacio
see detail map

GUANACASTE NATIONAL PARK

Belmopan City

Belize River

George Price Hwy.

Hummingbird Hwy.

Rio Mopan

Georgeville

Santa Elena

Rumors Resort

Xunantunich

Cristo Rey

Pacbitun

San Antonio

Benque Viejo del Carmen

San José Succotz

Macal River

0   6 miles

0   6 kilometers

KEY
⛰ Mayan Site

everyone's liking. $ *Rooms from: BZ$131* ✉ *Roar River Dr., Belmopan* ☎ *610/0400* ⊕ *www.belizebirdrescue.org* ↺ *5 rooms* ⦿ *Some meals.*

$$$$
RESORT
Fodor's Choice
★

⛺ **Sleeping Giant Rainforest Lodge.** This well-run lodge, just off the Hummingbird Highway near the Sibun River, offers luxury in a remote rain-forest setting. **Pros:** air-conditioned luxury accommodations in the foothills of the Maya Mountains; attractive grounds bordered by Sibun River; good food. **Cons:** caters to many groups; expensive. $ *Rooms from: BZ$735* ✉ *Mile 36.5, Hummingbird Hwy., Belmopan* ☎ *786/472–9664 in U.S.* ⊕ *www.sleepinggiantbelize.com* ↺ *20 rooms* ⦿ *No meals.*

$$
B&B/INN
FAMILY

⛺ **Twin Palms B&B.** This unpretentious, pleasant B&B in Belmopan offers affordable, comfortable rooms with televisions, fans, and refrigerators, plus the bonus of two swimming pools. **Pros:** comfortable and friendly; reasonable rates. **Cons:** no a/c. $ *Rooms from: BZ$230* ✉ *8 Trio St., off Hummingbird Hwy., Belmopan* ✛ *From Hummingbird Hwy. at Belmopan look for Uno gas station. Entrance to Trio St. is across highway. Look for Twin Palms sign* ☎ *822/2831* ⊕ *www.belmopanbedandbreakfast.com* ↺ *10 rooms* ⦿ *Breakfast.*

SPORTS AND THE OUTDOORS

Belmopan and San Ignacio offer a similar lineup of outdoor activities, and since they're only about 20 miles (33 km) apart, even if you are staying in San Ignacio you can enjoy the activities near Belmopan.

BIRDING

Although there's good birding in many areas around Belmopan, Pook's Hill Lodge, 5.5 miles (9 km) off the George Price Highway at Mile 52.5, is in a league of its own. The birding list from Pook's Hill includes the Mealy Parrot, Spectacled Owl, Aztec Parakeet, and Keel-billed Toucan.

CANOEING AND KAYAKING

The Belize River, wide and mostly gentle (Class I–II) offers good canoeing and kayaking. It was once used by loggers to transport mahogany to Belize City and hosts the annual La Ruta Maya Mountains to the Sea Canoe Race. The multiday race is held in March during the Baron Bliss holiday. You can also canoe or kayak portions of the Caves Branch River (also Class I–II). Many hotels and lodges arrange canoe or kayak trips, including **Caves Branch Adventure Co. & Jungle Lodge** (*822/2800*), off the Hummingbird Highway. Full-day canoe or kayak trips start at around BZ$120 per person.

CANOPY TOURS

You may feel a little like Tarzan as you dangle 80 feet above the jungle floor, suspended by a harness, moving from one suspended platform to another.

CAVING

The area around Belmopan, with its karst limestone topography, is a paradise for cavers.

Fodor's Choice
★

Actun Tunichil Muknal. The Actun Tunichil Muknal (ATM) cave system runs some 3 miles (5 km) through the limestone of Cayo, just a few miles from Belmopan. ATM is the resting place of the Crystal Maiden, a

Maya girl who was sacrificed here, along with at least 13 others, including seven children, hundreds of years ago. If you visit Actun Tunichil Muknal ("Cave of the Stone Sepulcher" in the Mayan language), you will experience what many say are the most awesome sights in all of Central America. You'll see amazing limestone formations, thousand-year-old human calcified skulls and skeletons, and many Mayan artifacts including well-preserved pottery. As long as you are in adequate physical condition—you have to hike almost an hour, swim in neck-deep water, and clamber through dark, claustrophobic underground chambers—this is sure to be the most memorable tour you'll take in Belize. Cameras are banned from the cave, and the tour is not suitable for young children. ■TIP→ **Although you can drive on your own to the staging area for ATM, you must have a licensed guide to visit it, as you'll be up close and personal with priceless Mayan artifacts.** It's easiest to do an all-day tour from San Ignacio or Belmopan. These tours run around BZ$200–BZ$280, including transportation, lunch, and the government admission fee. ⊠ *Off Mile 52.5, George Price Hwy., road entrance at junction of Price Hwy. and Teakettle Village, Belmopan* ☎ *822/3302 National Institute of Culture & History (NICH)* 🖾 *BZ$50, plus required guide fee.*

Caves Branch Adventure Co. & Jungle Camp. First on the scene was Ian Anderson of Caves Branch Adventure Co. & Jungle Camp. He and his friendly staff of highly trained guides run exhilarating adventure-themed caving, tubing, and hiking trips from an upscale jungle camp just south of Belmopan. They also run day and overnight kayaking trips in the Cayo District. ⊠ *12 miles (19.5 km) south of Belmopan, Mile 42.5, Hummingbird Hwy., Belmopan* ☎ *866/357–2698 toll-free in U.S. and Canada, 610/3451 in Belize* ⊕ *www.cavesbranch.com.*

St. Herman's Blue Hole National Park. At St. Herman's Blue Hole National Park, at Mile 42 of the Hummingbird Highway, there are two large caves, St. Herman's and the Crystal Cave. Both require a guide to explore (guides are available at the national park visitor center), though you can go without a guide into the first 300 yards of St. Herman's. ⊠ *Mile 42, Hummingbird Hwy., Belmopan* ⊕ *www.belizeaudubon.org* 🖾 *BZ$10.*

CAVE TUBING

An activity you'll find in few places outside Belize is cave tubing. You drift down a river, usually the Caves Branch River in the Cayo District, in a large rubber inner tube. At certain points the river goes underground, and you float through eerie underground cave systems, some with Mayan artifacts still in place. The only light is from headlamps.

In the last years since Jaguar Paw Lodge (now no longer operating as a lodge) and Caves Branch Adventure Co. & Jungle Lodge (☎ *673/3454, 866/357–2698* ⊕ *www.cavesbranch.com*) first introduced it, cave tubing has become one of the most popular soft-adventure activities in Belize. It's the number one mainland shore excursion of cruise-ship passengers, and on days when several large ships are docked in Belize City you should expect inner-tube traffic jams.

Caves Branch River has two main entry points: near the former **Jaguar Paw Lodge** (✉ *off Mile 37 of George Price Hwy.*), at **Nohoch Che'en Caves Branch Archeological Reserve**, and near **Caves Branch Adventure Co. & Jungle Lodge** (✉ *off Hummingbird Hwy.* ☎ *822/2800*). The Jaguar Paw access attracts more people, and when several cruise ships are in port at Belize City the river here can be jammed. There's a parking area about 0.5 mile (1 km) from Jaguar Paw, and here you'll find a number of independent tour guides for cave-tubing tours, which vary in length. Cave-tubing trips from Caves Branch Lodge are longer, require more hiking, and cost more.

Cave tubing is subject to changes in the river levels. In the dry season (February–May or June), the river levels are often too low for cave tubing. Also, after heavy rains, the water level in the river may be too high to safely float through caves, so in the rainy season (June–November) cave-tubing trips may occasionally be canceled. Always call ahead to check if tours are operating.

Nohoch Che'en Caves Branch Archeological Reserve. Often still referred to as Jaguar Paw (the name of the jungle lodge formerly at this site), Nohoch Che'en Caves Branch is the most-visited archaeological site in Belize, mainly because of the number of cruise-ship day-trippers who come here. However, that doesn't diminish the grandeur—and just plain fun—you'll experience when you float on inner tubes in the Caves Branch River through caves that the ancient Maya held sacred. Many Belize City, Belmopan, and San Ignacio tour companies offer cave-tubing tours that include transportation, equipment, and a guide. If you have a rental car, you can drive to the park and do cave tubing on your own with a guide for lower cost. The site is at the end of a paved road off Mile 37 of the George Price Highway, and is now quite commercial with a large paved parking lot, changing rooms, concession stands, a bar, and shops. Tour operators at the site provide guides and equipment, and independent guides will also be around to offer tours. Tours start with a 30-minute hike to the cave entrance, and then you float back to a point near the parking lot. Cave tubing is not recommended for young children—some operators have a 12-year-old age requirement. At times during the rainy season, and occasionally during other parts of the year, water may be too high for safe tubing. ✉ *Nohoch Che'en Caves Branch, off Mile 37, George Price Hwy.* ✛ *From Belize City, follow George Price Hwy. to Mile 37. Turn south (left) on paved road and follow about 6 miles (10 km) to Nohoch Che'en Caves Branch Archeological Reserve parking lot* ☎ *226/2882* ⊕ *www.nichbelize.org* ✉ *BZ$30.*

GOLF

Roaring River Golf Course. The only public golf course on the mainland is Roaring River Golf Course. This 9-hole, 1,933-yard, par-32 jungle course (watch out for the crocs in the water traps) with double tees that let you play 3,892 yards at par 64, was the pet project of an expat South African, Paul Martin, who found himself with some extra time and a lot of heavy earth-moving equipment on his hands. Before long, he'd carved out the greens and bunkered fairways. It's not Pebble Beach, but it's fun, and affordable, too, as fees are only BZ$35 for 9 holes or BZ$50 for 18 holes. After a round of golf, you can sip a Belikin at the clubhouse. Roaring River Golf Course also has five air-conditioned cottages for rent, and a restaurant, The Meating Place, for guests and groups, with advance reservations only. ✉ *Off Mile 50.25, George Price Hwy., Roaring River Dr., near Camalote village, Belmopan ✚ Turn south at Camalote village at Mile 50.25 of Price Hwy. and follow signs* ☎ *820/2031* ⊕ *www.belizegolf.net.*

HORSEBACK RIDING

FAMILY **Banana Bank Lodge & Jungle Horseback Adventures.** The largest equestrian operator in this part of Belize is Banana Bank Lodge, off the George Price Highway near Belmopan. Run by John Carr, a former Montana cowboy and rodeo rider, Banana Bank has more than 90 horses, mostly quarter horses, a large round-pen riding arena, stables, and miles of jungle trails on a 4,000-acre ranch. They offer occasional agricultural tours that introduce visiting farmers or others interested in agriculture to Mennonite and other farm operations in Belize. A two-hour ride costs BZ$120, and a four- to five-hour ride is BZ$180. A full-day jungle ride is BZ$200 per person and includes lunch. Night rides and horseback riding packages are also available. ✉ *Banana Bank, Belmopan* ☎ *832/2020* ⊕ *www.bananabank.com.*

SHOPPING

FAMILY **Art Box.** With one of the largest selections of arts and crafts in Belize, Art Box offers handcrafted gift items, books, jewelry, tons of souvenirs, and more. Upstairs is a gallery featuring Belizean artists including Carolyn Carr. ✉ *Mile 46, George Price Hwy., Belmopan* ☎ *623/6129* ⊕ *www. artboxbz.com.*

FAMILY **Farmhouse Deli.** Jungle lodge owner Ian Anderson (he owns Caves Branch Jungle Lodge on the Hummingbird Highway) developed an interest in making cheese, which evolved into opening this New York–style deli and cheese shop in Belmopan. Here you'll find a selection of more than a dozen cheeses that are otherwise rarely available in Belize, along with mostly organic and natural goods including artisanal breads, prepared foods, and sandwiches. ✉ *Rio Grande Ave., Belmopan* ☎ *822/3354.*

SAN IGNACIO AND ENVIRONS

23 miles (37 km) southwest of Belmopan.

When you see the Hawksworth Bridge, built in 1949 and the only public suspension bridge in Belize, you'll know you've arrived at San Ignacio, the hub of the Cayo district. San Ignacio, with its twin town Santa Elena just to the east, is an excellent base for exploring western Belize. Nearby are three Mayan ruins, as well as national parks and a cluster of butterfly farms.

With its well-preserved wooden structures, San Ignacio is a Belizean town where you might want to linger. Evenings are comfortable and usually mosquito-free, and the colonial-era streets are lined with funky bars and restaurants. It's worth coming at sunset to listen to the eerily beautiful sounds of the grackles, the iridescent black birds that seem to like the town.

San Ignacio is less than two hours by car on the George Price Highway from Belize City. Note that coming into San Ignacio can be a little confusing, especially since the main bridge was damaged during Hurricane Earl in August 2016. As you go through the "twin town" of Santa Elena and head into San Ignacio, you'll see the Hawksworth Bridge straight ahead. Normally, this is one-way with east-going traffic only, but until a new bridge opens nearby (most likely sometime in 2017), the one-lane bridge is used for traffic going both east and west, with flag persons alternating car traffic. This has resulted in traffic delays in both directions. Check local news and information before leaving for more information on the progress of the new bridge and how traffic patterns might be affected at the time of your trip.

San Ignacio and the jungle lodges around it are used by many visitors to explore western Belize, which easily takes a week or more if you want to see it all.

EXPLORING

TOP ATTRACTIONS

Most tours to **Actun Tunichil Muknal** leave from San Ignacio, although this amazing cave is actually near Belmopan.

FAMILY

Fodor'sChoice

★

Belize Botanic Gardens. The life's work of Ken duPlooy, an ornithologist who died in 2001, the personable Judy duPlooy, and their family, is the 45-acre Belize Botanic Gardens. It's an extensive collection of hundreds of trees, plants, and flowers from all over Central America. Enlightening tours of the gardens, set on a bank of the Macal River at duPlooy's Jungle Lodge, are given by local guides who can tell you the names of the plants in Mayan, Spanish, and English as well as explain their varied medicinal uses. An orchid house holds the duPlooys' collection of more than 100 orchid species, and there also is a palm exhibit. The lodge offers a shuttle from San Ignacio for BZ$70 per-person, minimum two persons, including admission to the gardens; call ahead to reserve. The Botanic Gardens also run gardening programs for Belize residents as well as great birding opportunities. ⊠ *Big Eddy, Chial Rd.* ✛ *From San Ignacio, head 4.75 miles (7.5 km) west on Benque Rd., turn left on unpaved Chial Rd. and go about 5 miles (8 km) to duPlooy's Jungle Lodge* ☎ *824/3201* ⊕ *www.belizebotanic.org* ☜ *BZ$15 self-guided tour; BZ$30 guided tour.*

FAMILY

Cayo Welcome Center. The largest tourism information center in the country, the BZ$4 million Cayo Welcome Center was established in San Ignacio due to the Cayo's archaeological sites and rain-forest jungle lodges getting an increasing number of visitors. Besides friendly staff who provide information on tours, lodging, restaurants, and sightseeing, the center has exhibits and photos of Mayan artifacts found in San Ignacio, along with contemporary art and cultural displays. Free Wi-Fi is available throughout. Food stalls and a burger restaurant are in or near the center complex, and there is easy access to the pedestrian-only section of Burns Avenue, with its tour guide offices, restaurants, bars, banks, shops, and budget hotels. The center also functions as a community center, with free movies and musical concerts by local bands some nights. ⊠ *Savannah St.* ☎ *623/3918, 800/624–0686 Belize Tourism Board in Belize City* ⊕ *www.travelbelize.org.*

WORTH NOTING

FAMILY **Cahal Pech.** Just at the western edge of San Ignacio, on a tall hill, is a small, intriguing Mayan site, the unfortunately named Cahal Pech ("Place of the Ticks"). You probably won't be bothered by ticks now, however. It was occupied from around 1200 BC to around AD 900. At its peak, in AD 600, Cahal Pech was a medium-size settlement of perhaps 10,000 people with some three dozen structures huddled around seven plazas. It's thought that it functioned as a guard post, watching over the nearby confluence of the Mopan and Macal rivers. It may be somewhat less compelling than the area's other ruins, but it's no less mysterious, given that these structures mark the presence of a civilization we know so little about. Look for answers at the small visitor center and museum. ⊠ *Cahal Pech Hill* ☎ *822/2016 NICH Belize Institute of Archeology* ⊕ *www.nichbelize.org* ▨ *BZ$10.*

FAMILY **Chaa Creek Natural History Centre & Blue Morpho Butterfly Farm.** The Natural History Centre at The Lodge at Chaa Creek has a small library and lots of displays on everything from butterflies to snakes (pickled in jars). Outside is a screened-in blue morpho butterfly-breeding center. If you haven't encountered blue morphos in the wild, you can see them up close here and even peer at their slumbering pupae, which resemble jade earrings. Once you're inside the double doors, the electric blue beauties, which look boringly brown when their wings are closed, flit about or remain perfectly still, sometimes on your shoulder or head, and open and close their wings to a rhythm akin to inhaling and exhaling. Tours are led by a team of naturalists. You can combine a visit here with one to the Belize Medicinal Plants Trail. ⊠ *The Lodge at Chaa Creek, Chial Rd.* ☎ *834/4010 in Belize, 877/709–8708 Chaa Creek* ⊕ *www. chaacreek.com* ▨ *BZ$10 self-guided tour; BZ$20 combined with self-guided Belize Medicinal Plant Trail tour.*

El Pilar. Near the border of Belize and Guatemala, El Pilar is still being excavated under the direction of Anabel Ford, a professor at the University of California at Santa Barbara, and the MesoAmerican Research Center. El Pilar is three times larger than Xunantunich, but because it's at the end of a 7-mile (12 km) rough dirt road, it gets only a few hundred visitors a year. Excavations of Mayan ruins have traditionally concentrated on public buildings, but at El Pilar the emphasis has been on reconstructing domestic architecture—everything from houses to gardens with crops used by the Maya. El Pilar, occupied from 800 BC to AD 1000, at its peak may have had a population of 20,000. Several well-marked trails take you around the site. Because the structures haven't been stripped of vegetation, you may feel as if you're walking through a series of shady orchards. ■ TIP→ **Don't forget binoculars: In the 5,000-acre nature reserve there's terrific bird-watching.** Behind the main plaza, a lookout grants a spectacular view across the jungle to El Pilar's sister city, Pilar Poniente, on the Guatemalan border. There is a visitor center, the Be Pukte Cultural Center of Amigos de El Pilar, in

Bullet Tree Falls (usually open daily 9–5), where you can get information on the site and pay the admission fee. Note that several incidents of robbery have occurred at or near El Pilar. You may want to visit this site on a tour, available from several tour operators in San Ignacio including duPlooy's and Crystal Paradise/Birding in Paradise. ⊠ *7 miles (12 km) northwest of Bullet Tree Falls, off Bullet Tree Rd., Bullet Tree Falls ✥ Take Bullet Tree Rd. in San Ignacio to Bullet Tree Falls. In Bullet Tree Falls, just before bridge over Mopan River on left you will see Be Pukte Cultural Center of Amigos de El Pilar. To go on to El Pilar, you will see signs to El Pilar Rd.* ☎ *822/2106 NICH Institute of Archeology in Belmopan* ⊕ *www.nichbelize.org* ✆ *BZ$10.*

FAMILY   **Belize Medicinal Plants Trail.** Also called the Rainforest Medicine Trail, this trail was originally developed by natural medicine guru Rosita Arvigo and gives you a quick introduction to traditional Mayan medicine. The trail takes you on a short, self-guided walk through the rain forest, giving you a chance to study the symbiotic nature of its plant life. Learn about the healing properties of such indigenous plants as red gumbo-limbo and see some endangered medicinal plants. The shop here sells Mayan medicinal products like Belly Be Good and Flu Away. ⊠ *The Lodge at Chaa Creek, Chial Rd.* ☎ *834/4010 in Belize, 877/709–8708 toll-free number in U.S. and Canada* ⊕ *www.chaacreek.com* ✆ *BZ$10 self-guided tour; BZ$20 guided tour. BZ$20 for self-guided tour including Natural History Centre and Blue Morpho Breeding Center.*

FAMILY   **Spanish Lookout.** The hilltop community of Spanish Lookout, popula-
Fodor's Choice   tion 3,000, about 5 miles (8 km) north of the George Price Highway, is
★   one of the centers of Belize's 11,000-strong Mennonite community, of which nearly 3,000 are in Cayo District. The easiest access to Spanish Lookout is via the paved Route 30 at Mile 57.5 of the Price Highway. The village's blond-haired, fair-skinned residents may seem out of place in this tropical country, but they're responsible for much of the construction, manufacturing, and agriculture in Belize. They built many of Belize's resorts, and most of the chickens, eggs, cheese, and milk you'll consume during your stay come from their farms. Many of the small wooden houses that you see all over Belize are Mennonite prefabs built in Spanish Lookout. In Belize's conservative Mennonite communities, women dress in cotton frocks and head scarves, and the men don straw hats, suspenders, and dark trousers. Some still travel in horse-drawn buggies. However, most Mennonites around Spanish Lookout have embraced pickup trucks and modern farming equipment. The cafés and small shopping centers in Spanish Lookout offer a unique opportunity to mingle with these sometimes world-wary people, but they don't appreciate being gawked at or photographed any more than you do. Stores in Spanish Lookout are modern and well-stocked, the farms wouldn't look out of place in the U.S. Midwest, and many of the roads are paved (the Mennonites do their own road paving). Oil in commercial quantities was discovered in Spanish Lookout in 2005, and several wells are still pumping, although the amount of oil pumped has diminished in recent years. ⊠ *Spanish Lookout.*

FAMILY   **Tropical Wings.** Besides thoughtful displays on the Cayo flora and fauna, Tropical Wings, a little nature center, raises about 20 species of butterfly including the blue morpho, owl, giant swallowtail, and monarch varieties. The facility, at The Trek Stop, also has a small restaurant and gift shop, along with cabins. ✉ *Mile 71.5, George Price Hwy., 6 miles (10 km) west of San Ignacio, San José Succotz* ☎ *823/ 2265* 🌐 *www.thetrekstop.com/tropwings.htm* 🎟 *BZ$10.*

WHERE TO EAT

Besides the restaurants listed here, most of the jungle lodges in the Cayo have their own restaurants. Those at Table Rock Lodge, Mystic River Lodge, The Lodge at Chaa Creek, and duPlooy's Lodge are especially good. Nearer town, the restaurants at Ka'ana Boutique Resort and San Ignacio Resort Hotel also are noteworthy. On the other end of the price scale, street vendors set up barbecue grills and food stalls on the Price Highway just east of the Hawksworth Bridge in Santa Elena, and you can get big plates of food for little money.

5

$$$ ECLECTIC

🍴 **The Crave.** At what might be the smallest restaurant in Cayo, there's room for just one table inside and one outside, but you'll be rewarded with San Ignacio's take on gourmet dining. Choose from a small number of menu options that change daily (steak, pasta, lamb ribs, and pork chops are usually served in some way) selected by the chef/owner and cooked in an open kitchen beside the inside table. Wine is served (but not beer or cocktails). [$] *Average main: BZ$35* ✉ *24 West St.* ☎ *602/0737* 💳 *No credit cards.*

$$ LATIN AMERICAN FAMILY

🍴 **Erva's.** Nothing fancy here, just down-home Belizean dishes at moderate prices, and that's exactly why it's popular. Go for the traditional beans-and-rice dishes or a fish platter; the ceviche is good, too. If you're in the mood for something else, you can get a pizza. It's a couple of blocks off the main drag, so it's quieter and more relaxing here, whether you dine on the veranda or inside in the homey dining room. [$] *Average main: BZ$20* ✉ *4 Far West St.* ☎ *824/2821* 🕒 *Closed Sun.*

$$ ECLECTIC FAMILY Fodor's Choice ★

🍴 **Guava Limb Café.** Located in a remodeled colonial framehouse on the far end of Burns Avenue, Guava Limb Café serves an eclectic mix of delicious soups, seafood, salads, and local and American dishes that have given it a reputation as the best restaurant in San Ignacio. Run by the owners of the Lodge at Chaa Creek, there's open-air seating and a bar on the first level, while a second-level veranda overlooks Macal River Park. You'll enjoy fresh, artful dishes like herb and garlic pan-seared shrimp with butternut squash bisque and jasmine rice, or glazed spare ribs with potato croquettes. [$] *Average main: BZ$26* ✉ *79 Burns Ave.* ☎ *824/4837.*

$ LATIN AMERICAN FAMILY

🍴 **Hode's Place Bar & Grill.** Popular for cold beers, karaoke, and billiards, Hodes is often the busiest place in town. It has a large shaded patio next to a citrus grove, and with swings, slides, and an ice-cream bar (it's much bigger than it looks from the outside). The fried chicken with french fries are some of the best in Cayo. Prices are very reasonable, and there's a full bar. [$] *Average main: BZ$14* ✉ *Savannah St., across from sports stadium* ☎ *804/2522.*

$$
ECLECTIC
FAMILY
Fodor'sChoice
★

✕ **Ko-Ox Han-Nah.** From the Maya language Ko-Ox Han-Nah roughly translates to "let's go eat." It's far from fancy—you eat on simple tables in what is essentially a large open-front building on busy Burns Avenue—but service is cheerful, and the food is inexpensive and well-prepared. Much of the food is raised on the farm of the Zimbabwe-born owner. In addition to the usual Belizean beans-and-rice dishes, Ko-Ox Han-Nah serves fusion food influenced by Mexican, Southeast Asian, and North and South Indian cooking, with salads, sandwiches, burritos, Burmese dishes, Cambodian and Korean chicken dishes, and Indian lamb curries. $ *Average main: BZ$19* ✉ *5 Burns Ave.* ☎ *824/3014.*

$
LATIN AMERICAN
FAMILY

✕ **Pop's Restaurant.** The most popular place for breakfast in San Ignacio is here at Pop's, where it's served all day from 6:30 am to 3 pm. You can get an American full breakfast here, but you can also try a Belizean breakfast such as a cheese and chaya omelet, Belizean bacon, refried beans, and fry jacks. $ *Average main: BZ$14* ✉ *West St., near Waight St.* ☎ *824/3366* ▭ *No credit cards.*

$$
LATIN AMERICAN
FAMILY

✕ **Sanny's Grill.** With sizzling spices, this restaurant transforms basics like chicken or pork chops beyond standard fare. Try the pork in brandy-mustard sauce, the coconut chicken, or the piña colada fish. Eat in the casual dining room or out on the covered deck, with views through the vines and flowers. In a residential area off Benque Road, the place can be hard to find, especially after dark so consider taking a taxi. $ *Average main: BZ$26* ✉ *E. 23rd St.* ☎ *824/2988* ☾ *No lunch.*

WHERE TO STAY

SAN IGNACIO

Hotels in downtown San Ignacio are all budget-to-moderate spots. On the western edge of town, with hotels such as the San Ignacio Resort Hotel and Ka'ana, lodgings become more upscale. The lodges along the Mopan River, a river that winds into Belize from Guatemala, tend to be in the budget-to-moderate range. Most lodges on the Macal River, such as The Lodge at Chaa Creek and duPlooy's Lodge, are upmarket, though there are some exceptions. A number of lodges, including Mystic River, Inn the Bush, Table Rock, and Mariposa have opened on the Cristo Rey Road en route to the Mountain Pine Ridge, most also with access to the Macal River.

$
HOTEL
FAMILY

▦ **Aguada Hotel & Restaurant.** Frugal travelers jump at the opportunity to stay in this tidy, attractive, and inexpensive hotel with air-conditioned rooms and saltwater swimming pool in Santa Elena, the low-key town adjoining San Ignacio. **Pros:** clean, inexpensive rooms with a/c; one of the few budget hotels with a pool. **Cons:** a bus or short taxi ride away from downtown San Ignacio; traffic near the hotel may increase when the new San Ignacio bridge opens. $ *Rooms from: BZ$90* ✉ *La Loma Luz area, off George Price Hwy. across from La Loma Luz hospital, Santa Elena* ☎ *804/3609* ⊕ *www.aguadabelize. com* ⇥ *25 rooms* ⦿⏐ *No meals.*

$$$
B&B/INN

▦ **Amber Sunset Jungle Resort.** Owned by a family originally from Belize City, this jungle resort makes a real effort to show the diversity of Belize; the five cabañas, built into the jungle canopy, are each decorated

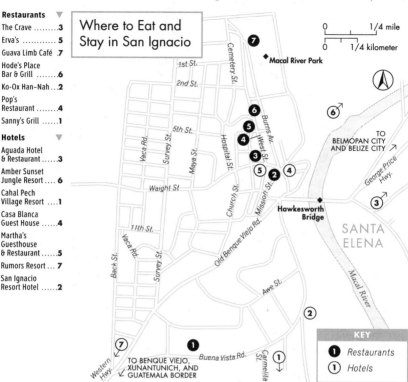

Where to Eat and Stay in San Ignacio

0 _____ 1/4 mile

0 _____ 1/4 kilometer

◆ **Macal River Park**

1st St.

2nd St.

Cemetery St.

5th St.

Burns Av.

West St.

Hospital St.

Maya St.

Survey St.

Vaca Rd.

Waight St

Church St.

Mission St.

Old Benque Viejo Rd.

11th St.

Back St.

Survey St.

Vaca Rd.

Awe St.

TO
BELMOPAN CITY
AND BELIZE CITY ↗

George Price Hwy.

**Hawkesworth
Bridge**

SANTA
ELENA

Macal River

Buena Vista Rd.

Carmelita St.

Western Hwy.

TO BENQUE VIEJO,
XUNANTUNICH, AND
GUATEMALA BORDER

KEY

❶ *Restaurants*

① *Hotels*

5

to reflect one of Belize's major population groups (Creoles, Mestizos, Maya, Garifuna, and the Mennonites). **Pros:** unique theme focusing on diversity; nice swimming pool. **Cons:** no a/c; steep climbs required to reach cabañas and restaurant. Ⓢ *Rooms from: BZ$382 ⊠ Mile 59, George Price Hwy.* ☎ *824/3141 ⊕ www.ambersunsetbelize.com ⇌ 5 cabañas* ⦿ *No meals.*

$$
RESORT
▦ **Cahal Pech Village Resort.** Once you make it up the steep hill, you'll enjoy the best views in Cayo at this hotel at the western edge of San Ignacio, near the Cahal Pech Mayan site. **Pros:** great views; enticing pool; good value. **Cons:** some rooms and cabañas need upgrading; limestone dirt road up to hotel is very steep, especially if you're walking. Ⓢ *Rooms from: BZ$245 ⊠ 1 mile (2 km) west of town, off George Price Hwy., Cahal Pech Rd., Cahal Pech Hill* ☎ *824/3740, 239/494–3281 in U.S.* ⊕ *www.cahalpech.com ⇌ 56 rooms* ⦿ *Breakfast.*

$
HOTEL
▦ **Casa Blanca Guest House.** Though it's in the center of San Ignacio, on bustling Burns Avenue, this small hotel is an oasis of peace and one of Belize's top budget choices. **Pros:** central downtown location; clean and simple rooms; good value. **Cons:** limited parking nearby. Ⓢ *Rooms from: BZ$45 ⊠ 10 Burns Ave.* ☎ *824/2080 ⊕ www.casablancaguesthouse.com ⇌ 9 rooms* ⦿ *No meals.*

$ ⬛ **Martha's Guesthouse and Restaurant.** With clean rooms, a good restau-
B&B/INN   rant, and convenient tours, the four-story Martha's Guesthouse pro-
FAMILY   vides just about everything you need right in the heart of downtown San
Ignacio. **Pros:** handy downtown location; tasty food on-site. **Cons:** can
be noisy; rates are higher than most other downtown hotels. $ *Rooms
from: BZ$142* ✉ *10 West St.* ☎ *804/3647* ⊕ *www.marthasbelize.com*
🛏 *16 rooms* ⦿ *No meals.*

$ ⬛ **Rumors Resort.** This roadside hotel just west of San Ignacio provides
HOTEL   a pool, an affordable restaurant and bar, and a convenient location, all
at moderate prices. **Pros:** easy access to San Ignacio without the parking and traffic; pleasant rooms with a/c and Wi-Fi. **Cons:** some standard rooms could use upgrades. $ *Rooms from: BZ$196* ✉ *Mile 68,
George Price Hwy., about 3 miles (5 km) west of downtown San Ignacio* ☎ *824/2795* ⊕ *www.rumorsresort.com* 🛏 *11 rooms* ⦿ *No meals.*

$$$$ ⬛ **San Ignacio Resort Hotel.** Queen Elizabeth II once stayed at this resort
RESORT   with comfortable if not "royal" rooms that have verandas facing a
Fodor's Choice   lovely hillside. **Pros:** safe, comfortable choice at the edge of town; good
★   restaurant and bar. **Cons:** a little pricey for what you get. $ *Rooms
from: BZ$571* ✉ *18 Buena Vista Rd.* ☎ *824/2034, 855/488–2624 toll-
free in U.S. and Canada* ⊕ *www.sanignaciobelize.com* 🛏 *26 rooms*
⦿ *No meals.*

ALONG THE MOPAN RIVER

$ ⬛ **Clarissa Falls Resort.** The low gurgle of nearby Mopan River rapids is
RESORT   the first and last sound of the day at Clarissa Falls Resort. **Pros:** quiet,
FAMILY   pastoral riverside setting; good food; very friendly and welcoming owners. **Cons:** resort is on a ranch and not in a true jungle setting. $ *Rooms
from: BZ$164* ✉ *Mile 70, George Price Hwy., 5.5 miles (9 km) west of
San Ignacio* ☎ *833/3116* ⊕ *www.clarissafallsresort.com* 🛏 *11 cabañas,
1 bunkhouse with 10 beds* ⦿ *Some meals.*

$$$$ ⬛ **Ka'ana Boutique Resort.** Ka'ana brings a level of luxury to San Igna-
RESORT   cio with tranquil gardens, a wine cellar, and spacious rooms outfitted
with 500-count cotton sheets, high-end toiletries, and flat-screen TVs.
Pros: convivial staff; luxury amenities; good bar and restaurant. **Cons:**
not a true jungle lodge; pricey. $ *Rooms from: BZ$675* ✉ *Mile 69.25,
George Price Hwy.* ☎ *824/3350 in Belize, 866/494–2807 toll-free in
U.S.* ⊕ *www.kaanabelize.com* 🛏 *15 rooms* ⦿ *No meals.*

$$$$ ⬛ **Mahogany Hall Boutique Resort.** An upmarket alternative to fancy jun-
HOTEL   gle lodges is this resort in Bullet Tree Falls, on the banks of the Mopan
River. **Pros:** gorgeous suites; lovely views of the Mopan River. **Cons:**
somewhat unusual location—neither a jungle lodge nor in-town hotel;
steep stairs with no handrails and no elevator. $ *Rooms from: BZ$535*
✉ *Paslow Falls Rd., Bullet Tree Falls* ⤡ *From east, turn left off Bullet
Tree Rd. just before bridge over Mopan River* ☎ *622/4325, 800/610–
9821* ⊕ *www.mahoganyhallbelize.com* 🛏 *8 rooms* ⦿ *No meals.*

$ ⬛ **Parrot Nest.** If ever since you were a kid you've wanted to sleep in a
HOTEL   tree house by a river, this is your chance. **Pros:** rustic but cute cabañas
and tree houses; good value; helpful and friendly owners. **Cons:** not
truly in the jungle; cabañas are small. $ *Rooms from: BZ$109* ✉ *Off
Bullet Tree Rd., on Mopan River, Bullet Tree Falls* ☎ *669/6068* ⊕ *www.
parrot-nest.com* 🛏 *7 cabañas, 2 treehouses* ⦿ *No meals.*

ALONG THE MACAL RIVER

$$ RESORT FAMILY Fodor's Choice ★ **Black Rock River Lodge.** Some 800 feet above limestone cliffs and the Macal River gorge, across from Elijio Panti National Park, Black Rock Lodge has one of the most beautiful settings of any lodge in the country. **Pros:** remote, gorgeous setting; eco-conscious management. **Cons:** isolated setting means you're stuck here for somewhat pricey meals and tours. [$] *Rooms from: BZ$262* ✉ *On Macal River, 13 miles (22 km) upriver from San Ignacio* ☎ *834/4038* 🌐 *www.blackrocklodge.com* 🛏 *20 rooms* 🍴 *No meals.*

$$$ RESORT FAMILY **duPlooy's Lodge.** High above a bend in the Macal River is this remarkable, relaxing lodge whose grounds include the 45-acre Belize Botanic Gardens. **Pros:** botanic gardens on-site; first-rate birding; eco-conscious management. **Cons:** costs for meals, transfers, and tours all add up. [$] *Rooms from: BZ$488* ✉ *Chial Rd.* ✥ *From San Ignacio head 4.75 miles (7.5 km) west on George Price Hwy., turn left on Chial Rd., and go about almost 5 miles (8 km) to duPlooy's* ☎ *824/3101 in Belize, 512/243–5285 in U.S.* 🌐 *www.duplooys.com* 🛏 *14 rooms* 🍴 *Breakfast.*

$$$$ RESORT FAMILY Fodor's Choice ★ **The Lodge at Chaa Creek.** This was the first true jungle lodge in the Cayo, and owners Mick and Lucy Fleming (he's from England, she's from the United States) have spent more than three decades polishing The Lodge at Chaa Creek to a fine, rich patina, while adding features like a gorgeous bi-level swimming pool. **Pros:** stunningly landscaped grounds; excellent staff and service; green and socially conscious owners. **Cons:** lodging, meal, and tour prices may strain your budget. [$] *Rooms from: BZ$798* ✉ *Chaa Creek Rd., off Chial Rd.* ✥ *From San Ignacio go 4.75 miles (7.5 km) west on Benque Rd., aka George Price Hwy., turn left on Chial Rd. and go about 4.5 miles (7 km). Follow signs to Chaa Creek* ☎ *824/2037 local reservations, 877/709–8708 toll-free in U.S. and Canada* 🌐 *www.chaacreek.com* 🛏 *37 rooms* 🍴 *Breakfast.*

SPORTS AND THE OUTDOORS

San Ignacio is the center for touring in western Belize. Just walk along busy Burns Avenue and you'll see signs for all kinds of tours and find the offices of several tour operators. Individual tour guides, who by law must be Belizean citizens and be licensed by the government, may work for tour operators, for a lodge or hotel, or they may freelance on their own. Some hang out at restaurants in town, especially those on Burns Avenue, and post notices at bulletin boards in downtown hotels and restaurants. PACZ Tours, Mayan Heart World, and others have offices downtown. You can compare prices and sign up for the next day's tours. Obviously, the more layers of costs involved, the higher the price for you, but on the other hand larger operators and hotel tour companies have more resources, and they have their long-term reputations to protect, so they may be more reliable. Tours from lodges usually are more costly than if booked with an independent tour operator. Also, some lodges try to sell packages of tours rather than individual ones.

Most jungle lodges offer a full range of day trips, using either their own guides or working with independent guides and tour companies. The largest lodge-affiliated tour operation is Chaa Creek Expeditions, but

Black Rock Lodge, Crystal Paradise, duPlooy's, Cahal Pech Village, San Ignacio Resort Hotel, and other hotels and lodges also do many tours and trips.

If you have a rental car, you can visit all of the Mayan sites in the Cayo on your own, along with other attractions such as the butterfly farms, the Belize Botanic Gardens, Medicinal Plants Trail, and many of the attractions in the Mountain Pine Ridge. However, for most caving tours, notably Actun Tunichil Muknal, you'll need a guide, and for canoe and kayak trips, you'll need drop-off and pickup. Local guides also are critical for nature hikes and birding trips, as many of these guides have remarkable local knowledge and ability to spot things you probably wouldn't see otherwise.

BIRDING

The area around San Ignacio is good for birding because it contains such a variety of habitats—river valleys, foothills, lagoons, agricultural areas, and broadleaf jungle—each of which attracts different types of birds. For example, Aguacate Lagoon near Spanish Lookout attracts waterbirds such as night herons, neotropic cormorants, and whistling ducks. Open land and pastures are good for spotting laughing falcons, vermillion flycatchers, eastern meadowlarks, and white-tailed kites.

There's good birding on the grounds of most of the lodges along the Mopan and Macal rivers, including **Chaa Creek, duPlooy's, Crystal Paradise,** and **Clarissa Falls.** In addition, local guides and tour companies run birding trips.

FAMILY **Paradise Expeditions.** Based in Cayo and connected with Crystal Paradise Lodge, Paradise Expeditions is a family operation with decades of experience in Cayo. The Tut family group has five- to 11-night birding trips to various parts of Belize, starting at BZ$2,500 per person for a five-night, six-day birding trip in Central Belize, and ranging up to around BZ$3,000 per person for a 12-day, 11-night expedition that covers much of the country. ⊠ *Cristo Rey Rd.* ☎ *610/5593* ⊕ *www. birdinginbelize.com.*

CANOEING AND KAYAKING

The Cayo's rivers, especially the Mopan and Macal, make it an excellent place for canoeing and kayaking. Most of the larger resorts, like **Chaa Creek** and **duPlooy's,** have canoes or inflatable kayaks. Generally you put in the Macal and paddle and float down to the Hawksworth Bridge at San Ignacio, a trip that takes two or three hours depending on your starting point. You'll pay about BZ$50 to BZ$75 per person for canoe rental and pickup. You'll see iguanas and birdlife on the banks, and if you dip in for a swim, don't be surprised if tiny (toothless) fish school around you to figure out whether you're food.

Do exercise caution. You won't believe how fast the rivers, especially the Macal, can rise after a heavy rain. Following rains in the Mountain Pine Ridge, it can reach a dangerous flood stage in just a few minutes. Also, in the past there have been a few rare incidents of visitors in canoes being stopped and robbed on the Macal. Watch weather forecasts, and ask locally about safety on the rivers.

CAVING

Fodor's Choice ★ Over the millennia, as dozens of swift-flowing rivers bored through the soft limestone, the Maya Mountains became pitted with miles of caves. The Maya used them as burial sites, and, according to one theory, as subterranean waterways that linked the Cayo with communities as far north as the Yucatán. Previously, the caves fell into a 1,000-year slumber, disturbed only by the nightly flutter of bats. In recent years, the caves have been rediscovered by spelunkers.

Belize Magnificent Mayan Tours. Operated by Albert Williams and his family, Belize Magnificent Mayan Tours (usually known as BZM) has a large variety of caving tours in Cayo, including day trips to ATM, Barton Creek Cave, Crystal Cave, and Chechem Ha. It also does trips to the Chiquibul, Mountain Pine Ridge, and other destinations. ⊠ *16 B. San José Succotz, San José Succotz* ☎ *621/0312* ⊕ *www.bzmtours.com.*

Fodor's Choice ★ **PACZ Tours.** Arguably the top Actun Tunichil Muknal tour operator, PACZ has been operated by Emilo Awe since 1998, with a sizeable group of tour guides. The ATM tour costs around BZ$220 from downtown San Ignacio, including lunch and admission. PACZ also does a Barton Cave trip, for BZ$170. You can meet the PACZ tour guides at the office on Burns Avenue, or they will pick you up at hotels around San Ignacio. ⊠ *30 Burns Ave.* ☎ *824/0536* ⊕ *www.pacztours.net.*

HIKING

Most of the lodges have hiking trails. **Black Rock River Lodge, Chaa Creek, Table Rock,** and **duPlooy's** all have especially good areas for hiking. If you want even more wide-open spaces, head to the Mountain Pine Ridge, which offers hundreds of miles of hiking trails, mostly old logging roads. For more adventurous hikes and overnight treks, you'll want to go with a guide.

Maya Guide Adventures. Marcos Cucul and son Francis, who run Maya Guide Adventures, are Ket'chi Mayans who are trained in cave and wilderness rescue. They can take you on day adventures, overnight caving, canoeing, and kayaking trips, or guide you in Elijio Panti National Park or other national parks and reserves. Overnight trips start at around BZ$700 per person, depending on length and number of people. ⊠ *Yaxche Jungle Camp, Belmopan* ☎ *600/3116* ⊕ *www.mayaguide.bz.*

HORSEBACK RIDING

The Lodge at Chaa Creek. With its stable of well-cared-for riding horses, the Lodge at Chaa creek offers two- to three-hour guided horseback trips, with morning or afternoon options. The trips cost BZ$90 per person, and rides cover about 5 miles (8 km). ⊠ *Chaa Creek Stables, Chaa Creek Rd., off Chial Rd.* ☎ *834/4010 in Belize, 877/709–8708 toll-free in U.S. and Canada* ⊕ *www.chaacreek.com.*

Mountain Equestrian Trails. When it comes to horseback-riding adventures, whether on the old logging roads of the Mountain Pine Ridge or on trails in the Slate Creek Preserve, the local experts are found at Mountain Equestrian Trails. Five-night riding packages including accommodations, meals, and daily rides are around BZ$5,500 for two people in-season. Day rides also are offered for around BZ$180 per person. ⊠ *Mile 8, Mountain Pine Ridge Rd.* ☎ *669/1124 in Belize, 800/838–3918 toll-free in U.S.* ⊕ *www.metbelize.com.*

SHOPPING

Creek Art Walter Castillo Home Art Gallery. Noted artist Walter Castillo, a San Pedro native, has moved his gallery workshop from Bullet Tree Falls. His highly collectible paintings are among the best known contemporary works on Belizean life. Call ahead for directions to the gallery and to arrange a time to visit. ⊠ *Walter St., Bullet Tree Falls* ☎ *670/4351* ⊕ *www.waltercastilloart.com.*

Fodor'sChoice ★   **Orange Gallery.** This has one of the best selections of Belizean and Guatemalan crafts in Belize. It has an especially good selection of wood items from tropical hardwoods, including bowls, small pieces of furniture, and carvings. There's also a small restaurant and guesthouse here. ⊠ *Mile 60, George Price Hwy., east of San Ignacio* ☎ *824/3296* ⊕ *www.orangegifts.com.*

FAMILY
Fodor'sChoice ★   **San Ignacio Market.** On Saturday morning, San Ignacio Market comes alive with farmers selling local fruits and vegetables. Vendors also hawk crafts, clothing, and household goods. Some vendors show up on other days as well, but Saturday has by far the largest market. A smaller vegetable and fruit market is open weekdays near Burns Avenue, closer to town. ⊠ *Savannah St., across from soccer stadium.*

BENQUE VIEJO

7 miles (11 km) southwest of San Ignacio

Old Bank, or Benque Viejo in Spanish, is the last town in Belize before you reach Guatemala. Modest in size and population (about 9,000), Benque is low-key in other ways, too, but the little House of Culture is worth a short stop, and neighboring San José Succotz village is home to the Xunantunich Mayan site. The Poustinia Land Art Park is perhaps the most unusual element of Belize's art scene.

EXPLORING

TOP ATTRACTIONS

FAMILY   **Xunantunich.** One of the most accessible Mayan sites in Belize, Xunantunich, *(pronounced shoo-nan-too-nitch),* is located on a hilltop site above the Mopan River west of San Ignacio. You take a hand-pulled ferry across the river (it carries pedestrians and up to four vehicles), near the village of San José Succotz. The ferry is free, but tip the operator a Belizean dollar or two if you wish. Tour guides offer their services as you board the ferry, but you do not need a guide to see the ruins. After crossing the Mopan on the ferry, drive or hike about a mile to the visitor center and the ruins. Although settlement of Xunantunich occurred much earlier, the excavated structures here, in six plazas with about two dozen buildings, date from 200 to 900 A.D. El Castillo, the massive 120-foot-high main pyramid and still the second-tallest structure in Belize after Caana at Caracol, was built on a leveled hilltop. The pyramid, which you can climb if you have the energy, has a spectacular 360-degree panorama of the Mopan River valley into Guatemala. On the eastern wall is a reproduction of one of the finest Mayan sculptures in Belize, a frieze decorated with jaguar heads, human faces, and abstract geometric patterns telling the story of the Moon's affair with Morning Light. ⊠ *Near San José Succotz Village, 6.5 miles (11 km) southwest of San Ignacio, George Price Hwy. (Benque Rd.), San José Succotz* 🕾 *822/2106* ⊕ *www.nichbelize.org* 🖃 *BZ$10.*

WORTH NOTING

Actun Chechem Ha. On private land, Actun Chechem Ha, which means "Cave of the Poisonwood Water," is a Mayan burial cave with artifacts that date back three millennia. There are many pots and a stela used for ceremonial purposes. This cave may have the largest collection of Mayan pottery in one place anywhere in Belize, possibly the world. To examine the pottery, you'll have to climb ladders, and getting to the cave requires a 35- to 45-minute walk, mostly uphill. The cave is on private property, and the landowner's family sometimes gives tours. Tour companies, with registered guides, also visit here from San Ignacio and Belmopan, charging from BZ$150 per person. ■ TIP➜ **Belize Magnificent Tours in San Ignacio, which charges BZ$190 per person, is one recommended tour company for this trip.** Due to the hike to the cave entrance and climbing in the cave, you need to be reasonably physically fit to visit Chechem Ha. ⊠ *10 miles (17 km) south of Benque Viejo, Mile 7, Hydro Rd., near Vaca Falls, Benque Viejo del Carmen* 🕾 *653/0799* 🖃 *Tours to Chechem Ha including transportation from San Ignacio or your lodge, lunch, admission fee, and sometimes swimming at Vaca Falls are around BZ$150–BZ$200 per person.*

Benque House of Culture. The mission of Benque House of Culture, one of the government-sponsored houses of culture in Belize (others are in Belize City, Orange Walk Town, Corozal Town, San Pedro, and San Ignacio/Santa Elena), is "promoting beauty and goodness." Housed in the former Benque police station, this little museum (and we do mean *little*) has displays on the history of Benque Viejo, and also offers classes for local schoolchildren and their teachers. There is also a large rosewood and mahogany marimba (a xylophone-like musical instrument) on display. ⊠ *64 Joseph St., 7 miles (11.5 km) west of San Ignacio, Benque Viejo del Carmen* 🕾 *823/2697* ⊕ *www.nich.org* 🖃 *By donation.*

Poustinia Land Art Park. One of the most unusual and least-known attractions in Belize, Poustinia Land Art Park is a collection of about 30 original works by artists from a dozen countries, including Belize, Norway, Guayana, Brazil, Guatemala, and England, scattered about some 60 acres of a former cattle ranch. It's owned by an architect, who calls Poustinia an "environmental project." Among the works of outdoor art, which some would call funky and others fascinating, are "Downtown," by Venezuelan artist Manuel Piney, and "Returned Parquet," a reference to Belize's colonial history in mahogany parquet flooring by Tim Davies, a British artist. Nature is taking over the art works, which apparently is part of the plan. Getting around the park, which is open by appointment only, requires sometimes strenuous hiking; bring insect repellent. Make arrangements to visit the park and for a tour guide at the Benque House of Culture in Benque Viejo. ✉ *2.5 miles (5 km) south of Benque Viejo, 8 miles (13 km) southwest of San Ignacio, Mile 2.5, Hydro Rd., Benque Viejo del Carmen* ☎ *823/269 Benque House of Culture* 🎟 *BZ$20.*

WHERE TO EAT

$ LATIN AMERICAN Fodor's Choice ★ 🍴 **Benny's Kitchen.** This little open-air restaurant near Xunantunich has won many fans who come for hearty Mayan, Mestizo, and Creole dishes at rock-bottom prices. You'll find mostly locals here, many from San Ignacio, Benque Viejo, and other parts of Cayo District. Most items on the menu are BZ$12 or less, including *chilimole* (chicken with mole sauce), cow-foot soup, Belizean *escabeche*, and stew pork with rice, beans, and plantains. You can make a meal of the Mestizo appetizers including *salbutes,* tostadas, and empanadas, most under BZ$2 each. The classic Mayan *pibil* (pork cooked in an underground oven) is sometimes on the menu. The banana and mango *licuados* (milk shakes) are delicious, and you can also enjoy the official national drinks of Belize, Belikin and Fanta. [$] *Average main: BZ$10* ✉ *Across Benque Rd., (George Price Hwy.) from ferry to Xunantunich, San José Succotz* ✣ *Turn south just west of Xunantunich ferry and follow signs about 3 blocks* ☎ *823/2541.*

WHERE TO STAY

$ RENTAL 🏨 **The Trek Stop.** After a day spent out and about, a cold Belikin and filling Mexican and Belizean dishes await you at this cluster of neat-as-a-pin cabins on a hilltop near Xunantunich ruins. **Pros:** top value for the money; friendly local management. **Cons:** just a couple of steps up from camping; location means you'll have to take a bus or taxi to most sights, except Xunantunich. [$] *Rooms from: BZ$52* ✉ *6 miles (9 km) west of San Ignacio, George Price Hwy. (aka Benque Rd.), near Xunantunich, San José Succotz* ☎ *823/2265* 🌐 *www.thetrekstop.com* 🛏 *9 cabins, 7 with shared bath* 🍽 *No meals.*

MOUNTAIN PINE RIDGE

17 miles (27 km) south of San Ignacio.

The best way to describe Mountain Pine Ridge is to paraphrase Winston Churchill: it's a puzzle wrapped in an enigma. Instead of the tropical vegetation you'd expect to find, two-thirds of this large reserve is pine forest, mainly Honduras pines. Most pines are young, due to losses from wildfires and beetle infestations. Old logging roads cut through red clay, giving the region an uncanny resemblance to northern Georgia in the United States. Sinkholes, caves, and waterfalls are common in limestone areas. With elevations up to 3,335 feet, winter temperatures can drop into decidedly untropical low 40s, yet exotic wildlife abound, including orange-breasted falcons, toucans, tapirs, jaguars, and crocodiles. It's widely considered the best place in Belize to see waterfalls and to go mountain biking.

GETTING HERE AND AROUND

From the George Price Highway, there are two routes into the Mountain Pine Ridge, both just east of San Ignacio: the Mountain Pine Ridge Road (also sometimes called the Chiquibul Road or the Georgeville Road), at Georgeville at Mile 61.6 of the George Price Highway; and the Cristo Rey Road, with the turnoff at Mile 66.5 of the George Price Highway. From the George Price Highway, the entrance to the Mountain Pine Ridge is 10.2 miles (17 km) via the Mountain Pine Ridge Road and 14.8 miles (25 km) via the Cristo Rey Road. Note that Cristo Rey Road is now partly paved, and even the nonpaved portions are well-maintained, while the Georgeville Road is often filled with ruts and limestone shards that can easily cause a flat tire.

Heading southeast from San Ignacio on the Cristo Rey Road, a little beyond San Antonio, the Cristo Rey Road meets the Mountain Pine Ridge Road coming from Georgeville. Turn right to go into the Mountain Pine Ridge. After 2.5 miles (4 km) a guard at a gatehouse will record your name, destination, and license-plate number. The main road through the Mountain Pine Ridge is a mostly dirt road that can become almost impassable after heavy rains, but is otherwise a decent road without the bumps that plague many other backroads in Cayo.

There is no public bus transportation into the Mountain Pine Ridge. Charter flights by Javier's Flying Service and Tropic Air can fly into private airstrips at Blancaneaux Lodge and Hidden Valley Inn. Tour operators in San Ignacio offer day trips to the Pine Ridge and also to Caracol in the Chiqibul.

Entrance into the Mountain Pine Ridge is free, though there is a nominal charge collected if you go to the viewing area for Thousand Foot Falls.

Contacts Javier's Flying Service. ⊠ *Central Farm Airstrip, Central Farm, San Ignacio* ☏ *824/0460* ⊕ *www.javiersflyingservice.com.* **Tropic Air.** ☏ *226/2626 reservations in Belize, 800/422–3435 toll-free in U.S. and Canada* ⊕ *www. tropicair.com.*

TIMING

You could spend a week or longer exploring the streams, waterfalls, and distant trails of the Mountain Pine Ridge.

SAFETY AND PRECAUTIONS

The Mountain Pine Ridge is a remote and lightly populated area. Occasionally, bandits have taken advantage of this to stop and rob visitors, and some Guatemalan squatters have tried to move across the border in search of free land, prompting run-ins with Belize authorities. Guatemalan *xateros,* hunters for the prized xate palm, also are a problem in parts of the area. Currently, Belize Defence Forces soldiers accompany vehicles to Caracol. If you drive on your own to Caracol, it is at your own risk. However, the main danger to most visitors is not bandits but getting sunburned on a hiking trail or old logging road.

EXPLORING

TOP ATTRACTIONS

FAMILY   **Green Hills Butterfly Ranch and Botanical Collections.** The largest and the best of Belize's butterfly farms open to the public, Green Hills has about 30 native species in a huge flight area on display at any given time. Jan Meerman, who has published a book on Belize's butterflies and moths, runs the place with Dutch partner Tineke Boomsma and other staff, who speak a variety of English, Spanish, Dutch, Yucatec Maya, and Creole. On the 100-acre grounds there are also many flowers, including passion flowers, bromeliads, heliconias, and orchids. Birding is good here as well, with more than 300 speciies sighted in the area. Bring lunch and eat it in the Green Hills picnic area. ⊠ *Mile 8, Mountain Pine Ridge Rd. (aka Chiquibul Rd., aka Georgeville Rd.), El Progresso/7 Mile* ☎ *834/4017* ⊕ *www.green-hills.net* ⊠ *Guided tour BZ$25.*

Mountain Pine Ridge Forest Reserve. This reserve is a highlight of any journey to Belize and an adventure to explore, although the scenery may remind you more of the piney woods of the far southern Appalachians than of tropical jungle. The Mountain Pine Ridge Forest Reserve is in the high country of Belize—low mountains and rolling hills are covered in part by vast pine forests and crisscrossed with old logging roads. Waterfalls and streams abound, and there are accessible caves, such as Rio Frio. The higher elevations, up to near 3,400 feet, provide cooler temperatures and outstanding views. The best way to see this area, which covers more than 106,000 acres, is on a mountain bike, a horse, or your own feet. It's also not a bad ride from an SUV, which you'll need to get you through the Pine Ridge to the Chiquibul wilderness and the magnificent ruins of Caracol. Aside from the Honduras pines, 80% of which were damaged in recent years by the Southern pine beetle but are now recovering, you'll see lilac-color mimosa, Saint-John's-wort, and occasionally a garish red flower appropriately known as hotlips. Look for the craboo, a wild tree whose berries are used in a brandylike liqueur believed to have aphrodisiac properties (the fruit ripens June through August). Birds love this fruit, so any craboo is a good place to spot orioles and woodpeckers. You may not see them, but the Pine Ridge is home to many of Belize's large mammals, including tapirs, cougars, jaguars, and ocelots, and in the streams are a few Morelet's crocodiles. ⊠ *Mountain Pine Ridge, San Antonio Village.*

WORTH NOTING

FAMILY   **Barton Creek Cave and Archeological Reserve.** This wet cave, now a part of the Barton Creek Archeological Reserve in a remote area off the Mountain Pine Ridge Road, offers a canoeing adventure in Xibalba (the Mayan underworld.) You'll float through about a mile of a long underground chamber—the cave is nearly 5 miles (8 km) long and parts have never been completely explored. You'll see Mayan ceramics along with ancient calcified skeletal remains and skulls. You can go on a tour from San Ignacio or from your lodge. PACZ Tours, for example, offers a six-hour tour, including lunch and admission to the cave, for BZ$170 plus tax per person, and Chaa Creek offers a half-day tour for one to four persons for BZ$310 plus BZ$50 per person for park admission and equipment plus tax. You can also drive to the cave yourself, rent a boat and gear, and hire a guide near the cave. Getting to the cave is an adventure in itself, requiring a long drive on rough roads. Parts of the road and the cave itself may be inaccessible after hard rains. Be careful in the cave; it's best to tour with a reputable tour company with an experienced tour guide and reliable, well-maintained equipment such as float vests. ⊠ *Barton Creek Cave* ✛ *Turn at Mile 62 of George Price Hwy. (formerly Western Hwy.) onto Mountain Pine Ridge Rd. aka Georgeville Rd. or Chiquibul Rd. Go about 3 miles (5 km) and, at Cool Shade, turn left. Go 4 miles (6.4 km) on a rough, unpaved road through Lower Barton Creek Mennonite community to Upper Barton Creek and cave. Watch for signs for Barton Creek Outpost, Mike's Place, and cave* ☎ *822/2106 Institute of Archeology* ⊕ *www.nichbelize.org* ✉ *BZ$10.*

Noj K'a'ax Meen Elijio Panti National Park. Named after the famed Guatemala-born herbal healer who died in 1996 at the age of 106, Elijio Panti National Park was a 2001 addition to Belize's extensive national parks system. It spans about 13,000 to 16,000 acres (the exact area is undetermined) around the villages of San Antonio, Cristo Rey, and El Progreso and along the Macal River. In the park are Sakt'aj waterfalls and two dry caves known as Offering and Cormorant. The hope is that with no hunting in this park, more birds and wildlife will return to western Belize. Development of the park has been slowed by differing perspectives among those in San Antonio village, including Maria Garcia (a relative of Elijio Panti) of the Itzamna Society, various departments of the government of Belize, and other parties. Even today, there is no one official website for the park. Currently you must be accompanied by a licensed tour guide to enter the park. For information on the park and how to visit it, check with tour guides in San Ignacio or San Antonio. ⊠ *Off Cristo Rey Rd., San Antonio Village* ⊕ *www.epnp.org* ✉ *BZ$10.*

Thousand Foot Falls (*Hidden Valley Falls*). Inside the Mountain Pine Ridge Forest Reserve, Thousand Foot Falls actually drops nearly 1,600 feet, making it the highest waterfall in Central America. A thin plume of spray plummets over the edge of a rock face into a seemingly bottomless gorge below. The catch is that the viewing area, where there is a shelter with some benches and a public restroom, is some distance from the falls. Many visitors find the narrow falls unimpressive from this vantage point. To climb closer requires a major commitment: a steep climb down and up the side of the mountain is several hours. ⊠ *Mountain Pine Ridge, 1000 Foot Falls* ✛ *From the Mountain Pine Ridge gate, go 2 miles (3 km) and turn left toward Hidden Valley Inn. Go 4 miles (6.4 km) to the falls observation area. It's well-signed* ✉ *BZ$4.*

FAMILY **Río Frio Caves.** These caves are only a few miles by car down a steep track, but ecologically speaking, they are in a different world. In the course of a few hundred yards, you drop from pine savanna to tropical forest. Few other places in Belize illustrate its extraordinary geological diversity as clearly as this startling transition. A river runs right through the center of the main cave—actually it's more of a tunnel, open at both ends—and, over the centuries, has carved the rock into fantastic shapes. Swallows fill the place, and at night ocelots and margays pad silently across the cold floor in search of slumbering prey. Seen from the dark interior, the light-filled world outside seems more intense and beautiful than ever. About a mile away (2 km) are the Cuevas Gemelas (Twin Caves), best seen with a guide. Due to occasional bandit activity in the area, at times a Belize Defence Forces escort is required to visit the Rio Frio Caves—if driving on your own, ask at your hotel or at the Douglas de Silva forestry station, where private vehicles meet up with a Defence Force escort. ✉ *Mountain Pine Ridge* ✥ *From entrance gate of Mountain Pine Ridge, go 14 miles (23 km). Turn right Douglas de Silva forestry station at Rio Frio sign and drive 5 miles (8 km) to caves* 🎟 *Free.*

WHERE TO STAY

NEAR MOUNTAIN PINE RIDGE

$$ B&B/INN 🏨 **Crystal Paradise Resort.** This jungle lodge is operated by the Tut (pronounced *Toot*) family—Mom and Dad Tut and their 10 children. **Pros:** Belizean-owned; good guided tours. **Cons:** no-frills rooms and cabañas. [$] *Rooms from: BZ$207* ✉ *Cristo Rey Rd., Cristo Rey Village* ☎ *615/9361* 🌐 *www.crystalparadise.com* 🛏 *12 rooms* 🍴 *Some meals.*

$$$ HOTEL 🏨 **Gumbo Limbo Jungle Resort.** Well-priced, with a lovely hilltop setting, and amenities such as a pool, this small lodge is an attractive option just 2 miles (3 km) from the George Price Highway at Georgeville. **Pros:** attractive cottage accommodations; lovely views; nice swimming pool. **Cons:** steep hill on dirt access road is a doozy. [$] *Rooms from: BZ$316* ✉ *Mile 2, Mountain Pine Ridge Rd. (aka Chiquibul Rd. or Georgeville Rd.), Georgeville* ☎ *650/3112* 🌐 *www.gumbolimboresort.com* 🛏 *4 cottages.*

$$ B&B/INN 🏨 **Inn the Bush Eco-Jungle Lodge.** With only three cabañas, every guest gets personal attention at this small ecolodge where you can lounge in a four-poster king bed and then jump in the pool for a refreshing swim. **Pros:** personal service; reasonable rates; peace and quiet. **Cons:** access road is rough. [$] *Rooms from: BZ$273* ✉ *Mile 6, Cristo Rey Rd., Macaw Bank, off Cristo Rey Rd., Cristo Rey Village* ☎ *670/6364* 🌐 *www.innthebushbelize.com* 🛏 *3 cabañas* 🍴 *No meals.*

$$ B&B/INN 🏨 **Macaw Bank Jungle Lodge.** This small, laid-back ecolodge on 50 acres adjoining the Macal River is for travelers seeking a no-frills spot where you can hear the jungle hum outside your doorstep and where the air bristles with the promise of bird and animal sightings. **Pros:** laid-back ecolodge with moderate rates; great food. **Cons:** not a luxury lodge; need a rental car. [$] *Rooms from: BZ$283* ✉ *Cristo Rey Rd., Cristo Rey Village* ☎ *665/7241* 🌐 *www.macawbankjunglelodge.com* 🛏 *5 cottages* 🍴 *No meals.*

$$ HOTEL 🏨 **Mountain Equestrian Trails.** MET, as most people call it, is one of Belize's top equestrian spots. **Pros:** equestrian charm abounds; reasonable prices for cabañas. **Cons:** facilities a bit too rustic for some. [$] *Rooms from: BZ$288* ✉ *Mike 8, Mountain Pine Ridge Rd. (aka Chiquibul Rd. or Georgeville Rd.), El Progresso/7 Mile* ☎ *669/1124 in Belize, 800/838–3918 toll-free U.S. reservations* 🌐 *www.metbelize.com* 🛏 *10 cabañas* 🍴 *Some meals.*

$$$$ RESORT Fodor's Choice ★ **Mystic River Resort.** Operated by a French-American couple, this jungle resort on the Macal River is a step up in luxury, service, and dining from other run-of-the-mill lodges in the area. **Pros:** stylishly decorated cottages all with views and fireplaces; excellent food; friendly management. **Cons:** a little pricey; no a/c. [$] *Rooms from: BZ$595* ✉ *Mile 6, Cristo Rey Rd., San Antonio Village* ☎ *834/4100* 🌐 *www.mysticriverbelize.com* 🛏 *6 cottages* 🍴 *No meals.*

$$$ B&B/INN FAMILY Fodor's Choice ★ **Table Rock Lodge.** At this intimate jungle eco-spot, cobblestone walkways and thick awnings of foliage gracefully blend into a jungle setting, perched just above the Macal River. **Pros:** low-key, relaxing, off-the-beaten-path ecolodge; good value; wonderful food. **Cons:** it's a bumpy 20-minute ride to San Ignacio; Wi-Fi only in dining room. [$] *Rooms from: BZ$345* ✉ *Cristo Rey Rd., San Antonio Village* ☎ *672/4040* 🌐 *www.tablerockbelize.com* 🛏 *6 cottages* 🍴 *Some meals.*

MOUNTAIN PINE RIDGE

$$$$ RESORT Fodor's Choice ★ **Blancaneaux Lodge.** As you sweep down Blancaneaux's hibiscus- and palm-lined drive, past the big main swimming pool, you may get a whiff of Beverly Hills, and indeed the lodge is owned by film director Francis Ford Coppola. **Pros:** fabulous grounds; deluxe cabañas and villas; wonderful food and service. **Cons:** many steep steps may pose problems for some; very expensive. [$] *Rooms from: BZ$900* ✉ *Mountain Pine Ridge* ✣ *Turn right at Blancaneaux sign 4.5 miles (7.5 km) from Mountain Pine Ridge entrance gate* ☎ *866/356–5881 toll-free reservations number in U.S. and Canada* 🌐 *www.thefamilycoppolaresorts.com/en/blancaneaux-lodge* 🛏 *10 cabañas, 7 villas, 1 house* 🍴 *Breakfast.*

$$$ RESORT **Gaia Riverlodge.** Drive deep into the Mountain Pine Ridge and you'll find, perched on a steep hill above the Five Sisters waterfalls, this elegant lodge and staging ground for exploration. **Pros:** appealing small lodge; a little less expensive than other lodges in the Mountain Pine Ridge; eco-friendly. **Cons:** some standard cabañas don't have much of a view; no pool or TV. [$] *Rooms from: BZ$476* ✉ *Mountain Pine Ridge* ✣ *From main Mountain Pine Ridge Rd., turn right at Blancaneaux and Five Sisters signs 4.5 mile (7.2 km) from Pine Ridge entrance gate. Continue past Blancaneaux airstrip about 1 mile (1.6 km)* ☎ *834/4024* 🌐 *www.gaiariverlodge.com* 🛏 *16 cabañas* 🍴 *Some meals.*

$$$$ B&B/INN Fodor's Choice ★ **Hidden Valley Inn & Reserve.** Sitting on 7,200 acres, Hidden Valley has more than a dozen waterfalls, at least two private caves, and 90 miles (150 km) of hiking and mountain biking trails. **Pros:** charming lodge atmosphere; wonderful waterfalls; excellent birding and stunning pool. **Cons:** meals are pricey; loss of many mature pines due to the pine beetle means it can be hot and dry on the trails. [$] *Rooms from: BZ$670* ✉ *4 Cooma Cairn Rd.* ✣ *From main Mountain Pine Ridge Rd., turn left at Hidden Valley Inn sign 3.75 miles (6.25 km) from Pine Ridge entrance gate* ☎ *822/3320, 877/773–1774 toll-free reservations number in U.S. and Canada* 🌐 *www.hiddenvalleyinn.com* 🛏 *12 cottages* 🍴 *Some meals.*

SPORTS AND THE OUTDOORS

BIRDING

Birding is great in the Mountain Pine Ridge, and, surprisingly, it's even better now that many of the pines were felled by the Southern pine beetle. Without the tall pines, it's much easier to spot orange-breasted falcons, blue crown motmots, white king vultures, stygian owls, and other rare birds.

CAVING

Easily accessible in the Cayo is the Río Frio Cave. You can also do trips to Barton Creek Cave, about 8 miles (13 km) northwest of Mountain Pine Ridge entrance gate, off Mountain Pine Ridge Road, and to Actun Tunichil Muknal from Mountain Pine Ridge. Hidden Valley Inn has two caves open only to guests of the inn.

HIKING

With its karst limestone terrain, extensive network of old logging trails and roads, and cooler temperatures, the Mountain Pine Ridge is ideal for hiking. All the lodges here have miles of marked trails. You can also hike along the roads (mostly gravel or dirt), as there are very few cars in the Pine Ridge. Most people find this more pleasant than trying to fight their way through the bush. The mountain area around Baldy Beacon, the highest point in the Pine Ridge at around 3,335 feet, is especially beautiful; it may remind you of part of the Highlands of Scotland.

All of the Mountain Pine Ridge and Chichibul Wilderness is lightly populated, and some of the residents, such as unemployed squatters who have moved into this remote area, may not always have your best interests at heart. Cell phones don't usually work here, although there has been talk of installing some cell-phone towers as a security measure. Lodges such as Hidden Valley Inn provide radio phones to guests who are hiking. Always leave word with a responsible party about your hiking plans and time of expected return. Carry plenty of water, food, a compass, and basic medical supplies, especially on long hikes to remote areas. You may want to hire a guide.

HORSEBACK RIDING

In this remote area with virtually no vehicular traffic and many old logging roads, horseback riding is excellent. **Blancaneaux Lodge** and **Hidden Valley Inn** offer horseback riding, and **Mountain Equestrian Trails** runs horseback tours into the Pine Ridge.

MOUNTAIN BIKING

Mountain Pine Ridge has the best mountain biking in Belize on hundreds of miles of remote logging roads. Mountain biking is especially good on the 90 miles (150 km) of private hiking and mountain biking trails at Hidden Valley Inn. Blancaneaux and Hidden Valley Inn provide complimentary mountain bikes to guests. The Lodge at Chaa Creek also offers mountain biking.

ZIP-LINING

FAMILY **Calico Jack's Jungle Canopy & Zip Line.** Calico Jack's zip line is more than a half mile (1 km) long. The "Ultimo Explorer" zip-line tour has 9 runs on 15 platforms more than 2,700 feet. Zip-lining starts at BZ$80 plus tax. There also are five caves on the grounds, two open for exploring with a guide. Calico Jack's Village also has cabañas for rent, and a restaurant. ⊠ *Off Mile 7, Mountain Pine Ridge Rd., El Progresso/7 Mile* ☎ *832/2478* ⊕ *www.calicojacksvillage.com.*

CARACOL

55 miles (98 km) south of San Ignacio

Caracol (Spanish for "snail") is the most spectacular Mayan site in Belize, as well as one of the most impressive in Central America. It was once home to as many as 200,000 people (almost two-thirds the population of modern-day Belize).

GETTING HERE AND AROUND

Caracol is about 55 miles (92 km) from San Ignacio, and about 35–40 miles (57–66 km) from the major lodges in the Mountain Pine Ridge. Because roads are mostly unpaved and often in poor condition, cars or tour vans take about two hours from the Pine Ridge lodges and about three hours from San Ignacio, sometimes longer after heavy rains.

Advance permission to visit Caracol is no longer required. Although only about a 10-mile (17-km) section of the road to Caracol from San Ignacio is paved, once into the Mountain Pine Ridge the road is generally in good shape, except after heavy rains. The Belize government has plans to eventually pave the entire road to Caracol.

SAFETY AND PRECAUTIONS

Occasional holdups of tourists by armed gangs believed to be from Guatemala occurred here over the past several years. For caution's sake, trips to Caracol are now in a group convoy, protected by Belize Defence Forces troops. The meet-up point is Augustine De Silva village, a few miles into the Pine Ridge. As off-putting as that may seem, Caracol is well worth seeing. The robbery incidents have occurred very rarely, and the tour operators to Caracol know the ropes and will work to make sure your trip to Caracol is rewarding and safe.

TIMING

You generally can't overnight at Caracol, so you have to visit on a day trip. You can see the excavated area of Caracol in a few hours.

TOURS

Most visitors to Caracol come as part of a tour group from San Ignacio, or from one of the lodges in the Mountain Pine Ridge. Full-day tours from San Ignacio, which often include a picnic lunch and stops at Río Frio Cave, Río On, and other sights in the Mountain Pine Ridge, cost from about BZ$160 to BZ$220 per person, including the BZ$20 admission fee to Caracol, depending on what is included and the number of people going. Tours from independent operators generally cost less than those from lodges. Lodges in the Mountain Pine Ridge charge around BZ$200–BZ$250 per person for tours to Caracol, including tax.

Because of its remote location, Caracol gets only about 12,000 visitors a year. That's about one-tenth the number who visit Altun Ha, one-fifth the number who visit Xunantunich, and a smaller fraction of the number who see Tikal. Thus, you're in exclusive company, and on some slow days you may be one of only a handful of people at the site. Excavations by a team from the University of Central Florida usually are carried out in the winter, typically January through March.

EXPLORING

FAMILY

Fodor's Choice
★

Caracol. Once a metropolis with five plazas and 32 large structures covering almost a square mile, Caracol once covered an area larger than present-day Belize City. Altogether it is believed there are some 35,000 buildings at the site, though only a handful of them have been excavated. Excavations at Caracol are being carried on by Diane and Arlen Chase of the University of Central Florida. The latest excavations are in an area approximately 500 yards southeast of Caracol's central plaza. Once Caracol has been fully excavated it may dwarf even the great city of Tikal, which is a few dozen miles away (as the toucan flies) in Guatemala. The evidence suggests that Caracol won a crushing victory over Tikal in the mid-6th century, a theory that Guatemalan scholars haven't quite accepted. Until a group of *chicleros* (collectors of gum base) stumbled on the site in 1936, Caracol was buried under the jungle of the remote Vaca Plateau. It's hard to believe it could have been lost for centuries, as the great pyramid of Caana, at nearly 140 feet, is still Belize's tallest structure.

The main excavated sections are in four groups, denoted on archaeological maps as A, B, C, and D groups. The most impressive structures are the B Group at the northeast end of the excavated plaza. This includes Caana (sometimes spelled Ca'ana or Ka'ana), or "Sky Palace," listed as Structure B19-2nd, along with a ball court, water reservoir, and several large courtyards. Caana remains the tallest structure in Belize. The A Group, on the west side of the plaza, contains a temple, ball court, and a residential area for the elite. The Temple of the Wooden Lintel (Structure A6) is one of the oldest and longest-used buildings at Caracol, dating back to 300 BC. It was still in use in AD 1100. To the northwest of the A Group is the Northwest Acropolis, primarily a residential area. The third major plaza forming the core of the site is at the point where a causeway enters the "downtown" part of Caracol. The D Group is a group of structures at the South Acropolis.

Near the entrance to Caracol is a small but interesting visitor center. If you have driven here on your own (with a Belize Defence Forces escort) instead of with a tour, a guide usually can be hired at the site, but you can also walk around on your own. Seeing all of the excavated area involves several hours of hiking around the site. Wear sturdy shoes and bring insect repellent. Also, watch for anthill mounds and, rarely, snakes. This part of the Chiquibul Forest Reserve is a good place for birding and wildlife spotting. Around the ruins are troops of howler monkeys and flocks of oscellated turkeys, and you may also see deer, coatimundis, foxes, and other wildlife at the site or on the way. ✛ *From Mountain Pine Forest Ridge reserve entrance, head south 14 miles (23 km) to village of Douglas DiSilva (where you can meet up with a Belize Defence Forces escort), turn left and go 36 miles (58 km)* ⊕ *www. caracol.org* ✉ *BZ$20.*

THE SOUTHERN COAST

By Lan Sluder

The transition from one landscape to another is often swift and startling in Belize. As you approach the Hummingbird Highway's end in coastal Dangriga, the lush, mountainous terrain of the north gives way to flat plains bristling with orange trees. Farther south, the Stann Creek Valley is where bananas, the nation's first bumper crop, and most other fruits are grown. Equally noticeable is the cultural segue: whereas San Ignacio has a Spanish air, the Southern Coast is strongly Afro-Caribbean.

The Southern Coast isn't so much a melting pot as a tropical stew full of different flavors. A seaside Garífuna Village recalls Senegal, while just down the road a Creole village evokes the Caribbean. Inland, Maya live much as they have for thousands of years next door to Mestizos from Guatemala and Honduras who've come to work the banana plantations or citrus groves. Sprinkled in are expats from the northern climes, looking for a retirement home or trying to make a buck in tourism.

Tourist dollars, the staple of contemporary Belize, have largely bypassed Dangriga to land in Hopkins, and, even more tellingly, in Placencia, the region's most striking destination. Just a decade or so ago there were only three small resorts on the peninsula north of Placencia Village. Now there are more than 20, stretching up to the villages of Seine Bight, Maya Beach, and beyond. Despite the global recession, plans are in the works for new condos and hotels, although some of these developments were stalled by a shortage of financing and a scarcity of buyers. A few shut down, victims of the real-estate bust, or are rotting away in the tropical humidity. Still, owners of small beach resorts and inns are cashing in, selling out to developers, who are in turn combining several small tracts into one, hoping to put together larger residential or resort projects.

With the paving of the Placencia road now completed, and, the possibility of a new airstrip in Hopkins, an international airport just north of the peninsula, and a new cruise-ship port on a caye off Placencia, many believe that the tipping point for this area has been reached and that the new wave of resorts and residential developments will be larger, more upscale, and more multinational. Local residents appear divided about the dramatic changes. Some embrace the development in hopes of a better economic future; others bitterly oppose it, citing the impact on the narrow peninsula's fragile ecosystems. With the exception of a few shop owners and some guides, most Placencia residents appear to oppose the coming of mass cruise-ship tourism to the Southern Coast, but powerful political and economic forces in the country seem to be winning out.

TOP REASONS TO GO

Beaches. The mainland's best beaches are on the Placencia Peninsula and around Hopkins. Although they're narrow ribbons of khaki rather than wide swaths of talcum-powder sand, they're ideal for lazing in a hammock under a coco palm. And you don't have to fight the crowds for a spot—at least not yet.

Jaguars. The world's first and only jaguar preserve is the Cockscomb Basin Wildlife Sanctuary. Chances are you won't actually see one of these big, beautiful cats in the wild, as they roam the high bush mainly

at night, but you may see tracks or hear a low growl in the darkness.

Water Sports. Anglers won't be disappointed by the bonefish, tarpon, and other sportfishing. The Barrier Reef here is generally 15 miles (25 km) or more off the coast, so it's a long trip out, even with the fast boats the dive shops use. However, there are patch reefs around closer islands, with excellent snorkeling. Serious divers will find two of Belize's three atolls, Turneffe and Glover's, within reach. In a charter sailboat you can island-hop in the protected waters inside the reef.

The surfacing of the Southern Highway from Dangriga all the way to Punta Gorda has made the region much more accessible. Off the main highway, however, most roads consist of red dirt and potholes. The road that once was the worst in the region, the dirt track from the Southern Highway to Placencia Village, has been transformed, thanks to a loan from the Caribbean Development Bank, into a smooth, paved, two-lane thoroughfare. The repaving of the Hopkins Road has also been completed, although the main road through Hopkins village is still like a bed of nails.

Real-estate sales are a driving force in Placencia, Hopkins, and elsewhere along the coast. The lure is the beaches. The Southern Coast has the best beaches on the mainland, although as elsewhere inside the protecting Barrier Reef, the low wave action means the beaches are narrow and there's usually sea grass in the water close to shore. (Sea grass—not seaweed, which is an algae—may be a nuisance for swimmers, but it's a vital part of the coastal ecosystem, acting as a nursery for sea life.) Much of the seafront land has been divided into lots awaiting development; if things continue at this pace, the area will one day rival Ambergris Caye as Belize's top beach destination.

ORIENTATION AND PLANNING

GETTING ORIENTED

From the north, two roads lead from the George Price Highway (formerly Western Highway) to the Southern Coast: the Hummingbird Highway from Belmopan, and the Coastal Road from La Democracia. The Hummingbird is paved, and the most scenic drive in all of Belize. The Coastal Road is unpaved, dusty, or muddy, depending on the amount of rain. Despite the name, it does not hug the coast; in fact you never glimpse the sea from it. The loose gravel roadway is an accident waiting to happen. In short, if you're driving, take the Hummingbird.

Off the spine of the Southern Highway, various shorter roads lead to villages on the coast and inland: from the highway it's about 4 miles (7 km) on a newly paved road to Hopkins; 25 miles (42 km) to Placencia Village, nicely paved all the way, although the speed bumps are irritating; and 5 miles (8 km) to Big Creek/Independence on a paved road.

Gales Point and Dangriga. Gales Point is a small Creole village, with a beautiful waterside setting, known for the manatees in nearby lagoons. Dangriga is the largest Garífuna settlement in Belize, and a jumping-off spot for several offshore cayes. However, neither Gales Point nor Dangriga is a tourism center.

Hopkins. The most accessible and friendly Garífuna Village in Belize, Hopkins has good beaches and a growing tourism industry. It's similar to what Placencia was like 15 years ago.

Placencia Peninsula. This peninsula has the best beaches on the mainland. With the paving of the Placencia road, real-estate development and tourism are taking off, bringing more high-quality accommodations and dining, along with problems associated with development.

PLANNING

WHEN TO GO

The weather on the Southern Coast is similar to that in central and northern Belize, only a little wetter. On average, for example, the Cayo District has rain, or at least a shower, on 125 days a year, while in Stann Creek District there's some rain on 183 days—usually thanks to late fall and winter cold fronts or summer tropical fronts passing through. These showers are generally followed by sunshine. Summer daytime temperatures along the coast reach the high 80s, occasionally the 90s. Humidity is high most of the year, typically 80% or more.

GETTING HERE AND AROUND

AIR TRAVEL

You'll arrive fresher if you fly. From Belize City (both international and municipal airports) there are frequent flights to Dangriga and Placencia on Maya Island Air and Tropic Air. There are more than 20 flights daily between Belize City and Placencia, and more than a dozen to Dangriga. You'll generally fly in small aircraft, such as the 14-passenger Cessna Caravan C208. Fares tend to be slightly lower on Maya Island Air. There's an effort to open an airstrip in Hopkins, but as of this writing it has not been approved by the Belize government.

Contacts Maya Island Air. ✉ *Placencia airstrip, Placencia Rd., Placencia Village* ☎ *523/3443 at Placencia airstrip, 223/1403 in Belize City for reservations countrywide, 522/0617 at Dangriga airstrip* ⊕ *www.mayaislandair.com.* **Tropic Air.** ✉ *Placencia airstrip, Placencia Rd., Placencia Village* ☎ *523/3410 at Placencia airstrip, 226/2626 in Belize for reservations, 800/422–3435 in U.S. for reservations, 522/2129 at Dangriga airstrip* ⊕ *www.tropicair.com.*

BOAT AND FERRY TRAVEL

There is a well-established water taxi, a small boat named the *Hokey Pokey,* between Placencia Village and Independence, a village on the west side of Placencia Lagoon. Currently there are eight round trips each way daily, except on Sunday, when there are six or seven. Schedules for the boat are set to coincide with James Bus Line stops in Independence, so you can make connections to Punta Gorda to the south, or Dangriga, Belmopan, and Belize City to the north.

From Placencia, a weekly boat, the *D'Express,* runs to Puerto Cortes, Honduras, on Friday, with a stop in Big Creek across the lagoon to clear immigration and customs. It departs from the Placencia Municipal Pier at the south end of Placencia Village. In Puerto Cortes, the boat arrives at Laguna and returns from Puerto Cortes on Monday morning. You can buy tickets at Barefoot Beach Bar, which is on the beachfront next to Tipsy Tuna in Placencia.

From Dangriga, boats go out daily to Tobacco Caye. There are no fixed schedules, but the boats generally leave around 9 to 9:30 am. Ask at the Riverside Café or at the boats docked in the Stann Creek River near the café.

Happy Go Luckie Tours in Hopkins has a water-taxi service from Hopkins to Dangriga, Tobacco Caye, Placencia, and a few other destinations. There is no fixed schedule; passengers must book trips in advance and prices are based on a minimum of two persons. The company also provides sea and river tours, fishing and snorkeling tours, and custom charter tours to cayes and atolls off the Southern Coast.

Contacts D' Express. ⊠ *Placencia Municipal Pier, at south end of Main St., Placencia Village* ☎ *626/8835 D'Express.* **Happy Go Luckie Tours.** ☎ *635/0967* ⊕ *www.hgltours.com.* **Hokey Pokey.** ⊠ *MNM Gas Station Dock, Placencia Rd., Placencia Village* ✧ *Follow signs for MNM Gas Station Dock, just north of heart of village* ☎ *667/1821.*

BUS TRAVEL

In the south, James Bus Line runs from Belize City via Belmopan to Dangriga and Independence and then Punta Gorda. Schedules are subject to change, but James Bus Line has about 10 buses daily. The buses don't stop in Placencia, they stop across the lagoon in Independence, where you can connect with the Hokey Pokey boat to Placencia Village. Ritchie's Bus Service has four buses daily each way between Dangriga and Placencia, with reduced service on Sunday. BEBB Bus Line has twice-daily service between Placencia and Dangriga, with a stop in Hopkins. Fares on all buses between Placencia and Dangriga are BZ$10. With connections, the trip from Belize City to Dangriga and Hopkins is three to five hours; Placencia is around five to six hours, depending on the number of stops and connections. Buses are usually old U.S. school buses or ancient Greyhound buses, are often crowded, and don't have air-conditioning or restrooms. The James Bus Line buses generally are in the best condition. In Placencia, buses are not supposed to go into the main part of Placencia Village due to traffic congestion and the narrow street, but some do. A temporary bus station is in a vacant parking lot on the east side of the main road at the north end of the Placencia

Village. △ **Several charter buses bring workers from nearby villages to Placencia, but they do not pick up other passengers.**

Contacts BEBB Bus Line. ✉ *BEBB, Placencia Rd., Placencia Village.* **James Bus Line.** ✉ *7 King St., Punta Gorda* ☎ *702/2049 in Punta Gorda* ⊕ *www.jamesbusline.com.* **Ritchie's Bus Service.** ✉ *Ritchie's Bus Service, Main Rd., Placencia Village* ☎ *631/7073* ⊕ *www.ritchiesbusservice.com.*

CAR TRAVEL

To get to Placencia, head southeast from Belmopan on the Hummingbird Highway. The highway is one of Belize's better roads, as well as one of its most scenic. On your right rise the jungle-covered Maya Mountains, largely free of signs of human habitation except for the occasional field of corn or beans. As you approach Dangriga you'll see large citrus groves. South of Dangriga on the Southern Highway you'll pass a number of large banana plantations—the blue plastic bags protect the bananas from insect damage.

Several small local outfits, including Barefoot Services and Placencia Car Rental, rent cars in Placencia. Some companies also rent scooters and golf carts, which can be driven on the roads. Budget, based in Belize City, has a branch in Placencia. The car rental companies in Placencia will deliver cars to Dangriga, Hopkins, and other areas nearby, but you'll probably have to pay a small delivery fee.

Contacts Barefoot Services. ✉ *Caribbean Travel and Tours Office, Main St., Placencia Village* ⚓ *In Placencia Village on east side of main road, near Rumfish y Vino* ☎ *523/3066* ⊕ *www.barefootservicesbelize.com.* **Budget.** ✉ *Live Oak Plaza, south of airstrip, Placencia Village* ☎ *223/2435 in Belize City, 523/3068 in Placencia* ⊕ *www.budget-belize.com.* **Placencia Car Rental.** ✉ *Placencia Rental, Placencia Rd., Seine Bight Village* ⚓ *On main road just north of Robert's Grove* ☎ *523/ 3284* ⊕ *www.placenciacarrental.com.*

TAXI TRAVEL

If you need a ride to the airport in Dangriga, have your hotel call a taxi. Taxis usually meet arriving flights at the Dangriga and Placencia airstrips, but many hotels in Placencia provide free pick-up services at the airstrip and also provide scheduled van service from the hotel to and from Placencia Village. Taxis are expensive in Placencia.

ABOUT THE HOTELS

There are two kinds of lodging to choose from on the Southern Coast: small, basic hotels, often Belizean-owned, and upscale beach resorts, usually owned and operated by Americans or Canadians. The small hotels are clustered in Placencia Village, Hopkins Village, and in Dangriga Town. The beach resorts are mostly on the Placencia Peninsula north of Placencia Village and also just to the south of Hopkins Village. Several of these resorts, including Hamanasi in Hopkins, are among the best hotels in Belize. There also are some vacation rental houses near Hopkins and on the Placencia Peninsula.

More than two dozen condo developments have opened, are under construction, or are in the planning stages on Placencia Peninsula and near Hopkins.

HOTEL AND RESTAURANT PRICES
For expanded lodging reviews and current deals, visit Fodors.com.

WHAT IT COSTS IN BELIZE DOLLARS			
$	**$$**	**$$$**	**$$$$**
RESTAURANTS under BZ$15	BZ$15–BZ$30	BZ$31–BZ$50	over BZ$50
HOTELS under BZ$200	BZ$200–BZ$300	BZ$301–BZ$500	over BZ$500

Restaurant prices are per person for a main course at dinner. Hotel prices are for two people in a standard double room, including tax and service.

ABOUT THE RESTAURANTS
Broiled, grilled, fried, sautéed, cooked in lime juice as ceviche, or bar-becued on the beach: any way you eat it seafood is the life-stuff on the Southern Coast. Restaurants serve fish, lobster, conch, and shrimp, often fresh from the boat, or, in the case of shrimp, straight from the shrimp farms near Placencia.

Expect mostly small, locally owned restaurants; some breezy beachside joints with sand floors, others wood shacks. Placencia has by far the largest number of eateries, with Hopkins a distant second. Chef Rob's is Hopkins' best restaurant. Some of the upscale restaurants are in resorts, such as Turtle Inn. The Bistro at Maya Beach Hotel is one of the country's best restaurants. And it's worth making a trip to Placencia just to sample the incredible gelato at Tutti-Frutti.

Off-season, especially in late summer and early fall, restaurants in Placencia and Hopkins may close for a few weeks, and on any day the owners may decide to close early if there are no customers, so call ahead. It's also a good idea to make reservations so the cooks will have enough food on hand.

TOURS
Altogether, Placencia has about 150 licensed tour guides and around two dozen licensed tour operators; Hopkins and Dangriga also have licensed tour guides and operators. Most of the guides, except some fishing guides, work on a contract basis for resorts or tour operators. These tour guides and operators offer dive and snorkel trips to Laughing Bird, the Belize Barrier Reef, and Turneffe and Glover's atolls; wildlife tours to Monkey River; birding tours to Red Bank and elsewhere; hiking trips to Cockscomb Basin Wildlife Sanctuary and Mayflower Bocawina National Park; and, excursions to Mayan ruins near Punta Gorda.

The larger resorts on the Placencia Peninsula, including Chabil Mar, Turtle Inn, and Robert's Grove, offer a variety of tours and trips, using tour guides they have come to trust. Likewise, in Hopkins the larger resorts such as Hamanasi offer both land and sea tours. *See Where to Eat and Stay sections for contact information.*

To book tours and trips, check with your hotel; in Placencia Village, several of the tour operators have small offices along Main Street. Also check with the Belize Tourism Industry Association's (BTIA) visitor information office; the staff in Placencia can advise you on tours. You'll probably pay a little less by booking in the village instead of at your hotel, but the savings may not be worth the effort.

ADVENTURE TOURS

Toadal Adventures Belize. Dave Vernon's Toadal Adventure provides top-notch multiday sea and river expedition kayak trips in southern Belize. Trips can be customized to your specific schedule and interests. Dave and Deb Vernon also operate a budget guesthouse, Deb & Dave's Last Resort, and a more upscale lodging, The North, in Placencia Village. ⊠ *Near Sidewalk, Placencia Village* ☎ *523/3207* ⊕ *www.travelbelize. org/toadal-adventure-belize.*

BOATING, SAILING, AND WATER SPORTS

Snorkeling trips inside the reef, to Laughing Bird Caye and other snorkel spots, are popular tour options, as are half-day boat trips to Monkey River and boat excursions on the Placencia Lagoon to look for mana-tees. Most full-day trips include a picnic lunch. If you're going to an area with an admission or marine reserve fee often the fee is additional. Also available from Placencia are bareboat and crewed sailboat charters by charter operators such as The Moorings.

Fodor's Choice ★ **Destinations Belize.** Owner Mary Toy, a former attorney in the United States, has been offering tours in the Placencia area since 1998. Destina-tions Belize is especially strong in arranging guided fishing trips, but it also offers land and sea tours of all kinds. In addition, Mary Toy can help with overall Belize trip planning, including booking hotels and transportation. ⊠ *Placencia Village* ☎ *253/4018, 610/4718* ⊕ *www. destinationsbelize.com.*

Joy Tours. Joy Tours offers a wide range of land and sea tours. Sea tours include whale shark trips, fishing, diving, kayaking, and snorkeling. Land tours include hiking in Cockscomb and other destinations near Placencia. ⊠ *Placencia Village* ☎ *523/3325* ⊕ *www.belizewithjoy.com.*

The Moorings. An international yacht charter company, the Moorings offers 5- to 14-night sailing charters from Placencia aboard a catamaran or monohull sailboat. Stops include a number of small cayes including Hatchett Caye. Prices in-season for a weekly bareboat charter for two ranges from BZ$5,000 to BZ$10,000, not including provisions. An all-inclusive skippered charter with a cook for a week in high season can cost from BZ$20,000 to BZ$38,000. ⊠ *The Moorings, Placencia Rd., Laru Beya Marina, Seine Bight Village* ☎ *888/979–1198 toll-free in U.S. and Canada, 523/3351 in Placencia* ⊕ *www.moorings.com.*

SCUBA DIVING AND SNORKLING

This far south, the reef is as much as 20 miles (33 km) offshore, neces-sitating boat rides of 45 minutes to nearly two hours to reach dive sites. Because this part of the reef has fewer cuts and channels, it's also more difficult to get out to the seaward side, where you'll find the best div-ing. As a result, most of the diving in this region is done from offshore cayes, which are surrounded by small reefs, usually with gently sloping drop-offs of about 80–100 feet. This isn't the place for spectacular wall dives—you're better off staying in the north or heading out to the atolls. Near Moho Caye, southeast of Placencia, you'll find brilliant red-and-yellow corals and sponges that rarely appear elsewhere in Belize.

Two marine reserves off Placencia are popular snorkeling and diving spots. Laughing Bird Caye, Belize's smallest marine reserve, about 13 miles (22 km) off Placencia, is a popular spot for snorkeling. Whale sharks, *Rhincodon typus,* gentle giants of the sea, appear off Placencia in the Gladden Spit area, part of the Gladden Spit and Silk Caves Marine Reserves 26 miles (43 km) east of Placencia, in late spring and early summer. You can snorkel or dive with them on day trips from Placencia. The best time to see whale sharks is three or four days before and after a full moon, March through June. Admission fee to each of these marine reserves is BZ$20; the admission typically is included in the dive or snorkel shop fee.

Diving costs a little more in Placencia than most other places in Belize, in part due to the distance to the reef and the atolls. Most of the larger resorts, like the Inn at Robert's Grove and Turtle Inn, have dive shops and also offer snorkel trips. Avadon Divers and the Splash Dive Center are considered two of the best dive shops in the region.

Ocean Motion. For snorkeling trips check with Ocean Motion, on the Sidewalk in the heart of Placencia Village. A full-day snorkeling trip to Laughing Bird Caye is BZ$150 per person (half-day, BZ$120), and a day trip to Frigate Caye is BZ$100. Rates include taxes, snorkel gear, and a lunch grilled on a caye, but not park fees, if any. ⊠ *Ocean Motion, Placencia Village* ☎ *523/3363* ⊕ *www.oceanmotionplacencia.com.*

FAMILY **Ranguana Caye.** For an idyllic island getaway with good snorkeling from the shore, consider a day trip to Ranguana Caye. The trip, run by the people who manage the caye, includes kayaking, paddleboarding, and snorkeling, as well as a beach barbecue. ■TIP→ **If you have time, grab a few cold ones at Billy's Beach Bar on the island (Drinks are extra.).** The fee is BZ$250 per person. ⊠ *Placencia Municipal Pier, Placencia Village* ☎ *674/7264* ⊕ *www.ranguanacaye.com.*

Fodor's Choice ★ **Splash Dive Center.** One of the best dive shops in southern Belize, Splash Dive Center offers many dive and snorkel trips that include visits to the inner and outer reefs and Glover's atoll. Opportunities to dive with whale sharks at Gladden Spit ire also available in late spring and early summer. ⊠ *Splash Dive Center, Placencia Village* ☎ *523/3080* ⊕ *www. splashbelize.com.*

VISITOR INFORMATION

The Placencia location of the Belize Tourism Industry Association (BTIA) is located behind Re/Max Real Estate on Main Street across from ScotiaBank. The BTIA publishes the *Placencia Breeze,* an informative monthly newspaper; it has a helpful website that lists accommodations, restaurants, and bars. Destinations Belize is another helpful site about Placencia that's put together by local resident Mary Toy. Hopkins has several interesting websites put together by local residents, including Visit Hopkins Belize.

Information Belize Tourism Industry Association. ⊠ *Main St., Behind Re/ Max Property Center, Placencia Village* ☎ *523/4045* ⊕ *www.placencia.com.* **Visit Hopkins Belize.** ⊕ *www.visithopkinsvillagebelize.com.*

6

GREAT ITINERARIES

IF YOU HAVE 3 DAYS ON THE SOUTHERN COAST

Base yourself in Placencia. On your first full day, walk the Sidewalk in Placencia Village, hear the latest gossip, and get to know a little of village life. Hang out on the beach at your hotel and get on Belize time, then have drinks and dinner in the village, perhaps at Rumfish y Vino, Secret Garden, or La Dolce Vita. If you still have energy, have some Belikins at the Barefoot Bar or Tipsy Tuna, both directly on the beach. On your second day, take a snorkel trip to Laughing Bird Caye or another snorkel area, or, if you dive, do a full-day dive trip to Turneffe or Glover's atoll. On your final day, drive or take a guided tour to Cockscomb Basin Wildlife Sanctuary. Be sure to stop at the Maya Center craft coopera-tive for gift shopping. If there's time, also visit the Mayflower/Bocawina National Park, with its Mayan sites and waterfalls. End the day with dinner at The Bistro at Maya Beach Hotel, one of the best restaurants in Belize.

IF YOU HAVE 5 DAYS ON THE SOUTHERN COAST

Drive or fly to Dangriga (the closest airport to Hopkins). While in Dangriga, stop by the Garífuna Museum, then proceed by taxi or rental car to Hopkins to stay at one of its beach resorts such as Hamanasi, one of the top beach resorts in Belize, or in a luxurious beachfront suite at Villa Margarita. On your first full day, take a walk on the beach in the morning, then tour Cockscomb Basin Wildlife Sanctuary and hike the jungle trails. Be sure to stop at the Maya Center craft cooperative. Have dinner at

one of the local restaurants in Hopkins Village such as Innie's or at Chef Rob's. On your second full day, get an early start and visit the Mayflower/Bocawina National Park with its small Mayan sites and big waterfalls, perhaps doing the zip line at Bocawina Rainforest Resort. Return to Hopkins and spend the late afternoon napping and recover-ing on the beach. On your third day, rise early and drive (or go by taxi) to Placencia. If the weather's good, take a snorkel trip. Have dinner in Placencia Village (don't miss gelato at Tutti-Fruitt) or at the Bistro at Maya Beach Hotel. End the evening with a drink on the beach at Tipsy Tuna. On your fourth day, if you dive, do a day dive trip to Turneffe or Glover's atoll. If you're there April to June around a full moon, consider doing a snorkel or dive tour to see the huge but gentle whale sharks at Gladden Spit. Alternatively, you could go fishing for tarpon or permit, and if you catch a snapper or something else edible, have one of the local restaurants prepare it for you for dinner. Or simply spend a lazy day in a hammock at the beach and around the pool. On your final day, if you're interested in Mayan sites, do a day trip to Lubaantun and Nim Li Punit near Punta Gorda, or go on a boat tour to Monkey River. You're guaranteed to see howler monkeys, crocs, and lots of birds.

FROM GALES POINT TO PLACENCIA

Thanks to its good beaches, the Southern Coast—the area from Gales Point to Placencia—is the up-and-coming part of Belize, with a growing number of resorts and restaurants, especially in Hopkins and Placencia.

DANGRIGA

99 miles (160 km) southeast of Belmopan.

With a population of around 9,000, Dangriga is the largest town in the south and the home of the Garífuna or Black Caribs, as they're also known (though some view the latter term as a remnant of colonialism). Strictly speaking the plural is Garinagu. There's not much to keep you in Dangriga. Though the town is on the coast, there are no good beaches, no truly first-class hotels, few restaurants, and, except for a small museum on Garífuna culture in the outskirts of town, not much to see. Rickety clapboard houses on stilts and small shops line the downtown streets, and the town has a kind of end-of-the-road feel. Dangriga isn't really dangerous, and in fact it's friendlier than it first seems, though it has a rough vibe, a little like Belize City, that's off-putting for many visitors.

Each year, on November 19 and the days around it, the town cuts loose with a week of Carnival-style celebrations. Garífuna drumming, costumed Jonkunu dancers, punta music, and a good bit of drinking make up the festivities of Garífuna Settlement Day, when these proud people celebrate their arrival in Belize and remember their roots.

GETTING HERE AND AROUND

You can arrive in Dangriga by car, bus, or airplane. The Hummingbird, one of Belize's most scenic roads, runs 54 miles (89 km) from Belmopan to Dangriga. As it approaches Dangriga, it technically becomes the Stann Creek District Highway, but most people simply refer to the entire road as the Hummingbird Highway. James Line and other bus lines have frequent service during the day from Belize City via Belmopan to Dangriga. The bus station in Dangriga is seven blocks south of town on the main road. By air, Maya Island and Tropic together have more than a dozen flights daily to Dangriga's airstrip from the international and municipal airports in Belize City. The airstrip is at the north edge of town.

TIMING

Candidly, Dangriga isn't exactly a mecca for tourists. (Some hotels have Dangriga mailing addresses, even though they're physically located in Hopkins or on an offshore caye or elsewhere.) Unless you have a special interest in Garífuna culture, need to overnight there on your way to Tobacco Caye, Southwater Caye, or another offshore caye, or simply have a yen to visit quirky, Graham Greene-ish spots, you'll probably spend only a few hours in Dangriga, if that. We do note that the best french fries we've ever had in Belize are at the Pelican Beach Hotel in Dangriga, the best hotel in town.

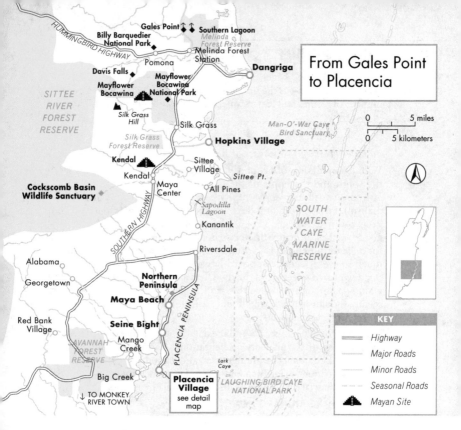

From Gales Point to Placencia

KEY
Highway
Major Roads
Minor Roads
Seasonal Roads
Mayan Site

SAFETY AND PRECAUTIONS

Visitors may get hassled a little on the streets of Dangriga, and care should be exercised if walking around town after dark.

EXPLORING

TOP ATTRACTIONS

FAMILY
Fodor'sChoice
★
Gulisi Garífuna Museum. Named after a Garífuna heroine who came to Belize with her 13 children and founded the village of Punta Negra in Toledo District, this museum has a number of displays on Garífuna history and life. Exhibits cover the Garífuna migration from Africa to St. Vincent, then to Roatan and Belize. Another exhibit is on Thomas Vincent Ramos, a visionary Garífuna leader who, in 1941, established the first Garífuna Settlement Day. Other displays are on Garífuna food, clothing, medicinal plants, and music and dance. The museum also has rotating displays of paintings by Garífuna artists including Pen Cayotano. ⊠ *Chuluhadiwa Park, Stann Creek Valley Rd.* ⊹ *About 2 miles (3 km) west of Dangriga* ☎ *699/0639* ⊕ *www.ngcbelize.org* 🎟 *BZ$10* ☾ *Closed Sun.*

Fodor'sChoice
★
Mayflower Bocawina National Park. Declared a national park in 2001, Mayflower Bocawina has small Mayan ruins, lovely waterfalls, and good hiking on more than 7,000 acres. A private lodge, Bocawina Rainforest Resort, (formerly Mama Noots) is in the park and has upscale

HISTORY

As elsewhere in Belize, the Maya were here first. They had settlements in what is now Stann Creek District at least from the Early Classic period (around AD 300) until the Post-Classic period (about AD 1200). However, this part of Belize did not have the large Mayan cities that existed elsewhere. Few of the known Mayan sites in the area have been extensively excavated, but they appear to have been small ceremonial centers.

In the 1600s, small numbers of English, some of whom were pirates, settled on the Placencia Peninsula, though most eventually left the area. Creoles, slaves from Jamaica, came to Stann Creek in the 1700s, mainly to work in logging, and, later, in fishing. In the next century English traders and farmers arrived in what is now Dangriga. They called their coastal trading posts "stands," which was corrupted to "stann." Hence the name Stann Creek. On November 19, 1823, a group of Garinagu from the Bay Islands of Honduras, Africans who had intermarried with Carib Indians in the southern Caribbean, arrived at the mouth of the Stann Creek River, at what was then called Stann Creek Town. This date is still celebrated in Belize as Garífuna Settlement Day. Later, the name of Stann Creek Town (but not the district) was changed to Dangriga, which means "sweet water" in the Garífuna language.

In the late 1800s several families, originally from Scotland, Portugal, Honduras, and elsewhere, arrived in Placencia. The names of these families—Garbutt, Leslie, Westby, and Cabral—are still common on the peninsula. In the 19th and early 20th centuries the fertile soils of the coastal plain were found to be ideal for growing bananas and citrus, and soon agriculture became the most important industry in the region. The first railroad in Belize, the Stann Creek Railway, built by the United Fruit Company to transport bananas, started operation around World War I. The railroad closed in the 1950s.

The first small tourist resorts were developed on the Placencia Peninsula in the 1960s and '70s, but the lack of infrastructure meant that few visitors got this far south. The first fishing cooperative was established in Placencia in 1962. Although fishing is still a way of life for a few people on the coast, the big money now is real-estate development and tourism. Shrimp farming, once an up-and-coming industry around Placencia, has run into problems due to competition from Asia, and several Belize shrimp farms have closed.

Hurricane Iris in 2001 devastated much of the Southern Coast south of Maya Beach, Tropical Storm Arthur in 2008 caused extensive flooding, and a minor earthquake in 2009 damaged some homes in Placencia and Monkey River. Luckily, Hurricane Earl, in August 2016, did little damage this far south and the area is rebounding stronger than ever, and you will see few signs of the natural disasters.

6

lodging, food and drink, and the longest zip line in Belize. The park has three minor Mayan ceremonial sites: Mayflower, T'au Witz, and Maintzunum, near Silk Grass Creek. Nearby are the three waterfalls: Bocawina Falls, Three Sisters Falls, and Antelope Falls. Access to Mayflower is easiest from Hopkins, about 20 minutes by car. However, tours are offered from Placencia and Dangriga as well as from Hopkins. The entrance to the park is about 4.5 miles (7.5 km) on a dirt road off the Southern Highway. From the visitor center, to get to Bocawina and Three Sisters Falls, which are close together, it's an easy hike of about 1.25 miles (2 km) on the marked Bocawina Falls trail. The trail to Antelope Falls, about 1.75 miles (3 km), is somewhat more difficult due to some steep sections that can be slick after rains. Maps of the trails are available at the small visitor center. So far, little excavation has been conducted at the Mayan sites, but the parklike setting at the base of the Maya Mountains is beautiful. ⊠ *Southern Hwy.* ✛ *From Mile 6 on Southern Hwy., go west 4.5 miles (7.5 km) on dirt road to park visitor center* 🖼 🖾 *BZ$10.*

FAMILY **Southern Lagoon.** One of the most beautiful lagoons in Belize, Southern Lagoon, is about 25 miles (41 km) north of Dangriga—a 45-minute car ride. This lagoon is home to many West Indian manatees, and on beaches nearby, hawksbill turtles nest May to October. The Northern and Western lagoons also are in this area. ⊠ *Southern Lagoon, Gales Point* ✛ *From Dangriga, drive west on Stann Creek Hwy./Hummingbird Hwy. to Melinda; turn right on unpaved Coastal Hwy. and go about 12 miles (20 km) to turnoff for Gales Point and follow 2.5 miles (4 km) to lagoon and Gales Point village.*

WORTH NOTING

FAMILY **Billy Barquedier National Park.** This 1,600-acre park lies along the Hummingbird Highway between Mile 16.5 to 19 in Stann Creek District. Established in 2001, the park is still relatively young, and although it offers no spectacular sights, it does have primitive hiking trails and the Barquedier Waterfall (locally sometimes called Bak-a-Der Waterfall), about a 20-minute hike from the entrance. The park is part of a community co-management program for parks and reserves, in this case with the Steadfast Tourism and Conservation Association of Steadfast village, which co-manages it with the Belize Forest Department. It's best to enter the park via the northern entrance at Mile 16.5 of the Hummingbird Highway. Camping is available in the park for BZ$20 per person, plus the park entrance fee. ⊠ *Main entrance, Mile 16.5, Hummingbird Hwy., Steadfast Village* 🖼 *668/0183* ⊕ *www.billybarquedier. org* 🖾 *BZ$8.*

FAMILY **Davis Falls.** The falls are about 500 feet high and are the second highest in the country (after Thousand-Foot Falls in the Mountain Pine Ridge), and the natural pool at the base of the falls is 75 feet deep. The swimming is wonderful, and the undisturbed forest around the falls is great for a picnic or enjoying nature. Before going to Davis Falls, stop at the Citrus Products of Belize plant (Mile 14.5 of Hummingbird Highway/Stann Creek District Highway), for information and to pay your admission fee. Tours of Davis Falls are offered by several tour guides including Holistic Eco Tours at Steadfast village. ∎TIP➜ **Getting to**

Davis Falls requires a four-wheel-drive vehicle to tackle the extremely rough 8-mile dirt road, before you set out on the arduous 2 mile (3.3 km) hike. ⊠ *Mile 14.5, Hummingbird Hwy.* ☎ *603/2339 for Holistic Eco Tours* 🎫 *BZ$10.*

Gales Point. The small Creole village of Gales Point, population about 500, has an idyllic setting on the Southern Lagoon. The lagoon and nearby waters are home to many manatees. You can drive to Gales Point via the unpaved Coastal Highway, and tours are available from Dangriga and Hopkins. ⊠ *Gales Point* ✛ *To Gales Point: From Dangriga, go northwest on Hummingbird Hwy. 8.5 miles (14 km) to village of Melinda; turn right on Manatee Hwy. (Coastal Rd.) and follow 13 miles (21 km) to turnoff, a sharp right turn. This dirt road to Gales Point Village runs about 2.5 miles (4 km) until it ends at lagoon and Manatee Lodge* ☎ *209/8031 community phone for Gales Point.*

Fodor's Choice
★
Marie Sharp's Factory. You can visit the source of one of Belize's few well-known exports, Marie Sharp's Hot Sauce, made in about a dozen different heat levels from Mild to Beware. The small factory, with about 25 workers, established and still run by Marie Sharp and family, is open to interested visitors weekdays, but for a tour it's best to call in advance. Besides the factory tour, you can also see the entire selection of products manufactured by Marie Sharp, and most are offered for sale along with Marie Sharp T-shirts and tote bags. Her products are sold in nearly every grocery in Belize and are on tables in most restaurants in Belize. ■TIP→ **Marie Sharp's main office is in Dangriga, where there also is a small shop.** ⊠ *1 Melinda Rd., 8 miles (13 km) west of Dangriga—watch for sign on east side of Hummingbird Hwy. as you near junction of Hummingbird and Southern Hwys., Stann Creek Valley* ☎ *520/2087* ⊕ *www.mariesharps-bz.com* 🎫 *Free.*

WHERE TO EAT

$
LATIN AMERICAN
✕ **King Burger.** Formerly called Burger King, but a far cry from the U.S. chain of a similar name, this is one of the best places in Dangriga to get an honest plate of chicken and rice and beans. Prepared by the Cuban owner, the fresh fish is good, and, yes, so are the hamburgers. Everything's affordable, too. No alcohol is served, but you can BYOB (Bring Your Own Belikin). $ *Average main: BZ$13* ⊠ *135 Commerce St., on Dangriga's main street just north of the bridge of North Stann Creek River* ☎ *522/2476* ▭ *No credit cards* ☉ *Closed Sun.*

$
LATIN AMERICAN
✕ **Riverside Café.** The Creole and Garífuna dishes here are hearty, tasty, and prepared fresh. The restaurant is often busy with fishermen and the guys who run boats out to Tobacco Caye and other offshore cayes, but it's basic and clean. If you're going to the islands you can arrange transportation while sipping a beer or having breakfast or a plate of rice and beans. $ *Average main: BZ$12* ⊠ *Riverside and Oak Sts., on west side of North Stann Creek River* ☎ *661/6390* ▭ *No credit cards.*

WHERE TO STAY

$$
RESORT
🏨 **Bocawina Rainforest Resort.** Located within the beautiful Mayflower Bocawina National Park, the Bocawina Rainforest Resort has comfortable, newly renovated accommodations that include four spacious deluxe suites (with two queen beds, a table and chairs in a sitting area

with jungle views through large windows), two thatched casitas (one has two bedrooms that can be rented together or as individual units), and six standard rooms that share a single verandah. **Pros:** hard-to-beat location in national park; lots of wildlife and birds; on-site zip line. **Cons:** you may need lots of bug spray; no a/c. [$] *Rooms from: BZ$281* ✉ *Mayflower Bocawina National Park, near Mayflower archaeological site, 5 miles (8 km) off Mile 6, Southern Hwy.* ☎ *670/8019, 844/894–2311 toll-free in U.S. and Canada* 🌐 *www.bocawina.com* 🛏 *12 rooms* 🍴 *Breakfast.*

$$ B&B/INN 🏨 **Manatee Lodge.** This colonial-era lodge, just feet from the Southern Lagoon and surrounded by flowers, has a stunning setting, though the facilities do not live up to its location. **Pros:** beautiful waterside setting; interesting colonial, Graham Greenesque atmosphere. **Cons:** off-the-beaten-path location; lodge needs updates and upgrades. [$] *Rooms from: BZ$220* ✉ *Manatee Lodge, on Southern Lagoon, Gales Point* ☎ *532/2400* 🌐 *www.manateelodge.com* 🛏 *8 rooms.*

$$ HOTEL 🏨 **Pelican Beach Resort.** This waterfront hotel on the north end of Dangriga, near the airstrip, is the best the town has to offer. **Pros:** charming colonial-era main building; breezy seaside location; the best lodging in Dangriga. **Cons:** not the beach of your dreams. [$] *Rooms from: BZ$294* ✉ *Scotchman Town, North End* ☎ *522/2044* 🌐 *www.pelicanbeachbelize.com* 🛏 *20 rooms.*

SHOPPING

Dangriga has some interesting, offbeat shopping, notably for Garífuna arts and crafts. Collectors may want to spend a day looking for items that are rarely available outside Belize and in some cases may not be available elsewhere in Belize. Noted Garífuna artist Pen Cayetano has a studio and gallery. Garífuna cultural expert Frank Swaso has a gallery selling local drums, dolls, masks, and wood carvings.

Pen Cayetano Studio Gallery. Punta rocker and internationally known Garífuna artist Pen Cayetano displays his bold, colorful paintings at his studio and gallery at his home in Dangriga. Work by his wife, Ingrid Cayetano, and daughter, Mali, are also displayed. The house, built around 1900 and totally redone by Cayetano, including painted murals on the exterior walls, alone is worth a visit, as it is one of the most interesting old buildings in Dangriga. ✉ *3 Aranda Crescent at Gallery St.* ☎ *628/6807* 🌐 *www.cayetano.de* 🎫 *BZ$5* 🕒 *Closed Mon.*

HOPKINS VILLAGE

10 miles (17 km) south of Dangriga on the Southern Hwy., then 2 miles (3.3 km) east on a partially paved road.

Hopkins is an intriguing Garífuna coastal village of about 1,800 people, halfway between Dangriga and Placencia. Garífuna culture is more accessible here than in Dangriga. Hopkins has the same toast-color beaches as those in Placencia, and a number of new resorts have opened to take advantage of them, including resorts, restaurants, and shops just to the south of Hopkins Village. Americans, Canadians, and Europeans are snapping up beachfront land here at prices only slightly lower than

CLOSE UP

The Garífuna Struggle

Perhaps the most unusual of the ethnic groups calling Belize home, the Garífuna have a story that is both bizarre and moving, an odyssey of exile and dispossession in the wake of the confusion wrought in the New World by the Old. The Garífuna are descended from a group of Nigerians who were shipwrecked on the island of St. Vincent in 1635. (Although the Nigerians were taken as slaves, their descendents vociferously deny they were ever slaves.) The Caribs, St. Vincent's indigenous population, fiercely resisted the outsiders at first, but they eventually overcame their distrust.

In the eyes of the British colonial authorities, the new ethnic group that developed after years of intermarriage was an illegitimate and troublesome presence. Worse still, the Garífuna sided with, and were succored by, the French. After nearly two centuries of guerrilla warfare, the British decided that the best way to solve

the problem was to deport them en masse. After a circuitous and tragic journey across the Caribbean, during which thousands perished of disease and hunger, some of the exiles arrived in Belize, while others ended up on the coast of Honduras, Guatemala, and Nicaragua.

That the Garífuna have preserved their cultural identity testifies to Belize's extraordinary ability to encourage diversity. They have their own religion, a potent mix of ancestor worship and Catholicism; their own language, which, like Carib, has separate male and female dialects; their own music, a percussion-oriented sound known as punta rock; and their own social structure, which dissuades young people from marrying outside their community. In writer Marcella Lewis, universally known as Auntie Madé, the Garífuna also had their own poet laureate. In 2002 the United Nations designated the Garífuna as a World Heritage culture.

6

in Placencia or on Ambergris Caye. If there's a downside to the area, it's the biting sand flies, which can be vicious at times.

GETTING HERE AND AROUND

The turnoff to Hopkins from the Southern Highway is 10 miles (16 km) south of the junction of the Hummingbird and Southern highways. The once potholed Hopkins Road is now nicely paved. James Bus Line will drop you at the entrance road to Hopkins along Southern Highway, and a few stop in Hopkins itself. Shuttles also transfer visitors from the international airport to Hopkins, as there is no direct air service to the village yet. Until that happens, you can fly to Dangriga and take a taxi to Hopkins, if your hotel doesn't provide a shuttle.

TIMING

The highlights of Hopkins can be seen in much less than a day, but if this is your beach destination, you can profitably spend several days, or longer, here enjoying activities on the water.

EXPLORING

Lebeha Drumming Center. In Hopkins you can watch young Garífuna boys hone their drumming skills at the Lebeha Drumming Center. *Lebeha* means "the end" in the Garífuna language, a reference to the school's location at a small guesthouse with a bar, budget rooms, and cabins near the north end of the village. Visitors are welcome. The drums are of mahogany or mayflower wood, with deerskin on the drumhead. Other instruments include *shakas,* or shakers, calabash gourds filled with fruit seeds and turtle shells. The drumming goes on nightly, though most activity is on weekends. Donations are accepted. You can take drumming lessons and purchase a CD of Lebeha drumming. ✉ *Lebeha Drumming, Main Rd., near north end of village, Hopkins* ☎ *665/9305* 🌐 *www.lebeha.com.*

WHERE TO EAT

$$$ SEAFOOD 🍴 **Barracuda Bar & Grill.** Owners Tony and Angela Marsico traded running a restaurant in Alaska for operating a beachside bistro in Belize. They've turned this restaurant, part of Beaches and Dreams Seafront Inn, into one of the better eateries on the Southern Coast, with delicious dishes like fresh grilled snapper and smoked chicken or ribs. Catch the sea breezes on the covered, open-air deck while you munch a handmade pizza or enjoy a burger. [$] *Average main: BZ$40* ✉ *Sittee Point, Hopkins* ☎ *523/7259* 🌐 *www.beachesanddreams.com.*

$$$ CARIBBEAN Fodor's Choice ★ 🍴 **Chef Rob's Gourmet Cafe.** You'll recognize this restaurant by the big sign out front made from one side of a red 1964 Peugeot 404, but inside the restaurant at Parrot Cove Lodge, Chef Rob Pronk's eclectic Caribbean-style, locally sourced food is surprisingly contemporary and delicious. You can order a four-course meal (soup, salad, entrée, and dessert) from the prix-fixe menu or order à la carte. The menu changes daily, but the entrée might be lobster, fresh fish, or ribs, all presented creatively and with interesting sauces. The restaurant is on the beach at Parrot Cove Resort, which Rob and his wife Corrie Pronk also manage. In 2016, Chef Rob expanded the restaurant and consolidated his Love on the Rocks restaurant with this one, giving diners the option of the regular restaurant menu or the Love on the Rocks concept, where guests cook their own food on a hot lava rock. [$] *Average main: BZ$50* ✉ *Parrot Cove Lodge, Sittee River Rd., Hopkins* ☎ *663/1529* 🌐 *www.chefrobbelize.com/* ✍ *Reservations essential.*

$$ PIZZA 🍴 **Driftwood Beach Bar and Pizza Shack.** Driftwood arguably has the best pizza in Southern Belize, served up by outgoing British-American owners in a friendly, casual atmosphere in a beachfront thatch palapa. Try the Driftwood combo pizza, with red sauce, pepperoni, Italian sausage, peppers, onion, mushrooms, and black olives (in three sizes). If pizza isn't your thing, go for the catch of the day or one of the pasta dishes. Plenty of cold beer and rum at reasonable prices. There's usually a beach barbecue on Sunday afternoons, with beach volleyball. [$] *Average main: BZ$25* ✉ *North end of Hopkins, Hopkins* ☎ *667/4072* 🌐 *www.driftwoodpizza.com* ⏲ *Closed Wed.*

$$ CARIBBEAN 🍴 **Geckos Restaurant.** One of the best-loved eateries in Hopkins, Geckos is a place where everybody knows your name; James cooks and Tina tends bar. Within minutes, you'll be friends with everybody, and you'll

be enjoying a rum and tonic, jerk chicken, Gecko Balls (don't ask, just try'em), and world-class, fresh-cut fries. TIP→ **Call ahead if you want a table in the open-air dining room.** [$] *Average main: BZ$24* ✉ *Main St. at Hopkins Rd., Hopkins* ✣ *Just north of T-intersection at entrance to Hopkins* ☎ *629/5411* 🌐 *www.geckosrestaurant.com* 🕒 *Closed Sun. and Tues.* 💳 *No credit cards.*

$ LATIN AMERICAN 🍴 **Innies Restaurant.** At Innies, as at most local restaurants in Hopkins, you're eating in a spot that was once somebody's house or back porch. Here, you can dine inside, or outside and get the full flavor of village life. The food is authentic (though some dishes cater to the taste of tourists), delicious, and inexpensive. You'll find the staff very friendly. Traditional Garífuna dishes such as *hudut* (fish cooked in coconut milk and served with mashed plantains) and *ereba* (grated cassava bread) with *bundiga* (a gravy of grated plantains and coconut) are available, but less exotic dishes like fried chicken and rice and beans with stew chicken are also served. [$] *Average main: BZ$14* ✉ *191 South, south end of village, Hopkins* ☎ *503/7333.*

$$ AMERICAN 🍴 **Lucky Lobster Bar and Grill.** You might feel like you've stumbled into a bar in the States, but this open-air bar just has all those trappings—several TVs tuned to sports channels, nice restrooms, and efficient service. If you're craving fried-not-greasy food, get the Chicklets (chicken tenders skillfully battered in buttermilk and cornmeal), or the Lucky Clucker Lollipops (chicken skewers). Come back for the great night scene. TIP→ **"I Got Lucky at Lucky Lobster" visors, koozies, and T-shirts can be purchased.** [$] *Average main: BZ$18* ✉ *Sittee River Rd., Lot 6, Hopkins* ☎ *676/7777* 🕒 *Closed Mon. and Tues.*

$ CAFÉ 🍴 **Thongs Café.** This European-run coffee shop and bistro is small but stylish, with Belizean wood carvings and paintings on the walls and free Wi-Fi. Expect good coffee, well-prepared breakfast omelets, and satisfying smoothies. For lunch, try the salads. TIP→ **The prime tables on the front patio fill up quickly so get here early.** [$] *Average main: BZ$14* ✉ *Main St., south of main T-intersection, Hopkins* ☎ *622/0110* 🕒 *Closed Mon.*

WHERE TO STAY

In addition to the resorts and hotels, Hopkins has about 20 small guesthouses, mostly run by local villagers but also by some expats who have found that the easygoing Hopkins life suits them. Most don't look like much from the outside, but have the necessities including electricity and, usually, private baths. At these guesthouses it's usually not necessary to make reservations. When you arrive in the village, just walk around until you find one that suits you.

$$$ RESORT 🏨 **Almond Beach Resort & Spa.** Variety is the spice of beach life here, with an assortment of rooms, suites, and villas, some of which can be combined into über-suites for families. **Pros:** variety of accommodations; full-service spa; full-service resort. **Cons:** not inexpensive. [$] *Rooms from: BZ$495* ✉ *Sittee Rd., Hopkins* ☎ *786/472–9664 U.S. for Almond Beach and all Viva Belize properties, 533/7040 Belize for Almond Beach* 🌐 *www.vivabelize.com/almond-beach* 🛏 *25 rooms* 🍽 *No meals.*

6

CLOSE UP

Development, Belize-Style

"People are building $500,000 houses on $5,000 roads!" This is the sentiment of many who watch in amazement as huge condos and luxury houses sprout up along narrow, muddy golf-cart trails. In some areas huge 4,000- to 6,000-square-foot homes are being built where there is no municipal water or sewage system, and in more remote parts of the country no electricity or telephone. One stretch of road on the Placencia Peninsula is now sprinkled with massive McMansions, gated communities, and condo projects, built on filled land next to the lagoon.

Belize's lack of infrastructure is nothing new. As late as the 1980s open sewers were common all over Belize City. Even today, in some rural villages, especially in Toledo District, telephone service is a rare commodity, and drinking water comes from a community well. With the unemployment rate in Belize in the low double digits, and with good, high-paying jobs scarce, many hope that the new housing boom will provide a needed economic boost and sustainable job growth. But environmentalists are taking a darker view.

In the Hopkins area, near Sittee Point, environmentalists worry that some of the tallest mangroves in the Western Hemisphere will fall prey to developers. It is illegal to remove endangered mangroves in Belize without a government permit, but this rule, like many other environmental protections, is often ignored. It isn't unusual for homeowners and developers with waterfront property to simply tear out these precious trees and deal with possible fines later.

Belize effectively has no zoning or comprehensive land-use planning, though there is now a countrywide building code that applies to individual buildings and houses. Environmental regulations, while strict in theory—every development is required to have a formal Environmental Impact Plan approved by the national government—often fail in practice. Protective regulations and permit procedures are circumvented, flouted, or just plain ignored. Government officials, whose resources are stretched thin, often can't provide oversight on development projects. According to environmentalists, some government officials are corrupt; they believe that developers can do what they like, if the price is right.

Economic growth, the environment, and the housing boom in Belize are complex, with parties facing off on a multitude of issues. Who knows if everyone will ever see eye-to-eye?

$$ RESORT FAMILY 🏨 **Beaches and Dreams Seafront Inn.** Refugees from Alaska's harsh winters purchased this small beachfront inn, turning it into a popular laid-back beach spot. **Pros:** kick-off-your-shoes atmosphere; steps from the sea; good restaurant. **Cons:** comfort, not luxury; restaurant prices not cheap. [$] *Rooms from: BZ$286* ✉ *Sittee Point Rd., Hopkins* ☎ *523/7259* 🌐 *www.beachesanddreams.com* 🛏 *11 rooms (6 in main hotel building, 1 cabin, and 4 rooms in original octaganol buildings)* 🍴 *No meals.*

$$$$ RESORT 🏨 **Belizean Dreams.** This collection of seaside condos is among the most upmarket accommodation choices on the Southern Coast. **Pros:** deluxe condo apartments; units can be combined and configured to meet your

needs; friendly service. **Cons:** pool is small; some units have a minimum stay. $ *Rooms from: BZ$590* ✉ *Sittee River Rd., Hopkins* ☎ *523/7271, 800/456–7150 toll-free in U.S. and Canada* ⊕ *www.belizeandreams. com* ⇨ *9 villas* ❍❘ *No meals.*

$$ **Coconut Row.** This property is made up of three different accommoda-
RENTAL tion types—Coconut Row, Palm Cove Cabins, and Buttonwood Guest-
house—which provides guests with a range of options to choose from
including standard rooms, apartments, and cabins. **Pros:** beachfront
units with Wi-Fi and fridges; a step up from other village accommoda-
tions; reasonable prices. **Cons:** a/c only at night unless you pay extra;
a few units don't have sea views. $ *Rooms from: BZ$218* ✉ *Front
St., Hopkins* ☎ *670/3000* ⊕ *www.coconutrowbelize.com* ⇨ *12 rooms*
❍❘ *No meals.*

$$$$ **Hamanasi Adventure and Dive Resort.** With beautifully landscaped
RESORT grounds, top-notch accommodations, and an excellent dive program,
Fodor'sChoice Hamanasi (Garífuna for "almond") is among Belize's very best beach
★ and dive resorts. **Pros:** well-run resort; deluxe lodging in beautiful
beachside setting; high-quality dive trips and inland tours. **Cons:** expen-
sive restaurant; pricey accommodations (but worth it); diving requires
a long boat trip to the reef or atolls. $ *Rooms from: BZ$931* ✉ *Ha-
manasi, Sittee River Rd., Hopkins* ☎ *533/7073, 844/235–4930 toll-free
in U.S. and Canada* ⊕ *www.hamanasi.com* ⇨ *25 rooms* ❍❘ *Breakfast.*

$ **Hopkins Inn.** New owners have taken over at Hopkins Inn, updating
B&B/INN and remodeling the rooms, while retaining the cosy, beachfront cot-
FAMILY tage feel that keeps the guests returning. **Pros:** on the beach; helpful,
Fodor'sChoice enthusiastic young owners. **Cons:** you may be awakened by the sound
★ of roosters. $ *Rooms from: BZ$185* ✉ *Hopkins* ☎ *665/0411* ⊕ *www.
hopkinsinn.bz* ⇨ *4 cottages* ❍❘ *Breakfast.*

$$$$ **Jaguar Reef Lodge.** The original upscale resort in Hopkins, Jaguar
RESORT Reef Lodge has updated its original whitewashed duplex garden and
FAMILY beachfront thatch cabañas and has added newer colonial suites with
local artwork, salt-tile floors, and custom-made hardwood furnish-
ings. **Pros:** attractive and well-kept grounds; lovely beachside loca-
tion. **Cons:** beautiful restaurant but meals are pricey; parking for guest
vehicles is limited. $ *Rooms from: BZ$540* ✉ *Sittee River Rd., Hopkins*
☎ *786/472–9664 U.S. for Jaguar Reef Lodge and all Viva properties,
533/7040 in Belize* ⊕ *www.vivabelize.com/jaguar-reef* ⇨ *20 units.*

$$$ **Parrot Cove Lodge.** This small beachfront resort with rooms in earth
RESORT tones arranged around a courtyard with a pool, is an attractive option
FAMILY if you don't need all the amenities of the larger resorts but want an
excellent restaurant. **Pros:** beachfront location; excellent restaurant on-
site. **Cons:** bit of a hike to activities in Hopkins Village. $ *Rooms from:
BZ$385* ✉ *False Sittee Point, Sittee River Rd., Hopkins* ☎ *523/7225*
⊕ *www.parrotcovelodge.com* ⇨ *10 units* ❍❘ *No meals.*

$ **Tipple Tree Beya Hotel.** This small beachfront guesthouse in the heart
B&B/INN of Hopkins Village, in business since 1998, provides a comfortable,
no-frills alternative to the coast's upmarket resorts. **Pros:** steps from the
water; hammocks on the porch. **Cons:** basic, not overly large rooms; no
a/c. $ *Rooms from: BZ$87* ✉ *Hopkins* ⊹ *On beach in heart of village*
☎ *615/7006* ⊕ *www.tippletree.com* ⇨ *7 units* ❍❘ *No meals.*

6

$$$$ RESORT FAMILY Fodor's Choice ★ **Villa Margarita.** For a total, top-notch, luxury splurge, take a suite at this new three-story, six-unit villa on the beach just south of Hopkins Village. **Pros:** gorgeous beachfront suites with balconies; designer furnishings and full kitchens; shared private pool. **Cons:** not inexpensive; no elevator. [$] *Rooms from: 600* ✉ *Sittee River Rd., Hopkins* ✣ *Just south of Almond Beach, next door to Villa Verana; check in at Jaguar Reef* ☎ *786/472–9664 in U.S.* 🌐 *www.vivabelize.com/villa-margarita* 🛏 *6 rooms* 🍴 *No meals.*

SPORTS AND THE OUTDOORS

BIRD-WATCHING

Cockscomb Basin Wildlife Sanctuary has excellent birding, with some 300 species identified in the reserve. You can also sometimes see the jabiru stork, the largest flying bird in the Western Hemisphere, in the marsh areas just to the west of Hopkins Village. Keep an eye out as you drive into the village from the Southern Highway. North of Hopkins is Fresh Water Creek Lagoon, and south of the village is Anderson Lagoon. These lagoons and mangrove swamps are home to many waterbirds, including herons and egrets. A kayak trip on the Sittee River should reward you with kingfishers, toucans, and various flycatchers. About 30 minutes by boat off Hopkins is Man-o-War Caye, a bird sanctuary that has one of the largest colonies of frigate birds in the Caribbean, more than 300 nesting birds. Hamanasi, Jaguar Reef, and other hotels arrange bird-watching trips.

CANOEING AND KAYAKING

When kayaking or canoeing on the Sittee River, you can see many birds and, possibly, manatees and crocodiles. Manatees and porpoises are often spotted in the sea just off the Hopkins shore. Several hotels in Hopkins, including Tipple Tree Beya Hotel, Hopkins Inn, and Jungle Jeanie's rent kayaks, canoes, and other water equipment by the hour or day. Although it's possible to do sea kayaking from Hopkins, often the water is choppy. Long sea-kayaking trips should be tried only by experienced kayakers, preferably with a guide.

CAVING

Caving tours from Hopkins typically go to St. Herman's Cave and the Crystal Cave at Blue Hole National Park on the Hummingbird Highway.

DISTANCES

Hopkins is less than 10 minutes by road (rough and potholed) from the paved Southern Highway and is ideally situated for a variety of outdoor adventures, both land and sea. Here's the distance from Hopkins to selected points of interest:

- Belize Barrier Reef: 10 miles (17 km)
- Cockscomb Basin Wildlife Sanctuary: 10 miles (17 km)
- Glover's and Turneffe atolls: 25 miles (42 km)
- Mayflower Bocawina National Park: 15 miles (25 km)

HIKING

Most hiking trips go to Cockscomb Basin Wildlife Sanctuary, where there are a dozen short hiking trails near the visitor center. If you're a glutton for punishment, you can go on a guided hike to Victoria Peak, the second-highest mountain peak in Belize. The 40-mile (67-km) hike from the visitor center at Cockscomb Basin Wildlife Sanctuary to the top entails inclines of 45 to 60 degrees. Most of these trips require at least three days up and back. One guide who will take you on jungle tours is Marcos Cucul, a jungle survival guide who is a member of the Belize National Cave and Wilderness Rescue Team.

Marcos Cucul. Marcos Cucul is a jungle survival guide who is a member of the Belize National Cave and Wilderness Rescue Team. ⊠ *Hopkins* ⊕ *www.mayaguide.bz.*

HORSEBACK RIDING

Local lodges arrange horseback-riding trips, working with ranches near Belmopan and Dangriga. A full-day horseback trip usually includes transportation to the ranch and lunch.

MANATEE-WATCHING TOURS

Local lodges offer trips to Gales Point and the Southern Lagoon to try to spot Antillean manatees, a subspecies of West Indian manatees. These large aquatic mammals—adults weigh 800 to 1,200 pounds—are related to elephants. They're found in shallow waters in lagoons, rivers, estuaries, and coastal areas in much of Belize, and are especially common in the lagoons around Gales Point. These gentle herbivores can live 60 years or longer. Under Belize government guidelines, you're not permitted to feed manatees, to swim with them, or to approach a manatee with a calf.

SCUBA DIVING AND SNORKELING

Diving and snorkeling off Hopkins is very good to terrific, though expensive compared with the northern cayes. The Barrier Reef is closer here—about 10 miles (17 km) from shore—than it is farther south. Dive shops with fast boats can also take you all the way to the atolls—Turneffe, Glover's, and even Lighthouse. These atoll trips generally start early in the morning, at 6 or 7 am, and last all day. In late spring, when whale sharks typically show up, local dive shops offer dives to see the Belizean behemoths at Gladden Spit Marine Reserve. Keep in mind that there are marine park fees (sometimes included in dive trip charges) for South Water Caye, Glover's, and Gladden Spit marine reserves, as well as additional rental fees for regulators, BCD, wet suits, and other equipment.

Fodor's Choice ★ **Hamanasi.** One of the best diving operations in Southern Belize is at Hamanasi. They have three large, well-equipped dive boats, including a 45-foot boat with three 200-horsepower outboard engines. ⊠ *Hopkins* ☎ *533/7073* ⊕ *www.hamanasi.com.*

WINDSURFING

Windsurfing is a growing sport in Hopkins, as the wind is a fairly consistent 10 to 15 knots, except in August and September, when it sometimes goes calm. The best winds are in April and May.

Windschief. Windschief rents well-maintained windsurfing equipment for BZ$20 for the first hour, then BZ$10 for additional hours, or BZ$60 a day. Private lessons are BZ$60 an hour. Windschief also has beach cabañas and a bar. ⊠ *Hopkins* ☎ *668/6087* ⊕ *www.windsurfing-belize.com.*

SHOPPING

Shopping is limited in Hopkins, where the local "shopping center" is a small clapboard house. Locals traditionally make much of what they use in daily life, from cassava graters to fishing canoes and paddles, and drums and *shakas* (shakers made from a calabash gourd filled with seeds). Around the village, you'll see individuals selling carvings and other local handicrafts made from shells and coconuts. Also, several small shops and stands are scattered around the main part of the village. You can bargain for the best price, but remember that there are few jobs around Hopkins and that these craftspeople are trying to earn money to help feed their families.

Garimaya. The biggest and newest gift shop in the area, Garimaya has a large selection of Garífuna and Maya crafts, including masks, clothing, jewelry, and wood carvings, although some items appear to be imported from Guatemala and Mexico. It also sells souvenirs such as T-shirts. ⊠ *Sittee River Rd., Hopkins* ☎ *666/7970.*

COCKSCOMB BASIN WILDLIFE SANCTUARY

10 miles (17 km) southwest of Hopkins Village.

The mighty jaguar, once the undisputed king of the Central and South American jungles, is now endangered. But it has a haven in the Cockscomb Basin Wildlife Sanctuary, which covers 128,000 acres of lush rain forest in the Cockscomb Range of the Maya Mountains. With the Bladen Nature Reserve to the south, the jaguars have a continuous corridor of about 250,000 acres. Thanks to these reserves, as well as other protected areas around the country, Belize has the highest concentration of jaguars in the world.

GETTING HERE AND AROUND

Maya Center, at the entrance of the road to Cockscomb, is at Mile 15 of the Southern Highway. You can drive here, or any local bus on the Southern Highway will drop you. From Maya Center it's 6 miles (10 km) to the park. You can drive, hike (about two hours), or take a local taxi. There is a co-op crafts shop at Maya Center, which is a good place to buy locally made Mayan crafts; however, prices here generally are no lower than elsewhere in Belize.

TIMING

Most visitors come to Cockscomb only on a day visit. However, for the best chance to see wildlife and even a jaguar, a stay of several nights is best.

EXPLORING

FAMILY

Fodor's Choice
★

Cockscomb Basin Wildlife Sanctuary. Some visitors to Cockscomb are disappointed that they don't see jaguars and that wildlife doesn't jump out from behind trees to astound them as they hike the trails. The experience at Cockscomb is indeed a low-key one, and seeing wildlife requires patience and luck. You'll have the best chance of seeing wild animals, perhaps even a jaguar or one of the other large cats, if you stay overnight, preferably for several nights, in the sanctuary. You may also have better luck if you go for an extended hike with a guide. Several nearby lodges, such as Hamanasi, offer night hikes to Cockscomb, departing around dusk and returning around 9 pm.

Cockscomb Basin has native wildlife aside from the jaguars. You might see other cats—pumas, margays, and ocelots—plus coatis, kinkajous, deer, peccaries, and, last but not least, tapirs. Also known as the mountain cow, this shy, curious creature appears to be half horse, half hippo, with a bit of cow and elephant thrown in. Nearly 300 species of birds have been identified in the Cockscomb Basin, including the keel-billed toucan, the king vulture, several hawk species, and the scarlet macaw, a species of parrot.

Within the reserve is Belize's best-maintained system of jungle and mountain trails, most of which lead to at least one outstanding swimming hole. The sanctuary also has spectacular views of Victoria Peak and the Cockscomb Range. Bring serious bug spray with you—the reserve swarms with mosquitoes and tiny biting flies called no-see-ums—and, if you can tolerate the heat, wear long-sleeve shirts and long pants. The best times to hike anywhere in Belize are early morning, late afternoon, and early evening, when temperatures are lower and more animals are on the prowl.

The road from Maya Center to the Cockscomb ranger station and visitor center winds 6 miles (10 km) through dense vegetation—splendid cahune palms, purple mimosas, orchids, and big-leaf plantains—and as you go higher the marvelous sound of tropical birds, often resembling strange windup toys, grows stronger and stronger. This is definitely four-wheel-drive terrain. You may have to ford several small creeks as well as negotiate deep, muddy ruts. At the end, in a clearing with hibiscus and bougainvillea bushes, you'll find a little office, where you can buy maps of the nature trails, along with restrooms, several picnic tables, cabins, and a campground. The Belize Audubon Society manages the Cockscomb and can assist in making reservations for the simple accommodations in the sanctuary.

Altogether there are some 20 miles (33 km) of marked trails. Walking along these 12 nature trails is a good way to get to know the region. Most are loops of 0.5–1.5 miles (1–2 km), so you can do several in a day. The most strenuous trail takes you up a steep hill; from the top is a magnificent view of the entire Cockscomb Basin. Longer hikes, such as to Victoria Peak, require a guide and several days of strenuous walking.

Hotels and tour operators and guides in Hopkins, Placencia, and Dangriga offer tours to Cockscomb; Hopkins is closest to the sanctuary but easily accessible from any of these coastal areas. ✉ *Maya Center, Mile 15, Southern Hwy.* ☎ *227/7369 Maya Center, 223/5004 Belize Audubon Society in Belize City* ⊕ *www.belizeaudubon.org* ✎ *BZ$10.*

Although most visitors come to Cockscomb on day trips and stay in Hopkins, Placencia, or Dangriga, you can camp at one of three campgrounds in the reserve.

$ **Cockscomb Campgrounds and Cabins.** You can camp at one of three
RENTAL   campgrounds in the Combscomb Wildlife Reserve for BZ$10 per night per person, or for a little more money you can stay in rooms in a dormitory with solar-generated electricity, starting at BZ$40 per person. **Pros:** true jungle setting; inexpensive. **Cons:** don't expect upscale amenities. $ *Rooms from: BZ$20* ⊠ *Cockscomb Basin Wildlife Sanctuary* ✛ *Near visitor center* ☎ *223/5004 Belize Audubon Society in Belize City* ⊕ *www.belizeaudubon.org* ⇗ *10 rooms* ⏻ *No meals.*

$ **Tutzil Nah Cottages.** Gregorio Chun and his family, Mopan Maya
RENTAL   people who've lived in this area for many generations, provide afford-
FAMILY   able accommodations in simple thatch cabañas. **Pros:** near Maya Center; owners highly knowledgeable about Cockscomb; interesting tours available. **Cons:** very basic accommodations; furnishings and beds need repairs and upgrading. $ *Rooms from: BZ$50* ⊠ *Mile 13.5, Southern Hwy., near Maya Center* ☎ *533/7045* ⊕ *www.mayacenter.com* ⇗ *4 rooms* ⏻ *No meals.*

PLACENCIA PENINSULA

28 miles (47 km) south of Dangriga by road.

The Placencia Peninsula is fast becoming one of the major visitor destinations in Belize, one that may eventually rival Ambergris Caye as the most popular resort area in the country. It's one 16-mile- (26-km-) long peninsula, with three different but complementary areas: Northern Peninsula/Maya Beach, Seine Bight, and Placencia Village.

The former dirt track that ran 25 miles (41 km) from the Southern Highway to the tiny community of Riversdale and then down the peninsula to Placencia Village has been paved, and the road is now in excellent condition (beware the speed bumps, however). Beginning at Riversdale, at the elbow where the actual peninsula joins the mainland, you'll get a quick glimpse through mangroves of the startlingly blue Caribbean. As you go south, the Placencia Lagoon is on your right, and behind it in the distance rise the low Maya Mountains, the Cockscomb Range ruffling the tropical sky with its jagged peaks. On your left, a few hundred feet away, beyond the remaining mangroves and a narrow band of beach, is the Caribbean Sea. A broken line of uninhabited cayes grazes the horizon.

The northern end of the peninsula from Riversdale south to Maya Beach once had just a few small seaside houses, and Maya Beach was a sleepy beach community. Now the towering five-story buildings of the Copal Beach condominium development, currently under construction, with a small casino on the first floor, rise up out of the flat peninsula land. "For Sale" signs dot the roadside, supersize beach- and lagoon-side mansions are going up at The Placencia Residences and elsewhere, and several new condominium communities and resorts are open or planned (though some are struggling to find buyers). These new resorts and condo developments join a group of laid-back seaside hotels and cabins. The beaches toward the upper end of the peninsula are some of the best on mainland Belize, and more restaurants and shops are starting to open here. One of the best restaurants in all of Belize, the Bistro at Maya Beach Hotel, is usually packed. There's now even a small bowling alley in Maya Beach, Jaguar Lanes.

Roughly midway down the peninsula is the Garífuna Village of Seine Bight, struggling to adapt to change. At both the north and south ends of the village upscale resorts and condo developments have sprung up to take advantage of the appealing beaches.

On a sheltered half-moon bay at the southern tip of the peninsula is Placencia Village. Founded by pirates, and long a Creole village, the community is now inhabited by an extraordinary mélange of people, local and expatriate. Most of the hotels in the village are modest, and most shops have tiny selections. Never mind, once you arrive you'll probably just want to lie in a hammock with a good book, perhaps getting up long enough to cool off in the gentle waves or to sip a Belikin at one of the village saloons.

From anywhere on the Placencia Peninsula you can dive along the Belize Barrier Reef, swim in the warm seawater, look for scarlet macaws in Red Bank village to the southwest (mainly between December and February), explore the Mayan ruins at Mayflower and hike to the waterfalls there, or, on a full day trip, travel to the Mayan sites at Lubaantun and Nim Li Punit near Punta Gorda, or treat yourself to some of the best sportfishing in the country.

GETTING HERE AND AROUND

Both Tropic Air and Maya Island Air fly from Belize City to Placencia, usually with a quick stop in Dangriga, and also from Punta Gorda. The airstrip is about 2 miles (3 km) north of the center of Placencia Village. A so-called international airport, privately financed, was partially built but then left to revert to jungle. Its remains are about 2 miles (3 km) northwest of the Placencia Peninsula.

By road, from the Southern Highway at Mile 22.2, it's about 8.25 miles (14 km) to Riversdale, 15.25 miles (26 km) to Maya Beach, 19 miles (31 km) to Seine Bight, and 25 miles (41 km) to Placencia Village. The road is completely paved. Ritchie's Bus Line and BEBB have buses between Dangriga and Placencia several times a day. James Bus Lines, the dominant bus service in the south, has nine or 10 buses a day each way between Belize City and Punta Gorda, but these buses stop across the lagoon in Independence rather than on the Placencia Peninsula itself.

Since there's no point-to-point bus service on the peninsula, and taxis are expensive, a rental car can be handy. If you haven't rented one in Belize City, you can rent one locally. Currently there are several car-rental agencies on the peninsula, plus a branch of Belize City's Budget agency.

TIMING

It takes but a couple of days to explore all of the Placencia Peninsula. How long you spend here depends on how much beach and water-sports time you want. Many visitors stay a week or longer, and some end up buying a lot or a house with the intention of living here permanently.

SAFETY AND PRECAUTIONS

The influx of construction workers to the peninsula, some from Guatemala and Honduras, has somewhat changed the security situation here. Petty thefts and break-ins are more common. However, overall the Placencia Peninsula is safe.

NORTHERN PENINSULA AND MAYA BEACH

36 miles (61 km) south of Dangriga by road.

Some of the best beaches on the Placencia Peninsula—and therefore on mainland Belize—are at the northern end of the peninsula and the Maya Beach areas. The light khaki-color sand is soft, the surf is gentle, and, while the Barrier Reef is miles off the coast here as it is elsewhere in this part of Belize, there is good snorkeling a short kayak ride away, around False Caye just east of Maya Beach.

GETTING HERE AND AROUND

From the Southern Highway you go about 8.25 miles (14 km) east to Riversdale, where the Placencia Peninsula formally meets the mainland. From there, head south through the northern end of the peninsula 7 miles (12 km) to Maya Beach.

WHERE TO EAT

$$ CARIBBEAN FAMILY Fodor's Choice ★

🍴 **Mango's of Maya Beach.** Award-winning chef Frank Da Silva, who for years ran the restaurant at Robert's Grove, took over Mango's in 2011 and quickly raised this casual beachside, three-story thatch-roofed eatery and bar to a new level. In 2016, he and a partner expanded the restaurant, roughly doubling its seating capacity. Da Silva brought with him some of his most well-known dishes including conch fritters with chipotle mayonnaise. The menu also includes bar staples like fajitas, peel-and-eat shrimp, fish-and-chips, and chicken wings or bigger dishes like filet mignon or baby back ribs. There are two or three specials each day, and you won't go wrong with any of them. You can also sip a beer or rum and Coke, and just enjoy the stunning sea view and cool breezes from the water. [$] *Average main: BZ$24* ✉ *Maya Beach, Placencia Rd., Maya Beach* ☎ *523/8102* 🕒 *Closed Mon.*

$$$ SEAFOOD FAMILY Fodor's Choice ★

🍴 **Maya Beach Hotel Bistro.** Before ending up on the Placencia Peninsula, Maya Beach Bistro owners John and Ellen Lee (he's Australian, she's American, he's the executive chef, she meets and greets) traveled the world and worked in 20 countries. They obviously figured out what travelers love, because their bistro by the beach is one of the best restaurants in all of Belize. It has won "Restaurant of the Year" honors from the Belize Tourism Board more than once. The setting, in a covered patio by the swimming pool with breezes from the sea, which is just a few yards away, is everything you come to the Caribbean to enjoy. The menu changes regularly, but among the standards you'll go gaga over are nut-encrusted snapper and cocoa-dusted pork chop on a risotto cake. There also are nightly seafood specials. The bistro has a selection of small plates and appetizers including fish cakes, baked garlic (wonderful spread on fresh-made crackers with chutney) coconut shrimp, and honey-coconut ribs. No matter what you choose, you'll find the flavors and presentation interesting and creatively inspired. At breakfast, don't miss the fresh-made bagels or the cinnamon roll—it's big enough for Godzilla. $ *Average main: BZ$38* ⊠ *Placencia Rd., Placencia Peninsula, Maya Beach* ☎ *533/8040* ⊕ *www.mayabeachhotel. com* ⌂ *Reservations essential.*

WHERE TO STAY

$$
RENTAL
FAMILY

⌂ **Barnacle Bill's Beach Bungalows.** "Barnacle Bill" Taylor, known as the wit of Maya Beach, and wife Adriane rent a pair of wooden Mennonite bungalows set among palm trees on a lovely beach; each cottage is on stilts and has a private bath and a kitchen where you can prepare your own meals. **Pros:** friendly spot; helpful owners; nice place just to relax. **Cons:** don't expect luxury. $ *Rooms from: BZ$250* ⊠ *23 Maya Beach Way, Maya Beach* ☎ *533/8110* ⊕ *www.barnaclebills-belize.com* ⌫ *2 cottages* ⏇ *No meals.*

$$$$
RESORT

⌂ **Belize Ocean Club Resort & Spa.** Stretching across the narrow Placencia Peninsula from sea to lagoon, this resort has one- and two-bedroom suites that are luxuriously outfitted with travertine marble floors, balconies, and custom kitchens with granite countertops. **Pros:** large, luxurious condo suites. **Cons:** staff eager but not highly trained. $ *Rooms from: BZ$712* ⊠ *Placencia Rd., Maya Beach* ⚓ *4 miles (6.4 km) north of Seine Bight* ☎ *786/233–8587 U.S. number, 671/4500* ⊕ *www.belize-oceanclub.com* ⌫ *60 rooms.*

$$
B&B/INN
FAMILY
Fodor$Choice
★

⌂ **Maya Beach Hotel.** This is the kind of small, unpretentious beachfront hotel that many come to Belize to enjoy, but few actually find. **Pros:** like a small Caribbean beach hotel should be; good value; excellent restaurant. **Cons:** rooms are only a couple of steps up from basic; Wi-Fi is a little spotty. $ *Rooms from: BZ$260* ⊠ *Placencia Rd., Maya Beach* ☎ *533/8040* ⊕ *www.mayabeachhotel.com* ⌫ *10 rooms* ⏇ *No meals.*

$$$$
RESORT
FAMILY
Fodor$Choice
★

⌂ **NAïA Resort and Spa.** Opened in late 2016, this resort—part of the 200-acre Cocoplum master-planned development established by former Belizean media entrepreneur Stewart Krohn—aspires to be the country's ultimate spa-centric seaside luxury resort. **Pros:** luxury villas and houses, some with private pools; large spa complex with the latest treatments and technologies; beautiful beach and lake setting. **Cons:** not inexpensive. $ *Rooms from: BZ$981* ⊠ *Cocoplum, Placencia Rd., Maya Beach* ☎ *523/4600* ⊕ *www.naiaresortandspa.com* ⌫ *35 villas* ⏇ *No meals.*

$$$
RESORT

⌂ **The Placencia.** Transplant an upscale, gated Florida condo community to Belize, and you might end up with something like The Placencia, with tennis courts, four restaurants (though only one or two may be open at a time), and the country's largest swimming pool. **Pros:** beautiful beach; huge pool; has a casino. **Cons:** meal plans very pricey; rarely many guests; high-rise condos and McMansions out of character with rest of peninsula; no golf course, airport, or some other amenities mentioned on website. $ *Rooms from: BZ$447* ⊠ *Placencia Rd., Maya Beach*

6

✣ Northern end of Placencia Peninsula ☎ 533/4117, 800/810–8567 in U.S. and Canada 🌐 www.theplacencia.com 🛏 100 rooms 🍴 No meals.

$$$ B&B/INN 🏨 **Singing Sands Inn.** The six free-standing thatched-roof cabañas face the beach, and are nicely decorated with polished hardwood floors. **Pros:** small beach hotel with pleasant cottages; reasonable prices; good restaurant; tropical gardens. **Cons:** smallish cabaña rooms. [$] *Rooms from: BZ$309 ✉ 714 Maya Beach Rd., 6 miles (10 km) north of airstrip, Maya Beach ☎ 533/3022, 440/579–3386 in U.S. 🌐 www.singingsands.com 🛏 10 rooms 🍴 No meals.*

SEINE BIGHT

47 miles (77 km) south of Dangriga.

Like Placencia, its Creole neighbor to the south, Seine Bight is a small village. It may not be for long, though, as Placencia's resorts are stretching north to and through this Garífuna community, one of six predominantly Garífuna centers in Belize. The beach, especially south of Seine Bight, is excellent, though near the village garbage sometimes mars the view. Hotels do rake and clean their beachfronts, and several community cleanups have been organized in an effort to solve this problem. All the businesses catering to tourists are along the paved main road (actually, it's the only road) that leads south to Placencia Village. The name Seine Bight derives from a type of net, called a seine, used by local fishermen. *Bight*means an indentation or inward bend in the coastline.

GETTING HERE AND AROUND

By road, Seine Bight is around 19 miles (31 km) from the Southern Highway. By air, you'll fly into the Placencia airstrip.

TIMING

You can explore Seine Bight in a few hours at most. How long you stay depends on how much beach and water time you want. Many visitors stay a week or more.

WHERE TO STAY

$$$ RENTAL 🏨 **Laru Beya Resort.** A condo colony whose name means "on the beach" in the Garífuna language, Laru Beya sits on 7 beachfront acres, with well-priced rooms and suites that are bright and sunny. **Pros:** well-designed rooms and suites; a good value. **Cons:** minigolf course needs maintenance. [$] *Rooms from: BZ$476 ✉ Off Placencia Rd., Seine Bight Village ✣ 0.5 miles (1 km) south of Seine Bight, south of Robert's Grove ☎ 523/3476, 800/890–8010 in U.S. and Canada 🌐 www.larubeya.com 🛏 30 units 🍴 Breakfast.*

$$$ RESORT 🏨 **Robert's Grove Beach Resort.** Robert's Grove is one of the largest (72 units including standard rooms, suites, and one-, two- and three-bedroom apartments, and new lagoon-side villas) and most complete resorts in southern Belize, with kayaks, windsurfers, small sailboats,and boats for diving. **Pros:** complete resort facilities; lovely seaside rooms and suites; lots of tours and on-site activities. **Cons:** nothing particularly exotic here; expensive; not what it used to be. [$] *Rooms from: BZ$405 ✉ Placencia Rd., Placencia Village ✣ 0.5 mile (1 km) south of*

Seine Bight ☎ *523/3565, 800/565–9757 in U.S. and Canada* ⊕ *www. robertsgrove.com* ⇦ *72 units* ⦿ *Breakfast.*

SHOPPING

Lola's Art. Painter and writer Lola Delgado moved to Seine Bight from Belize City in the late 1980s. Her workshop, Lola's Art, displays her bold, cheerful acrylic paintings of local women and scenes (BZ$100 and up). She also sells hand-painted cards, painted gourd masks, and some of her husband's wood carvings. Espresso and pastries are available. The workshop is up a flight of steps in a tiny wooden house off the main street, behind the football field. ⊠ *Seine Bight Village* ☎ *601/1913, 523/3342* ⊕ *www.lolasartinbelize.blogspot.com.*

PLACENCIA VILLAGE

5 miles (8 km) south of Seine Bight, 52 miles (85 km) south of Dangriga.

Placencia Village is a mini, downscale version of Key West, laid-back, hip, and full of atmospheric watering holes. At the end of the road, the village is the main residential center on the peninsula, with a population of close to 1,000, predominantly Creoles. It is also the peninsula's commercial hub—if you can call a small village a hub—with a half-dozen grocery stores, a couple of hardware stores, and the majority of the region's restaurants and bars. Traffic on the Main Road (also called Main Street, and farther north Placencia Road) through the village is surprisingly heavy, and parking can be problematic. Most of the hotels in the village proper are budget spots, but just north of the village, between it and the airport, are several upscale beach resorts and condo developments.

Sometimes billed as the world's narrowest street or longest sidewalk, the Sidewalk is a single concrete path that winds through the village. Setting off purposefully from the southern end of the village near the harbor, the path meanders through everyone's backyard. It passes wooden cottages on stilts overrun with bougainvillea and festooned with laundry, along with a few shops and tour offices, and then, as if it had forgotten where it was headed in the first place, peters out abruptly in a little clearing. Paved sidewalks and dirt paths run between the Sidewalk and the Main Road through Placencia Village. Stroll along the Sidewalk, and you've seen the village. If you don't mind its being a little rough around the edges, you'll be utterly enchanted by this rustic village, where the palm trees rustle, the waves lap the shore, and no one is in a hurry.

Along the Sidewalk and the Main Road are most of the village's guesthouses and cafés, which serve rice and beans, burgers, and seafood.

A large dock complex sits at the foot of the village, just off the Sidewalk and near the end of the main road. At this writing it's still unclear how exactly the dock will be used. The NCL cruise terminal on Harvest Caye, opening in 2017 (it's only a couple of years behind schedule) is supposed to tender passengers into Independence, across the lagoon, and not to Placencia, but that could change. Polls and straw votes show that a large majority of local residents opposed large-scale cruise

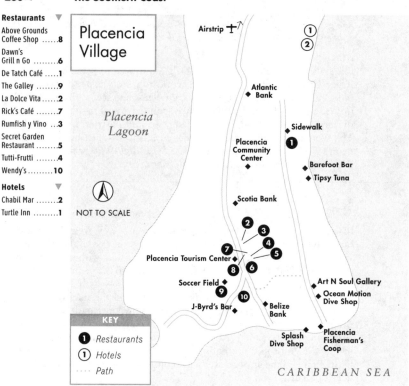

ship tourism in the area, but powerful political interests and financial magnets saw that the port was approved.

GETTING HERE AND AROUND

By road, Placencia Village is around 25 miles (41 km) from the Southern Highway. By air, you'll fly into the Placencia airstrip. From the airstrip to the village is a BZ$12 taxi ride for up to two people, BZ$6 each for three or more. You can also get here by boat, the Hokey Pokey, from Independence/Mango Creek across the Placencia Lagoon, BZ$10. There are several Ritchie and BEBB buses a day between Placencia Village and Dangriga, and the BEBB buses stop in Hopkins. James Bus Line buses don't go to Placencia but stop in Independence, connecting with the Hokey Pokey to Placencia Village.

TIMING

Placencia Village is small and can be seen in a day or less. How long you choose to stay depends on how much relaxing and beach and water time you desire. Many visitors stay a week or longer, and a few never leave.

SAFETY

Most visitors say they feel safe on the Placencia Peninsula. However, petty theft is a perennial problem, especially in Placencia Village. Quite a few budget travelers report thefts from their hotel rooms. A few Placencia hotels, and most of the more upscale resorts up the peninsula, have security guards. Note that at night the village and its beachfront are not well lighted.

WHERE TO EAT

$ CAFÉ Fodor's Choice ★ 🍴 **Above Grounds Coffee Shop.** Above Grounds sells shade-grown, organic Guatemalan coffee straight up, in lattes, iced, or however you like it. Fresh-roasted coffee by the pound is also for sale. The bagels come from The Bistro at Maya Beach, and the fresh donuts from a lady who sells them in the village. [$] *Average main: BZ$6* ✉ *Main St.* ✣ *South end of village across from south end of football field* ☎ *634/3212* 💳 *No credit cards.*

$$ LATIN AMERICAN FAMILY 🍴 **Dawn's Grill 'n Go.** Friendly service, local atmosphere, good food simply prepared, modest prices, ice-cold beer—what more could you want? Dawn's Grill 'n Go is in a small no-frills building with screened windows (no a/c) on the main street in Placencia Village. For breakfast, try an omelet with local sausage; for lunch, we like the fish tacos; and for dinner go for the grilled or fried chicken, or the fish of the day. [$] *Average main: BZ$20* ✉ *Main St., next to BTL office* ☎ *602/9302* 💳 *No credit cards* ⏲ *Closed Sun., closed several wks in late summer.*

$$ SEAFOOD 🍴 **De Tatch Café.** This open-air bar and restaurant near the sea with a "tatch" (thatch) roof has long been a popular hangout in the village. Try the huge shrimp burrito and wash it down with a few cold Belikins. If you go fishing and catch something, the restaurant will prepare it for you. Breakfasts are good here, too. [$] *Average main: BZ$20* ✉ *Placencia Village* ✣ *In village near Seaspray Hotel* ☎ *503/3385* ⏲ *Closed Wed.*

$$ SEAFOOD 🍴 **The Galley.** One of Placencia's oldest restaurants is making a comeback under new management (though the manager is part of the original family of owners). Located in an old building behind the football (soccer) pitch on the lagoon side of Placencia Village—the local team, the Placencia Assassins, play here—The Galley serves seafood such as fried shrimp and garlic conch, along with pizza and other dishes. It's one of a few places in the area where you can still get a seaweed shake, which is, well, an acquired taste. [$] *Average main: BZ$25* ✉ *Placencia Village* ✣ *Behind soccer field* ☎ *523/3133* ⏲ *Closed Sun.*

$$ ITALIAN FAMILY Fodor's Choice ★ 🍴 **La Dolce Vita.** In a slightly Fellini-esque setting, upstairs over Wallen's Store, the often-underrated La Dolce Vita brings authentic antipasti, bruschetta, and pasta dishes to Placencia. The spaghetti carbonara, with the owner's own home-smoked bacon, is amazing. Try the signature penne dolce vita, with a shrimp and zucchini sauce or the linguini with calamari, octopus, squid, and shrimp. Most dishes are in large portions. The Rome-born chef-owner, Simone DeAngelis, imports Italian pastas, olive oils, and wines to make sure everything is top quality. (The wine is always a generous pour.) With opera music playing softly in the background, it's like being in a small, family-run restaurant in Italy. [$] *Average main: BZ$29* ✉ *Main St., above Wallen's Store* ☎ *523/3115.*

$$ CARIBBEAN FAMILY 🍴 **Rick's Café.** This little place on the sidewalk is a nice stop for fresh ceviche and cold beer at lunch; just sit on the open-air veranda and watch the village life pass by. If you're craving greens, it also has some of Placencia's best salads. For dinner, try the pizza or pineapple shrimp quesadillas. The chef-owner, Rick, is well experienced in the hospitality business in Belize and treats his customers well. [$] *Average main: BZ$20* ✉ *Sidewalk* ✣ *Near center of village, on west side of sidewalk* ☎ *666/ 8466* 💳 *No credit cards.*

$$$ SEAFOOD 🍴 **Rumfish y Vino.** This hip spot run by transplanted New Yorkers, in a breezy second-floor location near Tutti-Fruitti, is a good place to have drinks, tapas, interesting seafood creations, and Italian pasta. Try the small plates of Thai shrimp cakes or *pescado relleño* (red snapper stuffed with shrimp). Bigger dishes include fish stew and several pasta and seafood dishes. There's a good selection of Italian and California wines. [$] *Average main: BZ$34* ✉ *Placencia Village Square, off Main St., near Tutti-Fruitti* ☎ *523/3293* 🌐 *www.rumfishyvino.com* ⏲ *No lunch.*

$$$ ECLECTIC Fodor's Choice ★ 🍴 **Secret Garden Restaurant.** What was once Placencia's first coffeehouse has gone upmarket under new management, serving sophisticated international meals at dinner in an open-air, palm-lined, romantically lighted garden. Enjoy the friendly service and an eclectic mix of dishes including ceviche, jerk chicken, black bean soup, and bacon-wrapped steak. The chef can do vegan and gluten-free dishes. Save room for the delicious key lime pie. ■ TIP→ **Cats are welcome.** [$] *Average main: BZ$35* ✉ *Sunset Pointe, in village* ☎ *523/3420* 🌐 *www.secretgardenplacencia.com* ⏲ *No lunch.*

$ CAFÉ Fodor's Choice ★ 🍴 **Tutti-Frutti.** Authentic, Italian-style gelato is the thing here, and it's absolutely delicious, the equal of any you'll find in New York, Buenos Aires, or even Rome. Try the tropical fruit flavors, such as banana, lime, coconut, papaya, and mango, or an unusual flavor such as sugar corn, all created from natural ingredients by Italian owner Tiziana Del Col. Beware: you may become addicted and return day after day to sample new flavors. [$] *Average main: BZ$8* ✉ *Main Square, Main Rd.* 💳 *No credit cards* ⏲ *Closed at least 2 months at end of summer.*

$$ LATIN AMERICAN FAMILY 🍴 **Wendy's.** No, not that Wendy's. This Wendy's is a long-established restaurant operated by Wendy Lemus that seems to have caught a second wind. It's open for breakfast, lunch, and dinner seven days a week, and always seems to deliver good, no-frills food at reasonable prices. The Belizean breakfast of fry jack (the local version of beignets without the sugar), bacon, eggs, and refried beans is nearly perfect. The grilled fish is fresh and delicious, and at lunch there are many dishes to choose from on the lengthy menu, including Creole items like cow-foot soup or Mestizo soups like *escabeche* or *chirmole*with fresh flour tortillas. On Monday, there's usually gibnut (a ground-dwelling, herbivorous rodent that is commonly hunted for food in Belize). You can dine inside or outside on the veranda, and both are pleasant. [$] *Average main: BZ$24* ✉ *Main St.* ☎ *523/3335* 🌐 *www.wendyscuisine.com.*

WHERE TO STAY

$$$$ RESORT FAMILY Fodor's Choice ★ 🏨 **Chabil Mar.** Chabil Mar means "beautiful sea" in Ket'chi Mayan, and the sea and almost 400 feet of beach are indeed gorgeous at this gated luxury condo resort. **Pros:** beautiful grounds; luxurious condos; lovely stretch of beach; every comfort and convenience at hand. **Cons:** walls hide the beauty of the grounds and beach; expensive, but you get your money's worth. [$] *Rooms from: BZ$785* ✉ *2284 Placencia Rd.* ✥ *Between airstrip and Placencia Village* ☎ *523/3606, 866/417–2377 toll-free in U.S. and Canada* 🌐 *www.chabilmarvillas.com* 🛏 *20 villas* 🍽 *No meals.*

$$$$ RESORT FAMILY Fodor's Choice ★ **Turtle Inn.** Francis Ford Coppola's second hotel in Belize is nothing if not exotic, with the furnishings, art, and most of the construction materials bought in Bali by the film director and his wife. **Pros:** exotic Balinese furnishings; delightful outdoor showers; beautiful seaside setting. **Cons:** no a/c; lodging, food, and drink are surprisingly pricey; you'll need your Platinum Amex. [$] *Rooms from: BZ$1,190* ✉ *Placencia Rd., 2 miles (3 km) north of Placencia Village* ☎ *824/4912, 866/356–5881 toll-free reservations in U.S. and Canada* 🌐 *www.thefamilycoppolaresorts.com/en/turtle-inn* 🛏 *25 villas* 🍴 *Breakfast.*

SHOPPING

The highlight of shopping on the Placencia Peninsula is going to the grocery store, and the largest (Wallen's Market and Top Value) are about the size of convenience stores, so you get the picture. The larger resorts, including Robert's Grove and Turtle Inn, do have gift shops. In Placencia Village a few small gift shops and arts-and-craft galleries are on the Sidewalk and the Main Street.

Art 'n Soul Gallery. This little gallery on the south end of the Sidewalk has paintings by owner Greta Leslie, along with work by other Belizean artists and some locally made jewelry from seashells, too. ✉ *South end of the Sidewalk* ☎ *503/3088.*

Treasure Box. A small gift shop on the main street of Placencia Village, Treasure Box has locally made jewelry, mostly from seashells. ✉ *Main St.* ☎ *503/3145.*

FAMILY **Wallen's Market & Pharmacy.** The oldest grocery in Placencia, though no longer the largest, Wallen's Market has the basics, and it's even air-conditioned. Wallen's also has a pharmacy and a separate hardware store. ✉ *Main St., across from soccer field* ☎ *503/3128 grocery, 523/3346 pharmacy.*

NIGHTLIFE

Nightlife in Placencia is generally limited to drinking at a handful of local bars, of which Barefoot and Tipsy Tuna are perhaps the most popular. You can hear live music on weekends at Barefoot, Tipsy Tuna, and J-Byrds.

Barefoot Beach Bar. After dark, Barefoot gets its share of seaside sippers. For a bar, the food is good, and it has one of the best selections of rums on the peninsula. ✉ *Beachfront, next to Tipsy Tuna* ☎ *523/3515.*

Casino at The Placencia. In mid-2016, this small casino, promised for years, finally opened on the first floor of one of the unfinished five-story Copal Beach condos at The Placencia Hotel and Residences. Was it worth the wait? You be the judge. The casino has about 150 gaming machines, not all operational, plus four or five live tables for blackjack and roulette. The parking lot is a big sandy field, and outdoor lighting is limited. Most nights, the dealers and casino staff outnumber the players, but players do get free drinks. ✉ *Copal Beach at The Placencia Hotel and Residences, Placencia Rd., Maya Beach* ✥ *Separate entrance to Copal Condos just north of entrance to The Placencia Hotel, on east side* ☎ *807/6868* 🌐 *www.theplacencia.com.*

6

The Flying Pig. This busy roadside sports bar serves ribs, burgers, pizza, and other bar food, along with quantities of Belikin. TFP features local musicians at open-mike nights. ⊠ *Placencia Rd., 0.5 mile (1 km) north of airstrip on east side of road* ☏ *602/6391.*

J-Byrds Bar. J-Byrds Bar attracts a fairly hard-drinking crowd, and there's live music on Friday nights. ⊠ *Near docks, Placencia Village* ☏ *523/3412.*

Tipsy Tuna. Known for friendly service, Tipsy Tuna is Placencia's largest and most popular open-air beach bar. There's live music some weekend nights, and you can always shoot pool or watch sports on a big-screen TV. Fill up on bar snacks like burgers, fajitas, tacos, and shrimp baskets. There's karaoke some nights and Garífuna drumming occasionally. ⊠ *Beachfront* ☏ *523/3089* ⊕ *www.tipsytunabelize.com.*

SPORTS AND THE OUTDOORS

BOWLING

FAMILY **Jaguar Lanes.** About the last place you'd expect to find a bowling alley is Maya Beach, but Jaguar Lanes is here, and it's fun! This little four-lane alley, air-conditioned, with jaguar murals on the walls and pine ceilings, has everything your lanes back home have, except you have to keep score on paper. ⊠ *Maya Beach* ☏ *629/3145* ☾ *Closed Thurs.*

FISHING

The fly-fishing on the flats off the cayes east of the Placencia Peninsula is some of Belize's best. This is one of the top areas in the world for permit. The area from Dangriga south to Gladden Caye is called "Permit Alley," and the mangrove lagoons off Punta Ycacos and other points south of Placencia are also terrific permit fisheries. You'll encounter plentiful tarpon—they flurry 10 deep in the water at times—as well as snook. You can also catch king mackerel, barracuda, wahoo, and cubera snapper. However, a lingering impact of Hurricane Iris in 2001 is that there are no longer as many good bonefish flats close to shore at Placencia. Bonefish are still around, but they're now several miles away, off the cayes.

Most of the better hotels also can arrange guides, many of whom pair with specific hotels. Fishing guides in Placencia are down-to-earth, self-taught guys who have fished these waters for years. They use small skiffs called *pangas.* For more information and help matching a local guide to your specific needs, get in touch with Mary Toy at Destinations Belize. ▮TIP→ **If you're on a budget, you can rent a canoe and try fishing the Placencia Lagoon on your own, where you may catch snook, barracuda, and possibly other fish.**

Guides usually provide trolling gear for free, but they'll charge you to rent light spin-casting tackle gear. If you're serious about fly-fishing, of course you'll want to bring your own gear. Don't forget to bring polarized sunglasses, a good fishing hat, insect repellent, lots of sunscreen and lip salve, and, if you're wading, thick-soled flats boots.

Destinations Belize. Owner Mary Toy can connect you with local fishing guides and arrange fishing trips of all kinds. ☏ *523/4018 in Belize, 603/386–6632 in U.S.* ⊕ *www.destinationsbelize.com.*

7

THE DEEP SOUTH

By Lan Sluder

Toledo District in the Deep South has Belize's only extensive, genuine rain forest, and its canopy of trees conceals a plethora of wildlife, including jaguars, margays, tapirs, and loads of tropical birds. The area's rich Mayan heritage is just being unearthed, with archaeologists at work at Pusilha, Nim Li Punit, Uxbenká, and elsewhere. Contemporary Maya—mainly Mopan and Ket'chi (other transliterations into English include Kekchi, Kekche, Q'eqchi', and others)—still live in villages around the district, as they have for centuries, along with the Garífuna, Creoles, East Indians, and others who constitute the Toledo population of about 32,000.

Lush, green, tropical Toledo also calls to chocolate lovers, as it's home to hundreds of small cacao growers. Cadbury's Green & Black gets some of its organic chocolate for Maya Gold chocolate bars from Toledo, and several small Belizean chocolate makers, including Cotton Tree, Goss, Ixcacao, Belcampo, and others, create gourmet chocolate from organic Toledo cacao beans. In 2007 a cacao festival was organized, and it continues annually as the Chocolate Festival of Belize, held on Commonwealth Day weekend in late May (dates vary—see ⊕ *www.chocolatefestivalofbelize.com*).

Toledo also has rice plantations, citrus orchards, and stands of mangos, pineapples, bananas, and coconuts, so you'll never go hungry here.

For many years, ill-maintained roads, spotty communications, and the country's highest annual rainfall—as much as 180 to 200 inches—kept Belize's southernmost region off-limits to all but the most adventurous of travelers. The precipitation hasn't changed, but with improvements to the Southern Highway—beautifully paved the entire way from Dangriga to Punta Gorda—and the opening of new lodges and hotels, the riches of Toledo District are finally becoming accessible. The San Antonio Road, from the area called "The Dump" on the Southern Highway to the Guatemala border, has been paved opening up easy access to a number of Mayan villages. Eventually, when a border crossing is completed and approved by the Guatemalan and Belizean governments, perhaps in 2018, new development, trade, and immigration will be introduced to Toledo.

Local residents are split on the wisdom of this. Some say it will mean not only more tourism dollars but also new Guatemalan markets for Toledo farm products. Others worry that the new border crossing will increase crime and create new problems for Toledo.

TOP REASONS TO GO

Rain Forests. The greenest, lushest jungles in Belize are in Toledo, fed by heavy rains and temperatures that stay mostly above 70°F. Red ginger, bright yellow-and-orange lobster claw, masses of pink on mayflower trees, and orchids of all colors splash the emerald-green landscape. Scarlet-rumped tanagers, black-headed trogans, green kingfishers, several species of parrots, and roseate spoonbills join hundreds of other birds in the rain-forest cacophony.

Outpost Atmosphere. Punta Gorda has that end-of-the-road feel, as if it's the last outpost on Earth. Yes, the Southern Highway does end here—but it's more than that. Here you get the feeling that even in today's world of 7 billion people there are still places where you could, if you needed to, hide out for a while and not be found.

Fishing. Among serious anglers, Southern Belize has a reputation for having one of the world's great permit fisheries, and for its large populations of tarpon and bonefish. The flats off Punta Ycacos are prime permit and bonefish grounds, and freshwater lagoons near Punta Negra hold snook, small tarpon, and other fish.

Other areas of Belize (not to mention Guatemala and Honduras) may have more spectacular ruins than Toledo, but where the Deep South shines is in its contemporary Mayan culture. Dozens of Mopan and Ket'chi villages exist much as they have for centuries, as do the Garífuna villages of Punta Negra and Barranco and the town of Punta Gorda (PG). You can visit some of the villages and even stay awhile in guest-houses or homestay programs. If don't have time to do an overnight, you can participate in a new, one-day Maya learning experience tour in local homes in Big Falls village or take a tour of an organic cacao farm.

Don't expect to come to Toledo and lounge on the sand. The area doesn't have good beaches except for a few accessible only by boat. The coastal waters of the Gulf of Honduras are often muddy from silt deposited by numerous rivers flowing from the Maya Mountains. What *can* you expect? Exceptional fishing (Toledo has one of the world's best permit fisheries) and cayes off the coast that are well worth exploring. The closest are the Snake Cayes; farther out are the Sapodilla Cayes, the largest of which is Hunting Caye, with a horseshoe-shaped bay at the caye's eastern end with beaches of white coral where turtles nest in late summer. The downside is that visits to the cayes and to inland sites usually require expensive tours, as distances are considerable, and public transportation is limited. The completion of the new road to Guatemala in 2016 should make trips and tours to many inland sites easier and, perhaps, a little cheaper.

ORIENTATION AND PLANNING

GETTING ORIENTED

The main road to the Deep South is the paved Southern Highway, which runs 100 miles (164 km) from the intersection of the Hummingbird Highway/Stann Creek District Highway to Punta Gorda (PG).

As you travel south on the Southern Highway, the Great Southern Pine Ridge is on your right, starting at about Mile 55. Farther in the distance are the Maya Mountains. On your left (though not visible from the highway) is the Caribbean Sea, and farther south, beyond Punta Negra, the Gulf of Honduras.

Branching off the Southern Highway are mostly unpaved roads, some barely more than muddy trails that lead to small villages. The San Antonio Road, from the Southern Highway about 14 miles (23 km) north of PG, has been beautifully upgraded and paved all the way to the Guatemala border, where an official border crossing is expected to be established. Currently, local residents cross back and forth freely, but there is no legal way to get exit and entrance permits.

Punta Gorda. Many of the handful of restaurants and shops in PG open and close at the whim of their owners, and therein lies some of the charm of this little town. It's a sleepy, friendly, overgrown village with a beautiful setting on the bay.

The Maya Heartland. Nothing else in Belize is quite like the Maya Heartland, where contemporary Mayan villages sit next to ancient ruins. Here also you'll see verdant rain forests, rice plantations, and cacao farms.

PLANNING

WHEN TO GO

June through September is the peak of the rainy season in Toledo, and when we say rainy we mean it—sometimes up to a foot of precipitation a day. Until you've experienced the roaring thunder, screeching lightning, and torrential rains of a summer storm in Toledo, you've never really seen tropical weather. Unless you love a good thunderstorm, come between December and early May, when most of Toledo gets only about an inch of rain a week.

GETTING HERE AND AROUND

AIR TRAVEL

Maya Island Air and Tropic Air fly south to Punta Gorda from both the municipal and international airports in Belize City, sometimes with brief stops at Dangriga and Placencia. Depending on stops, flights take from 1 to 1½ hours. There are four or five flights daily to PG on each airline. The Punta Gorda airstrip is on the town's west side; from the town's main square, walk four blocks west on Prince Street.

Contacts Maya Island Air. ⊠ *Punta Gorda Airstrip, Punta Gorda* ☎ *722/2072 at PG airstrip, 233/1403 in Belize City and reservations countrywide* ⊕ *www.mayaislandair.com.* **Tropic Air.** ⊠ *Punta Gorda Airstrip, Prince St., Punta Gorda*

☎ 722/2008 at PG airport, 226/2626 in San Pedro (main office) and for reservations countrywide, 800/422–3435 in U.S. ⊕ www.tropicair.com.

BOAT TRAVEL

Requena's, a long-established and generally reliable operator, provides daily boats to Puerto Barrios, Guatemala; departure is at 9:30 am from the docks on Front Street, Punta Gorda (PG). The trip takes about an hour and can be rough. The Pichilingo boat, as of this writing, departs PG at 2 pm, Tek-Dat at 1 pm, and Shark Boy at 4 pm. From Puerto Barrios, Pichilingo departs at 10 am, Tek-Dat at 3 pm, and Shark Boy at 1 pm. On Tuesday and Friday only, most boats have service at 10 am from PG to Livingston, Guatemala. Memo runs a daily boat from Punta Gorda to Livingston at 1 pm and returns daily at 3 pm (fare varies depending on the number of passengers). ■ TIP➜ **Times and fares are subject to change, especially during the off-season and bad weather.**

These boats are small open boats for pedestrians only; there is no auto ferry between Guatemala and Punta Gorda. You must pay an exit fee when departing from PG to Guatemala and when departing from Guatemala for Belize. For those traveling on to Honduras, Pichilingo offers a daily connecting shuttle bus at Puerto Barrios to Corinto on the Honduran border. From Corinto buses leave daily at 4:30 and 6 pm for Puerto Cortes, Honduras.

Contact Memo's Boat Service. ⊠ Punta Gorda Docks, Front St., Punta Gorda ☎ 651/4780 ✎ memosboatservicandtours@yahoo.com. **Pichilingo.** ⊠ Punta Gorda Docks, Front St., Punta Gorda. **Requena's Charter Service.** ⊠ 12 Front St., Punta Gorda ☎ 722/2070 ⊕ www.puntagordabelize.com/pg/requena/index. htm. **Shark Boy.** ⊠ Punta Gorda Docks, Front St., Punta Gorda.

BUS TRAVEL

James Bus Lines dominates the route between PG and points north. Currently there are nine daily local bus departures from PG to Belize City, and one express. The first bus is at 3:50 am and the last one at 3:50 pm. Eight local and two express James Line buses come from what is still called the Novelo's bus station in Belize City (Novelo's bus company no longer exists) to Punta Gorda daily, beginning at 5:15 am with the last bus at 3:45 pm. It's a six- to seven-hour trip to or from Belize City via Belmopan, Dangriga, and Independence, depending on whether it's an express or local bus. Most buses are old U.S. Bluebird school buses—they're usually crowded, cramped, and have no air-conditioning. If you have the budget, fly. Any nonexpress bus will pick up and drop you anywhere along the route.

Off the Southern Highway in Toledo public transportation is limited. On market days (generally Monday, Wednesday, Friday, and Saturday) buses leave the main plaza near the clock tower in PG around noon. Buses, mostly old American school buses operated by local entrepreneurs, go to different villages, returning on market days very early in the morning. There's no published schedule—you have to ask locally. As of this writing, buses from PG serve the villages of Aguacate, Barranco, Big Falls, Crique Sarco, Dolores, Golden Stream, Indian Creek, Jalacte, Laguna, Medina, San Antonio, San Benito Poite, San Jose, San Miquel, San Pedro Columbia, Santa Ana, San Vicente, Pueblo Viejo, and Silver

Creek. Bus service to villages along the new San Antonio Road, including Manfredi, San Antonio, Santa Cruz, and Jalacte has increased in frequency and quickness because of the new road.

Contact James Bus Line. ⊠ *7 King St., Punta Gorda* ☎ *702/2049 in PG* ⊕ *www.jamesbusline.com.*

CAR TRAVEL

The paving of the Hummingbird and Southern highways has made the journey to Punta Gorda much shorter and more pleasant. The drive from Belize City to PG can be done in around four hours, all on paved roads. Off the Southern Highway most Toledo roads, excepting the new San Antonio Road, are unpaved. In dry weather they're bumpy yet passable, but after heavy rains the dirt roads can turn into quagmires even for four-wheel-drive vehicles. Most tertiary roads are not well marked, so you may have to stop frequently for directions. Despite this, expensive taxis and infrequent bus service to and from the Mayan villages and elsewhere in Toledo are arguments for renting a car. There are no major car-rental companies in Punta Gorda. Your best option is to rent at the international airport in Belize City, where there are about 10 rental car companies, or in Placencia, especially if you're staying there on your way south. Bruno Kuppinger at SunCreek Lodge about 14 miles (22.5 km) northwest of Punta Gorda has a few cars available to rent. Belize City–based Budget has a satellite office in Placencia and can deliver a rental car from its Placencia fleet in PG for an extra fee. Barefoot Services in Placencia also will bring a vehicle to PG for a similar drop fee.

Barefoot Services. Barefoot Services in Placencia will deliver rental cars to Punta Gorda and elsewhere in Toledo. A one-time drop fee applies. Check with Barefoot for current drop rate. ⊠ *Main St., Placencia Village* ☎ *523/3066* ⊕ *www.barefootservicesbelize.com.*

Fodor's Choice ★ **Budget Belize.** This satellite office of Budget's main offices at the Belize international airport and on the Philip Goldson Highway in Belize City will deliver a vehicle to Punta Gorda for a one-time drop fee of BZ$250. High-season rates are around BZ$450 to $570 a week, plus 12.5% tax. ⊠ *Live Oaks Plaza, South of Placencia airstrip, Placencia Village* ☎ *523/3068, 800/284-4387 toll-free number outside Belize* ⊕ *www.budget-belize.com.*

TAXI TRAVEL

Taxis in the Deep South are available mostly in PG. Your hotel can call one for you. You can also hire a taxi to take you to nearby villages, but negotiate the rate in advance.

SAFETY

Punta Gorda is generally a safe, friendly town. Indeed, Toledo District has the lowest murder rate in Belize, and one of the lowest rates of other serious crimes. With normal precautions you should have no problem walking around, even after dark. The nearby Mayan villages are also relatively free of crime. Guatemala's Caribbean coast, just a short boat ride away, has a reputation for lawlessness, which can occasionally spill over into Toledo.

ABOUT THE HOTELS

The entire Toledo District has only about 30 hotels, most of them in and around Punta Gorda. Most are small and owner-run. You can usually show up without reservations and look for a place that suits you. Belcampo is among the most expensive lodges in the entire country.

HOTEL AND RESTAURANT PRICES

For expanded lodging reviews and current deals, visit Fodors.com.

WHAT IT COSTS IN BELIZE DOLLARS			
$	$$	$$$	$$$$
RESTAURANTS under BZ$15	BZ$15–BZ$30	BZ$31–BZ$50	over BZ$50
HOTELS under BZ$200	BZ$200–BZ$300	BZ$301–BZ$500	over BZ$500

Restaurant prices are per person for a main course at dinner. Hotel prices are for two people in a standard double room, including tax and service.

ABOUT THE RESTAURANTS

With relatively few tourists coming to the region, and most local residents unable to afford to eat out regularly, restaurants in Toledo often are here today and gone tomorrow. Even those that stick around often open and close at the whim of the owner or the cook. Those that do make it are usually basic spots serving local fish and staples like stew chicken with beans and rice. Prices are low—you'll rarely pay more than BZ$30 for dinner, unless you're eating at an expensive lodge such as Belcampo. Nearly all Toledo restaurants are in PG.

HOMESTAYS

A few programs offer the chance to live with the modern-day Maya or Garífuna at a homestay or village guesthouse. They are very inexpensive, but keep in mind that accommodations and meals are extremely basic; lodging usually lacks electricity and running water. You can also spend several days learning how to process cacao or learning to cook Belizean—including Mayan—recipes.

FAMILY **Aguacate Homestay Program.** Established in 2010, the Aguacate Homestay Program gives you the opportunity to have an authentic Mayan cultural experience in a Ket-chi (Qeqchi) Mayan village of fewer than 400 people. Guests live in a Mayan home, eat with the family, and participate in household and farm chores. Keep in mind that the living conditions are spartan at best. The homes are traditional thatch huts with dirt floors and no electricity, running water, or indoor plumbing. You pay BZ$16.35 per person including tax for lodging, BZ$7 per person per meal, and a BZ$10 per person registration fee. Part of the money goes to the host family and part to the village for improvements. Transportation by bus between Aquacate village and Punta Gorda is available four or five days a week at nominal cost. ✉ *Aguacate Village* ☎ *633/9954 Louis Cocul in Aguacate village* ⊕ *www.aguacatebelize.com.*

Living Maya Experience. Learn about Kek'chi crafts, culture, and cuisine in a hands-on private experience in Maya homes of participating villages in Big Falls. You could be involved in anything from building a traditional thatch house to making corn tortillas. Call in advance for what's available, times, and charges, or ask at your hotel or the BTIA Visitor Information Center in Punta Gorda to help arrange the Living Maya trip. If you're traveling solo, any nonexpress James Line bus will drop you off and pick you up at Big Falls village (watch for Las Faldes restaurant on the Southern Highway) near the Living Maya Experience homes where hosts Anita Cal and Marta Chiac live. Costs vary depending on which learning experiences you choose and the length of them, but most are under BZ$40 (not including transportation and additional tour company fees). ⊠ *Southern Hwy., Big Falls* ☎ *627/7408 Anita Cal, 632/4585 Marta Chiac.*

FAMILY

Fodor's Choice
★

Toledo Ecotourism Association (T.E.A.) Maya Village Guesthouse Program. The T.E.A. program allows visitors to participate in the village life of the Maya while maintaining some personal privacy. You stay overnight in small guesthouses in one of five Mopan and Kek'chi Mayan villages in Toledo District, currently including Santa Elena, San Antonio, San Jose, San Miguel, and Laguna; village guesthouse locations change from time to time. The guesthouses are very simple, with traditional thatch roofs and outdoor latrines. There is no running water or electricity in the guesthouses. You take meals in the homes of villagers and participate in the routines of village life. The program, endorsed by the Belize Tourism Board, is a collective owned by more than 200 members and is designed to promote cultural exchange. The cost is around BZ$100 a day per person, including meals and village activities. Other packages start at BZ$80 per person for a day trip to BZ$190 per person for a two-night stay. ⊠ *BTIA Office, 46 Front St., Punta Gorda* ☎ *702/2119* ⊕ *www. teabelize.org* ⊠ *From BZ$80 per person.*

TOURS

ADVENTURE TOURS

Big Falls Extreme Adventures. Big Falls Extreme Adventures offers zip-lining, river tubing, and hiking over, on, and around Rio Grande. Rates vary, but zip-lining and river tubing are around BZ$80 each, and if you do both there's a combination rate. Food is available at Las Faldas restaurant; lunch is around BZ$20. ⊠ *Southern Hwy., Big Falls* ☎ *634/6979* ⊕ *bigfallsextremeadventures.com* ⊠ *BZ$80 and up.*

Romero's Charter and Tours. Romero's Charters and Tours has a driver service with vans and other vehicles that can take you to any of the inland destinations. ⊠ *Cattle Landing, Forest Home* ☎ *222/5791* ✎ *rcharters@btl.net.*

Toledo Cave & Adventure Tours. Operated by German expat and longtime Toledo resident Bruno Kuppinger, Toledo Cave & Adventure Tours is not for couch potatoes. Kuppinger, who also has a woodworking business in Toledo, offers such high-energy tours as multiday trips to the Maya Divide and to Doyle's Delight, Belize's highest peak. ⊠ *San Antonio Rd., Punta Gorda* ☎ *604/2124.*

CULTURAL TOURS

Chocolate Week. In Toledo, Cotton Tree Lodge has a chocolate-making program in connection with Sustainable Harvest International, which teaches farmers to grow food on a sustainable basis. Chocolate Week, held for a week in the spring, lets you "work your way through the entire practical process [of making chocolate] from scratch, starting with the cacao fruit on the tree and ending with the chocolate in your mouth." ⊠ *Cotton Tree Lodge, Moho River, San Felipe* ☎ *670/0557, 212/529–8622 in U.S.* ⊕ *www.cottontreelodge.com.*

FAMILY **Eladio's Chocolate Adventure.** Eladio Pop provides a tour of his Agouti Cacao Farm in San Pedro Columbia village, followed by a chocolate tasting and a traditional Mayan lunch. Cost for this combination is BZ$50 per person, with à la carte tour options starting at BZ$25. Mr. Pop also offers a homestay with meals for BZ$30 per person. ⊠ *Agouti Cacao Farm, San Pedro Columbia Village, San Pedro Columbia* ☎ *624/0166* ✎ *eladiopop@gmail.com* ⊕ *www.agouticacaofarm. wordpress.com/.*

PG Tours. From her storefront on Front Street, Jo at PG Tours arranges land and sea trips around Punta Gorda, including visits to area Mayan sites, cacao farm tours, cooking lessons, and drumming lessons. ⊠ *42 Front St., Punta Gorda* ☎ *636/6162* ⊕ *www.pgtoursbelize.com.*

Toledo Cacao Growers Association. During the Chocolate Festival in May, and by advance arrangement at other times, the Toledo Cacao Growers Association (TCGA), which represents more than 1,100 small organic cacao growers in southern Belize, offers tours of working cacao farms. ⊠ *Main Middle St., Punta Gorda* ☎ *722/2992* ⊕ *www.tcgabelize.com.*

Warasa Garifuna Drum School. To learn more about the Garífuna culture, investigate the Warasa Garífuna Drum School, which approaches the Garífuna experience through drumming, drum making, and dance. Master Garifuna drummer and teacher Ronald Raymond McDonald is a self-taught drummer who has been performing since age five with his family group. McDonald gives private lessons in the Garifuna community of PG, with private lessons starting at BZ$25. Call or email to arrange lessons or demonstrations, or you can do so through your hotel or the BTIA Visitor Information Center on Front Street in PG. ⊠ *New Rd., St. Vincent Garifuna Reserve, Punta Gorda* ☎ *632/7701 Ray McDonald* ⊕ *www.warasadrumschool.com* ✉ *Garifuna drumming lessons start at BZ$25 for one-on-one lessons.*

VISITOR INFORMATION

The office of the Belize Tourism Industry Association (BTIA), at 46 Front Street near the water-taxi dock, is open weekdays 8–4, and Saturday 8–11:30.

Information Belize Tourism Industry Association. ⊠ *Toledo Tourism Information Center, 46 Front St., Punta Gorda* ☎ *722/2531* ✎ *btiatoledo@btl.net* ⊕ *www.btia.org.* **Toledo Tour Guides Association.** ⊠ *Visitor Information Center at BTIA, 46 Front St., Punta Gorda* ☎ *722/2531 at BTIA office.*

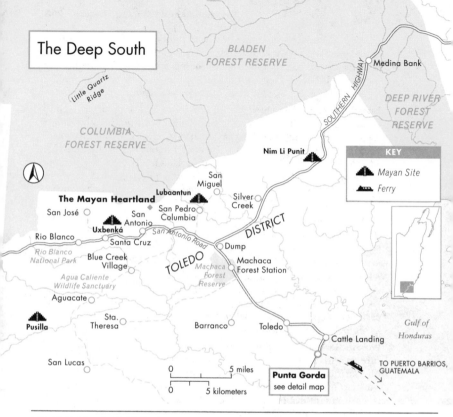

The Deep South

BLADEN
FOREST RESERVE

Medina Bank

Little Quartz Ridge

SOUTHERN HIGHWAY

DEEP RIVER
FOREST
RESERVE

COLUMBIA
FOREST RESERVE

Nim Li Punit

KEY

🔺 *Mayan Site*

🚢 *Ferry*

San
Miguel

The Mayan Heartland Lubaantun

Silver
Creek

San José

San Pedro
Columbia

San
Antonio

Uxbenká

DISTRICT

Rio Blanco

Santa Cruz

San Antonio Road

Dump

Rio Blanco
National Park

Blue Creek
Village

Machaca
Forest Station

TOLEDO

Machaca
Forest
Reserve

Agua Caliente
Wildlife Sanctuary

Aguacate

Pusilla

Sta.
Theresa

Barranco

Toledo

Gulf of
Honduras

Cattle Landing

San Lucas

0   5 miles

0   5 kilometers

Punta Gorda
see detail map

TO PUERTO BARRIOS,
GUATEMALA

PUNTA GORDA

102 miles (164 km) south of Placencia.

Most journeys south begin in the region's administrative center, Punta Gorda. PG (as it's affectionately known) isn't your typical tourist destination. Though it has a wonderful setting on the Gulf of Honduras, it has no real beaches. There are few shops of interest to visitors, a few simple restaurants, and little nightlife. Don't expect many tourist services.

So why, you ask, come to PG? First, simply because it isn't on the main tourist track. The accoutrements of mass tourism are still, refreshingly, missing here. Schoolchildren may wave at you, and residents will strike up a conversation. Toledo has stunning natural attractions, too, such as clean rivers for swimming and cave systems with Mayan artifacts that rival those in the Cayo District. Also, with several new or upgraded hotels to choose from, it's a comfortable base from which to visit surrounding Mayan villages, offshore cayes, and the high bush of the Deep South.

Settled in 1867 by ex-Confederate immigrants from the United States and later a magnet for religious missionaries, Punta Gorda once had 12 sugar estates, each with its own mill, but the sugar industry in Toledo has been replaced by rice farming, citrus groves, and small cacao plantations. After World War II, Great Britain built an important military base here, but when that closed in 1994 the linchpin of the local economy was yanked out. With some increase in tourist dollars and foreigners' growing interest in real estate here, PG is starting to pick up again, but hasn't lost its frontier atmosphere.

GETTING HERE AND AROUND

To best see the sights of Toledo, a rental car is ideal. Otherwise you'll be stuck paying high tour rates or waiting for infrequent bus service. Many people drive down from Belize City, Hopkins, or Placencia. If you've flown or bused in to PG, have a vehicle delivered to you from Budget in Placencia. If you'd like a knowledgeable local guide to ride with you in your rental car, that's also possible.

From the intersection of the Hummingbird and Southern highways it's a straight shot 100 miles (164 km) down the Southern, with only a well-marked right turn near Independence to slow you down. On the Southern Highway about 20 miles (33 km) north of Punta Gorda, at about Mile 83, you'll come to an intersection. If you turn left you'll stay on the Southern Highway to PG; if you bear right onto the San Antonio Road, you'll go comfortably to Lubaantun, San Antonio Village, and other Mayan villages, as well as the Guatemala border. Assuming that you continue on the Southern Highway, at about Mile 95 you have two options for reaching downtown PG. You can turn right on the mostly unpaved Saddleback Road and go 5 miles (8 km). To enter from the prettier Bay of Honduras side, as most visitors do, stay straight on the paved Southern Highway and go the same distance.

EXPLORING

TOP ATTRACTIONS

FAMILY **Agua Caliente Wildlife Sanctuary.** Hot springs, freshwater lagoons, caves, and hiking trails dot the 6,000-acre Agua Caliente Wildlife Sanctuary. The sanctuary is known for its water birds, including ibises, herons, egrets, woodstorks, and kingfishers. A half-mile boardwalk gives access to the visitor center. A local guide is recommended. During the dry season you can hike under the forest canopy and through wetlands to the warm springs at the base of the Agua Caliente hills. During the rainy season, canoes are available for hire. ■ TIP→ **Some local tours include Agua Caliente.** ⊠ *About 13 miles (21 km) west of Punta Gorda, Toledo* ✚ *From Punta Gorda, take Southern Hwy. 10 miles (16 km) north. Turn left on Laguna Rd. and go 3 miles (5 km). The trail to wildlife sanctuary begins in Laguna village.*

FAMILY **Bladen Nature Reserve.** Ever been freshwater snorkeling? Check out the Bladen River in the Bladen Nature Reserve. The river snakes through the reserve, allowing for excellent kayaking, canoeing, swimming, and, yes, some freshwater snorkeling. The 100,000-acre Bladen Reserve is co-managed by the Belize Forestry Department and the Ya'axche Conservation Trust, an environmental NGO based in Punta Gorda. Bladen is the center piece of the Maya Mountain Corridor, creating a crucial link in the last remaining large, intact block of forest in the region.

Additional parts of this corridor are protected by the Cockscomb Basin Wildlife Sanctuary, the Columbia River Forest Reserve, and the Chiquibul National Park and Forest Reserve, all bordering Bladen. Tours of the Bladen Reserve also are given by interns from a private reserve managed by the Belize Foundation for Research and Environmental Education (BFREE). Camping and simple bunkhouse accommodations are available for around BZ$80–BZ$120 per person per day, meals included. Additional charges may apply for transportation, canoe rental, laundry, and other services. ⊠ *Bladen Nature Reserve* ☎ *352/231-2772 in U.S. for BFREE, 722/0108 Ya'ache Conservation Trust in Punta Gorda* ⊕ *www.bfreebz.org.*

> **TO MARKET, TO MARKET**
>
> On market days—Monday, Wednesday, Friday, and Saturday, with Wednesday and Saturday usually being the largest—the town comes to life with vendors from nearby Mayan villages and even from Guatemala. They pack the downtown market area at the central plaza (look for the large clock tower) with colorful fruit and vegetable stands. Fresh fish also is sold in a building at the market, daily except Sunday, and for a small fee you can have your fish cleaned. On Front Street is the renovated main market with stalls selling clothing, crafts, and other items.

Columbia Forest Reserve. One of the largest undisturbed tropical rain forest areas in Central America is the Columbia Forest Reserve. It's in a remote area north of San José Village. The karst terrain—an area of irregular limestone in which erosion has produced sinkholes, fissures, and underground streams and caves—is difficult to navigate, so the only way to see this area is with a guide and with advance permission from the Belize Forestry Department. It has extremely diverse ecosystems because the elevation ranges from about 1,000 to more than 3,000 feet, with sinkholes as deep as 800 feet. You'll find areas of true "high bush" here: old-growth tropical forest with parts that have never been logged at all. Much of the rich flora and fauna of this area has yet to be documented. For example, one brief 12-day expedition turned up 15 species of ferns never found before in Belize, along with several new species of palms, vines, and orchids. Check with the Toledo Tour Guide Association at the BTIA visitor information office in Punta Gorda to try to find a guide to take you to this remote reserve. ⊠ *Columbia Forest Reserve, north of San José village, San José* ☎ *637/2000 Toledo Tour Guide Association.*

WORTH NOTING

FAMILY **Cotton Tree Chocolates.** From cacao beans to final candy bars, you can see how chocolate is made at Cotton Tree Chocolates, a small chocolate factory on Front Street in PG. It's associated with Cotton Tree Lodge. You'll get a short guided tour of the chocolate-making process and you can buy bars of delicious milk or dark chocolate. Cotton Tree Lodge also offers guests a program on sustainable cacao growing, producing, and harvesting. ⊠ *2 Front St.* ☎ *670/0557* ⊕ *www.cottontreechocolate. com* ▨ *Free* ☺ *Closed Sun.*

FAMILY **Golden Stream Spice Farm and Botanical Gardens.** See exotic spices such as cardamom, vanilla, nutmeg, clove, cinnamon, and sandalwood growing at this spice farm just off the Southern Highway at Golden Stream. Currently, only black pepper is grown in enough quantity (about 10,000 pounds of peppercorns per year) for commercial sales in Belize, but plans are to expand other spice production for domestic and, eventually, international sales. The spice farm is part of a 500-acre tract now producing mostly citrus, owned by Dr. Thomas Matthew, an Indian-born U.S. physician, and his wife, Tessie Matthew. Visitors are given a guided tour of the farm on a cart with seats pulled by a tracked tractor; walking tours are also available. Usually the last stop on the tour is the drying room, full of wonderful spice aromas. Tours (BZ$20 per person) generally start every hour on the hour from 8 to 4, but it's advisable to call ahead. The restaurant was expanded in 2016 to accommodate tour groups and other visitors. ✉ *Southern Hwy., Golden Stream* ☎ *732/4014* ⊕ *www.belizespicefarm.com* 🎟 *BZ$20.*

SPORTS AND THE OUTDOORS

Punta Gorda and Toledo offer great opportunities for outdoor activities—fishing, diving, snorkeling, sea and river kayaking, and caving. The problem has been that due to so few visitors to the Deep South and the limited number of tour operators, visitors often arrived to find that few tours were actually available on a given day, or if they were running, tended to cost much more than in other parts of Belize. An attempt to schedule tours to always run on specific days—for example, to Port Honduras Marine Reserve for snorkeling on Monday and to Blue Creek for caving on Tuesday—has fizzled out. Still, with tourism slowly increasing, more tours are being offered, and most prices are reasonable, given the high cost for gasoline and supplies. Try to go with a group of four to six, as many tours have a price based on a group of up to six people, not per person.

Among the most popular tours are those to the Snake Cayes with a full day of snorkeling, fishing, and beach bumming. Another popular tour combines Blue Creek caves and Agua Caliente Wildlife Sanctuary or a tour to Lubaantun, that's often combined with a visit to Rio Blanco National Park and its waterfall.

FISHING

For bonefish and tarpon, head to the estuary flats in the Port Honduras marine reserve at the end of the Río Grande, or go northward to Punta Ycacos. Anglers must pay a park fee in the Marine Reserve, but there is no fee for the Punta Ycacos, unless you fish in the Port Honduras reserve. To arrange for a guide with a boat, contact TIDE Tours or Garbutt's Marine.

Fodor's Choice
★ **TIDE Tours.** TIDE Tours has trained more than 60 tour guides in Toledo, and can arrange fly-fishing guides for bonefish or permit in Payne's Creek National Park and Port Honduras Marine Reserve, from around BZ$900 per day for two persons, not including tax or reserve fees. TIDE Fish Fest Weekend is an annual event held in October that raises awareness for environmental issues and also celebrates the region's

HISTORY

The Maya, mostly a group called the Manche Chol Maya, established sizable ceremonial centers and midsize cities in Toledo beginning almost 2,000 years ago. Uxbenká is one of the oldest centers, dating to AD 200. In the Classic period, Lubaantun, which flourished in the 8th and 9th centuries, is thought to have been the administrative center of the region, but for reasons still unclear it was abandoned not long after this. In southern Belize as elsewhere in Mesoamerica, the Mayan civilization began a long, slow decline a little more than 1,000 years ago.

Spanish conquistadors, including Hernán Cortés himself in 1525, came through southern Belize in the early 16th century, but the Maya resisted Spain's and, later, Britain's attempts to control and tax them. The British,

who arrived as loggers, tried to put the Maya in "reservations," and eventually, in the 18th and 19th centuries, moved nearly the entire Manche Chol population to the highlands of Guatemala.

In the late 19th century, groups of Mopan and Ket'chi Maya began moving into southern Belize from Guatemala, establishing more than 50 villages around Toledo. Around the same time, Garífuna from Honduras settled in Punta Gorda, Barranco, and Punta Negra.

Southern Belize, with its rain and remoteness from Belize City, has languished economically for most of the 20th century. The paved Southern Highway and new road from Guatemala should help boost tourism and development in the region in coming years.

natural resources. ■TIP→ TIDE can also arrange a variety of other tours throughout Toledo. ✉ Front St., Hopeville area ☎ 722/2274 TIDE office ⊕ www.tidetours.org.

SCUBA DIVING AND SNORKELING

This far south the reef has pretty much broken up, but individual cayes have their own small reef systems. The best of the bunch is at the Sapodilla Cayes with great wall dives. Lime Caye has camping, and Hunting Caye has a lighthouse. The only drawback is that because they're 40 miles (64 km) off the coast, a day's dive trip can be pricey, depending on how many people go. The Snake Cayes, with several notable dive sites, are closer in, about 18 miles (30 km) northeast of Punta Gorda. The four Snakes—East, West, South, and Middle—are so named because of boa constrictors that once lived there.

The turquoise waters lapping up the shores of the usually deserted white-sand beach on Snake Caye are good for snorkeling, as are the Sapodilla Cayes at the southern end of the Belize Barrier Reef.

Garbutt's Marine. All-day diving and snorkeling trips are available to the Snake and Sapodilla cayes as well as to Port Honduras Marine Reserve; overnight stays at Lime Caye is also an option. The three Garbutt's brothers, Scully, Oliver, and Eworth, also do guided fishing trips and have cabins for rent. ✉ Joe Taylor Creek, Southern Hwy. ☎ 722/0070 ⊕ www.garbuttsfishinglodge.com.

Reef Conservation International. Reef Conservation International operates marine conservation trips in the Sapodilla Cayes Marine Reserve from PG. You can stay at the ReefCI camp based on Tom Owens Caye, in basic accommodations—there's Internet but no hot water. You'll get plenty of snorkeling and diving, but you can also assist marine biologists and other Reef CI staff in monitoring and preserving the reef. One-week dive packages including diving, dive equipment, lodging, and meals start at BZ$2,660 per person, not including air fare to Belize or transfers to southern Belize. ✉ *Mile 18, Placencia Rd., Stann Creek District* ☎ *626/1429 in Placencia, 800/624–0686 U.S. toll-free number* 🌐 *www.reefci.com.*

WHERE TO EAT

$$ LATIN AMERICAN FAMILY Fodor's Choice ★

🍴 **Asha's Culture Kitchen.** In a rustic wood shack built right over the water, Asha's has the best views of any restaurant in Punta Gorda. From the main dining room or the breezy deck you can look across the Gulf of Honduras to Guatemala. Asha's chef-owner Ashton Martin specializes in fresh seafood served Creole-style, such as fried conch with mashed potatoes or grilled snapper with plantains and beans and rice. The menu changes daily. [$] *Average main: BZ$22* ✉ *74 Front St.* ☎ *722/2742* 💳 *No credit cards* 🕒 *Closed Tues.*

$$ VEGETARIAN FAMILY

🍴 **Gomier's Restaurant and Soy Centre.** This is one of the better restaurants in Punta Gorda—when and if it's open. Posted hours don't necessarily mean anything, as Gomier's opens when the friendly St. Lucia–born owner, Ingnatius "Gomier" Longville, feels like cooking. When it is open, Gomier's does excellent vegetarian meals, from organic ingredients grown locally by the owner, along with some seafood. Go with the vegetarian dish of the day, which could be stir-fried tofu or vegan spaghetti. Fresh seafood dishes, such as shrimp curry, sometimes are available. Garífuna *hudut* (green and ripe mashed plantains with fish and coconut stew) lunches are on Friday, and there's live music or documentary movies some nights. Prices are reasonable. The owner also offers tofu-making and cooking classes. [$] *Average main: BZ$20* ✉ *Alejandro Vernon St., behind "Welcome to Punta Gorda" sign on Front St.* ☎ *722/2929* 💳 *No credit cards* 🕒 *Closed Sun.*

$ LATIN AMERICAN

🍴 **Grace's.** An established spot, Grace's has genuine value, a down-home feel, and hearty plates of beans and rice and other Belizean staples on the menu. Get a seat near the entrance and eye the town's street life. This is a good place for a full breakfast of eggs, bacon, fry jacks (a Belizean version of a sopapilla), and, of course, beans. For lunch and dinner you can always get chicken, but you can usually get fresh fish, too, plus pizza, chow mein, hamburgers, and several dozen other dishes. [$] *Average main: BZ$14* ✉ *21 Main St.* ☎ *702/2414.*

$$ LATIN AMERICAN FAMILY

🍴 **Mangrove Inn at Casa Bonita.** No pretense here—instead, you're seated on the second floor verandah of the chef-owner's house across the street from the water in the Cattle Landing area of Punta Gorda. Iconie Williams cooks different dishes every evening, but you'll usually have a choice of seafood (snapper, snook, or shrimp) or a hearty dish like a thick pork chop or lasagna. It's all delicious and inexpensive, and a BYOB so bring your own beer or rum. Because it's a little away from

7

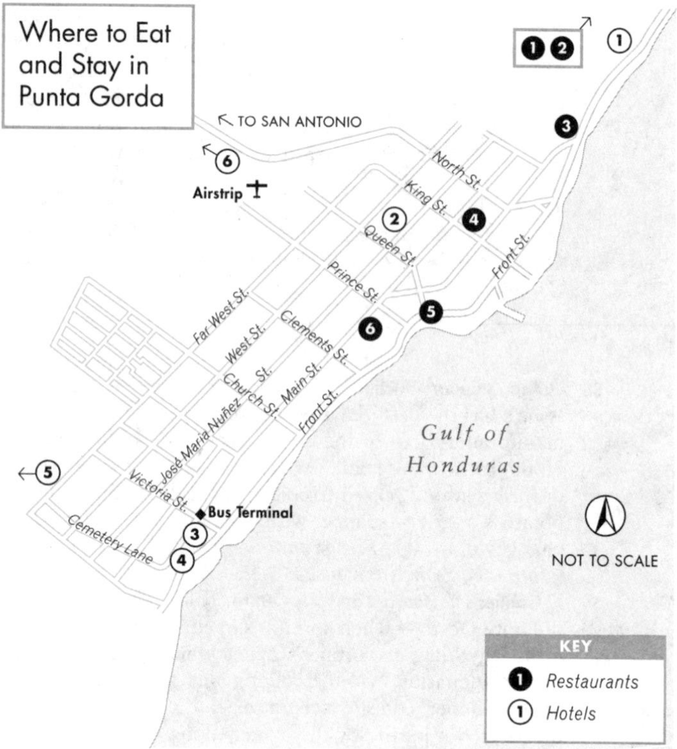

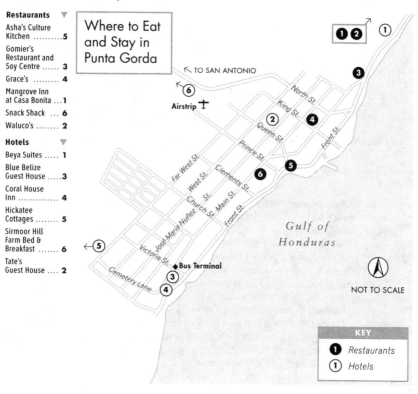

the main downtown area, most guests are local residents or expats, not tourists. [$] *Average main: BZ$16* ✉ *Southern Hwy., Cattle Landing area* ☎ *623/0497* 💳 *No credit cards* 🕑 *Closed Sun. and Mon.*

$ LATIN AMERICAN

🍴 **Snack Shack.** Burritos are the thing here, and in fact usually just about the only thing, except for smoothies, shakes, coffee, and the occasional daily special. You get a selection of fillings and type of flour tortilla. The huge breakfast burrito easily serves two. It's mostly a take-out spot, but there are a few tables on the patio for open-air dining, though the view is only of the Belize Telemedia parking lot. [$] *Average main: BZ$10* ✉ *Main St., in BTL parking lot* ☎ *620/3499* 💳 *No credit cards* 🕑 *Closed Sun.*

$$ LATIN AMERICAN Fodor's Choice ★

🍴 **Waluco's.** Formerly a rather rowdy bar, Waluco's was taken over by TIDE (restaurant profits go to support TIDE's conservation projects) in 2015 and turned into Punta Gorda's best and most pleasant restaurant. Go for the fresh-grilled fish of the day, which might be snook, snapper or another local catch. Prices are lower here than at most other restaurants in town, and if you come before dark, you'll enjoy views across the street of the Gulf of Honduras. Thursday is karaoke night, and there's occasional music by local acts other nights. [$] *Average main: BZ$16* ✉ *Hopeville, Mile 1, Southern Hwy.* ✣ *Across the street from the water, midway between downtown PG and Cattle Landing* ☎ *702/2129* 🕑 *Closed Mon.* 💳 *No credit cards.*

WHERE TO STAY

$
HOTEL
FAMILY
Beya Suites. From the verandas on the second- or third-floor rooftop terrace of this bright pink, waterfront hotel (*beya* means beachfront in the Garífuna language) within walking distance of downtown Punta Gorda, you have expansive views of the water. **Pros:** views of the water; Belizean-owned. **Cons:** most units are not really suites. *$ Rooms from: BZ$174 ⊠ 6 Front St. ☎ 722/2956 ⊕ www.beyasuites.com ↝ 10 rooms ✵ No meals.*

$
B&B/INN
FAMILY
Blue Belize Guest House. At this pleasant small spot overlooking the water, you can settle in and do your own thing in one of the six attractive self-catering flats, with kitchens or kitchenettes, spacious bedrooms, TVs with DVD players, and verandas with hammocks. **Pros:** spacious self-catering apartments; reasonable rates; breezy waterfront location. **Cons:** no a/c but sea breeze generally keeps rooms cool. *$ Rooms from: BZ$185 ⊠ 139 Front St. ☎ 722/2678 ⊕ www.bluebelize.com ↝ 6 rooms ✵ Breakfast.*

$$
B&B/INN
Fodor's Choice
★
Coral House Inn. Americans Rick and Darla Mallory renovated this 1938 British colonial–era house and turned it into one of the most pleasant small guesthouses in the country, with breezy views of the Bay of Honduras and warm hospitality from owners and staff. **Pros:** one of the best small inns in Belize; a/c and Wi-Fi included; reasonable prices. **Cons:** no restaurant, so you'll have to go out for dinner. *$ Rooms from: BZ$214 ⊠ 151 Main St., across from Punta Gorda hospital ☎ 722/2878 ⊕ www.coralhouseinn.com ↝ 6 rooms ✵ Breakfast.*

$
B&B/INN
Fodor's Choice
★
Hickatee Cottages. Just a mile (1.5 km) from downtown PG, this delightful small lodge, which is under new ownership, has lovely Caribbean-style cottages with zinc roofs and private verandas; it's nestled in lush jungle foliage where you'll hear howler monkeys and see a wide variety of birds. **Pros:** lovely cottages; lush jungle setting but near town; excellent value. **Cons:** no a/c. *$ Rooms from: BZ$190 ⊠ Ex-Servicemen Rd., about 1 mile (1.5 km) from PG ✚ Coming into PG on the bay side, follow Front St. into town, past Uno gas station (formerly Texaco), through market area, and then turn right immediately past St. Peter Claver church. Take next left onto Main St. and continue past hospital; bear right where road becomes Cemetery La. Follow Cemetery La. for three blocks and, when you reach small children's playground, turn "half left" onto Ex-Servicemen Rd. (also known as Boom Creek Rd.). Go 1 mile (1.5 km) farther to Hickatee Cottages, on left ☎ 662/4475 ⊕ www.hickatee.com ↝ 6 rooms ✵ Breakfast.*

$$
B&B/INN
FAMILY
Fodor's Choice
★
Sirmoor Hill Farm Bed and Breakfast. In a restored century-old colonial home on a 775-acre farm near Punta Gorda, this B&B is among the most appealing small lodgings in Belize. **Pros:** gorgeous rural setting; beautifully restored colonial home; swimming pool. **Cons:** not much privacy; more like visiting friends' home. *$ Rooms from: BZ$240 ⊠ New Rd., near Belize Defence Forces camp ☎ 722/0052 ⊕ www.sirmoorhillfarm.com ↝ 2 rooms ✵ Breakfast.*

$
B&B/INN
FAMILY
Tate's Guest House. If you don't demand luxury, you couldn't find a nicer budget spot in Punta Gorda. **Pros:** clean accommodations with a/c, Wi-Fi, and cable TV at affordable rates; central location in downtown PG; friendly, helpful owner. **Cons:** no-frill rooms. *$ Rooms from: BZ$90 ⊠ 34 Jose Maria Nunez ☎ 722/0147 ▭ No credit cards ↝ 5 rooms ✵ No meals.*

7

SHOPPING

Maya Bags. About 90 Mayan women from eight local villages are employed to sew handbags, purses, fitness bags, travel bags, and other items, which are sold in a fair trade shop in Punta Gorda near the airstrip and, on a larger scale, to stores in the United States and elsewhere. ⊠ *Airport St., near Punta Gorda airstrip* ☎ *917/697–2203 in U.S.* ⊕ *www.mayabags.org.*

Punta Gorda Front Street Market. The old market area along Front Street has been renovated. There are food stalls, and vendors sell fruit and vegetables, along with some crafts and miscellaneous household items. Unfortunately, the renovation kept the market area facing away from the water, so you don't get the views or the breezes. ⊠ *Front Street Market, Front St.*

Punta Gorda Market at Central Plaza. Fresh fruits and vegetables, local coffee and cacao beans, and some craft items are sold at indoor and outdoor stalls at the central plaza near the clock tower. The busiest market days usually are Tuesday, Wednesday, Friday, and Saturday. ⊠ *Punta Gorda Central Park, Main Middle St., at Clock Tower* ⊗ *Closed Sun.*

THE MAYAN HEARTLAND

Drive a few miles out of town, and you find yourself in the heartland of the Mayan people. Half the population of Toledo is Maya, a far higher proportion than in any other region. The Toledo Maya Cultural Council has created an ambitious network of Mayan-run guesthouses, and in 1995 it initiated the Mayan Mapping Project. By collating oral history and evidence of ancient Mayan settlements, the project hopes to secure rights to land that the Maya have occupied for centuries, but that the Belizean government has ceded to multinational logging companies. There's also a separate Mayan homestay program, where you stay in local homes rather than in guesthouses. *See Where to Stay, below, for information on these two programs.*

Several notable jungle lodges also are in the Mayan Heartland, including Belcampo Lodge, The Lodge at Big Falls, Cotton Tree Lodge, and The Farm Inn. However, the largest and most ambitious group of lodges, Belize Lodge and Excursions, owned by Europeans and run by an American, was closed in 2012 after Ya'aché Conservation Trust rangers found one of two captive jaguars at Indian Creek dead of starvation, and a second captive jaguar near death in an emaciated condition. Local villagers working at the lodges complained they had not been paid for months. Later in 2012, much of one of the BL&E lodges burned down, allegedly by angry local villagers.

The Maya divide into two groups: Mopan Maya and Ket'chi-speaking peoples from the Guatemalan highlands. Most of the latter are recent arrivals, refugees from repression and overpopulation. Each group tends to keep to itself, living in separate villages and preserving unique traditions. Among the Ket'chi villages in Toledo are Crique Sarco, San Vincente, San Miquel, Laguna, San Pedro Columbia, Santa Teresa,

Sunday Wood, Mabelha, and Corazon. Mopan Maya villages include San Antonio, Pueblo Viejo, and San José.

GETTING HERE AND AROUND

Because bus service to rural villages is limited at best, a car is almost a necessity unless you want to take guided tours. Happily, the newly paved San Antonio road from the Southern Highway to Jalacte village at the Guatemalan border, has opened up much of the Maya Heartland, making it much faster and easier to see villages on and near this newly improved road.

TIMING

You can see the highlights in a day or two, but to explore the region thoroughly takes longer. Distances are not great, but most tertiary roads are poor to terrible, and it takes time just to get around the district.

HEALTH AND SAFETY

Malaria exists in rural areas of Toledo. If you're going to spend any time in the bush, discuss with your physician whether to use chloroquine or other malaria prophylaxis. In rural areas the water is often from community wells; you should drink bottled water. Otherwise, the Mayan Heartland is very safe.

EXPLORING

MAYAN VILLAGES

Blue Creek. Don't miss Blue Creek, a beautiful stretch of river dotted with turquoise swimming holes. A path up the riverbank leads to dramatic caves. The entrance to Hokeb Ha Cave is fairly easy to explore on your own (although you should be a strong swimmer), but others require a guide or a tour. TIDE Tours and other tour operators offer trips to Blue Creek, providing lights and other necessary equipment. ⚠ **Don't swim in the river at night—the fer-de-lance, a highly poisonous snake, likes to take nocturnal dips.** ⊠ *Hokab Ha Cave, Blue Creek Village* ✛ *If going on your own from PG, drive north on Southern Hwy. to area called The Dump and turn west on San Antonio Rd. (currently being paved). Drive to village of Mafredi and turn left toward Blue Creek. Go about 9 miles (15 km) to entrance to Blue Creek research station.*

Fodor's Choice ★ **San Antonio.** The Mopan Maya village of San Antonio, 35 miles (56 km) west of Punta Gorda, is Toledo's second-largest town, with a population of more than 2,200. It was settled by people from the Guatemalan village of San Luis, who revere their former patron saint. The impressive village church, built of stones carted from surrounding Mayan ruins, has a stained-glass window donated by another city with a connection to the saint: St. Louis, Missouri. The people of San Antonio haven't forgotten their ancient heritage: each June 13, they take to the streets for a festival that dates back to pre-Columbian times. The new road to the Guatemala border passes through San Antonio Village, making access much faster and easier. ⊠ *San Antonio Village* ✛ *Drive north on Southern Hwy. to Dump, and turn left and follow San Antonio Rd. to San Antonio Village.*

San Pedro Columbia. The Ket'chi Mayan village of San Pedro Columbia is a cheerful cluster of brightly painted buildings and thatch houses off the San Antonio Road. ■TIP→ **The Mayan site of Lubaatun is nearby.** ⊠ *San Pedro Columbia ✛ From PG, drive north on Southern Hwy. to Dump, and turn west on San Antonio Rd. Just before village of San Antonio, turn right on dirt track (watch for sign) to San Pedro Columbia.*

GARÍFUNA VILLAGE

FAMILY   **Barranco.** Although the Maya are by far the largest population in rural Toledo, this is also a home to the Garífuna. Barranco, a small village of fewer than 200 people about an hour by road from Punta Gorda, is the best-known Garífuna center in Toledo. The southernmost coastal village in Belize has electricity, a couple of shops, a bar, a police station, a health clinic, and a school. It was the birthplace of Andy Palacio, the famed Punta rock musician who died in 2008. Palacio is buried in Barranco. A guided village tour includes, in addition to a visit to the Palacio gravesite, stops at the Dabuyaba (Garífuna temple), the House of Culture, and a cassava factory. Lunch in a local home is also possible. TIDE, PG Tours, and other tour operators offer trips to Barranco, or you can drive yourself. ⊠ *Barranco ✛ From PG, drive north to Jacinto village (watch for water tower) and turn west on dirt road to San Felipe, Santa Ana, and Barranco villages. It's about 9 miles (15 km) on dirt road to Barranco, but it may take you as long as 45 mins after you leave Southern Hwy.* ☎ *709/2010 Barranco community phone.*

MAYAN RUINS

FAMILY   **Lubaantun.** Lubaantun, which lies beyond the village of San Pedro
Fodor's Choice   Columbia, is a Late Classic site discovered in 1924 by German archae-
★   ologist Thomas Gann, who gave it a name meaning "place of fallen stones." Lubaantun must have been an awe-inspiring sight: on top of a conical hill, with views to the sea in one direction and the Maya Mountains in the other, its stepped layers of white-plaster stone would have towered above the jungle like a wedding cake. No one knows exactly what function the structures served, but the wealth of miniature masks and whistles found suggests it was a center of ceramic production. The trio of ball courts and the central plaza with tiered seating for 10,000 spectators seems like a Maya Madison Square Garden. There's a small visitor center at the site. Most tour operators in PG can arrange trips to Lubaantun, or you can visit by rental car, a trip made easier by the completion of the San Antonio Road. ⊠ *20 miles (33 km) northwest of Punta Gorda, about 1 mile (1.5 km) from village of San Pedro Columbia, Lubaantun, San Pedro Columbia* ⊕ *www.nichbelize.org* ⊠ *BZ$10.*

FAMILY   **Nim Li Punit.** Nim Li Punit, a Late Classic site discovered in 1976, has
Fodor's Choice   26 unearthed stelae, including one, Stela 14, that is 30 feet tall—the
★   largest ever found in Belize and the second largest found anywhere in the Mayan world. Nim Li Punit, which means "Big Hat" in the Ket'chi Mayan (sometimes referred to as Kek'chi) language, is named for the elaborate headgear of a ruler pictured on Stela 14. Shady trees cool you off as you walk around the fairly small site (you can see it all in an hour or so). Stop by the informative visitor center on the premises to learn more about the site. Nim Li Punit is near the Ket'chi village of Indian

CLOSE UP

Lubaántun and the Crystal Skull

In the last century Lubaantun became the scene of what is allegedly the biggest hoax in modern archaeology. After it was excavated in the 1920s, a British adventurer named F. A. Mitchell-Hedges claimed to have stumbled on what became known as the Crystal Skull. Mitchell-Hedges described the incident in a potboiler, *Danger, My Ally*, in 1951. According to the book, the Crystal Skull was found under an altar at Lubaantun by his daughter Anna. Mitchell-Hedges portrayed himself as a serious archaeologist and explorer; in truth, he was a magazine hack who was later exposed in England as an adventurer. The Crystal Skull made good copy; also known as the Skull of Doom, it

was supposedly used by Mayan high priests to zap anyone they didn't like. Mitchell-Hedges claimed it was 3,600 years old and had taken 150 years to fashion by rubbing a block of pure rock crystal with sand. A similar skull, in the possession of the British Museum, shows signs of having been manufactured in modern times with a dentist's drill. However, some archaeologists believe the Crystal Skull may be authentic, possibly of Aztec origin. Anna Mitchell-Hedges, who died in 2007, adamantly refused to allow the Crystal Skull to be tested and denied all requests by the Belizean government to return it. It is now owned by her caregiver, Bill Homann.

7

Creek, and children (and some adults) from the village usually come over and offer jewelry and crafts for sale. It is easily accessible via a short dirt road off the Southern Highway. ⊠ *Mile 72.5, Southern Hwy., Indian Creek Village* ✛ *From PG, drive north on Southern Hwy. about 27 miles (44 km) to Indian Creek village. Turn west at Nim Li Punit sign and go about 0.5 mile (1 km) on dirt road to site. James Line buses (locals, not express) will drop you at entrance road* ☎ *822/2106 NICH Institute of Archeology* ⊕ *www.nichbelize.org* ⊠ *BZ$10.*

FAMILY **Uxbenká.** Uxbenká, or "ancient place," is on the eastern edge of Santa Cruz Village, about 3 miles (5 km) west of San Antonio. This small ceremonial site has a main plaza with six structures, and a series of smaller plazas. More than 20 stelae have been found here, six of them carved. This site is not officially open to visitors, but if you ask a villager in Santa Cruz, you can probably get an informal guided tour, or go with a TIDE or other tour from PG (about BZ$200), which also include a visit to the nearby Yok Balum cave. Access to the site is much improved by the new San Antonio Road—watch for signs to Uxbenká on the north side of San Antonio Road as you approach Santa Cruz village. ⊠ *Uxbenká, Santa Cruz* ✛ *From PG, drive north on Southern Hwy. to Dump and turn west on San Antonio Rd. Drive past San Antonio village about 3 miles (5 km) to Santa Cruz village* ⊕ *www.nichbelize. org* ⊠ *BZ$5–BZ$10 donation.*

WHERE TO EAT AND STAY

$ ✕**Coleman's Café.** This longtime local favorite serves simple but tasty
LATIN AMERICAN   Belizean dishes such as stew chicken or pork with beans and rice. Sit
at tables with oilcloth tablecloths under a covered patio, open to the
breezes, and enjoy genuine Belizean hospitality at lunch and dinner.
Some days Coleman's has a buffet of Belizean foods at lunch. Ⓢ *Average
main: BZ$14 ⊠ Main St., Big Falls Village, Big Falls ✛ Near rice mill
☎ 630/4069 ▭ No credit cards.*

$$$$ ⌂**Belcampo Lodge.** New ownership has moved this former fishing lodge
RESORT   far up the scale of luxury by renovating the main lodge, adding a gor-
FAMILY   geous spa, redoing the cottages, and adding four new luxury cottages.
Fodor's Choice   **Pros:** great views of jungle and the distant sea from hilltop location;
★   incredible spa; the top lodge option near Punta Gorda. **Cons:** very
pricey. Ⓢ *Rooms from: BZ$2,160 ⊠ Machaca Hill, Wilson Rd., Punta
Gorda ☎ 722/0050, 888/299–9940 reservations in U.S. and Canada
⊕ www.belcampobz.com ⇥ 16 suites ⧫All-inclusive.*

$$$$ ⌂**Cotton Tree Lodge.** This jungle lodge is named after the silk cotton
RESORT   tree (also called the kapok or ceiba), and, fittingly, the lodge strives to
FAMILY   provide a silky-smooth experience for guests. **Pros:** stunning riverside
setting, complete with rope swing to play Tarzan in the river; lots of
activities. **Cons:** sometimes buggy; no a/c. Ⓢ *Rooms from: BZ$1,111
⊠ Moho River, near San Felipe Village, San Felipe ☎ 866/480–4534|
toll-free in U.S. and Canada, 670/0557 in Belize ⊕ www.cottontreelo-
dge.com ⇥ 15 rooms ⧫All-inclusive.*

$ ⌂**The Farm Inn.** On a 52-acre farm near San Antonio village, off the
B&B/INN   newly redone San Antonio Road, this South African-run lodge has six
FAMILY   nicely designed rooms and suites. **Pros:** quiet, natural setting near traditional Mayan villages; friendly international management; reasonable
prices. **Cons:** no a/c. Ⓢ *Rooms from: BZ$174 ⊠ San Antonio Rd., San
Antonio Village ✛ From PG, drive north on Southern Hwy. to Dump,
turn left on San Antonio Rd. Drive to San Antonio Village, and continue
about 2 miles (3.3 km). Watch for Farm Inn sign on right. Turn right
and follow drive a few hundred yards to lodge ☎ 732/4781 ⊕ www.
thefarminnbelize.com ⇥ 6 rooms ⧫Breakfast.*

$$$ ⌂**The Lodge at Big Falls.** Relax beside a meandering jungle river, listen to
HOTEL   otters splash, and admire colorful tropical birds and butterflies at this
FAMILY   small lodge on 30 placid acres beside the Rio Grande River. **Pros:** it's fun
to tube or swim in the river; excellent birding; good food. **Cons:** meals
are pricey. Ⓢ *Rooms from: BZ$351 ⊠ Off Mile 79, Southern Hwy.,
Rio Grande River, Big Falls ☎ 732/4444 ⊕ www.thelodgeatbigfalls.
com ⇥ 9 rooms ⧫No meals.*

SIDE TRIP TO
GUATEMALA

Updated
by Rose
Lambert-Sluder

The jungles of El Petén were once the heartland of the Mayan civilization. The sprawling empire—including parts of present-day Mexico, Belize, Honduras, and El Salvador—was once made up of a network of cities that held hundreds of thousands of people, but a millennium ago this fascinating civilization went into a mysterious decline and soon virtually disappeared. The temples that dominated the horizon were swallowed up by the jungle.

Today ancient ruins seem to emerge as if nourished by El Petén's soil. In comparison with the rest of Guatemala, which has 15 million people in an area the size of Tennessee, El Petén is relatively sparsely populated, although this is changing. Fifty years ago El Petén had fewer than 20,000 residents. Due to massive immigration from other areas of Guatemala, El Petén now has more than half a million people (almost twice the population of the entire country of Belize). Still, nature reigns supreme, with vines and other plants reclaiming everything that stands still a little too long. Whatever your primary interest—archaeology, history, birding, biking—you'll find plenty to do and see in this remote region.

Four-wheel-drive vehicles are required to get to many of the archaeological sites (but not to Tikal), while others, such as those in the Mirador Basin, are reachable only by boat or on foot. The difficulty doesn't just enhance the adventure, it gives you time to take in the exotic scenery and rare tropical flora and fauna that are with you all the way. Most major roads in the Petén are now beautifully paved, and the towns of Flores and Santa Elena bustle with activity.

The Petén may be vast and remote, but the traveler's focus takes in a far more limited area. Ruins dot the entire region, but excavation has begun on only a few of them. In the center of the region on Lago Petén Itzá sits Flores, its administrative center, and its twin town of Santa Elena, the site of the regional airport. Northeast lie the famed ruins of Tikal.

HISTORY

At its peak, the Mayan civilization developed one of the earliest forms of writing, the very first mathematical system to use zero, complex astronomical calculations, advanced agricultural systems, and an inscrutable belief system. It was during this zenith that spectacular cities such as Tikal were built. By the time the Europeans arrived, the Mayan civilization had already mysteriously collapsed.

Until the 1960s the Petén region was a desolate place. This all changed when the Guatemalan government began offering small tracts of land in El Petén for US$25 to anyone willing to settle it. The landless moved in droves, and today the population is more than 500,000—a 25-fold increase in around 50 years.

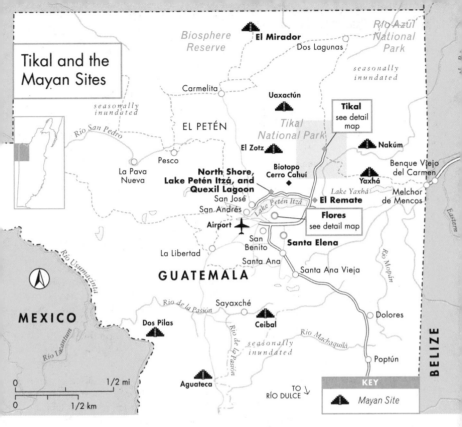

Unemployment in El Petén is high, and tourism—mostly associated with Tikal and other Mayan sites—is the main industry. Many make ends meet through subsistence farming, logging, hunting for *xate* (palm leaves used in the floral industry) in the wild, and marijuana cultivation. Exploration for oil is under way in a few areas as well.

ORIENTATION AND PLANNING

GETTING ORIENTED

The Petén is rugged country, where major roads are few and far between and traffic is thin. Because there are only two airports—one in Guatemala City, the other in Flores—you'll do most of your travel by land. Most roads you'll traverse are paved, such as the road from Santa Elena–Flores to Tikal, the road from Río Dulce in the south to Santa Elena–Flores, and a few others.

Proximity to Las Verapaces and the Atlantic lowlands—it's four to five hours from either region—make the Petén a reasonable overland combination with either, and air links to Guatemala City simplify travel here from almost any other region of the country.

Tikal. Arguably the most impressive of all Mayan sites, and rivaling even Machu Picchu in Peru and Angkor Wat in Cambodia in its ancient splendor, Tikal is a must-see.

Tikal Environs. Set at the end of the causeway in Lake Petén, the town of Flores is an enchanting and walkable small town, tourist-oriented, with almost a charmed Mediterranean air. The village of El Remate, closer to Tikal and on the lake, is another pleasant (though perhaps less enchanting) base for exploring the region.

Other Mayan Sites in El Petén. The complexes of Yaxhá, Nakúm, Uaxactún, and El Zotz, among others, are scattered around Tikal. They're all close, but poor roads limit the number of visitors, especially during the rainy season.

PLANNING

WHEN TO GO

It's very warm here year-round. The rainy season is May to November, and the rain takes itself seriously. Occasional showers are a possibility the rest of the year, but shouldn't interfere with your plans. March and April are the hottest months, with December and January a few degrees cooler than the rest of the year. July and August see an influx of visitors during prime North American and European vacation time.

GETTING HERE AND AROUND

AIR TRAVEL

Aeropuerto Internacional Santa Elena (FRS), or the Mundo Maya International Airport, often just referred to as the Flores airport, is less than 0.5 mile (1 km) outside town. Taxis and shuttles meet every plane and charge about 20 quetzales per person to take you into Flores. The airport has service to and from Belize City, Guatemala City, and Cancún.

Avianca and TAG operate flights between Guatemala City and Santa Elena-Flores that take less than an hour and cost from around US$110 each way or US$190 round-trip (and sometimes less). Tropic Air runs flights to and from Belize City's international airport between US$120–US$160 each way.

Contacts Avianca Airlines. ☎ 800/284–2622 in U.S. ⊕ www.avianca.com. **TAG.** ☎ 502/2380–9494 in Guatemala ⊕ www.tag.com.gt. **Tropic Air.** ✉ Philip Goldson International Airport, Belize City ☎ 501/226–2626 in Belize, 800/422–3435 in U.S. ⊕ www.tropicair.com.

BUS TRAVEL

Linea Dorada and Autobuses Fuente del Norte offer daily direct bus service between the Marine terminal in Belize City and Santa Elena-Flores. The five-hour trip on air-conditioned buses with comfortable reclining seats, TVs, and bathrooms costs around US$25 one-way. Call at least one day ahead for reservations. Inexpensive local service is available, but those buses stop in every village along the way, which adds hours to the trip. The same lines also offer service between Guatemala City and Santa Elena-Flores.

In Santa Elena, the main local bus *terminal* is a bustling center where your questions can be easily answered. (To and from the bus station, a tuk-tuk should be a mere Q5.) Here you can catch a scheduled minibus shuttle, operated by San Juan Travel and other companies, that makes the 42-mile (70-km) trip on a good paved road to Tikal several times in the morning and return trips in the evening. Service is usually reduced during slow periods. They cost around Q50 one way per person and take 1½ hours or more, depending on stops.

From the town bordering Belize, Melchor de Mencos, there are frequent chicken buses, often packed, which cost about Q30 (around $4). They'll take you to Santa Elena-Flores but not to Tikal. To get to Tikal from the Belize border, you have to get off at El Cruce (the Crossroads), and wait for another bus en route to Tikal. The frequency of buses depends on the time of year and is not wholly reliable, but roughly every two hours until the early afternoon.

Contacts Autobuses Fuente del Norte. ⊠ *E Bus Terminal, 4a Calle, Santa Elena* ☏ *502/7947–7070 Grupo del Fuente, 501/223–1200 Mundo Maya Travel in Belize* ⊕ *www.travelmundomaya.com.* **Linea Dorada.** ⊠ *Mercado Nuevo Interior , Zona 2, Santa Elena* ☏ *502/7924–8434, 502/7924–8535* ⊕ *www. lineadorada.com.gt.* **San Juan Travel.** ⊠ *E Bus Terminal, 4a Calle, Santa Elena.*

CAR TRAVEL

Main roads in El Petén, such as between Flores/Santa Elena and Tikal, are paved and in very good shape. Secondary roads, however, often are in poor repair and not very well marked. Some roads are impassable during the rainy season, so check with the tourist office before heading out on seldom traveled roads, such as those to the more remote ruins surrounding Tikal.

If you're not booked on a tour, one way to get around El Petén is to rent a four-wheel-drive vehicle. Many rental agencies, including Hertz, have offices at Mundo Maya International Airport. Tabarini, a local company, also rents vehicles from an airport office. Prices start at around US$35 a day, or US$50 a day for an SUV, cheaper than Belize. You need a valid driver's license from your own country to drive in Guatemala.

Most rental companies in Belize don't allow the car to leave the country. Crystal Auto Rental in Belize City does, however; though you need to coordinate this two days in advance to get paperwork ready. Insurance through Crystal will not cover you in Guatemala. It is ill-advised to drive after dark in Guatemala; use extreme caution when driving. ⚠ **Armed attacks on cars have happened both between Guatemala City and Petén, and between the Belize border and Tikal. Check official crime and safety reports before traveling.**

Local Agencies Hertz. ⊠ *Mundo Maya Airport, Santa Elena* ☏ *502/3274–4424 Hertz in Santa Elena, 800/654–3001 Hertz international rentals* ⊕ *rentautos.com. gt.* **Tabarini.** ⊠ *Mundo Maya International Airport, Santa Elena* ☏ *502/2444– 4200* ⊕ *www.tabarini.com.*

8

BORDER FORMALITIES

The Belize border is about 9 miles (15 km) from San Ignacio, just west of the town of Benque Viejo del Carmen. Border crossings at the newer customs and immigration building here are usually quick and easy.

Upon arrival at the border, you'll be approached on the Belize side by money changers asking if you want to exchange U.S. or Belize dollars for Guatemalan quetzales. Another group will approach you on the Guatemala side. The rate given by money changers will be a little less than you'll get at an ATM or bank, but you may want to exchange enough for your first day in Guatemala. You'll usually get better rates on the Guatemala side.

Belize formalities include paying your US$20 (BZ$40) exit fee. You may see a Q20 entrance fee when entering Guatemala. This fee is known to be unofficial; however, it's smarter to pay it than to argue with the officers at your own risk. Most visitors to Guatemala, including citizens of the United States, Canada, and European Union, do not need visas, and passports are normally stamped with a permit to enter for 90 days. Customs officials rarely check baggage.

Melchor de Mencos is a scruffy border town with unpaved streets. Shops on the main drag sell Guatemalan crafts. Other than extremely basic hotels (some of which are brothels), the only good place to stay nearby is the Río Mopan Lodge, where you can snag a room for under US$35.

There's no safe long-term parking at the border, so if you are driving a rental car, you should arrange to park it elsewhere. Only a handful of Belize rental companies allow their vehicles to be taken into Guatemala (try Crystal in Belize City or Safe Cars in San Ignacio). Note, however, that Belize insurance isn't valid in Guatemala, and Guatemalan insurance currently isn't sold at the border.

■TIP➡ **As you cross at Melchor de Mencos, you'll be pounced on by taxi drivers. If taxi is your planned transport, be vigilant. Don't take the first offers, and work the cost down (showing uncertainty or disinterest works best).**

TAXI TRAVEL

Taxis from the Santa Elena–Flores airport to Tikal are around US$30. A taxi from the Santa Elena airport into Flores is Q20 (about US$2.50) per person.

EMERGENCIES

El Petén's only hospital is in San Benito, a suburb of Santa Elena. Medical facilities in El Petén are not as modern as in the rest of the country. If you're really sick, consider getting on the next plane to Guatemala City. Centro Médico Maya in Santa Elena has physicians on staff, though little or no English is spoken.

Contact Emergency Services Centro Médico Maya. ⊠ *2 Av y 4 Calle, Zona 1, Santa Elena* ☏ *502/7926–0180.* **Hospital Nacional.** ⊠ *Calle Principal, San Benito* ☏ *502/7926–1459.* **Police.** ☏ *110 for police emergency, 120 for ambulance,.* **Tourist Emergency Assistance.** ☏ *502/2421–2810, 1500 for tourist emergency assistance.*

SAFETY

Most crimes directed at tourists in El Petén have been pickpocketings, muggings, and thefts from cars. However, there have been a number of incidents over the years involving armed groups stopping buses, vans, and private cars at Tikal park.

In town, don't wear flashy jewelry and watches, keep your camera in a secure bag, and don't handle money in public. Hire taxis only from official stands at the airport, outside hotels, and at major intersections. If you can avoid it, don't drive after sunset. One common ploy used by highway robbers is to construct a roadblock, such as logs strewn across the road, and then hide nearby. When unsuspecting motorists get out of their cars to remove the obstruction, they are waylaid. ■TIP→ **If you come upon a deserted roadblock while driving, don't stop; turn around.**

INGUAT, the national institute for tourism, has voluntary security caravans to escort cars from Santa Elena-Flores to Tikal. To inquire about an escort, it is recommended to contact INGUAT directly by email at least three days in advance (info@inguat.gob.gt).

The increase in adoption of Guatemalan children has caused some people—particularly rural villagers—to fear that children will be abducted by foreigners. Limit your interaction with children you do not know, and be discreet when taking photographs.

ABOUT THE HOTELS

El Petén now has a wide range of lodging options, from suites at luxurious lakeside resorts to stark rooms in budget hotels. Flores has many lodging choices, though most are merely adequate, and the number of hotels there keeps prices competitive. The hotels in the much larger Santa Elena, the gateway to the island town of Flores, are generally larger and more upscale than the places in Flores, but with less atmosphere. El Remate, about 22 miles (35 km) from Flores on the road to Tikal, is a pleasant alternative, with several excellent small, mostly inexpensive hotels. At Tikal itself are three lodges that have the great advantage of being right at the park. On the north side of Lago de Petén Itzá are several hotels, including a couple of the most upscale in the region: Francis Ford Coppola's La Lancha and the largest resort hotel in the area, Hotel Camino Real Tikal.

WHAT IT COSTS IN GUATEMALAN QUETZALES			
$	**$$**	**$$$**	**$$$$**
Restaurants under Q70	Q70–Q100	Q101–Q130	over Q130
Hotels under Q360	Q360–Q560	Q561–Q760	over Q760

Restaurant prices are per person for a main course at dinner. Hotel prices are for two people in a standard double room, including tax (up to 22%) and service.

Many hotels in El Petén have high and low seasons. They charge higher rates during the dry season, December through April, especially at the peak times of Christmas and Easter, and sometimes also during the

July-to-August vacation season. Advance reservations are a good idea during these periods, especially at Tikal park lodges.

ABOUT THE RESTAURANTS

In El Petén you have a couple of choices for dining: *comedores,* which are small eateries along the lines of a U.S. café or diner, with simple and inexpensive local food; and restaurants, that, in general, are a little nicer and serve a wider selection of food, often with an international or American flavor. Restaurants are mostly in Flores and other towns. In more remote lodgings, you'll probably eat in the hotel dining room.

Some restaurants serve wild game, or *comida silvestre.* Although often delicious, the game has usually been taken illegally. You might see *venado* (venison), *coche del monte* (mountain cow or peccary), and *tepezcuintle* (paca, a large rodent) on the menu.

EXTENDED TOURS

Aside from hotel-run overnight or multiday tours, ARCAS runs special ecotours. Martsam Travel offers many different types of tours in the area. Tip tour guides about 10% of the tour price.

Contacts ARCAS EcoTours. ⊠ *Mayan Biosphere Reserve, Flores ⊹ Near Zoológico Petencito* ☎ *502/5208–0968.* **Martsam Travel.** ⊠ *Calle 30 de Junio, lobby of Capitán Tortuga, Flores* ☎ *502/7926–0346 in Flores, 866/832–2776 in U.S. and Canada* ⊕ *www.martsam.com.*

FROM BELIZE

Many tour operators in the San Ignacio, Belize, area operate day and overnight or multinight Tikal tours. You'll pay more in Belize than in Guatemala, but you reduce the hassle factor significantly—you'll probably be picked up at your Cayo hotel, whisked across the border, provided with a guide to Tikal, and fed lunch (hotel accommodations are arranged if you're staying overnight). You'll typically pay US$150 for a day tour to Tikal from San Ignacio. Overnight tours can be as much as US$450, but include a sunrise tour. When comparing tour costs, check to see if border fees and Tikal admission are included.

VISITOR INFORMATION

Contacts ARCAS. ⊠ *Mayan Biosphere Reserve, Flores ⊹ Near Zoológico Petencito* ☎ *502/5208–0968 Dr. Fernando Martinez (Rescue Center Director)* ⊕ *www.arcasguatemala.org.* **CINCAP.** ⊠ *In central plaza, Av. Libertad, Flores.* **INGUAT.** ⊠ *Mundo Maya International Airport, Santa Elena* ☎ *502/2421–2800* ⊕ *www.visitguatemala.com.*

TIKAL

22 miles (35 km) north of El Remate, 42 miles (68 km) northeast of Flores.

Fodor's Choice ★

GETTING HERE AND AROUND

There are several ways to get to Tikal. If you're in Belize City, you can take a bus on the Fuente del Norte or Linea Dorada lines to Santa Elena-Flores. At higher cost, you can fly Tropic Air from the Philip Goldson International Airport, which has flights every day. If in San Ignacio, Belize, take a taxi or cheaper collective taxi to the Guatemalan border.

TOP REASONS TO GO

TIKAL

Tikal is usually ranked as the most impressive of all Mayan sites. You can climb many of the structures and, looking across the jungle canopy, feel humbled by the history's gravitas.

OTHER MAYAN RUINS

Tikal is the best known, but hardly the only important Mayan site in El Petén. El Mirador was a giant city-state, perhaps larger than Tikal, and in the Mirador Basin are the remains of at least four other centers, including Nakbé, El Tintal, Xulnal, and Wakná.

WILDLIFE

The ancient world amazes, but when you see a spider monkey munching allspice berries just feet away, you may think the best part of the Mayan world is what still inhabits it.

FLORES AND LAGO PETÉN ITZÁ

The island town of Flores has a muted, old-world ambience in the middle of an oceanic lake.

SHOPPING FOR HANDICRAFTS

The indigenous population is known for a variety of handicrafts. There's an open-air market in Santa Elena, and Flores has a number of little shops. The village of El Remate has unique wood carvings, and the border town of Melchor also has shops catering to tourists.

From there you'll cross the border and either take a taxi straight to Tikal, or a bus to El Cruces (the crossroads between Santa Elena-Flores and Tikal), where you'll wave down another bus. From the border (referred to as Melchor de Mencos), a taxi is by far the easier option, cheaper in a group if you can find friendly passengers at the border with whom to split the cost. *See Petén Getting Here and Around for more information.*

If you choose to rent a car, a paved, well-patrolled 42-mile (70-km) highway connects Flores-Santa Elena and Tikal, passing through the town of El Remate at about its halfway point. Most expensive but least stressful of the options is an escorted tour from San Ignacio.

TIMING

You can visit Tikal on a day trip and get a good sense of its grandeur. Depending on your schedule, you may choose to spend the night either at Tikal National Park so you can see the ruins in the morning (a must for birders), or in Flores, El Remate, or elsewhere along the shores of Lake Petén Itzá. You can easily spend two days, or longer, exploring the ruins. You may want to hire a guide for your first day, then wander about on your own on the second. If you have additional time, consider an extension in El Petén. The town of Flores, with its lakeside bistros and cobblestone streets, merits at least a half-day stroll.

SAFETY AND PRECAUTIONS

Taxis and tourist buses seem to be magnets for bandits in El Petén. The bandits take passengers' valuables; occasionally passengers have been assaulted. Keep in mind that some 300,000 international visitors come to Tikal every year, and the vast majority of them have no problems with crime.

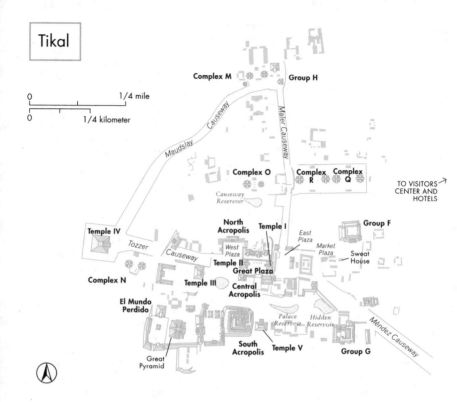

Tikal

FAMILY
Fodor's Choice
★

Tikal. Although the region was home to Mayan communities as early as 600 BC, Tikal itself wasn't established until sometime around 200 BC. One of the first structures to be built here was a version of the North Acropolis. Others were added at a dizzying pace for the next three centuries. By AD 100 impressive structures like the Great Plaza had already been built. But even though it was a powerful city in its own right, Tikal was still ruled by the northern city of El Mirador. It wasn't until the arrival of a powerful dynasty around AD 300 that Tikal arrogated itself to full power. King Great Jaguar Paw sired a lineage that would build Tikal into a city rivaling any of its time. It's estimated that by AD 500 the city covered more than 18 square miles (47 square km) and had a population of close to 100,000.

The great temples that still tower above the jungle were at that time covered with stucco and painted with bright reds and greens, and the priests used them for elaborate ceremonies meant to please the gods and assure prosperity for the city. What makes these structures even more impressive is that the Maya had no metal tools to aid in construction, had no beasts of burden to carry heavy loads, and never used wheels for anything except children's toys. Of course, as a hierarchical culture they had a slave class, and the land was rich in obsidian, a volcanic glass that could be fashioned into razor-sharp tools.

By the 6th century Tikal governed a large part of the Mayan world, thanks to a leader called Caan Chac (Stormy Sky), who took the throne around AD 426. Under Caan Chac, Tikal became an aggressive military and commercial center that dominated the surrounding communities with a power never before seen in Mesoamerica. The swamps protected the city from attack and allowed troops to spot any approaching enemy. Intensive agriculture in the *bajos* (lowlands) provided food for the huge population. A valuable obsidian trade sprang up, aided by the city's strategic position near two rivers.

Tikal thrived for more than a millennium, forming strong ties with two powerful centers: Kaminal Juyu, in the Guatemalan highlands, and Teotihuacán, in Mexico City. The city entered a golden age when Ah-Cacao (Lord Chocolate) ascended the throne in AD 682. It was Ah-Cacao and his successors who commissioned the construction of the majority of the city's most important temples. Continuing the tradition of great structures, Ah-Cacao's son commissioned Temple I, which he dedicated to his father, who is buried beneath it. He also ordered the construction of Temple IV, the tallest temple at Tikal. By the time of his death in 768 Tikal was at the peak of its power. It would remain so until its mysterious abandonment around AD 900.

For almost 1,000 years Tikal remained engulfed by the jungle. The conquistadors who came here searching for gold and silver must have passed right by the overgrown ruins, mistaking them for rocky hills. The native Peténeros certainly knew of the ancient city's existence, but no one else ventured near until 1848, when the Guatemalan government dispatched archaeologists to the region. Tikal started to receive international attention in 1877, when Dr. Gustav Bernoulli commissioned locals to remove the carved wooden lintels from across the doorways of Temples I and IV. These were sent to a museum in Basel, Switzerland.

In 1881 and 1882 English archaeologist Alfred Percival Maudslay made the first map showing the architectural features of this vast city. As he began to unearth the major temples, he recorded his work in dramatic photographs—you can see copies in the museum at Tikal. His work was continued by Teobert Maler, who came in 1895 and 1904. Both Maler and Maudslay have causeways named in their honor. In 1951 the Guatemalan air force cleared an airstrip near the ruins to improve access for large-scale archaeological work. Today, after more than 150 years of digging, researchers say that Tikal includes some 3,000 significant buildings. Countless more are still covered by the jungle. ⊠ *Parque Nacional Tikal* ⊕ *www.tikalpark.com* ✆ *Q150*.

EXPLORING

WITH A GUIDE

Most people find a guide worth it. Guides can be booked at the concrete information kiosk near the parking lot; some can be booked ahead. They make the visit more interesting, though don't believe everything they tell you, as some guides have their own pet theories on the decline of the Maya or other subjects that they love to expound to tourists. Rates are highly negotiable, but expect to pay about US$60 for a tour for up to four or five people. In a large group you may pay as little as US$10 per person. If you're staying more than one day, hire a guide for the first day, and then wander on your own after that.

ON YOUR OWN

Pack well: Wear hiking or walking shoes and bring plenty of water (a liter a person per hour is advised)—you'll be walking about 6 miles (10 km) if you intend to see the whole site. Take along your bug spray, as you'll likely sweat off the first layer. Snacks and sunscreen are smart to have. There are bathrooms inside the park, but not potable water.

The ticket-taker and gate to Tikal is at the left of the roundabout where the information kiosk sits. (Signs are not plentiful.) When you pass the gate, keep to the middle trail. You'll soon arrive at the ancient city's center, filled with awe-inspiring temples and acropolises. The pyramid that you approach from behind is **Temple I**, known as the Temple of the Great Jaguar because of the feline represented on one of its carved lintels. It's in what is referred to as the **Great Plaza**, one of the most beautiful and dramatic in Tikal. The Great Plaza was built around AD 700 by Ah-Cacao, one of the wealthiest rulers of his time. His tomb, comparable in magnitude to that of Pa Cal at the ruins of Palenque in southern Mexico, was discovered beneath the Temple of the Great Jaguar in the 1960s. The theory is that his queen is buried beneath **Temple II**, called the Temple of the Masks for the decorations on its facade. It's a twin of the Temple of the Great Jaguar. In fact, construction of matching pyramids distinguishes Tikal from other Mayan sites.

The **North Acropolis**, to the west of Ah-Cacao's temple, is a mind-boggling conglomeration of temples built over layers and layers of previous construction. Excavations have revealed that the base of this structure is more than 2,000 years old. Be sure to see the stone mask of the rain god at Temple 33. The **Central Acropolis**, south of the Great Plaza, is an immense series of structures assumed to have served as administrative centers.

If you climb to the top of one of the pyramids, you'll see the gray roof combs of others rising above the rain forest's canopy but still trapped within it. **Temple V**, to the south, underwent a $3 million restoration project and is now open to the public. **Temple IV**, to the west, is the tallest-known structure built by the Maya. Although the climb to the top is steep the view is unforgettable.

To the southwest of the plaza lie the **South Acropolis**, which hasn't been reconstructed, and a 105-foot-high pyramid, similar in construction to those at Teotihuacán. A few jungle trails, including the marked Interpretative Benil-ha Trail, offer a chance to see howler monkeys and other wildlife. You also may see packs of the hook-tailed coatimundi (*pizote* in Spanish), adorable relatives of the racoon. Outside the park, a somewhat overgrown trail halfway down the old airplane runway on the left leads to the remnants of old rubber-tappers' camps, and is a good spot for bird-watching.

EXPLORING TIPS

Visitors are not allowed inside the ruins after opening hours, which are 6 am to 6 pm.

There are tales of tourists sneaking in or slipping guards bribes to pass, but we advise against that. The trails are not lit and climbing the pyramids is risky in the dark. There's also a slight menace of robbery.

If you stay at one of the three lodgings on the grounds, you get a jump-start on the day-tour visitors and have the advantage of being here late in the afternoon, after everyone else has left.

In order to take a famous sunrise tour, you must stay in the park the night before. Tours begin at 4 am, and you'll pay the day's Q150 ticket fee to the park, plus an extra Q100 for entrance before the park opens, plus the cost of the tour. They don't guarantee the sun, and there's often a cloud canopy; but seeing the park awaken is a marvel.

Signs indicate whether a structure cannot be climbed ("No Subrir"), which is not always obvious. Look for these signs and respect the rules.

In the past, if you purchased an entrance ticket after 3 pm, you could use the same ticket for your next day's entry, but at the time of writing that's unfortunately no longer the case. It doesn't hurt to ask upon purchase.

⚠ **There are no ATMs inside Tikal National Park. Hotels usually exchange dollars for quetzales or will direct you to a business that will. Be sure to have plenty of cash before heading to Tikal.**

At park headquarters are two small archaeological museums that display Mayan artifacts, plus a new exhibit on current restoration and conservation projects. These are good resources for information on the enigmatic rise and fall of the Maya people, though little information is in English. Don't confuse these structures for the ruins; though with their cracking walls and invasion of grass it would be understandable.

El Centro de Conservación e Investigación de Tikal. Founded in 2012, the Center of Conservation and Research is a collaboration with the government of Japan. There's a small exhibition and info center about its restoration and conservation work. ⊠ *Tikal* ⊕ *www.mcd.gob.gt/ el-centro-de-conservacion-e-investigacion-de-tikal.*

El Museo Lítico (*Stelae Museum*). El Museo Lítico or Stelae Museum has stelae (commemorative stone slabs) found at Tikal and interesting photos from early archaeological excavations. ⊠ *Near visitor center* 🖼 *Q30 admission to both museums.*

El Museo Tikal (*Tikal Sylvannus G. Morley Museum*). El Museo Tikal has a replica of Ha Sawa Chaan K'awil's burial chamber and some ceramics and bones from the actual tomb (the jade, however, is a replica). ⊠ *Near visitor center* 🖼 *Q30 admission to both museums.*

TIKAL TOURS

Many folks make a lifelong career out of guiding tours at Tikal, and can be found around the information kiosk centered in the roundabout inside the park. Inquire whether they are INGUAT certified, about their guidance experience, tour costs, and whether there's a chance a tour would be cancelled if not enough tourists sign on. If you prefer to book ahead of time, there are multiple options.

> ## WATCH FOR THE ANIMALS!
>
> Obey Tikal's 45 kph (27 mph) speed limit; it's designed to give you time to stop for animals that cross the road within the confines of the park. Be particularly careful of the raccoon-like coatimundi that locals call a *pizote*, which scurries with abandon across the road. At the park entrance a guard gives you a time-stamped ticket to be collected by another guard when you arrive at the visitor center. If you cover the 9-mile (15-km) distance in less than 20 minutes, you'll be deemed to have been speeding and possibly fined.

FAMILY   **Canopy Tours Tikal.** The fun folks at Canopy Tours Tikal have expeditions that take you to the true heart of the rain forest—not on ground level, but more than 100 feet up in the air, where you can *"vuele como Superman."* Even more exhilarating, you may see monkeys in their homes and/or other wildlife. Each zip line costs US$25 (approx. Q188) per person (plus park entrance fee). Inquire and they'll give transport from inside the park, Remate, or Flores for a small extra fee. Tikal Canopy Tour also offers hiking, birdwatching, and horseback riding. ✉ *Near entrance gate to Tikal park, El Remate ✤ About 40 mins by car from Flores* ☎ *502/5615–4988* ⊕ *www.tikalcanopy.com* 💲 *Q375.*

FAMILY   **Ecotourism & Adventure Specialists.** This company's professionally run tours include an option for hotel pickup in Flores in the morning, and then hotel drop-off in the late afternoon after a day of guided exploration. Tours can be reserved through their website. ✉ *Guatemala City* ☎ *502/2367–2837* ⊕ *www.tikalpark.com.*

EM Tours. These guides provide private and small group tours, including sunrise tours, with a bounty of knowledge to share. ✉ *Socotzal, at gate of Tikal Park* ☎ *502/4051–3805.*

WHERE TO STAY

There are three hotels on the park grounds: Tikal Inn, Jungle Lodge, and Jaguar Inn. At all of these you pay for the park location rather than good amenities and great service. Electric power is from generators, which usually run for part of the morning and evening, although batteries may provide limited lighting throughout the night. None of the hotels at the park have air-conditioning. Since the hotels here have a captive audience, service is not always as friendly or helpful as it could be, and reservations are sometimes "lost," even if you have confirming e-mail. However, when contrasted with the massive concessionaire-owned lodges inside national parks around the rest of the world, these hotels are intimate and atmospheric. If you want to be even closer to the cry of howler monkeys, good camping is available at the park campsite (Q50 per person plus approximately Q50 for tent or hammock), where you'll sleep under a small thatch gazebo. Or you can camp at the Jaguar Inn, which will provide an inflatable mattress and linens in a modern pop-up tent and access to public bathrooms and showers (approximately Q100 per person). Two *comedores* are at the entrance to the park; Comedor Tikal on the right of the entrance is the better and cheaper. The tiny Caffé Ital near the souvenir stands will serve coffee and candy bars. All three hotels have restaurants open to the public, with inflated pricing. The hotels have room-only rates, but if you are booking through a travel agent you may be required to take a package that includes meals and a Tikal tour.

$$
B&B/INN
FAMILY
Fodor'sChoice
★

Jungle Lodge. Easily the best accommodations in Tikal, this lodge's cobblestone footpaths will lead you through a tamed jungle (but not so tame as to deny you a hello from a spider monkey or an iguana) to remodeled bungalows, painted with elegant interpretations of Mayan motifs. **Pros:** dynamic interiors and exteriors; Edenic jungle gardens; swimming pool; suits a range of budgets. **Cons:** due to renovations, rooms are more expensive; dining options underwhelming and overpriced o r comedor. $ *Rooms from: Q510* ✉ *Parque Nacional Tikal, Jungle Lodge* ☎ *502/2477–0570* ⊕ *www.junglelodgetikal.com* ⇩ *49 rooms* ☉ *No meals.*

$$
B&B/INN
FAMILY

Tikal Inn. Step into the lobby and you feel like you've entered another decade, though which decade is up for debate: the walls are browning at the edges and the pool may be a crocodile-green, but the cashew trees and explosive ferns remind you that you're in a jungle wonderland, so what does modernity matter? The cluster of bungalows, set farthest from the park entrance, wraps around a well-manicured garden and a pool (cleanliness varies), which you will be very happy to see after trekking through the ruins. **Pros:** good location in the park; swimming pool; decent service; packages can be a bargain. **Cons:** rooms can be hot since there is no power for fans at night; limited hot water and electricity; accommodations are dated. $ *Rooms from: Q450* ✉ *Parque Nacional Tikal, Tikal Inn* ☎ *502/7861–2444* ✉ *tikalinn@gmail.com* ⊕ *www.tikalinn.com* ⇩ *25 rooms* ☉ *Some meals.*

TIKAL ENVIRONS

Flores is the blue-ribbon rose in the bouquet of green that is El Petén. If you're traveling in the region, it would be a shame to miss this historic little island, where you can stay in a cozy inn, eat well, and explore the hilly cobblestone streets on foot. Santa Elena, at the entrance to Flores, is a bustling commercial center but is far less frequented by tourists (hence it's the perfect place to get an authentic sense of how people live in El Petén). El Remate, a village on the shore of the lake, has a number of small, mostly budget, hotels, and is a handy jumping-off point for Tikal if you don't stay in the park.

FLORES

133 miles (206 km) north of Río Dulce, 38 miles (61 km) northeast of Sayaxché.

The red-roof town of Flores, on an island in the waters of Lago Petén Itzá connected to the mainland by a main road, is on the site of the ancient city of Tatyasal. This was the region's last unconquered outpost of Mayan civilization, until finally falling to the Spanish in 1697. The conquerors destroyed the city's huge pyramids.

Today, from afar the provincial capital looks like a toy village neatly assembled; up close it has narrow streets lined with buildings in buttermint pastels, and flowers spilling over balconies, making every corner photogenic. There's a central square presided over by a colonial church, and the pint-sized motorized tuk-tuks give you a real sense of being *elsewhere*. Touristy, yes, but still charming.

To stay in some of Flores' hotels is to experience a different era; you almost expect to see it through a yellow-tinted filter. Some hotels are quaint and unfussy; some are simply pedestrian, even mediocre. Frame your expectations well, and their eccentricities can enhance the experience.

Connected to the mainland by a bridge and causeway—don't be put off by the Burger King at the entrance to the causeway—Flores serves as a base for many travelers to El Petén. It's also the center of many nongovernmental organizations working for the preservation of the Mayan Biosphere, an endangered area covering nearly all of northern Petén. Flores is also one of the last remaining vestiges of the Itzá, the people who built Mexico's monumental Chichén Itzá.

GETTING HERE AND AROUND

Once in Flores, all will be a hop-skip-jump (or just a stroll) away. Wave down a zooming tuk-tuk if the hills are looking unfriendly.

TIMING   Even if you fall in love with Flores, which is possible and almost inevitable, a night or two is enough for most to steep in the charm of the *islita*.

WHERE TO EAT

$$ ⤬ **Achiote.** A broad menu features *comida típica* as well as familiar
INTERNATIONAL   plates, so you can order a tasty hamburger (with optional whiskey
FAMILY   sauce) or *pollo al achiote*, chicken spiced with the red, red pre-Colom-
Fodor'sChoice   bian herb. Picky eaters can choose a simple pasta dish. The atmosphere
★   is tasteful and relaxing, so you won't even miss the lake, which is a
couple of blocks away. At lunch look for the *menu ejecutivo*, a daily
special with included dessert that tends to be a bargain. Ⓢ *Average
main: Q70* ✉ *Av. Reformes, at Hotel Isla de Flores* ☎ *502/7867–5176*
⊕ *www.hotelisladeflores.com* ▭ *No credit cards.*

$ ⤬ **Café Arqueológico Yaxhá.** Combining a cultural and educational experi-
LATIN AMERICAN   ence with good food, this restaurant is the creation of German architect
Dieter Richter, who has worked on projects at Yaxhá and Naranjo. You
can browse a collection of books, photos, maps, and other information
about the Mayan world while you enjoy a *hamburguesa*or a Mayan dish
such as *Pollo Xni Pec* (chicken in a chili sauce served with rice and yucca).

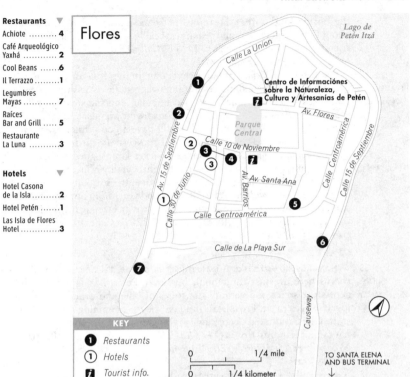

KEY

❶ *Restaurants*

① *Hotels*

🛈 *Tourist info.*

0 ————— 1/4 mile

0 ————— 1/4 kilometer

TO SANTA ELENA
AND BUS TERMINAL
↓

You can also book tours to Yaxhá and elsewhere. $ *Average main: Q60* ✉ *Av. 15 de Septiembre* ☎ *502/5830–2060* ⊕ *www.cafeyaxha.com.*

$
CAFÉ
✕ **Cool Beans** (*El Café Chilero*). You'll feel appropriately cool chilling in a hammock or shooting the breeze with another wanderer in this leafy garden café, sipping lemonade or an ice latte. Bored by the national beers, Gallo in Guatemala or Belikin in Belize? This café serves real IPAs and a selection of imported craft beers. You can eat breakfast for under Q40, and light meals are served the rest of the day. There's free Wi-Fi. $ *Average main: Q55* ✉ *Calle 15 de Septiembre* ☎ *502/5571–9240* ☾ *Closed Sun.*

$$
ITALIAN
FAMILY
Fodor's Choice
★
✕ **Il Terrazzo.** This terrace is so lovely and the Italian food so rich that the lake will seem swapped for the Mediterranean in a delicious sleight of hand. The best plates are the bowls of house-made pasta slick with olive oil and dense with shrimp, bacon, tomatoes, squash, basil, or whatever tops your dish of choice. Burgers, steak, and interesting pizzas are also on the menu. The avocado salad is a little wedding cake of vegetables; beautiful. Plus, if you've been jonesing for that clementine San Pel-ligrino, Il Terrazzo's got you covered. $ *Average main: Q80* ✉ *Calle la Union* ☎ *502 /7867–5479* ☾ *Closed Sun.* ▭ *No credit cards.*

$
VEGETARIAN
✕ **Legumbres Mayas.** "Legumes" might not be the sexiest feature of a restaurant name, but this little cinder-block, rickety-tabled joint has plates and plates of those fresh veggies you've been missing—and not

the boring kind, either. Heapings of beans and rice can be had for about Q20. Vegetarians and vegans especially will rejoice. The folks are friendly, too. $ *Average main: Q25* ⊠ *Calle 15 de Septiembre* ☏ *502 /4324–7259* ▭ *No credit cards.*

$

LATIN AMERICAN

Fodor'sChoice

★

╳ **Raíces Bar and Grill.** Grilled meats come piping hot off the *parrilla* (grill) and give this palapa restaurant swagger. Tacos with practically an artist's palette of sauces are also popular, and the steamed fish is excellent. Raíces is built over the water, so with friends, a margarita in hand, and the lake framing it all, you'll have a good time. $ *Average main: Q50* ⊠ *Flores* ☏ *502/7867–5743* ▭ *No credit cards.*

$$$

INTERNATIONAL

╳ **Restaurante La Luna.** With its plaited-wicker lampshades glowing, La Luna inspires romance on any moonlit night. Quality is inconsistent and prices may make you do a double-take, but entrées usually please, like the rich *pimiento relleno.* A handful of good vegetarian options include stuffed zucchini in white sauce. It's dreamy for an evening drink, despite the lack of lake view. $ *Average main: Q120* ⊠ *Calle 30 de Junio, at corner Calle 10 de Noviembre* ☏ *502/7867–5443.*

WHERE TO STAY

$$

HOTEL

FAMILY

▨ **Hotel Casona de La Isla.** A little musty in places, a little coarse-walled, rooms here are just functional; but Lake Petén Itzá is a few skips across the street and verandas in tones of blue and orange make for lovely places to sit. **Pros:** beautiful lake views; swimming pool; helpful staff. **Cons:** outdated decor; unless you get a special, rooms are not a bargain. $ *Rooms from: Q473* ⊠ *Calle 30 de Junio, at Calle 10 de Noviembre* ☏ *502/7867–5200* ⊕ *www.hotelesdepeten.com* ⇗ *26 rooms* ¶◎¶ *Breakfast.*

$$

HOTEL

FAMILY

▨ **Hotel Petén.** The common areas, with lake views and cheery colors are lovelier places to be than the simple rooms, but the oldest hotel in Flores remains a reliable one. **Pros:** classic hotel with great views of the lake from some balcony rooms; clean and quaint; decent value. **Cons:** four flights of stairs to get to top-floor rooms; modest rooms. $ *Rooms from: Q436* ⊠ *Calle 30 de Junio, off Calle Centroamérica* ☏ *502/2366–2841* ⊕ *www.hotelesdepeten.com* ⇗ *21 rooms* ¶◎¶ *No meals.*

$$

B&B/INN

FAMILY

Fodor'sChoice

★

▨ **La Isla de Flores Hotel.** A fresh sensibility, which includes distressed wood and acid-washed concrete tastefully layered over historic architecture and original beams, makes this Flores' most stylish hotel, and very easy to recommend. **Pros:** airy rooms with inspired design; lovely rooftop bar. **Cons:** not on the water; higher rates than older hotels. $ *Rooms from: Q540* ⊠ *Av. la Reforma* ☏ *7867–5176* ⊕ *www.hotelisladeflores.com* ⇗ *30 rooms* ¶◎¶ *No meals.*

NIGHTLIFE

The best of Flores nightlife involves having a mojito while watching the moon and the lake do their nightly dance. Not a bad way to close the day. In truth, there's not much partying; but Il Terrazzo, Raíces Bar and Grill, Cool Beans, and La Luna are all lovely places for a drink. Most have generous happy hours; many close before midnight. *See Where to Eat in Flores section.*

ACTIVITIES AROUND FLORES

BOATING

Boat trips on Lake Petén Itzá can be arranged through most hotels in Flores or by haggling with boat owners who congregate behind the Hotel Santana. Tours often include a stop at Paraíso Escondido, a small mainland park northwest of Flores.

FAMILY **Kinkajou Kingdom and ARCAS.** Take a 10-minute boat ride across the lake to the wonderful exhibit Kinkajou Kingdom, featuring the big-eyed honey-bear cuties, as well as spider monkeys, margays, and other nonreleasable animals. This education service of the conservation NGO ARCAS is seldom taken advantage of by visitors but you should try to make time for it. Though you can drop in, reservations are recommended. ✉ *Mayan Biosphere Reserve* ✥ *Near Zoológico Petencito* ☎ *502/5208–0968* ✎ *arcasguatemala@gmail.com* 🌐 *www.arcasguatemala.org* 🎫 *Q15.*

SANTA ELENA

0.25 mile (0.5 km) south of Flores.

Although it lacks the charms of neighboring Flores, gritty Santa Elena is pretty much unavoidable. Most services that you'll need for your trip to El Petén are usually offered here. There are also more upscale hotels here than in Flores.

GETTING HERE AND AROUND

Tuk-tuks—the motorized three-wheeled taxi rickshaws manufactured in Asia—ply the streets of Flores and Santa Elena. Five minutes and Q5 will get you between the two towns.

TIMING

Santa Elena is a place to sleep in a decent hotel, get money from an ATM, and buy picnic supplies. There's little to see in Santa Elena itself. At most, you'll use it as a base for exploring other parts of El Petén, so how long you stay here depends on your exploration plans.

SAFETY AND PRECAUTIONS

Some gas stations in Santa Elena have armed guards 24 hours a day, so that should tell you something. The better hotels are quite safe, however, and most visitors never experience any crime.

WHERE TO STAY

$$$$ HOTEL FAMILY 🏨 **Hotel La Casona del Lago.** Santa Elena's spiffiest hotel puts you in mind of an old-time lighthouse, dignified in blue and white and sitting lakeside, with splendid views of Flores across the water. **Pros:** short walk or tuk-tuk ride across causeway to Flores; views of Flores and the lake; pool. **Cons:** rooms on streetside can be noisy; gets a good deal of group business; expensive (for this part of Guatemala). [$] *Rooms from: Q767* ✉ *Calle Litoral on Lago* ☎ *502/7952–8700* 🌐 *www.hotelesdepeten.com* 🛏 *48 rooms.*

SPORTS AND THE OUTDOORS

There are several caves in the hills behind Santa Elena with interesting stalactite and stalagmite formations and subterranean rivers. The easiest to visit is Aktun Kan, just south of town.

FAMILY **Ixpanpajul Parque Natural.** Ixpanpajul Parque Natural is a private nature reserve sitting on a large stand of primary rain forest. Hiking the suspended bridges of the skyway will give you a bird's-eye view of the indigenous flora and fauna that make the rain forest the most biodiverse ecosystem on the planet. The park also offers myriad adventure opportunities, from nighttime ATV tours to horseback rides to mountain-bike excursions, and the Tarzán Canopy Tour zip line. Camping and rental cabañas are available. A restaurant has a limited menu averaging around Q70. ✉ *Km 468, via Rio Dulce* ✣ *6 miles (10 km) south of Santa Elena between Santa Elena and Tikal Park* ☎ *502/2336–0576, 502/4062–9812 in park* 🌐 *www.ixpanpajul.com.*

EL REMATE

GETTING HERE AND AROUND

El Remate is about a half hour from Flores by car.

TIMING

Most visitors use El Remate as a base for visits to Tikal and other nearby Mayan sites, so the length of stay depends on how much time you want to spend seeing ruins.

SIGHTS

Biotopo Cerro Cahuí. With around 1,500 acres of rain forest, Biotopo Cerro Cahuí near El Remate is one of the most accessible wildlife reserves in El Petén. It protects a portion of a mountain that extends to the eastern edge of Lago Petén Itzá, so there are plenty of opportunities for hiking. Two trails put you in proximity of birds like ocellated turkeys, toucans, and parrots. As for mammals, look up to spot the long-armed spider monkeys or down to see squat rodents called *tepezcuintles*. Tzu'unte, a 4-mile (6-km) trail, leads to two lookouts with views of nearby lakes. The upper lookout, Mirador Moreletii, is known by locals as Crocodile Hill, because from the other side of the lake it looks like the eye of a half-submerged crocodile. Los Ujuxtes, a 3-mile (5-km) trail, offers a panoramic view of three lakes. Both hikes begin at a ranger station (with toilets), where English-speaking guides are sporadically available. Some robberies and attacks on tourists have taken place in the reserve, so ask locally in El Remate about safety conditions before you explore on your own. ✉ *West of El Remate* 🎟 *Q40.*

WHERE TO EAT AND STAY

$$ HOTEL Fodor's Choice ★ 🏨 **La Casa de Don David.** Don David Kuhn has lived in the area for 40 years and is a great source for Tikal travel tips, while his lakeside hotel, an institution in Petén, also offers much to the visitor. **Pros:** gardens of a four-star resort; knowledgeable hosts; good restaurant. **Cons:** not a lot of frills. [$] *Rooms from: Q376* ✉ *On road to Biotopo Cerro Cahuí, near El Remate* ☎ *502/5306–2190, 502/5949–2164* 🌐 *www.lacasadedondavid.com* 🛏 *13 rooms* 🍴 *Some meals.*

$ HOTEL FAMILY 🏨 **La Mansión del Pájaro Serpiente.** Perched on a hillside in El Remate, the aged and charming Mansión del Pájaro Serpiente has some of the prettiest accommodations in El Petén. **Pros:** lakeview cabins (though it's not directly on the lake); larger rooms have canopied beds and oversize windows; swimming pool carved from stone; good value.

Cons: not for visitors who can't walk up and down steep hills; credit cards not accepted. $ *Rooms from: Q352* ⌂ *On main hwy. south of El Remate* ☏ *502/5967–9816 in English or Spanish* ✉ *tikalnancy@ hotmail.com* ⊕ *www.30minutesfromtikal.com* ▭ *No credit cards* ⤳ *11 rooms* ⦿| *Breakfast.*

SHOPPING

Although most souvenirs here are similar to those found elsewhere in Guatemala, the beautiful wood carvings are unique to El Petén. More than 70 families in this small town dedicate themselves to this craft. Their wares are on display on the side of the highway right before the turnoff for the Camino Real and La Lancha hotels on the road to Tikal, and also in small shops in El Remate.

NORTH SHORE, LAKE PETÉN ITZÁ AND QUEXIL LAGOON

8 miles (13 km) west of El Remate.

The small villages of San Pedro, San José, and San Andrés, on the northwest shore of Lake Petén Itzá, have beautiful vistas of the sparkling lake. Several upscale lodges and hotels have opened here or on nearby Quexil Lagoon, and the area is accessible via bus or car on an improved (but bumpy) dirt road from El Remate or Santa Elena, or in the clockwise direction from San Benito.

WHERE TO STAY

$$$$
RESORT
Fodor's Choice
★

La Lancha. Francis Ford Coppola's Guatemalan lodging is decorated in exquisite taste, with rich textures and all casitas glimpsing Lake Petén Itzá. **Pros:** lovely lake views; excellent restaurant; a/c in rooms; frequent specials. **Cons:** expensive (for Guatemala); somewhat remote; lots of steep steps; you can hear your neighbors in the cheaper duplex units. $ *Rooms from: Q1,520* ⌂ *8 miles (13 km) west of El Remate, San José* ☏ *502/7928–8331, 800/611–9774 in U.S. and Canada* ⊕ *www. coppolaresorts.com/lalancha* ⤳ *10 rooms* ⦿| *Breakfast.*

$$$$
RESORT
FAMILY

Las Lagunas. Las Lagunas' storied founder had a passion for hunting trophy game; now his resort brings a hunting lodge aesthetic to lagoon-side luxury, on the expansive grounds of a nature reserve with spider monkey acrobats giving frequent shows. **Pros:** 200-acre jungle preserve; well-oiled luxury with howler monkey wake-up calls. **Cons:** rates are sky-high, especially for Guatemala; remote enough that pricey on-site dining is your main option. $ *Rooms from: Q2,500* ⌂ *Desarrollo de Tayasal, Flores* ✛ *Left off Km 1.5 Carretera a San Miguel* ☏ *502/7790–0300* ⊕ *www.laslagunashotel.com* ⤳ *19 rooms* ⦿| *Breakfast.*

$$$$
B&B/INN
Fodor's Choice
★

Ni'tun Lodge and Private Reserve. After hiking through the jungle, you'll love returning to this charming cluster of bungalows, which feel almost subterranean with their rock walls and earthen tones. **Pros:** small, very personal lodge experience; wonderful food; engaging owners. **Cons:** off the beaten path; expensive; difficult for anyone with mobility issues. $ *Rooms from: Q1,400* ⌂ *Near San Andrés, across Lake Petén Itzá northwest of Flores, San Andrés Xecul* ☏ *502/5201–0759* ⊕ *www. nitun.com* ⊙ *Closed late May–early June* ⤳ *4 units* ⦿| *Breakfast.*

8

OTHER MAYAN SITES IN EL PETÉN

Although Tikal is the most famous, El Petén has hundreds of archaeological sites, ranging from modest burial chambers to sprawling cities. The vast majority have not been explored, let alone restored. Within a few miles of Tikal are several easy-to-reach sites. Because they're in isolated areas, it's a good idea to go with a guide.

EL MIRADOR

El Mirador. El Mirador, once equal in size and splendor to Tikal, may eventually equal Tikal as a must-see Mayan ruin. It's just now being explored, but elaborate plans are being laid to establish a huge park four times the size of Tikal. Dr. Richard D. Hansen of the University of Utah is director for the Mirador Basin Project, sponsored by the Foundation for Anthropological Research and Environmental Studies (FARES). The Mirador Basin contains the El Mirador site itself, four other known Mayan cities that probably were as large as Tikal (Nakbé, El Tintal, Xulnal, and Wakná), and many smaller but important sites—perhaps as many as 80 to 100 cities. The Mirador Basin is home to an incredible diversity of plant and animal life, including 200 species of birds, 40 kinds of animals (including several endangered ones, such as jaguars), 300 kinds of trees, and 2,000 different species of flora. It has been nominated as a UNESCO World Heritage Site. Currently, fewer than 2,500 visitors get to El Mirador annually, as it's a difficult trek requiring four to six days of hiking (round-trip). The jumping-off point for the trek is Carmelita Village, about 50 miles (84 km) north of Flores. There are no hotels in the Mirador Basin, and no roads except for dirt paths. Local tour companies such as Martsam Tours in Flores and elsewhere can arrange treks. For those with the budget, like actor Mel Gibson, you can visit by helicopter. ⌧ *40 miles (66 km) northwest of Tikal* ⊕ *www.miradorbasin.com.*

UNDERSTANDING BELIZE

FAST FACTS

Name: Officially changed from British Honduras to Belize in 1973

Capital: Belmopan City

Type of government: Parliamentary democracy

National anthem: "Land of the Free"

Population: 357,000 (2012 World Bank estimate)

National Tree: Mahogany (*Swietenia macrophilla*)

This prized tree has been heavily logged in Belize, and large specimens are found in only a few areas. The "big leaf" mahogany tree can grow more than 150 feet high and takes 80 years to reach maturity. The wood has a coppery red sheen, a tight, knot-free grain, and a single mature tree can be worth US$100,000 or more.

National Flower: Black Orchid (*Prosthechea cochleata*)

The name is deceiving. Only the lip of the flower is black, and the long, slender sepals and petals are yellow-green. These fragrant little flowers bloom year-round and can be found growing on trees in damp areas.

National Bird: Keel-Billed Toucan (*Ramphastos solfurantus*)

The toucan, with its huge canoe-shaped beak and bright yellow cheeks, can be found in open areas all over the country and loves to eat fruit.

National Animal: Baird's Tapir (*Tapirello bairdii*)

Called the mountain cow by most Belizeans, the tapir is actually related to the primitive horse and rhinoceros. A beefy vegetarian, it can weigh up to 600 pounds and is often found in heavy bush, near rivers and streams.

National Motto: *Sub Umbra Florero*

"Under the Shade I Flourish" refers to the shade of the mahogany tree, which is on Belize's coat of arms and flag.

National Drink: Orange Fanta and **Belikin Beer** (unofficially, of course).

Did You Know?

More than 40% of Belize's land is protected as national parks or reserves.

Belize has the longest barrier reef in the Western and Northern hemispheres.

The two tallest buildings in Belize, one at Caracol and one at Xunantunich, date back more than 1,000 years.

Belize is thought to have the largest population of manatees in the world.

Belize is the only country in Central America with English as the official language.

Belize has fewer than 400 miles (640 km) of paved roads.

The names of two of the four major highways in Belize officially changed in 2012. Western Highway is now George Price Highway and Northern Highway is Philip Goldson Highway.

The expanse of Selva Maya (Maya Forest), which Belize shares with Guatemala and Mexico, covers some 9,600 square miles (25,000 square km), the largest block of tropical forest north of the Amazon Basin.

At the height of the Mayan civilization, Belize may have had a population approaching 1 million people, about three times the population of the country today.

Belize is the only country in Central America without a border on the Pacific Ocean.

A MAYAN PRIMER

Traditionally, archaeologists have divided Mayan history into three main periods: Pre-Classic, Classic, and Post-Classic. Although some academics question the validity of such a uniform chronology, the traditional labels are still in use.

The **Pre-Classic** (circa 3,000 BC–AD 250) period is characterized by the influence of the Olmec, a civilization centered on the Gulf Coast of present-day Mexico. During this period cities began to grow, especially in the southern highlands of Guatemala and in Belize, and it's at this time that Belize's Cuello, Lamanai, Santa Rita, Cahal Pech, Pacbitun, and Altun Ha sites were first settled, along with El Mirador in Guatemala.

By the **Late Pre-Classic** (circa 300 BC–AD 250) period the Maya had developed an advanced mathematical system, an impressively precise calendar, and one of the world's five original writing systems. In Belize, Cerros (also called Cerro Maya) was established during the Late Pre-Classic period.

During the **Classic** (circa AD 250–900) period, Mayan artistic, intellectual, and architectural achievements literally reached for the stars. Vast city-states were crisscrossed by a large number of paved roadways, some of which still exist today. The great cities of Caracol (Belize), Palenque (Mexico), Tikal (Guatemala), and Quirigu (Guatemala) were just a few of the powerful centers that controlled the Classic Mayan world. In AD 562 Caracol—which at its height was the largest city-state in Belize, with a population of about 150,000—conquered Tikal. Other notable Classic period sites in Belize include Xunantunich, El Pilar, and Lubaantun.

The single largest unsolved mystery about the Maya is their rapid decline during the **Terminal Classic** (AD 800–900) period and the centuries following. Scholars have postulated that climate change, pandemic disease, extended drought, deforestation, stresses in the social structure, overpopulation, and changes in the trade routes could have been responsible. Rather than a single factor, several events taking place over time could well have been the cause.

The Maya of the **Post-Classic** (AD 900–early 1500s) period were heavily affected by growing powers in central Mexico. Architecture, ceramics, and carvings from this period show considerable outside influence. Although still dramatic, Post-Classic cities such as Chichén Itzá and Uxmal pale in comparison to their Classic predecessors. By the time the Spanish conquest reached the Yucatán, the Maya were scattered, feuding, and easy to conquer. Several sites in Belize, including Lamanai, were continuously occupied during this time, and even later.

Here are some key dates in the history of the Maya in Belize and in the El Petén area of Guatemala. Most of the dates are approximate, and some dates are disputed.

BC

3114	Date of the creation of the world, or 0.0.0.0.0 according to the Long Count calendar
3000	Early Olmec and Mayan civilizations thought to have begun
2500	Cuello established
2000	Santa Rita established
1500	Lamanai established
1000	Cahal Pech established
900	Olmec writing system developed; Caracol established
800	Tikal established
500	First Mayan calendars carved in stone
400–300	First written Mayan language
250	Altun Ha established
200	First monumental buildings erected at Tikal and El Mirador

AD

400–600	Tikal becomes leading city-state, with population of perhaps 200,000
553	Accession of Lord Water as Caracol ruler
562	Caracol conquers Tikal
599	Accession of Lord Smoke Ahau as Caracol ruler
618	Accession of Kan II as Caracol ruler
631	Caracol defeats Naranjo; Caracol's population is 150,000
700	Lubaantun established
800	Cahal Pech abandoned
895	Xunantunich abandoned
899	Tikal abandoned
900	Classic period of Mayan history ends
900–1500	Mayan civilization in decline, many cities abandoned
1000	Southern Belize Mayan centers mostly abandoned
1050	Caracol abandoned
1517	Spanish arrive in Yucatán and begin conquest of Maya
1517–1625	Diseases introduced from Europe cause death of majority of Maya
1524–25	Hernán Cortés passes through Belize en route to Honduras, after leading expeditions to conquer the Aztecs in Mexico
1546–1600s	Maya in Belize rebel against Spanish
1695	Tikal ruins rediscovered by Spanish
1700s	Lamanai continuously occupied over 3,000 years
1724	Spanish abolish *encomienda* system of forced Mayan labor
1839	John Lloyd Stephens and Frederick Catherwood visit Belize
1847	Caste Wars in Yucatán begin
1881	Early archaeological work begins at Tikal, by Alfred Maudslay
1894	Thomas Gann begins exploring Xunantunich and other Belize ruins
1926	Ruins of El Mirador, one of the earliest and largest Mayan cities, found in remote area of the Petén
1936	Caracol ruins rediscovered by a lumberman
1956	William Coe and others begin excavations at Tikal
1985	Drs. Arlen and Diane Chase begin excavations at Caracol, which continue to this day
1992	Rigoberta Menchu, a Maya from Guatemala, wins Nobel Peace Prize
2012	The time some predicted would be the end of the world, December 21, 2012, or 13.0.0.0.0 in the Long Count Mayan calendar passed as just another day
2013	The looting and export of Mesoamerican Mayan artifacts for illegal sale to collectors becomes an estimated $100-million-a-year business

MAYAN ARCHITECTURE

One look at the monumental architecture of the Maya, and you might feel transported to another world (perhaps that's why Tikal was used as the rebel base in the original 1977 *Star Wars*). The breathtaking structures are even more impressive when you consider that they were built 1,000 to 2,000 years ago or more, without iron tools, wheels, or pulleys. The following is a brief explanation of the architecture you see at a Mayan ruin.

Influences

Mayan architecture, even the great temples, may echo the design of the typical thatch hut ordinary Maya used for thousands of years. The rectangular huts had short walls made of a limestone mud and were topped by a steeply tilted two-sided thatch roof. Caves—ever-important Mayan ceremonial sites—were also influential. Many aboveground Mayan temples and other monumental structures have cave-like chambers, and the layout of Mayan cities probably reflected the Mayan cosmology, in which caves played a critical role.

Building Materials

With few exceptions, the large buildings in Mayan cities were constructed mostly from limestone, which was widely available in Belize and the Mexican Yucatán. Quarries were often established close to a building site so that workers didn't have to haul stone long distances. The Maya used limestone for mortar, stucco, and plaster. Limestone was crushed and burned in wood-fired kilns to make lime. A cement-like mortar was made by combining one part lime with one part of a white soil called *sahcab,* and then adding water.

The Maya also used wood, which was plentiful in Mesoamerica. In fact, some of the early temples were probably constructed of wood poles and thatch, much like the small houses of the Maya; unfortunately, these buildings are now lost.

Tools

The Maya were behind the curve with their tool technology. They didn't have iron tools, pulleys to move heavy weights, or wheels to build carts. They didn't have horses or other large animals to help them move materials. Instead, they used large numbers of laborers to tote and haul stones, mortar, and other building materials.

Obsidian, jade, flint, and other hard rocks were used to make axes, knives, and saws. The Maya had mason's kits to cut and finish limestone, and they had the equivalent of a plumb bob and other tools to align and level stones. The Maya were skilled stoneworkers, although the degree of finish varied from city to city.

City Layout

In most Mayan cities large plazas were surrounded by temples and large pyramids, probably used for religious ceremonies and other important public events. Paved causeways connected the plazas. Away from the city center were sprawls of "suburbs"—smaller stone buildings and traditional thatch huts.

Most cities had ball courts, and although the exact rules are unclear, players used a ball of natural rubber (rubber was discovered by the Olmecs) and scored points by getting the ball through a hoop or goalpost. "Sudden death" had a special meaning—the leader of the losing team was sometimes killed by decapitation.

The celebration of Belize's historic multiculturalism begins on its flag: the two young men—one black and the other white—are woodcutters standing beneath a logwood tree. Under them is a Latin inscription: *sub umbra floreat*—"In the shade of this tree we flourish."

BELIZE HISTORY

Anthropologists believe that humans from Asia crossed a land bridge, in what is now the Bering Strait in Alaska, into North America about 25,000 years ago. Gradually these Paleoindians, or "Old Indians," whose ancestors probably were Mongoloid peoples, made their way down the continent, establishing Native American or First Nation settlements in what is now the United States and Canada. Groups of them are thought to have reached Mesoamerica, which includes, besides Belize, much of central Mexico, Guatemala, Honduras, and Nicaragua, around 20,000 to 22,000 years ago.

These early peoples were hunter-gatherers. The Olmec civilization, considered the mother culture of later Mesoamerican civilizations including that of the Maya, arose in central and southern Mexico 3,000 to 4,000 years ago. The Olmecs developed the first writing system in the New World, dating from at least 900 BC. They also had sophisticated mathematics and created complex calendars. The Olmecs built irrigation systems to water their crops.

As long ago as around 3000 BC—the exact date is in question and has changed as archaeologists have made new discoveries—the Maya began to settle in small villages in Belize and elsewhere in the region. They developed an agriculture based on the cultivation of maize (corn), squash, and other fruits and vegetables. Some archeologists believe that the Maya—like other Indians in the region as well as in the South American Amazon—augmented soils with charcoal, pottery fragments, and organic matter to create *terra preta* (Portuguese for dark soil), very fertile earth that stood up to hard tropical rains. In Belize, small settlements were established as early as 2500 BC at Cuello in what is now Orange Walk District in northern Belize. Then, over the next 1,000 years or so, settlements arose at Santa Rita in Corozal and Lamanai in Orange Walk, and at Cahal

Pech, Caracol, and elsewhere in Cayo District in western Belize. What would become the great city-states of the region, including Tikal in today's Petén region of Guatemala and Caracol in the Cayo, were first settled around 900 to 700 BC.

Several centuries before the time of Christ, several Mayan villages grew into sizable cities. The Maya began to construct large-scale stone buildings at El Mirador, Tikal and elsewhere. Eventually, Tikal, Caracol, and other urban centers each would have thousands of structures—palaces, temples, residences, monuments, ball courts, even prisons. Although the Maya never had the wheel, and thus no carts or wagons, they built paved streets and causeways, and they developed sophisticated crop irrigation systems.

At its height, in what is known as the Classic period (250 BC to AD 900), the Mayan civilization consisted of about 50 cities, much like ancient Greek city-states. Each had a population of 5,000 to 100,000 or more. Tikal, the premier city in the region, may have had 200,000 residents in and around the city during its heyday, and Caracol in Belize probably had nearly as many. The peak population of the Mayan civilization possibly reached 2 million or more, and as many as a million may have lived in Belize alone—more than three times the current population.

The Mayan culture put a heavy emphasis on religion, which was based on a pantheon of nature gods, including those of the sun, moon, and rain. The Mayan view of life was cyclical, and Mayan religion was based on accommodating human life to the cycles of the universe.

Contrary to what scholars long believed, however, Mayan society had many aspects beyond religion. Politics, the arts, business, and trade were all important and dynamic aspects of Mayan life. Dynastic leaders waged brutal wars on rival city-states. Under its ruler Lord Smoke Ahau, Caracol, the largest city-state in Belize, conquered Tikal in AD 562, and less than a hundred years later conquered another large city, Naranjo (also in Guatemala).

The Maya developed sophisticated mathematics. They understood the concept of zero and used a base-20 numbering system. Astronomy was the basis of a complex Mayan calendar system involving an accurately determined solar year (18 months of 20 days, plus a five-day period), a sacred year of 260 days (13 cycles of 20 days), and a variety of longer cycles culminating in the Long Count, based on a zero date in 3114 BC, or 0.0.0.0.0—the date that the Maya believed was the beginning of the current cycle of the world.

The Mayan writing system is considered the most advanced of any developed in Mesoamerica. The Maya used more than 1,000 "glyphs," small pictures or signs, paired in columns that read from left to right and top to bottom. The glyphs represent syllables and, in some cases, entire words, that can be combined to form any word or concept. There is no Mayan alphabet. Mayan glyphs can represent either sounds or ideas, or both, making them difficult to accurately interpret. The unit of the writing system is the cartouche, a series of 3 to 50 glyphs, the equivalent of a word or sentence in a modern language.

As in most societies, it's likely that the large majority of the Maya spent much of their time simply trying to eke out a living. In each urban area the common people lived in simple thatch dwellings, similar to those seen in the region today. They practiced a slash-and-burn agriculture. Farmers cleared their small plots by burning the bush, then planting maize, squash, sunflowers, and other crops in the rich ash. After two or three years, when the soil was depleted, the plot was left fallow for several years before it could be planted again.

Beginning around AD 800, parts of the Mayan civilization in Belize and elsewhere in Mesoamerica began to decline. In most areas the decline didn't happen suddenly, but over decades and even centuries, and it took place at different times. For example, the cities in the Northern Lowlands of the Yucatán, such as Chichén Itzá, flourished for several more centuries after Tikal and Caracol were abandoned.

Scholars are still debating the reasons for the decline. Climatic change, lengthy droughts, overpopulation, depletion of arable land, social revolutions by the common people against the elites, epidemics, and the impact of extended periods of warfare all have been put forth as reasons. Earthquakes, hurricanes, and other natural disasters may have played a role at certain sites. It may well have been a combination of factors, or there may have been different causes in different regions.

Whatever the reasons, the Mayan civilization in Belize and elsewhere in Mesoamerica never regained its Classic period glory. By the time the Spanish arrived in the early 1500s only a few of the Mayan cities, mainly in the Highlands of Guatemala, were still thriving. Most of the great cities and trading centers of Belize and Guatemala, including Caracol and Tikal, had long been abandoned. Lamanai and a few other urban settlements were still inhabited.

Seeking gold and other plunder, the Spanish began their conquest of the Maya in the 1520s. Some Mayan states offered fierce resistance, and the last Mayan kingdom, in Mexico, was not vanquished until almost 1700. The Maya in Belize rebelled against the Spanish several times, but there was one enemy against which the Maya were defenseless: European disease. Smallpox, chicken pox, measles, flu, and other infectious diseases swept through the Mayan settlements. Scientists believe that within a century nearly 90% of the Maya had been wiped out by "imported" diseases.

Mayan resistance to European control continued from time to time. In 1847 Mayan Indians in the Yucatán rose up against Europeans in the bloody Caste Wars, which lasted until 1904. This had a major impact on Belize, as many Mexican Mestizos (persons of mixed Indian and European heritage) and Maya moved to northern Belize to escape the violence. Sarteneja, Orange Walk Town, and Ambergris Caye were among the areas at least partly settled by refugees from the Yucatán.

Much of the Mayan civilization was buried under the tropical jungles for centuries, and Westerners knew little about it. In the process of trying to convert the Maya to Christianity in the 16th century, the Spanish burned most of the codices, Mayan "books" made of deer hide or bleached fig-tree paper. Only in the last few decades have scholars made progress in deciphering Mayan glyphic writing.

In 1839 two British adventurers, John Lloyd Stephens and Frederick Catherwood, visited Central America, including Belize, and explored a number of the Mayan sites. Their books, especially *Incidents of Travel in Central America, Chiapas, and Yucatán,* with text by Stephens and illustrations by Catherwood, brought the attention of the world to the Mayan past.

In the late 1800s the first systematic archaeological excavations of Tikal and Mayan sites in Belize were begun. Alfred Maudslay, an Englishman, conducted excavations at Tikal in 1881–82, and Harvard's Peabody Museum did fieldwork there between 1895 and 1904. Sylvanus Morley, a well-known Maya expert, conducted work at Tikal at times between 1914 and 1928. In 1956 the University of Pennsylvania began the first large-scale excavation project at Tikal. In Belize, Thomas Gann, a British medical officer stationed in what was then British Honduras, carried out the first excavations of several major Belize Mayan sites, including Santa Rita, Xunantunich, Lubaantun, sites on Ambergris Caye, and others, starting in 1894. Since then, many university and museum teams, including ones from the University of Pennsylvania, the Royal Ontario Museum, Tulane University, the University of Texas, the University of California, and the University of Central Florida, have conducted extensive fieldwork in Belize. Drs. Diane and Arlen Chase, of the University of Central Florida, have been at work at the largest site in Belize, Caracol, since 1985.

About 30,000 Maya live in Belize today, according to the 2010 Belize Census, of which about 17,000 are Ketchi, 11,000 are Mopan, and 2,000 are Yucatec. In southern Belize they're predominantly Ketchi and Mopan Maya; in western Belize, Mopan Maya; and in northern Belize, Yucatec Maya. The largest concentration of Maya in Belize is in the small villages in Toledo District near Punta Gorda.

By some interpretations, the end of the world, or at least its current cycle, was supposed to have taken place on December 21, 2012, according to the Long Count calendar of the ancient Maya. A number of hotels and other tourism organizations in Belize, Guatemala, Mexico and elsewhere attempted to capitalize on this supposed apocalypse with tours and special lodging packages. However, other experts said that the Maya did not see this as the end of the world but rather as a transition from one age to another. In any event, the day passed like any other day.

Barry Bowen

When he died February 26, 2010, in the crash near San Pedro of the Cessna 206 he was piloting, Sir Barry Bowen not only was the most prominent and best-known businessman in Belize, whose products touched nearly every Belizean and every visitor to Belize, but he also was a central figure in the political and economic history of modern Belize and a key link to the British Honduras past.

Born September 19, 1945, in Belize City, Bowen connected in some way to nearly every major development in Belize. He owned the most storied (and also at times the most hated) business enterprise in the country's history, Belize Estate and Produce Company; he was a pioneer in the two industries that now dominate commerce in Belize, agriculture and tourism; he was a supporter, leader, and major financier of the most powerful political party in the country, the People's United Party, although he also had close friends and associates in the United Democratic Party; and he proved himself one of the toughest and most capable entrepreneurs in modern Belize, using a combination of savvy marketing, hardball tactics, and government connections to make Belikin beer and Coca-Cola soft drinks his personal cash cows.

Bowen could trace his roots in Belize back to the middle of the 18th century, when the first Bowen, from England, disembarked from a British ship and joined the ragtag band of Baymen at an encampment at the mouth of the Belize River.

In 1978, just before independence, Barry Bowen bought Bowen and Bowen from his father. Bowen moved quickly to develop and exploit the opportunities he saw in the backwater of Belize. He developed the Coca-Cola franchise and turned Belikin, first brewed in the late 1960s, into the national drink of Belize.

Today, thanks in part to the virtual monopoly status granted by the Belize government to Bowen Brewing, Belikin controls nearly all of the beer market in Belize.

Barry Bowen seemingly never believed in the great potential in mass tourism that some others saw, preferring instead to invest in industries such as aquaculture. Although he owned valuable seafront property on Ambergris Caye, Belize's number one tourist destination, he didn't open a resort there. However, in 1988, he did develop a pioneering upscale jungle lodge, Chan Chich Lodge, on Gallon Jug Estate lands, formerly part of the Belize Estate and Produce Company, which controlled hundreds of thousands of prime acres in Orange Walk District. Built literally on top of a Mayan plaza, Chan Chich Lodge is widely considered among the top few jungle lodges in Central America, and one of the best in the world.

Barry Bowen's life was not without its controversies and contradictions. Although he actively supported many conservation causes, and was a friend and supporter of the Belize Zoo and its director Sharon Matolo, he was an advocate of the construction of the Chalillo Dam, which Matolo strongly opposed due to destruction of habitat for the Scarlet Macaw and other birds and animals.

Bowen also was criticized for building his jungle lodge on a Mayan site. Lord Smoking Shell, an ancient Mayan chief, will roll over in his grave, some said. In defense, Bowen claimed the location of the lodge protected the site from looters.

Admired or distrusted, envied or loved, Sir Barry was a one of a kind. Bold and full of life, ambitious and willing to take a risk, a man of vision and large plans, he was a multimillionaire who certainly achieved things in little Belize.

THE MANY CULTURES OF BELIZE

Belize is a rich gumbo of colors and languages. Creoles, also known as Kriols, once the majority, now make up only about a quarter of the population. Creoles in Belize are descendants of slaves brought from Jamaica to work in the logging industry. By the early 18th century, people of African descent came to outnumber those of British origin in Belize. The two groups united early in the country's history to defeat a common enemy, the Spanish. Most of the Creole population today is concentrated in Belize City and in the rural villages of Belize District such as Gales Point and Crooked Tree, although there are predominantly Creole villages elsewhere, including Monkey River and Placencia. English is the country's official language and taught in school, although an English dialect, Creole, is widely spoken, and there are now more native Spanish speakers in Belize than English speakers.

Mestizos are the fastest-growing group in Belize and make up about half the population. These are persons of mixed European and Mayan heritage, typically speaking Spanish as a first language and English as a second. Some migrated to Belize from Mexico during the Yucatán Caste Wars of the mid-19th century. More recently, many "Spanish" (as they're often called in Belize) have moved from Guatemala, El Salvador, Honduras, or elsewhere in Central America. According to the 2010 Belize Census, more than 33,000 residents of Belize were born in other Central American countries. Mestizos are concentrated in northern and western Belize.

Numbering close to a million at the height of the Mayan kingdoms, the Maya today constitute less than one-tenth of the Belize population of 357,000. There are concentrations of Yucatec Maya in Corozal and Orange Walk districts, Mopan Maya in Toledo and Cayo districts, and also Ketchi Maya in about 30 villages in Toledo. Most speak their Mayan dialect and either English or Spanish, or both.

About one in twenty Belizeans is a Garífuna. The Garinagu (the plural of Garífuna) are of mixed African and Carib Indian heritage. Most originally came to Belize from Honduras in the 1820s and 1830s. Dangriga and Punta Gorda are towns with large Garífuna populations, as are the villages of Seine Bight, Hopkins, and Barranco. Besides their own tongue—an Arawakan-based language with smatterings of West African words—many Garinagu speak English and Creole and sometimes Spanish.

Other groups include more than 11,000 Mennonites, who tend to live in their own communities such as Spanish Lookout, Blue Creek, Barton Creek, Shipyard, and Little Belize; and sizable groups of East Indians and Chinese, mostly from Taiwan and Hong Kong. Belize's original white populations were English, but today's "gringos" are mostly expats from the United States and Canada, with some from the United Kingdom and various Commonwealth countries, together numbering several thousand. All these groups find in this tiny country a tolerant and amiable home.

Whatever the background of its citizens, Belize's population is young. More than two out of five Belizeans are under 15 years of age, and the median age is just 22.

FLORA AND FAUNA

Belize is home to thousands of species of trees and flowers, hundreds of kinds of birds, butterflies, and moths. An amazing array of creatures makes its home in Belize. Many are not terribly difficult to see, thanks to their brilliant coloring. Others are likely to elude you completely. A rundown of some of the region's most attention-grabbing mammals, birds, reptiles, amphibians—even a few insects—is provided below. Also, we've listed a few of the more colorful or interesting plants and trees. Common names, in English and Spanish or Mayan, are given, so you can understand the local wild things lingo.

Africanized Honeybee (killer bee): African honeybees were accidentally released in Brazil in the 1950s, interbred with European honeybees (a subset of the genus *Apis*) and spread north, reaching Belize in the 1980s. Now, most honeybees in Belize are Africanized. While their sting is no worse than a regular bee, they are highly aggressive. Many livestock animals have been killed by Africanized bees in Belize, and in 2013 a four-year-old Mennonite child was stung to death. If attacked, try to protect your face and get inside a building.

Bat (*murciélago*): There are more than 80 species of bats in Belize, making them by far the most common mammal found in the country. Belize has three species of vampire bats.

Black orchid (clamshell orchid, cockle-shell orchid): The national flower of Belize is the black orchid, now *Prosthechea cochleata* and formerly *Encyclia cochleata*. The very dark purple flower is unusual among orchids, as the flower is effectively upside down. It is pollinated not by bees but by a small fly.

Bukut (stinking toe): Howler monkeys love the leaves of the bukut, which grows to almost 100 feet (30 meters) in open fields and pastures. You can see bukut trees at Community Baboon Sanctuary, along the Hummingbird Highway, and elsewhere in Belize. In April and May they are loaded with salmon-pink flowers. The long brown seedpods also are eaten by monkeys and birds, but they have an unpleasant smell, like sweaty socks. Hence the common name, stinking toe.

Cacao (wild cacao, kakaw): Most prevalent in Toledo District, the wild cacao is a small tree that grows to about 32 feet (10 meters). Its fruit pods, which are directly on the trunk, contain seeds that are the source of chocolate and cocoa powder. The Toledo Cacao Growers' Association (TCGA) represents over 1,000 organic cacao growers in southern Belize.

Caiman (*cocodrilo*): The spectacled caiman is a small crocodile that subsists mainly on fish. It's most active at night (its eyes glow red when illuminated by a flashlight), basking in the sun by day. It's distinguished from its American cousin by its sloping brow and smooth back scales.

Cashew (*marañon*): This tree, related to the mango, is about the size of a small apple tree, growing up to about 40 feet (12 meters), often in a serpentine fashion. In late spring and early summer it bears cashew apples, pear-shaped bright red or yellow pseudofruit. These can be eaten, though they have a somewhat unpleasant aftertaste, but a wonderful grape-like aroma. But the true fruit is the cashew nut, attached to the base of the cashew apple. The cashew nut shell contains a poisonous liquid. Before the nuts can be safely eaten they must be roasted twice. Crooked Tree village is the center of cashew cultivation in Belize, and cashew wine is also available here.

Ceiba (cotton tree, kapok, *yaaxche*): The national tree of Guatemala and the sacred tree of the ancient Maya, who cultivated it in their plazas, the ceiba (*say-ba*) is one of the giants of the bush, sometimes growing more than 230 feet (70 meters), rising out of the jungle canopy. It has a gray, cylindrical trunk supported by large buttresses at the ground and, high up, nearly horizontal branches.

Cohune palm (*corozo* palm): The cohune is one of the most important trees for the Maya in Belize. Its leaves are used to thatch the roofs of buildings, its nuts are used for oil or soap and as fuel for fires, the sweet heart is eaten, traditionally in Belize during Easter week, and the heart sap can be used to make a wine. It is often a marker for ancient Mayan sites now hidden by jungle. Its distinctive fluted shape and tall height (up to 100 feet or more than 30 meters) make it easy to spot.

Cougar (puma): Growing to 5 feet (1½ meters) in length, mountain lions are the largest unspotted cats in Central America. Rarely seen, they live in most habitats in the region and feed on vertebrates ranging from snakes to deer.

Crocodile (*lagarto*): Although often referred to by Belizeans as alligators, crocodiles reign supreme in this region. They are distinguished from the smaller caiman by their flat heads, narrow snouts, and spiky scales. Crocodiles seldom attack humans, preferring fish, birds, and the occasional small mammal. Both species are endangered and protected by international law.

Fer-de-lance (*barba amarilla*): One of the most dangerous of all pit vipers, the fer-de-lance has a host of names, such as tommygoff, in Belize. This aggressive snake grows up to 8 feet in length and is distinguished by the bright yellow patches on its head.

Flamboyant (flame tree, royal Poinciana, *guacamayo*): This is perhaps the most visually striking tree in Belize, at least May through July when it is covered in blazing blossoms of flame-color orange. Originally from Madagascar, the flamboyant is easily identified, even when not in bloom, because of its umbrella shape, much wider than it is tall.

Frog (*rana*): More than 30 species of frogs can be found in Belize. Most are nocturnal in an effort to avoid being eaten, but the brightly colored poison dart frogs—whose brilliant red, blue, and green coloration warns predators that they don't make a good meal—can be spotted during the day. Red-eyed leaf frogs are among the showiest of nocturnal species.

Howler monkey (*mono congo*): These chunky-bodied monkeys travel in troops of up to 20. A bit on the lethargic side, they eat leaves, fruits, and flowers. The deep, resounding howls of the males serve as communication among and between troops. Erroneously termed "baboons" by Belizeans, these dark-faced monkeys travel only from tree to tree, limiting their presence to dense jungle canopy.

Iguana: The largest lizards in Central America, these scaly creatures can grow to 10 feet. They are good swimmers, and will often plop into a body of water when threatened by a predator. Only young green iguanas are brightly colored; adult females are grayish, while adult males are olive (with orangish heads during mating season). They are considered a delicacy among Belizeans, who call them "bamboo chicken."

Jaguar (*tigre*): The largest feline in the Western Hemisphere grows up to 6 feet (2 meters) long and can weigh up to 250 pounds. Exceedingly rare, this nocturnal predator is most often spotted near the Cockscomb Basin Wildlife Sanctuary in Belize or near Chan Chich Lodge.

Leaf-cutter ant (*zompopa*): Called wee wee ants in Creole, leaf-cutter ants are the region's most commonly noticed ants. They are found in all lowland habitats. Columns of these industrious little guys, all carrying clippings of leaves, sometimes extend for several hundred yards from plants to the underground nest. The leaves are used to cultivate the fungus that they eat.

Macaw (*lapas*): The beautiful scarlet macaw is the only species of this bird found in Belize. Huge, raucous birds with long tails, macaws use their immense bills to rip apart fruits to get to the seeds.

Their nests are in hollow trees. They are endangered because of poachers and deforestation.

Mahogany (*caoba*): The national tree of Belize appears on the Belize flag, and the country's motto, *Sub Umbra Florero* ("Under the Shade I Flourish"), refers to the mahogany tree. Mahogany was the mainstay of the Belize (then British Honduras) economy for almost two centuries, from the mid-1700s until the 1950s. Most of the largest trees—the mahogany can soar to over 150 feet (45 meters) and reach trunk widths of over 6 feet (2 meters)—were cut down and exported to Europe where they were made into fine furniture and railway carriages. Some large specimens remain in the Programme for Belize lands in Orange Walk District.

Manatee: An immense and gentle mammal, the manatee is often called the sea cow. Living exclusively in the water, particularly in shallow and sheltered areas, manatees are said to be the basis of myths about mermaids. Fairly scarce today, these vegetarians have been hunted for thousands of years for their tasty flesh; their image frequently appears in ancient Mayan art.

Morpho (*morfo*): This spectacular butterfly doesn't fail to astound first-time viewers. Easy to overlook when resting, their color is only apparent when they take flight. One species has brilliant-blue wings, while another is distinguished by its intense violet color. Adults feed on fallen fruit, never flowers.

Parrot (*loro*): A prerequisite of any tropical setting, there are five species of parrot in Central America. All are clad in green, which means they virtually disappear upon landing in the trees. Most have a splash of color or two on their head or wings.

Poisonwood (*che chem, chechem negro*): Avoid this low-growing small tree. Fairly common in Belize, it can be identified by the black, oily sap on the trunk. The bark, sap, and leaves of the poisonwood cause a reaction similar to poison ivy or poison oak. Fortunately, an antidote, the red gumbo limbo tree, usually grows next to or near the poisonwood. Rub a strip of gumbo limbo bark on the affected area, or boil the bark in water and apply with a sponge.

Scorpion (*escorpión*): *Centruroides gracilis* is the most common scorpion in Belize. It grows up to 6 inches in length. Its sting is poisonous, and painful—about like a wasp sting—but not serious or fatal except in the case of an allergic reaction. If you're stung, don't panic—wash the area with soap and water (the venom is water-soluble) and apply an icepack.

Sea turtle: Sea turtles on the coasts of Belize come in three varieties: green, hawksbill, and loggerhead. All have paddlelike flippers and have to surface to breathe.

Spider monkey (*mono colorado, mono araña*): These lanky, long-tailed monkeys hang out in groups of two to four. Their diet consists of ripe fruit, leaves, and flowers. Incredible aerialists, they can swing effortlessly through the trees using their long arms, legs, and prehensile tails.

Tapir (*danta*): The national animal of Belize is also known as the mountain cow. Like a small rhinoceros without the armor, it has a stout body, short legs, and small eyes. Completely vegetarian, it uses its prehensile snout for harvesting vegetation. The shy creature lives in forested areas near streams and lakes, where it can sometimes be spotted bathing.

Toucan (*tucán, tucancillo*): Recognizable to fans of Froot Loops cereal, the toucan is common in Belize. The keel-billed and chestnut-mandibled toucans can grow to 22 inches long. The smaller and stouter emerald toucanet and yellow-ear toucanet are among the most colorful. All eat fruit with their curved, multihued beaks.

A CREOLE PRIMER

The Creole language (also spelled Kriol) is associated with the Creole or black people of Belize, especially those around Belize City. But people all over Belize know the Creole language and speak it daily. You'll hear Creole spoken by Mennonite farmers, Chinese shopkeepers, and Hispanic tour guides. Creole was brought to Belize by African slaves and former slaves from Jamaica and elsewhere in the Caribbean. Creole words are primarily of English origin, with some words from several West African tongues, Spanish, Miskito (an indigenous language of Central America, spoken by some 200,000 people in Honduras and Nicaragua), and other languages.

Spoken in a lilting Caribbean accent and combined with a grammar and syntax with West African roots, the language, despite English word usage, is difficult for foreigners to understand. Plurals aren't used often in Creole. For some, knowing how to speak Creole is a test you have to pass before you can become a "real" Belizean. However, with the increasing number of Hispanic immigrants in Belize, it's heard less and less, while Spanish is heard more and more.

Here are a few Creole words and phrases. If you want to learn more, get the *Kriol-Inglish Dikshineri* (Paul Crosbie, Editor-in-Chief) published by the Belize Kriol Project and available in gift shops and bookstores in Belize.

Ah mi gat wahn gud guf taim: I had a really good time.

Bashment: Party

Bwah: Boy

Chaaly prise: A large rat, after Sir Charles Price, an 18th-century Jamaican planter

Chinchi: A little bit

Dis da fi wi chikin: This is our chicken (well-known slogan of a Mennonite chicken company).

Dollah: A Belize dollar

Fowl caca white and tink eh lay egg: A chicken sees its white droppings and thinks it laid an egg (said of a self-important person).

Grind mean: Ground meat

Gyal: Girl

Humoch dis kaas?: How much is this?

Ih noh mata: It doesn't matter.

Madda rass: Foolishness (literally, mother's ass)

Tiga maga but eh no sic: Tiger's skinny but he's not sick (that is, don't judge a book by its cover).

Waawa: Foolish

Wangla: Sesame seed or candy made from sesame seeds

Weh di beach deh?: Where's the beach?

Yerrisso: Gossip, from "Ah her so" (so I hear)

TRAVEL SMART
BELIZE

GETTING HERE AND AROUND

▌AIR TRAVEL

TO BELIZE

All international flights to Belize fly into Philip S. W. Goldson International Airport (BZE) in Ladyville about 9 miles (15 km) north of downtown Belize City. The airport has a 9,700-foot-long runway capable of handling all but the largest jets. U.S. gateway cities with nonstop service by international airlines to Belize include Atlanta, Charlotte, Chicago, Dallas-Fort Worth, Denver, Houston, Los Angeles, Miami, and Newark. International cities with nonstop service to Belize on international airlines include Panama City, Panama, San Salvador, El Salvador, and Toronto, Canada. Not all cities have daily service, and in some cases service is seasonal, typically during the high season from late November to April or May.

Seven international airlines fly into Belize from U.S. and Central American cities: American Airlines has multiple flights daily from Miami (MIA) and Dallas-Fort Worth (DFW) and nondaily, limited seasonal service from Charlotte (CLT). Avianca Airlines, formerly TACA, has daily service from its hub in San Salvador, El Salvador (SAL). Copa Airlines currently has three flights a week from Panama City, Panama (PTY). Delta Airlines has daily nonstop service from Atlanta (ATL) and some flights from Los Angeles (LAX), although service may be reduced during off-season months. Southwest Airlines has daily service from Houston Hobby (HOU) and, beginning spring 2017, weekly service from Denver (DEN). United Airlines has multiple daily flights from Houston's George Bush Intercontinental Airport (IAH) and a weekly flight from Chicago O'Hare (ORD). WestJet, a Canadian airline, began twice-weekly nonstop service from Toronto Pearson International (YYZ) to Belize in late 2016. Currently, there is no nonstop service to Belize from anywhere in Europe, but American has a flight from London connecting in Miami that allows a same-day arrival in Belize without an overnight layover.

To Belize City it's roughly 2½–3 hours from Miami and Atlanta; 2½–3½ hours from Dallas, Houston, and Charlotte; 4½ hours from Newark and Denver; and about 6 hours from Los Angeles and Toronto.

Tropic Air, one of two Belizean airlines and the only one with international flights, offers twice-daily service between Belize City's international airport and Flores, Guatemala, with continuing service (usually on a code-share with TAG, a Guatemalan airline) to and from Guatemala City. It also has service between Belize City and Cancún and Mérida, Mexico, and less-than-daily service to and from San Pedro Sula, Tegucigalpa, and Roatán, Honduras. Service frequency varies during the year, depending on demand. Maya Island Air, another Belizean airline, currently has domestic service only.

WITHIN BELIZE

Domestic planes are single- or twin-engine island-hoppers and puddle-jumpers, such as Cessna Caravans. They typically carry 4 to 14 passengers. The carriers are Tropic Air and Maya Island Air; both have about 250 domestic flights daily and fly to San Pedro on Ambergris Caye and Caye Caulker as well as to Corozal Town, Dangriga, Placencia, and Punta Gorda. Tropic Air also has domestic service to Orange Walk Town, Belmopan and San Ignacio. Maya Island Air also has service to Savannah and Kanantik, airstrips near Placencia.

Belize domestic flights on Maya Island and Tropic Air from and to the international airport are between BZ$250 and BZ$500 round-trip and somewhat less, about BZ$150 to BZ$400 round-trip, between the municipal airstrip (TZA) in Belize City and domestic destinations. A Belize Airports Authority Rider Fee of

BZ$5 is added into the cost of tickets, and BZ$1.50 security fee is added if using the international airport.

Charter services such as Javier Flying Service will take you almost anywhere for around BZ$400 per hour and up; Javier specializes in flights to Chan Chich Lodge, Blancaneaux Lodge, and Hidden Valley Inn on the mainland and the Phoenix Resort on Ambergris Caye. Both Maya Island and Tropic Air also offer charter services to remote lodges and resorts with airstrips such as Chan Chich and Blancaneaux. Astrum Helicopters, based near Belize City, offers transfers, aerial property tours, and custom sightseeing and photography tours anywhere in Belize. Costs for up to six people in the Bell 206 helicopters are around BZ$2,000 an hour. Fixed rates apply for transfers to specific resorts, starting at BZ$2,500 for one to four persons.

You'll save 10% to 40% on flights within Belize by flying to and from the municipal airport near downtown Belize City, rather than to or from the international airport north of the city in Ladyville. If you're arriving at the international airport, a transfer by taxi to the municipal airport is BZ$50 for two persons, plus an additional BZ$10 for each extra person; transferring to the municipal airport sometimes makes more sense for families or groups traveling together. If you need to fly between Belize City and another part of the country, it's always at least a little cheaper to fly to or from municipal airports. Be aware that the municipal airstrip is short, just 1,825 feet, suitable only for short-takeoff-and-landing aircraft. It sits right beside the sea. Landings and takeoffs sometimes can be a thrill.

Air Contacts American Airlines. ✉ *American Airlines, Philip S. W. Goldson International Airport, Ladyville* ☎ *800/433-7300 in U.S. and Canada, 223/2522 reservations in Belize, 225/4146* ⊕ *www.aa.com.* **Astrum Helicopters.** ✉ *Cisco Base, Mile 3.5 George Price Hwy., formerly Western Hwy., Western Suburbs* ☎ *222/5100* ⊕ *www.astrumhelicopters.com.*

Avianca Airlines. ✉ *Belize Global Travel Services, 41 Albert St., Commercial District* ☎ *800/284-2622 toll-free in U.S. and Canada, 227-7363 reservation in Belize City, 227/7363 at international airport* ⊕ *www.avianca.com.* **Copa Airlines.** ✉ *Philip S. W. Goldson International Airport, Ladyville* ☎ *800/359-2672 toll-free in U.S.* ⊕ *www.copaair.com.* **Delta Airlines.** ✉ *Philip S. W. Goldson International Airport, Ladyville* ☎ *888/750-3284 toll-free in U.S. and Canada, 255/2010 reservations and information in Belize* ⊕ *www.delta.com.* **Javier Flying Service.** ✉ *Central Farm Airstrip, San Ignacio* ☎ *824/0460* ⊕ *www.javiersflying-service.com.* **Maya Island Air.** ✉ *Belize City Municipal Airstrip, Marine Parade Harbor Front* ☎ *223-1403 reservations* ⊕ *www.mayais-landair.com.* **Southwest Airlines.** ✉ *Philip S. W. Goldson International Airport, Ladyville* ☎ *800/435-9792 toll-free in U.S. and Canada, 225/2045 reservations in Belize* ⊕ *www.south-west.com.* **Tropic Air.** ✉ *San Pedro Airstrip, San Pedro Town* ☎ *226/2626 reservations in Belize, 800/422-3435 toll-free reservations in U.S. and Canada* ⊕ *www.tropicair.com.* **United Air Lines.** ✉ *Whitfield Tower, 4792 Coney Dr., 1st fl., Northern Suburbs* ☎ *800/266-3822 toll-free reservations in Belize, 822/1062 in Belize, 800/864-8331 toll-free reservations in U.S. and Canada* ⊕ *www.united.com.* **WestJet.** ✉ *Philip S. W. Goldson International Airport, Ladyville* ☎ *888/937-8538 toll-free reservations in U.S. and Canada* ⊕ *www.westjet.com.*

AIRPORTS

International flights arrive at the Philip Goldson International Airport (BZE) in Ladyville, 9 miles (15 km) north of downtown Belize City. It's the world's only airport with a mahogany ceiling (it's in the original terminal building). Small domestic airports are mostly just landing strips with a one-room check-in. These Belize domestic airports include Belize City municipal (TZA), Belmopan (BCV), Corozal (CZH), Dangriga (DGA), Savannah (SVH), Placencia (PLJ), Punta Gorda (PND), Orange Walk Town (ORZ), San Pedro (SPR), Caye Caulker (CUK), Maya Flats near San Ignacio (MYF), and Sarteneja (SJX). An airstrip near Hopkins has been proposed, but as of this writing it has not received government approval. With the exception of the San Pedro airport, which has nighttime lighting, all the domestic airstrips operate only during daylight hours.

The future of a controversial, privately funded international airport near the north end of the Placencia Peninsula is unclear. As of this writing, construction work has stopped and the airport and landing strip remain unfinished. The current Belize government has also announced plans to build an international airport on North Ambergris Caye, but no time line has been given.

Philip Goldson International Airport has security precautions similar to those in the United States; the domestic airstrips have limited security systems, but there has never been an airline hijacking in Belize. For international flights, arrive at the airport at least two hours before departure; for domestic flights, about half an hour. For connections from international flights to domestic flights, allow 45 minutes. In Belize, domestic airlines with more passengers than seats sometimes simply add another flight.

A new visitor identification system including fingerprint scanners was introduced in 2013 by Belize immigration at Philip S. W. Goldson, paid for in part by the United States. The government is expanding this system for use at all land and sea arrival points to Belize. The new system includes computer workstations, webcams, and passport readers. It is managed through a central server at Immigration headquarters in Belmopan. U.S. PreCheck status doesn't apply in Belize.

Contacts Belize Municipal Airstrip (TZE).
✉ On seafront off Princess Margaret Dr., Belize City Municipal Airstrip, Marine Parade Harbor Front. **Philip S. W. Goldson International Airport (BZE).** ✉ 9 miles (15 km) north of Belize City center, off Philip Goldson Hwy., Philip S. W. Goldson International Airport, Ladyville ☎ 225/2045 ⊕ www.pgiabelize.com.

▮ BOAT TRAVEL

Since Belize has about 200 miles (325 km) of mainland coast and as many as 1,000 islands (most just tiny spits of sand, coral and mangroves) in the Caribbean, water taxis, passenger ferries, and private boats are key to moving around the islands and coastal areas.

To reach the more remote cayes and the atolls, you're basically left to your own devices, unless you're staying at a lodge or resort where such transfers are arranged for you. The resorts on the atolls run their own boats, but these usually aren't available to the general public.

FERRIES AND PRIVATE BOATS

A local ferry company, Coastal Xpress, provides scheduled boat transportation up and down the east side of Ambergris Caye. One-way rates start at BZ$10, and daily and weekly passes are available.

Several private boats make daily runs from Dangriga to Tobacco Caye; boats usually leave Dangriga around 9 or 9:30 am and return later in the day. Check at the Riverside Café in Dangriga or ask your hotel on Tobacco Caye, as several of these lodges include transport in the rate. Charter boats to Tobacco Caye also are available from Hopkins. Many hotels on Ambergris Caye and Caye Caulker and in coastal resort areas can arrange boat charters for you with a captain. Visitors can not pilot a boat unless they have a Belizean captain's license; exceptions include the use of small personal sailboats such as Hobie Cats and bareboat sailing charters, usually weekly, of catamarans and monohull sailboats. In the case of bareboat sailing charters, you need to demonstrate you are an experienced sailer to get a boat.

Information Coastal Xpress. ✉ Beachfront, Amigos del Mar Dock, San Pedro Town ☎ 226/2007 ⊕ www.coastalxpress.com.

WATER TAXIS

There are two main water-taxi companies that serve the Northern Cayes of Ambergris and Caulker: Ocean Ferry Belize and

San Pedro Belize Express. Fast boats that hold up to 50 to 110 passengers connect Belize City with San Pedro (Ambergris Caye) and Caye Caulker. From Belize City, water taxis make the 45-minute run to Caye Caulker, and then continue on to San Pedro, which requires another 30 minutes on the water. Ocean Ferry boats stop and pick up at Caye Chapel and St. George's Caye, on demand. These water taxis also connect San Pedro with Caye Caulker and both of these islands with Chetumal, Mexico. Thunderbolt connects San Pedro with Corozal Town in Northern Belize, with a stop on demand in Sarteneja.

Most scheduled water taxis allow two pieces of luggage per person, along with miscellaneous personal items. Seas, especially in the south between Dangriga and Placencia and Puerto Cortes, Honduras, and also between Punta Gorda and Puerto Barrios, Guatemala, can be rough. Postpone your trip if the weather looks bad, or, in the case of private charters, cancel if the boat offered looks unseaworthy or crowded.

Several water-taxi companies, including Requena's, offer daily service from Punta Gorda to Puerto Barrios, Guatemala. D'Express offers weekly service between Placencia and Puerto Cortes, Honduras.

The Belize water-taxi business is in a state of flux, with companies entering and leaving the business. Schedules and rates are subject to frequent change.

Information D'Express. ⊠ *Placencia Municipal Pier, Main St., Point Placencia, Placencia Village* ⚓ *Municipal Pier is at south end of Placencia village, near The Shack restaurant* ☎ *626/8835.* **Ocean Ferry Belize.** ⊠ *Marine Terminal, 10 N. Front St., Commercial District* ☎ *223/0033* ⊕ *www.oceanferrybelize.com.* **Requena's.** ⊠ *12 Front St., Punta Gorda* ☎ *722/2070* ✎ *watertaxi@btl.net* ⊕ *www.belizenet.com/requena.* **San Pedro Belize Express Water Taxi.** ⊠ *Brown Sugar Terminal, 111 N. Front St., near Tourism Village, Commercial District* ☎ *223/2225* ⊕ *www.*

belizewatertaxi.com. **Thunderbolt.** ⊠ *Thunderbolt, Municipal Pier, Corozal Town* ☎ *422/0026* ⊕ *www.ambergriscaye.com/thunderbolt/.* **Water Jets International.** ⊠ *Angel Coral St., on back (lagoon) side of island near soccer field, San Pedro Town* ☎ *226/2194* ⊕ *www.sanpedrowatertaxi.com.*

TRAVEL TIMES FROM BELIZE CITY		
To	**By Air**	**By Car or Bus**
San Pedro	20 minutes	n/a
Caye Caulker	15 minutes	n/a
Corozal Town	1–2 hours (via San Pedro)	2–3 hours
San Ignacio	30 minutes	2–2½ hours
Placencia	50 minutes	3–3½ hours
Punta Gorda	1 hour	4–6 hours
Cancún, Mexico	1½ hours	8–11 hours

▮ BUS TRAVEL

Bus service on the Philip Goldson and George Price highways (formerly the Northern and Western highways) and to southern Belize via the Hummingbird and Southern highways is frequent and generally dependable. Elsewhere service is spotty. There's limited municipal bus service from point to point within Belize City on several small local lines.

Buses can get you just about anywhere cheaply for inter-town trips) and quickly. Expect to ride on old U.S. school buses or retired Greyhound buses. Buses with restrooms and air-conditioning are rare to nonexistent in Belize. On some routes there are a few express buses, that stop only at bus stations. These cost a few dollars more.

▮TIP→ **Be prepared for tight squeezes— this can mean three people in a two- person seat—and watch for pickpockets around bus stations. On some busy routes, seats may be full, and you may have to stand. Drivers and their assistants** (in Guatemala, cobradors or ayudantes, fare collectors, who call out the stops) are knowledgeable and helpful. They can direct you to the right bus, and tell you when and where to get off. To be sure you're not forgotten, try to sit near the front of the bus. On most Belize buses, your luggage will be put at the back of the bus, behind the last seats.

Most buses on main routes run according to more-or-less reliable schedules; on less-traveled routes the schedules may not mean much. Buses operate mostly during daylight hours, but they run until around 9 pm on the western route between Belize City and San Ignacio, and service begins before sunrise on that route and on the northern route between Belize City and Corozal Town. Published bus schedules are rare, and almost no bus line has a website. Some lines post hand-written schedules in bus terminals. The Belize Tourism Board sometimes has schedules for popular routes. Also check online for the Belize Bus Blog, which has generally up-to-date information on Belize bus rates and schedules and also on other types of transportation in Belize. Buses in Belize accept only cash in U.S. or Belize dollars.

Inexpensive public buses, also of the converted school bus variety, crisscross Guatemala, but they can be slow and extremely crowded, with a three-per-seat rule enforced. Popular destinations from Guatemala City, such as Santa Elena/ Flores near Tikal, use first-class Pullman buses. Your hotel or INGUAT office can help you make arrangements. Fares on public buses in both Belize and Guatemala are a bargain.

■TIP➜ In Belize, in cities and towns where there are bus stations, you buy tickets at the station. When boarding elsewhere, you pay the driver's assistant. The same system applies in Guatemala.

Reservations are usually not needed or expected in Belize or Guatemala, even for express departures. Arrive at terminals about a half hour before departure.

Belize Companies Belize Bus Blog. ⊕ *www. belizebus.wordpress.com.* **James Bus Line.** ✉ *7 King St., Punta Gorda* ☎ *702/2049* ⊕ *www.jamesbusline.com.*

Guatemala Companies Autobuses del Norte. ✉ *Mercado Terminal, 6a Av., Flores* ☎ *7924–8131 in Santa Elena, Guatemala* ⊕ *www.adn.gt.* **Fuente del Norte.** ✉ *Terminal de Buses, Santa Elena* ☎ *223/0457 Marine Terminal in Belize City, 7926–29997 Terminal de Buses, Santa Elena* ⊕ *www.grupofuentedel-norte.com.*

■ CAR TRAVEL

GASOLINE

Modern gas stations—Shell, Uno, Puma, and other international or regional brands, some of them with convenience stores and 24-hour service—are in Belize City and most major towns and along major highways in Belize. In more remote areas, especially in the south, fill up the tank whenever you see a station. Unleaded gas costs around BZ$10–BZ$12 for a U.S. gallon. Diesel fuel is around BZ$8– BZ$9. Most stations have attendants who pump gas for you. They don't expect a tip, although they are happy to accept it. Most stations now accept credit cards, along with Belize and U.S. dollars.

Prices at Guatemala's service stations aren't quite as high as in Belize. At most stations an attendant will pump the gas and make change. Plan to use cash, as credit cards sometimes aren't accepted.

PARKING

In Belize City, with its warren of narrow and one-way streets, downtown parking is often at a premium. For security, try to find a guarded, fenced parking lot, and don't leave your car on the street overnight. Elsewhere, except in some areas of San Ignacio and Orange Walk Town, there's plenty of free parking. San Ignacio has a downtown municipal lot with guarded parking at modest rates—the lot is behind the Cayo Welcome Center.

There are no parking meters in Belize. In most cities and towns parking rules are laxly enforced, although cars with license plates from another district of Belize or a foreign country may attract a ticket.

FROM/TO	ROUTE	DISTANCE
Belize City–Corozal Town	Philip Goldson Highway	94 miles (160 km)
Belize City–San Ignacio	George Price Highway	72 miles (116 km)
Belize City–Placencia	George Price, Hummingbird, and Southern highways	147 miles (237 km)
Belize City–Punta Gorda	George Price, Hummingbird, and Southern highways	200 miles (323 km)
San Ignacio–Placencia	George Price, Hummingbird, and Southern highways	113 miles (182 km)

ROAD CONDITIONS

All four main roads in Belize—the George Price Highway (formerly Western Highway), Philip Goldson Highway (formerly Northern Highway), Southern Highway, and Hummingbird Highway—are completely paved. These two-lane roads are generally in good condition. The once-horrendous Placencia Road is now completely paved, as is the Hopkins Road. The San Antonio Road from the Southern Highway near Punta Gorda to the Guatemala border has been upgraded and paved all the way to Jalcate village near the Guatemala border, although an official border crossing may not open until 2018. Signage is good along the main highways; large green signs direct you to major sights. Large speed bumps are ubiquitous, and some of them are unmarked.

Elsewhere in Belize, expect fair to stupendously rough dirt, gravel, and limestone roads. Some unpaved roads, and occasionally stretches of even paved roads, may be impassable at times in the rainy season.

Immense improvements have been made to Guatemala's ravaged roads. A highway from Río Dulce to Tikal has cut travel time along this popular route significantly. In the Petén, the road from Belize to Tikal and Flores is paved and in very good condition. Roads in remote areas are frequently unpaved, rife with potholes, and treacherously muddy in the rainy season. Four-wheel-drive vehicles are recommended for travel off the beaten path. In the town of Flores, expect mostly narrow streets, some paved with cobblestones. Road signs are generally used to indicate large towns; smaller towns may not be so clearly marked. Look for intersections where people seem to be waiting for a bus—that's a good sign that there's an important turnoff nearby.

RULES OF THE ROAD

Driving in Belize and Guatemala is on the right. Seat belts are required, although the law is seldom enforced. There are few speed-limit signs, and speed limits are rarely enforced. However, as you approach villages and towns watch out for "sleeping policemen," a local name for speed bumps. The entire country of Belize has only about a dozen traffic lights, and only Belize City, downtown Orange Walk Town, and downtown San Ignacio have anything approaching congestion. In recent years, Belize has been changing many intersections to roundabouts. One unusual aspect of driving in Belize, likely a hold-over from British Honduras days when driving was on the left, is that vehicles turning left against traffic are not supposed to hold up cars behind them; instead, they signal a right turn, pull over to the right, and wait for a break in traffic to turn left.

Despite the relatively small number of private cars in Belize, traffic accidents are the nation's number one cause of death. Belizean drivers aren't always as skilled as they think they are, and drunk drivers can be a problem. Guatemala's narrow roads and highways mean you can be stuck motionless on the road for half an hour while a construction crew stands around a hole in the ground. Always allow extra travel time for such unpredictable events, and bring along snacks and water. In both Belize and Guatemala, be prepared to stop for police traffic and auto insurance checks. Usually tourists in rental cars are checked only cursorily. In Belize, auto liability insurance is mandatory (it's included in the cost of car rentals). In Guatemala, liability insurance isn't required but it's advised. If you observe the rules you follow at home, you'll likely do just fine. Just don't expect everyone else to follow them.

▎RENTAL CARS

Belize City and the international airport in Ladyville have most major car-rental agencies as well as several local operators. At the international airport, a line of about 10 rental-car offices is on the far side of the main parking lot across from the airport entrances. There also are car-rental agencies in Corozal Town, San Ignacio, Placencia, and Punta Gorda. Some Belize City car-rental companies will deliver vehicles to other locations in Belize, but there is always a drop fee that varies depending on destination. Prices for car rentals vary, but all are high by U.S. standards, and vehicles are often a few years old with quite a few miles. If renting from an agency at the international airport, there's a BZ$10 airport fee. Off-season, rates are a little lower. Weekly rates usually save you money over daily rates. Make sure you ask the agency what procedures are in place if your car breaks down in a remote area. Most agencies in Belize send a driver with a replacement vehicle or a mechanic to fix the car.

For serious safaris, a four-wheel-drive vehicle is invaluable. But since unpaved roads, mudslides in rainy season, and a general off-the-beaten-path landscape are status quo here, all drivers will be comforted with a four-wheel-drive vehicle.

Car rental has never really caught on in Guatemala, which, given the narrowness of some roads, is just as well. If you want to rent, several international and local car-rental companies, including Hertz, are based at the Flores airport, serving Tikal. If your car breaks down in Guatemala, your best bet is to call the National or Tourist Police.

In Belize and Guatemala, rental-car companies routinely accept driver's licenses from most other countries without question. Most car-rental agencies require a major credit card for a deposit, and some require you be over 25, but under 70.

Most Belize agencies don't permit their vehicles to be taken into Guatemala or Mexico. Crystal Auto Rental in Belize City does permit its vehicles to be taken into Guatemala, as do a couple of the car-rental companies in San Ignacio, although without any insurance coverage while in Guatemala. There is no place to buy Guatemalan liability insurance at the Belize-Guatemala border.

On Belize's cayes you can't rent a car, but you can rent a golf cart, at prices not much less than renting a car. You'll need a driver's license and a credit card.

CAR-RENTAL INSURANCE

Auto liability insurance is mandatory in Belize, and nearly all rentals include basic liability coverage in the rental rate. However, other damage to the car, such as from hitting a tree or stolen car, is not covered by basic liability insurance. If you own a car, your personal auto insurance may cover a rental to some degree, though not all policies protect you abroad; always read your policy's fine print. If you don't have auto insurance, then consider buying the collision- or loss-damage waiver (CDW or LDW) from the car-rental company, which eliminates some of your responsibility for damage to the car. Many credit cards offer CDW coverage, but it's usually supplemental to your own insurance and rarely covers trucks, minivans, luxury models, and the like. American Express and some other credit/charge card companies offer a premium CDW plan for a flat fee, usually around US$20–$25 per rental, not per day, that has more leeway than regular CDW plans—for example, covering SUVs, trucks, and driving off paved roads. If your insurance coverage is secondary, you may still be liable for loss-of-use costs from the car-rental company. But no credit-card coverage is valid unless you use that card for *all* transactions, from reserving to paying the final bill. All companies exclude car rental in some countries, so be sure to find out about the destination to which you are traveling.

Belize has agents or franchisees of international auto rental companies including Alamo, Avis, Budget, Enterprise, Hertz, and Thrifty along with local companies such as Crystal Auto Rental and AQ Auto Rental. Recommended auto rental agencies in Belize City have kiosks across the main parking lot at Philip S. W. Goldson International Airport in Ladyville as well as locations in Belize City. See individual chapters for vehicle rentals in other locations in Belize and Flores, Guatemala.

Major Agencies Alamo Car Rental. ⊠ *1 Slaughterhouse Rd., Commercial District* ☎ *223/0641 in Belize* ⊕ *www.alamo.com.* **AQ Auto Rental.** ⊠ *Mile 5.5, Goldson Hwy., Northern Suburbs* ☎ *222/5122 in Belize.* **Budget.** ⊠ *Mile 2.5 Goldson Hwy., formerly Northern Hwy., Northern Suburbs* ☎ *223/2435 in Belize* ⊕ *www.budget-belize.com.* **Crystal Auto Rental.** ⊠ *Mile 5, Goldson Hwy., formerly Northern Hwy., Northern Suburbs* ☎ *223/1600 in Belize, 800/777–7777 toll-free in Belize* ⊕ *www.crystal-belize.com.* **Hertz.** ⊠ *11A Cork St., Commercial District* ☎ *800/654–3001 in U.S. and Canada for international reservations, 225/3300 in Belize* ⊕ *www.carsbelize.com.*

▮ SHUTTLES

Belize has a variety of shuttle services. These operate primarily between Belize City and San Ignacio, although shuttles also are available to Belmopan, Placencia, Chetumal, Mexico, and elsewhere. Most hotels and lodges in Cayo will arrange round-trip van transfers for guests to and from the international airport in Belize City. Several private shuttle services transport visitors between the airports and water-taxi locations in Belize City to Belmopan and San Ignacio in Cayo District. Rates vary depending on the number of people, whether the service is on-demand or prescheduled and what other services, such as a stop at the Belize Zoo, are included. Among the recommended shuttles are William's Shuttle, Discounted Belize Shuttles, Mayan Heart World Adventure Tours, Belize Shuttles and Transfers, and PACZ Tours. In the north, Belize VIP Transfers will whisk you across the border to Chetumal, but the fee does not include the BZ$40 Belize exit fee. Mayan Heart World Adventure Tours has a daily shuttle from San Ignacio to Tikal. A BZ$40 Belize exit fee also is required when going to Tikal from Belize's western border.

Línea Dorada and Fuente del Norte run daily minibuses between Belize City and Flores, Guatemala. These fares don't include Belize exit fees when leaving by land.

Shuttles in Guatemala are private minivans that hold up to eight passengers. Minibus shuttles between Flores and Tikal run frequently, starting at 5 am from Flores.

Reservations are generally required for shuttle service in both Belize and Guatemala. Some may ask for payment up front; before obliging, be sure you're dealing with a reputable company.

Belize Companies **Belize Shuttles and Transfers.** ☎ *637/9922 in Belize* ⊕ *belize-shuttles.trekksoft.com/en.* **Belize VIP Transfers.** ✉ *Caribbean Village, South End, Corozal Town* ☎ *422/2725 in Belize* ⊕ *www. belizetransfers.com.* **Discounted Belize Shuttles and Tours.** ✉ *Philip S. W. Goldson International Airport, Ladyville* ☎ *620/1474 in Belize* ⊕ *www.discountedbelizeshuttlesand-tours.com.* **Mayan Heart World Adventure Tours.** ✉ *29 Burns Ave., San Ignacio* ☎ *824/3328 in Belize* ⊕ *www.mayanheart-world.net.* **PACZ Tours.** ✉ *30 Burns Ave., San Ignacio* ☎ *824/0536 in Belize* ⊕ *www. pacztours.net.* **William's Belize Shuttle.** ✉ *Parrot's Nest, Bullet Tree Falls* ☎ *620/3055 in Belize* ⊕ *williamshuttlebelize.com.*

Guatemala Companies **Fuente del Norte.** ✉ *Terminal de Buses, Santa Elena* ☎ *7926–2999 in Santa Elena, Guatemala, 223/0457 Marine Terminal, Belize City, 223/1200 Mundo Maya Travels in Brown Sugar Marketplace at 90 Front St. in Belize City sells tickets for Fuente del Norte buses* ⊕ *www.grupofuent-edelnorte.com.*

ESSENTIALS

■ ACCOMMODATIONS

Regardless of the kind of lodging, you'll usually stay at a small place, as only a few properties have more than 50 or 75 rooms, and most have fewer than 30. The owners often actively manage the property. Thus, Belize accommodations usually reflect the personalities of their owners, for better or worse.

APARTMENT AND HOUSE RENTALS

You can most easily find vacation home rentals on Ambergris Caye. Marty Casado's Ambergris Caye website has a good selection of rental houses and condos. Vacation Rentals By Owner (VRBO) and Airbnb have scores of rentals on Ambergris Caye and elsewhere in Belize. There also are some vacation rental houses in Placencia and Hopkins and on Caye Caulker. *Individual chapters in this guide direct you to vacation rental sources.*

Information Airbnb. ⊕ *www.airbnb. com/s/Belize?s_tag=GxLZEhHq.* **Ambergis Caye website.** ⊕ *www.ambergriscaye.com.* **Vacation Rentals By Owner (VRBO).** ⊕ *www. vrbo.com.*

BEACH HOTELS

Beach hotels range from a basic seaside cabin on Caye Caulker to a small, deluxe resort such as Victoria House on Ambergris Caye or Hamanasi near Hopkins. On Ambergris Caye many resorts are "condotels"—low-rise condo complexes with individually owned units that are managed like a hotel.

JUNGLE LODGES

Jungle lodges are concentrated in Cayo District, but they are also in Toledo, Belize, and Orange Walk districts and can be found most anywhere except the cayes. Jungle lodges need not be spartan; nearly all have electricity (though the generator may shut down at 10 pm), many have swimming pools, and a few have air-conditioning. The typical lodge has a roof of bay-palm thatch and may remind you of a Mayan house gone upscale.

STAYING ON REMOTE CAYES

Lodging choices on remote cayes appeal to the diving and fishing crowd. Amenity levels vary greatly, from cabins with outdoor bathrooms to simple cottages to comfortable villas with air-conditioning.

TRADITIONAL HOTELS

Traditional hotels, usually found in larger towns, can be basic budget places or international-style hotels such as the Radisson Fort George in Belize City.

CANCELLATIONS

As most hotels have only a few rooms, a last-minute cancellation can have a big impact on the bottom line. Most properties have a sliding scale for cancellations, with full refunds (minus a small administrative fee) if you cancel 60 or 90 days or more in advance, with reduced refund rates for later cancellations, and often no refunds at all for cancellation 30 to 45 days out. Practices vary, so check on them.

HOSTELS AND GUESTHOUSES

Belize has few traditional hostels, however, there are some on Caye Caulker, in San Ignacio, and Belize City, along with at least one in each of the following areas: Corozal Town, Orange Walk Town, Sarteneja, Punta Gorda, Belmopan, Hopkins, and Placencia. Inexpensive guesthouses, common all over Belize, function much like hostels, albeit generally with less opportunity for guest interaction.

RATES

In the off-season—generally May to November, though dates vary by hotel—most properties discount rates by 20% to 40%. Although hotels have published rates, in the off-season at least you may also be able to negotiate a better rate, especially if you're staying more than one or two nights. ■TIP➜ **Walk-in rates are usually lower than prebooked rates, and rooms booked direct on the Internet may be lower than those booked through agents.**

Most hotels allow children under a certain age to stay in their parents' room at no extra charge, but others charge for them as extra adults; find out the cutoff age for discounts.

All prices for Belize accommodations in this guide are in Belize dollars (2 Belize dollars = 1 U.S. dollar) for a standard double room in-season with no meals, including service charges if any and 9% hotel tax.

▮ COMMUNICATIONS

INTERNET

DSL high-speed Internet (though not always the "high speed" you may be accustomed to) is available in most populated areas, and cable Internet is offered in Belize City, Placencia, San Pedro, and elsewhere. Relatively high-speed cell Internet is becoming popular around the country. In more remote areas, there's the option of satellite Internet. Most offices of the main phone company, Belize Telemedia Ltd., have computers with DSL Internet connections (BZ$10 per half hour). BTL also has Wi-Fi hotspots at the international airport (free) and elsewhere. Most hotels, lodges, and inns now offer free Wi-Fi access for guests.

CYBERCAFES AND INTERNET CAFÉS

Cybercafes are now common in Belize City and in most towns and resort areas all over Belize. The problem is that these lightly capitalized businesses frequently are here today and gone tomorrow. Your best bet is just to scout the area where you're staying for an open Internet café.

INTERNET AT ACCOMMODATIONS

Nearly all mid-level and upscale hotels, and many budget ones, now provide Internet access, typically Wi-Fi, for your laptop, tablet computer, or Internet-enabled

smartphone, and also a computer or two in the office or lobby, at no charge. In towns and resort areas this is usually DSL, but with speeds of only 2 to 4 Mbps down or less. At jungle lodges and other remote properties, the access is usually via a satellite system, with very limited bandwidth. At these lodges you're usually asked to use the Internet for email only and not to upload or download large files. ■TIP➜ **If you're traveling with a laptop in Belize, be aware that the power supply may be uneven, and most hotels don't have built-in current stabilizers. At remote lodges power is often from fluctuating generators. Bring a surge protector and your own memory sticks to save your work.**

PHONES

CALLING WITHIN BELIZE

All Belizean telephone numbers are seven digits. (Guatemalan numbers, with a few exceptions, are eight digits.) The first digit in Belize is the district area code (2 for Belize District, 3 Orange Walk, 4 Corozal, 5 Stann Creek, 6 for mobile phones, 7 Toledo, and 8 Cayo). The second indicates the type of service (0 for prepaid services, 1 for mobile, 2 for regular landline). The final five digits are the phone number. Thus, a number such as 22x/xxxx means that it's a landline phone in Belize District.

To dial any number in Belize, local or long distance, you must dial all seven digits. When dialing from outside Belize, dial the international access code (011), the country code for Belize (501), and all seven digits. When calling from the United States, for example, dial 011/501–xxx–xxxx.

Belize has a good nationwide phone system. The largest telcom company in Belize is Belize Telemedia Ltd., which offers the only landline service in Belize and is dominant in mobile. There are BTL pay phones on the street in the main towns, but they only take prepaid phone cards, not coins. Phone cards are available in shops at BTL offices. Dial 113 for directory assistance and 115 for operator assistance. You can get phone numbers in Belize on the website of BTL.

CALLING OUTSIDE BELIZE

To call the United States, dial 001 or 10–10–199 plus the area code and number. BTL blocks many foreign calling cards and also attempts to block even computer-to-computer calls on Skype and similar services.

Resources Belize Telemedia Ltd. ☎ *800/225–5285 toll-free in Belize, 223/2368 main number in Belize City* ⊕ *www.belizetelemedia.net.*

MOBILE PHONES

If you have a multiband cell or smartphone and your service provider uses the GSM 850/1900 digital system (like AT&T) you can use your phone in Belize on the DigiCell system of Belize Telemedia Ltd. You'll need a new SIM card (your provider may have to unlock your phone for you to use a different SIM card), and a prepaid phone card to pay for outgoing calls (incoming cell calls are free). Both items and also rental cell phones are available at the BTL office at the international airport (near the rental car kiosks), at some BTL offices, and at a number of private shops and stores around Belize that are DigiCell distributors.

Another option is a BTL competitor, Smart!, which operates a nationwide cellphone system that uses CDMA technology (like Verizon in the United States). At one of its offices—in Belize City, Corozal Town, Orange Walk Town, Belmopan City, San Ignacio, San Pedro, or Benque Viejo—you can reprogram your unlocked 800 MHz or 850 MHz CDMA phone for use in Belize. There's an activation fee, and you'll need to purchase a prepaid plan with per-minute rates for outgoing calls; incoming calls, text messages, and voice mail are free.

You may also be able to activate your own cellular smartphone for use in Belize. Check with your service provider, but be aware that international roaming charges are high.

Contacts BTL International Airport Office. ⊠ *Philip S. W. Goldson International Airport, Ladyville ✛ Facing car-rental offices, BTL office is at far left end of group of car-rental offices across airport parking lot* ☎ *225/4162 office at international airport, 800/225–5285 toll-free in Belize* ⊕ *www.belizetelemedia.net.* **Smart!** ⊠ *Mile 2.5 Goldson Hwy., formerly Northern Hwy., Northern Suburbs* ☎ *280/1000 in Belize* ⊕ *www.smart-bz.com.* **Verizon Wireless.** ☎ *800/922-0204 in U.S.* ⊕ *www.verizonwireless.com.*

▮ CUSTOMS AND DUTIES

At the international airport in Belize City it rarely takes more than 30 minutes to clear immigration and customs.

Duty-free allowances for visitors entering Belize include 1 liter of liquor and one carton of cigarettes per person. Customs officials may confiscate beer, including beer from Guatemala or Mexico, as Belize protects its domestic brewing industry. The exception is beer from countries in CARICOM, of which Belize is a member.

▮TIP➔ **When arriving by international air at Philip Goldson International Airport you can buy up to four bottles of spirits or wine at the duty-free shop in the arrival terminal near the baggage claim area. These won't be counted toward your regular import allowance.**

In theory, electronic and electrical appliances, cameras, jewelry, or other items of value must be declared at the point of entry, but unless these are new items you plan to leave in Belize, you probably will not be required to declare them. You should have no trouble bringing in a laptop for personal use.

Firearms of any type, along with ammunition, are strictly prohibited, as are fresh fruits and vegetables. Although a couple of dozen food items, including meats, rice, beans, sugar, and peanuts, require an import license, grocery items other than fresh fruits and vegetables, in small amounts for personal use and in their original packages, are usually allowed.

To take home fresh seafood of any kind from Belize, you must first obtain a permit from the Fisheries Department. There's a 20-pound limit. It is illegal to export any Mayan artifact from Belize.

You may enter Guatemala duty-free with a camera, up to six rolls of film, any clothes and articles needed while traveling, 500 mg of tobacco, 3 liters of alcoholic beverages, two bottles of perfume, and 2 kg of candy. Unless you bring in a lot of merchandise, customs officers probably won't even check your luggage, although a laptop may be somewhat scrutinized.

It's illegal to export most Mayan artifacts from Guatemala. If you buy any such goods, do so only at a well-established store, and keep the receipt. You may not take fruits or vegetables out of Guatemala.

Information in Belize Belize Fisheries. ☎ 223/2623 in Belize ⊕ www.agriculture.gov.bz.

U.S. Information U.S. Customs and Border Protection. ☎ 877/227–5511 in U.S., 202/325–8000 for international callers ⊕ www.cbp.gov.

▌ EATING OUT

For information on food-related health issues, see Health.

MEALS AND MEALTIMES

You can eat well in Belize thanks to a gastronomic gumbo of Mexican, Caribbean, Mayan, Garífuna, English, and American dishes. On the American side, think fried chicken, pork chops, burgers, and steaks. On the coast and cayes, seafood—especially lobster, conch, snapper, snook, and grouper—is fresh, relatively inexpensive, and delicious.

Try Creole specialties such as cow-foot soup (yes, made with real cows' feet),

"boil up" (a stew of fish, potatoes, plantains, cassava and other vegetables, and eggs), and the ubiquitous "stew chicken" with rice and beans. Many Creole dishes are seasoned with red or black *recado,* a paste made from annatto seeds and other spices.

In border areas and elsewhere, enjoy Mestizo favorites such as *escabeche* (onion soup), *salbutes* (fried corn tortillas with chicken and a topping of tomatoes, onions, and peppers), or *garnaches* (fried tortillas with refried beans, cabbage, and cheese).

In Dangriga, Hopkins, and Punta Gorda or other Garífuna areas, try dishes such as *sere lasus* (fish soup with plantain balls) or cassava dumplings.

Breakfast is usually served from 7 to 9, lunch from 11 to 2, and dinner from 6 to 9. Few restaurants are open late. Remember, though, that small restaurants may open or close at the whim of the owner. Off-season, restaurants may close early if it looks as if there are no more guests coming, and some restaurants close completely for a month or two, usually in September and October. Unless otherwise noted, the restaurants listed *in this guide* are open daily for lunch and dinner.

▐TIP→ **Other than at hotels, Belize restaurants are often closed on Sunday.**

RESERVATIONS AND DRESS

Reservations for meals are rarely needed in Belize or the Tikal area. The exceptions are for dinner at jungle lodges and at small restaurants where the owner or chef needs to know in advance how many people are dining that night.

A couple of restaurants in Belize City have a dress code, which basically means that you can't wear shorts at dinner. We mention dress only when men are required to wear a jacket or a jacket and tie, which is nearly unheard of in Belize.

WINES, BEER, AND SPIRITS

Many restaurants serve beer—almost always the local brew, Belikin—and terrific, tropical mixed drinks. A growing number offer wine. Belikin is available in regular, stout, and premium versions. Lighthouse, a lighter lager by the same brewery, is also available at many bars and restaurants. A few American and other imported beers are available in some groceries, but prices are high. Due to restrictive import laws, the beers of neighboring Mexico and Guatemala are rarely available. However, beers brewed in CARICOM countries (of which Belize is a member), including Red Stripe from Jamaica and Heinekin from St. Kitts, are now sold in Belize. Presidente, a Pilsner brewed in the Dominican Republic, has been making a big marketing push in Belize, too.

Several Belize companies manufacture liquors, primarily rum, but also gin and vodka. Traveller's "One Barrel" Rum, with a slight vanilla flavor, wins the stamp of approval from many aficionados. In bars, local rum drinks are always much cheaper than drinks with highly taxed imported liquors. Grocery stores in Belize sell liquor, beer and wine.

Imported wines are available in supermarkets and better restaurants, at about twice the price of the same wines in the United States. There are wine specialty stores in Belize City and San Pedro. Cashew wine and other local wines are available around the country.

The drinking age in Belize is 18, although IDs are rarely checked. The official drinking age in Guatemala is 20.

▍ETIQUETTE

Patience and friendliness go a long way in Belize. Don't criticize local ways of doing things—there's usually a reason that may not be obvious to visitors—and, especially with officials, adopt a respectful attitude.

Belizeans generally are incredibly kind and friendly. Greet folks with a "Good morning" before asking for directions, for a table in a restaurant, or when entering a store or museum, for example. It will set a positive tone and you'll be received much more warmly for having done so.

Don't take pictures inside churches. Do not take pictures of indigenous people without first asking their permission. Offering them a small sum as thanks is customary.

With the exception of first-class buses based in Guatemala and Mexico, the seats on many buses often have three people seated abreast. Though tourists are often larger than the average local, you should respect the rule, and make room for others. It's fine to step into the aisle to let someone take a middle or window seat.

Business dress is casual. Men rarely wear suits and ties, and even the Belize prime minister appears at functions in a white shirt open at the neck.

English is Belize's official language. Spanish is widely spoken especially in northern and western Belize. Several Mayan dialects and the Garífuna language are also spoken. Some Mennonite communities speak a German dialect. Creole, or Kriol, which uses versions of English words and a West African–influenced grammar and syntax, is spoken as a first language by many Belizeans, especially around Belize City.

Around Tikal, wherever tourist traffic is heavy, you'll find a few English speakers; you'll have considerably less luck in places off the beaten path. In general, very little English is spoken in El Petén, and in some small villages in the region absolutely none. In addition, many Guatemalans will answer "yes" or "*si*" even if they don't understand your question, so as not to appear unkind or unhelpful. To minimize such confusion, try posing questions as "Where is so-and-so?" rather than asking "Is so-and-so this way?"

ELECTRICITY

There's no need to bring a converter or adapter, as electrical current in Belize and Guatemala is the same as in the United States, and outlets take U.S.-style plugs. In a few remote areas lodges and hotels generate their own electricity, and after the generators are turned off at night, power, if there's any, comes only from storage batteries.

EMERGENCIES

In an emergency, call 911 nationwide, or 90 in Belize City only. There are police stations in Belize City and in Belmopan City, in the towns of Benque Viejo, Corozal, Dangriga, Orange Walk, Punta Gorda, San Ignacio, and San Pedro, and in Placencia Village and a few other villages. Police try to respond quickly to emergencies, although lack of equipment, supplies, and training may sometimes reduce their effectiveness.

Police are generally polite, professional, and will do what they can to help. In Belize City and in most tourist areas, including Placencia and San Pedro, there are special tourist police whose job is to patrol areas where visitors are likely to go and to render any assistance they can, including providing directions.

There are checkpoints on most major highways in Belize, especially near border areas and around Belize City. Police officers may ask for your driver's license or passport; just as frequently, they will wave you through.

Most Belizeans are extremely solicitous of the welfare of visitors to the country. In an emergency, it's likely that bystanders or people in the area will gladly offer to help, usually going out of their way to render any assistance they can.

Your hotel can provide the names of nearby physicians and clinics. You can also go to the emergency room of public hospitals in Belize City and major towns. Don't worry about payment—in an emergency, you'll be treated regardless of your ability to pay, though after being treated you may be asked to pay what you can. Private hospitals (there are two in Belize City and one in San Ignacio) may ask for some guarantee of payment and may accept private medical insurance. The Belize Emergency Response Team, based in Belize City, provides ambulance and air transport all over the country. *For more information, see Health, below.*

Guatemala police, overwhelmed at times by the amount of crime—in 2014 there were 96 murders a week in Guatemala— may not be able to respond effectively to emergencies. For tourist assistance in Guatemala, dial 1500 from any phone, and for police emergencies call 110 or 911.

Emergency Services *Belize Police.* ☎ *911 for police and other emergencies nationwide, 90 for police, fire, and ambulance in Belize City only.* **Guatemalan National Police.** ☎ *110 for emergencies, 2421–2810 police.* **Guatemalan Tourist Police.** ☎ *2421–2810 for 24-hr security information provided by INGUAT, 1500 dial 1500 from anywhere in Guatemala to connect to bilingual operator at Asistur, who will put you in contact with police, fire, or ambulance, 911 for emergencies in most parts of Guatemala.*

HEALTH

Many medicines requiring a doctor's prescription at home don't require one in Belize. Drugstores often sell prescription antibiotics, sleeping aids, and painkillers to anyone who has the money. However, pharmacies generally have a very small inventory, and only the most commonly prescribed drugs are available. In Belize private physicians often own an associated pharmacy, so they sell you, usually at modest cost, the medicine they prescribe. A few pharmacies are open 24 hours and deliver directly to hotel rooms. Eye doctors in Belize City, Belmopan, and elsewhere sell prescription contact lenses and can replace your prescription eyeglasses. Most hotel proprietors will direct you to such services.

SPECIFIC ISSUES IN BELIZE

Sand flies (also sometimes referred to as no-see-ums, or as sand fleas, which are a different insect) are common on many beaches, cayes, and in swampy areas. They can infect you with leishmaniasis, a disease that can cause the skin to develop sores that can leave scars. In rare cases, the visceral form of leishmaniasis, if untreated, can be fatal.

Use repellent containing at least a 30% concentration of DEET to help deter sand flies. Some say lathering on Avon's Skin So Soft or any oily lotion such as baby oil helps, too, as it drowns the little bugs.

The botfly or beefworm is one of the most unpleasant of Central American pests. Botfly eggs are deposited under your skin with the help of a mosquito, where one can grow into larva, a large living worm. To rid yourself of your unwanted pal, cover the larva's airhole in your skin with Vaseline, and after it suffocates you can remove it with a sterile knife. Or see your doctor. The good news is that unless you spend a lot of time in the bush in Belize, you are unlikely to encounter botflies.

Virtually all honeybees in Belize and Guatemala are Africanized. The sting of these killer bees is no worse than that of regular bees, but the colonies are much more aggressive. Farm animals and pets frequently are killed by Africanized bees, and in 2013 a young Mennonite boy in northern Belize died after being stung hundreds of times in his backyard. If attacked by Africanized bees, try to get into a building, vehicle, or underwater; protect your mouth, nose, and other orifices.

Scorpions are common in Belize and around Tikal. Their stings are painful, but not fatal. There are many venomous snakes in Belize and lowland Guatemala, including the notorious fer-de-lance and small but deadly coral snakes. Most visitors never even see a snake, but if bitten can go to medical centers for antivenom.

Crocodiles (called alligators by many Belizeans) are present in many lagoons and rivers, but very rarely are they known to attack humans. Many Belizean children swim in lagoons and rivers where there are many crocodiles.

Divers and snorkelers may experience "itchy itchy" or *pica pica,* a skin rash, in spring and early summer, when the tiny larvae of thimble jellyfish may get on the skin. Putting Vaseline or other greasy lotion on the skin before entering the water may help prevent the itch, and applying Benadryl, vinegar, or even Windex to the affected area may help stop the itch.

If you're a light sleeper, you might want to pack earplugs. Monkeys howling through the night and birds chirping at the crack of dawn are only charming on the first night of your nature excursion.

FOOD AND DRINK

Belize has a high standard of health and hygiene, so the major health risk is sunburn, not digestive distress. You can drink the water in Belize City, Cayo, Placencia, on Ambergris Caye, and in most other areas you're likely to visit, though you may prefer the taste of bottled water. In remote villages, however, water may come from shallow wells or cisterns and may not be safe to drink.

On trips to Tikal or other areas in Guatemala, assume that the water isn't safe to drink. Bottled water—*agua mineral* or *agua pura* in Spanish—is available even at the smallest *tiendas* (stores) and is cheaper than in the United States or Canada. Eating contaminated fruit or vegetables or drinking contaminated water (even ice) could result in a case of Montezuma's revenge, or traveler's diarrhea. Also skip uncooked food and unpasteurized milk and milk products.

INFECTIOUS DISEASES

The Zika virus, spread by *Aedes aegypti* mosquitoes, has been confirmed in Belize, although as of this writing the number of cases in Belize and in the Petén area of Guatemala is very small. However, pregnant women, and women who may become pregnant, should consult with their physician before visiting Belize or Guatemala, as the virus can cause severe birth defects. Zika can also be transmitted sexually. Anyone visiting Belize, or whose partner has visited Belize, and who comes down with symptoms such as rash, fever, joint pain or conjunctivitis (pink eye), even if very mild, should consider being tested. There's currently no vaccine to prevent Zika, although several are in development.

HIV/AIDS is an increasing concern in Central America. This is especially true in Belize, where the incidence on a per capita basis is the highest in the region.

According to the U.S. Centers for Disease Control and Prevention, there's a limited risk of malaria, hepatitis A and B, dengue fever, typhoid fever, and rabies in Central America. In most urban or easily accessible areas you need not worry. However, if you plan to spend a lot of time in the jungles, rain forests, or other remote regions, or if you want to stay for more than six weeks, check the CDC website.

In areas where malaria and dengue are prevalent, sleep under mosquito nets. If you're a real worrier, pack your own—it's the only way to be sure there are no tears. Although most hotels in Belize have screened or glassed windows, your room probably won't be completely mosquito-proof. Wear clothing that covers your arms and legs, apply repellent containing at least 30% DEET, and spray for flying insects in living and sleeping areas.

Vaccines for dengue fever are being developed and tested but are not yet widely available. For malaria, there are effective antimalarial medications: Chloroquine (the commonly recommended antimalarial for Belize and Guatemala) is sold as Aralen in Central America. It must be started a week before entering an area with malaria risk. Malarone is prescribed as an alternative, and it can be started only two days before arrival in a risk area. Check the CDC website or consult with

your physician about malaria prevention, but don't overstress about this. In Belize there are fewer than 900 reported cases of malaria a year, mostly in the far south, actually fewer cases than are reported in the United States. In Guatemala, El Petén is a risk area.

You should be up-to-date on shots for tetanus and hepatitis A and B. Children traveling to Central America should have current inoculations against measles, mumps, rubella, hepatitis, and polio.

▌HOURS OF OPERATION

Belize is a laid-back place that requires a certain amount of flexibility when shopping or sightseeing. Small shops tend to open according to the whim of the owner, but generally operate 8–noon and 1–6. Larger stores and supermarkets in Belize City and in larger towns such as San Ignacio and San Pedro don't close for lunch.

Many shops are only open a half day on Saturday. On Sunday, Belize takes it easy: Few shops are open, and many restaurants outside of hotels are closed. Most Mayan sites in Belize are open daily 8–5. Guatemala's Tikal ruins are open daily 6–6, with longer hours for those staying at lodges in the park.

HOLIDAYS

New Year's Day (January 1); Baron Bliss Day (officially March 9, but observation date may vary); Good Friday; Holy Saturday; Easter Monday; Labour Day (May 1); Sovereign's Day, also called Commonwealth Day (May 24); National Day (September 10); Independence Day (September 21); Columbus Day, also known as Pan-American Day (October 12); Garífuna Settlement Day (November 19); Christmas Day; Boxing Day (December 26).

▌MAIL AND SHIPPING

When sending mail to Central America, be sure to include the city or town and district, country name, and the words

"Central America" in the address. Don't use the abbreviation "CA" or your mail may end up in California, USA. Belizean mail service is good, except to and from remote villages, and the Belizean stamps, mostly of wildlife or flora, are beautiful. An airmail letter from Belize City takes about a week to reach the United States, longer—sometimes several weeks—from other areas.

An airmail letter to the United States is BZ60¢, a postcard, BZ30¢; to Europe, BZ75¢ for a letter, BZ40¢ for a postcard. An airmail letter to Belize from the United States costs US$1.15. Packages mailed to Belize tend to require expensive postage and must have customs forms attached.

EXPRESS SERVICES

If you have to send something fast, use FedEx, UPS, or DHL Worldwide Express, which are expensive but (usually) do the job right. They have offices in Belize City and agents elsewhere. In San Pedro, Mail Boxes Etc. can wrap and ship your packages.

Express Services DHL Worldwide Express. ⊠ *38 New Rd., Commercial District* ☎ *223/1070 in Belize* ⊕ *www.dhl.com.* **FedEx.** ⊠ *6 Fort St., Fort George* ☎ *223/1577* ⊕ *www. fedex.com.* **Mail Boxes Etc.** ⊠ *Coconut Dr., San Pedro Town* ✛ *Across from Wings near San Pedro airstrip* ☎ *226/4770* ⊕ *www.mbe-belize. com.* **UPS.** ⊠ *Belize Global Travel Services, 41 Albert St., Commercial District* ☎ *227/2332 in Belize.*

POST OFFICES

The main post office in Belize City is on North Front Street in the main commercial district. There are post offices in all towns and many villages. Mail service from Belize City to and from the United States and other countries is generally fast and reliable (airmail to and from the United States usually takes about seven days). To and from outlying towns and villages service is slower, and for remote villages it may take weeks. For faster, though expensive, service use DHL and FedEx.

Post Office Main Post Office—Belize Postal Service. ⊠ *Biddles Bldg., 150 N. Front St., Commercial District* ☎ *227/2201* ⊕ *www. postoffice.bz.*

▌MONEY

There are two ways of looking at the prices in Belize: either it's one of the cheapest countries in the Caribbean or one of the most expensive countries in Central America. A good hotel room for two will cost you upward of BZ$250, and fancy beach resorts and jungle lodges run BZ$500 to BZ$800 or more; a budget one, as little as BZ$40. A meal in one of the more expensive restaurants will cost BZ$50–BZ$75 for one, but you can eat the classic Creole dish of stew chicken and rice and beans for BZ$8–BZ$10. Prices are highest in Belize City, Ambergris Caye, and the Placencia Peninsula.

ITEM	AVERAGE COST IN BELIZE
Cup of Coffee	BZ$2
Glass of Wine	BZ$10–BZ$18
Glass of Beer	BZ$3–BZ$10
Sandwich	BZ$6–BZ$18
One-Mile Taxi Ride in Belize City	BZ$7
Museum Admission	BZ$10–BZ$20

Prices throughout *this guide* are given for adults. Substantially reduced fees are usually available for children and students.

ATMS AND BANKS

Belize has four Belize-based banks: Atlantic Bank; Heritage Bank, which took over some assets of Caribbean International Bank; the new National Bank of Belize, which has only two offices; and Scotia-Bank, which is an independent outpost of the big Canadian bank. Banking hours vary but are typically Monday–Thursday 8–3 and Friday 8–4. There is a branch of Atlantic Bank at the international airport that has longer hours, along with an ATM. Belize Bank has an ATM at the airport. All the banks have ATMs across the country that are open 24/7, although occasionally machines may run out of cash or are out of order.

Your own bank will probably charge a fee for using ATMs abroad, as will the Belize bank ATM. However, extracting funds as you need them is a safer option than carrying around a large amount of cash. That said, machines sometimes are down or out of money. Also, newer ATM cards, especially those with imbedded chips, may not work in some Belize ATMs. As a backup, carry some U.S. currency, a credit card or two, and perhaps a few old-fashioned traveler's checks.

ATMs in Belize give cash in Belize dollars. There are ATMs in Belize City (including two at the international airport), Ladyville, Corozal Town, Orange Walk Town, San Pedro, Caye Caulker, Belmopan, San Ignacio, Spanish Lookout, Dangriga, Hopkins, Placencia, and Punta Gorda. Most ATMs in Belize have a BZ$500 daily limit, but Atlantic Bank and ScotiaBank have higher limits. Belize Bank's 26 ATMs around the country take ATM cards issued outside Belize on the CIRRUS, MasterCard, PLUS, and Visa networks. Atlantic Bank's 16 ATMs also accept foreign cards on the CIRRUS, MasterCard, PLUS and Visa networks. ScotiaBank's 14 ATMs around the country also accept foreign-issued ATM cards. Heritage Bank's approximately 20 ATMs (seven credit unions in Belize associated with Heritage Bank also have ATMs) and National Bank of Belize's nine ATMs as of this writing do not accept foreign-issued ATM cards. Other bank offices you see in Belize City or San Pedro are international, offshore banks; they are set up to do business with individuals and companies domiciled outside Belize and do not provide retail banking services in Belize.

In the Petén you can get cash in quetzales from ATMs in Melchor de Mencos, Flores, and Santa Elena. Across the border in Chetumal, Mexico, ATMs usually offer a choice of Mexican pesos or U.S. dollars.

The biggest employer in Belize—the Belize government—pays most employees on the 14th or 15th of the month, and on those days in particular banks in Belize are jammed, with customer lines often snaking around the outside of the building. Banks are also usually busy on Friday.

You should have a four-digit PIN. As noted, some newer ATMs with imbedded computer chips issued outside Belize may not work with all ATMs in Belize. ATM scams—where the ATM "eats" your card or your PIN is stolen—only rarely occur in Belize but are increasingly common in Guatemala. Most banks offer cash advances on credit cards issued by Visa and MasterCard for a fee ranging from BZ$10 to BZ$30.

BELIZE CITY

Banks Atlantic Bank. ⊠ *Main Office, Corner Freetown Rd. and Cleghorn St., Commercial District* ☎ *223/4123* ⊕ *www.atlabank.com.* **Belize Bank.** ⊠ *Main Office, 60 Market Sq., Commercial District* ☎ *227/7132* ⊕ *www. belizebank.com.* **Heritage Bank.** ⊠ *Main Office, 106 Princess Margaret Dr., Northern Suburbs* ☎ *223/5698* ⊕ *www.heritageibt.com.* **National Bank of Belize.** ⊠ *Forest Dr. and Hummingbird Hwy., Belmopan* ☎ *822/0957* ⊕ *www.nbbl.bz.* **ScotiaBank Belize.** ⊠ *Main Office, 4 Albert St., Commercial District* ☎ *227/7027* ⊕ *www.scotiabank.com/bz.*

CREDIT CARDS

It's a good idea to inform your credit-card company (debit-card companies, too) before you travel, especially if you're going abroad and don't travel internationally very often. Otherwise, the credit-card company might put a hold on your card owing to unusual activity—not a good thing halfway through your trip.

Record all your credit-card numbers—as well as the phone numbers to call if your cards are lost or stolen—in a safe place, so you're prepared should something go wrong. Both MasterCard and Visa have general numbers you can call (collect if you're abroad) if your card is lost, but you're better off calling the number of your issuing bank, since MasterCard and Visa usually just transfer you to your bank; your bank's number is usually printed on your card. If you report a lost or stolen card promptly, you are not responsible for fraudulent charges on your card. You can report lost or stolen cards by phone and, in most cases, online.

In Belize, MasterCard and Visa are widely accepted, American Express less so, and Discover and Diner's hardly at all.

■TIP➔ **Hotels, restaurants, shops, and tour operators in Belize occasionally levy a surcharge for credit-card use, usually 5% but ranging from 2% to 10%.** This practice happily has become less common, but it still happens. If you use a credit card, ask if there's a surcharge. Most credit-card issuers now charge an international exchange fee, usually 2% to 3%, even if the foreign purchase is denominated in U.S. dollars.

Reporting Lost Cards American Express.
☎ *800/327–1267 in U.S., to report lost or stolen card, 954/473–2123 collect from abroad, to report lost or stolen card* ⊕ *www.americanexpress.com.* **MasterCard.** ☎ *800/627–8372 in U.S. to report lost or stolen card, 636/722–7111 collect from abroad, to report lost or stolen card* ⊕ *www. mastercard.com.* **Visa.** ☎ *800/847–2911 in U.S., to report a lost or stolen card, 303/967–1096 from abroad, to report a lost or stolen card* ⊕ *www.visa.com.*

CURRENCY AND EXCHANGE

Because the U.S. dollar (bills only, not coins) is gladly accepted everywhere in Belize, there's no need to exchange it. When paying in U.S. dollars, you may get change in Belize or U.S. currency, or in both.

The Belize dollar (BZ$) is pegged to the U.S. dollar at a rate of BZ$2 per US$1, and nearly all shops, stores, hotels, restaurants, and other businesses honor that exchange rate. Note, however, that moneychangers at Belize's Mexico and Guatemala borders operate on a free-market system and pay a rate depending on the demand for U.S. dollars, sometimes as high as BZ$2.15 to US$1. Banks (and ATMs) generally exchange at BZ$1.98 or less.

The best place to exchange Belize dollars for Mexican pesos is in Corozal, or at the Mexico-Belize border where the exchange rate is quite good. At the Guatemala border near Benque Viejo del Carmen, you can exchange Belize or U.S. dollars for quetzales—moneychangers will approach you on the Belize side and also on the Guatemala side. Usually the money changers on the Guatemala side offer better rates.

As of late 2016, the U.S. dollar-Guatemalan quetzal bank exchange rate was about 7.5 quetzales to 1 U.S. dollar; the dollar-Mexican peso exchange rate was about 18.5 Mexican pesos to 1 U.S. dollar.

When leaving Belize, you can exchange Belizean currency back to U.S. dollars (up to US$100) at Atlantic Bank at the international airport. The Belize dollar is difficult if not impossible to exchange outside Belize, even in the neighboring countries of Mexico and Guatemala (except at border crossings).

In Belize most hotel, tour, and car-rental prices are quoted in U.S. dollars, while most restaurant prices, taxis charges, and store prices are in Belize dollars. *In this guide, all* Belize prices are quoted in Belize dollars. Because misunderstandings can happen, if it's not clear, always ask which currency is being used.

TRAVELER'S CHECKS

Traveler's checks should be in U.S. dollars, and the American Express brand is preferred. Most hotels and travel operators still accept traveler's checks, and some restaurants and gift shops do. However, even in Belize City and popular tourist areas such as San Pedro, clerks at groceries and other shops may be reluctant to accept traveler's checks or will have to get a supervisor's approval to accept them. Some places charge a small fee, around 1% or 2%, if you pay with a traveler's check.

Most banks will cash them for a fee of 1% to 2%, but it may require a wait in line. In all cases, you will need your passport in order to use or cash a traveler's check.

▮ PACKING

Pack light. Baggage carts are scarce at Central American airports, and international luggage limits are increasingly tight. Tropic Air and Maya Island Air officially have 70-pound (32-kilogram) weight limits for checked baggage. However, in practice the airlines in Belize rarely weigh luggage, and if you're a little over it's usually no problem. Occasionally, if the flight on the small Cessna or other airplane is full and there's a lot of luggage, some bags may be sent on the next flight, usually no more than an hour or two later.

Bring casual, comfortable, hand-washable clothing. T-shirts and shorts are acceptable near the beach and in tourist areas. More modest attire is appropriate in smaller towns, and the long sleeves and long pants will protect your skin from the ferocious sun and mosquitoes. Bring a hat to block the sun from your face and neck. If you're on a boat, you'll want a tight-fitting cap or hat with chinstrap to keep it from being blown away.

If you're heading into the mountains or highlands, especially during the winter months, bring a light cotton sweater, a jacket, and something warm to sleep in, as nights and early mornings can be chilly. Sturdy sneakers or hiking shoes or lightweight boots with rubber soles for wet or rocky surfaces are essential. A pair of sandals (preferably ones that can be worn in the water) are good, too.

Be sure to bring insect repellent, sunscreen, sunglasses, and an umbrella. Other handy items include tissues, a plastic water bottle, and a flashlight (for occasional power outages or use in areas without streetlights). A mosquito net for those roughing it is essential, but people staying in hotels or lodges—even budget-level ones—rarely need one. Snorkelers should consider bringing their own equipment, especially mask and snorkel, if there's room in the suitcase. Divers will save money—typically BZ$50 or more a day in rentals—by bringing their own equipment. Sand and high humidity are enemies of your camera equipment. To protect it, consider packing your gear in plastic ziplock bags. Also bring your own condoms and tampons. You won't find either easily or in familiar brands.

▮ PASSPORTS AND VISAS

To enter Belize, only a valid passport is necessary for citizens of the United States; no visa is required.

If upon arrival the immigration official asks how long you expect to stay in Belize, give the longest period you might stay—you can be granted a stay for up to 30 days on the free tourist stamp you'll get for your passport on entry—otherwise, the official may endorse your passport with a shorter period.

You can renew your entry permit at immigration offices for a fee of BZ$50 per month for the first six months; after six months, it costs BZ$100 a month for up to six more months, at which time you may have to leave the country for 72 hours to start the process over (sometimes this rule isn't enforced). Note that renewals aren't guaranteed, but normally are granted.

If you're young with a backpack and entering Belize by land from Mexico or Guatemala, there's a slight chance you'll be asked to prove you have enough money to cover your stay. You're supposed to have US$60 a day, though this requirement is rarely enforced. A credit card also may work.

Citizens of the United States do not need a visa when entering Guatemala from Belize.

Info in Belize **Belize Immigration and Nationality Department.** ✉ *Immigration General Office, Dry Creek St., Belmopan* ✛ *Near Mountain View Blvd.* ☎ *822/3860 in Belmopan* ⊕ *www.governmentofbelize.gov. bz.* **Belize Tourism Board.** ✉ *64 Regent St.,*

Commercial District ☎ 227/2420 in Belize, 800/624–0686 toll-free in U.S. and Canada ⊕ www.travelbelize.org. **Belize Tourism Industry Association (BTIA)**. ✉ 10 N. Park St., Fort George ☎ 227/1144 ⊕ www.btia.org.

U.S. Passport Information U.S. Department of State. ☎ 877/487–2778 passport information ⊕ www.state.gov.

GENERAL REQUIREMENTS FOR BELIZE	
Passport	Must be valid for 3 months after date of arrival
Visa	Not required for Americans, Canadians, and European Union citizens, among others; a tourist card (actually a stamp in your passport) good for up to 30 days is issued free upon arrival
Vaccinations	Yellow fever required only if coming from an infected area such as parts of Africa
Driving	Valid driver's license from your home country
Departure Tax	By international air: US$39.25, usually included in the cost of your airline ticket; if not, it must be paid in U.S. dollars or by credit card. By land border into Mexico or Guatemala: US$20, payable in U.S. or Belize dollars. By water taxi or boat: usually US$3.75, payable in U.S. or Belize dollars

▌ RESTROOMS

You won't find many public restrooms in Belize, but hotels and restaurants usually have clean, modern facilities with American-style—indeed American-made—toilets. Small restaurants and shops sometimes charge a small fee for noncustomers to use their bathrooms. Hot-water showers in Belize often are the on-demand type, powered by butane gas.

Restrooms in Guatemala use Western-style toilets, although bathroom tissue generally shouldn't be flushed but discarded in a basket beside the toilet.

▌ SAFETY

CRIME

Belize City has a bad rep for crime, especially in the poverty-ridden sections of Belize City's South Side, but it rarely involves visitors. When it does, Belize has a rapid justice system: the offender often gets a trial within hours or days and, if convicted, can be sent to prison ("the Hattieville Ramada") the same day. Tourist police patrol Fort George and other areas of Belize City where visitors convene. Police are particularly in evidence when cruise ships are in port. If you avoid walking around at night (except in well-lighted parts of the Fort George area), you should have no problems in Belize City.

Outside of Belize City, and possibly the rougher parts of Dangriga and Orange Walk Town, you'll find Belize to be safe and friendly. Petty theft, however, is common all over, so don't leave cameras, cell phones, and other valuables unguarded.

Thefts from budget hotel rooms occur occasionally. Given the hundreds of thousands of visitors to Belize, however, these incidents are isolated, and the vast majority of travelers never experience any crime in Belize.

The road from the Belize border toward Tikal has long been an area where armed robbers stopped buses and cars, and there also have been incidents at Tikal Park itself. Mexico's Los Zetas drug cartel and other drug groups have been active in Northern Guatemala. Ask locally about crime conditions before traveling to Tikal. Crime also spills over the border in Cayo from Guatemala, as poor Guatemalan squatters seek land in the Mountain Pine Ridge and elsewhere. Xateros, who are seeking the prized Xate palms used by florists, also cross the border into the Chiquibul wilderness or Pine Ridge, and a few violent incidents have occurred between them and members of the Belize Defence Force. Visitors to Caracol Maya site usually go in a caravan protected by Belize soldiers. In 2016, the long-standing claim by Guatemala to some Belize territory in southern Belize again arose as an issue between the two neighbors. Shots were exchanged between Guatemalan and Belize forces. Despite the tension between the two governments, tourist travel wasn't disrupted.

American citizens should consider enrolling in the U.S. Statement Department's Smart Traveler Enrollment Program (⊕ *travelregistration.state.gov/ibrs/ui*), which makes it easier to locate you and your family in case of an emergency. Many other countries have similar programs.

SCAMS

Most Belizeans and Guatemalans are extremely honest and trustworthy. It's not uncommon for a vendor to chase you down if you accidentally leave without your change. That said, most organized scams arise with tours and packages, in which you're sold a ticket that turns out to be bogus. Arrange all travel through a legitimate agency, and always get a receipt. If a problem does arise, the Belize Tourism Board or INGUAT in Guatemala may be able to help mediate the conflict.

LGBT TRAVELERS

The U.S. Embassy in Belize has issued a warning for LGBT visitors traveling outside of the tourist-friendly cayes, as some incidents of verbal or physical assault have been reported. Ambergris Caye, Cayo, Placencia, and Toledo are home to a number of Belize hotels, restaurants, and other small businesses that are owned and run by LGBT people.

Advisories and Other Information Transportation Security Administration (*TSA*). ☎ *866/289–9673* ⊕ *www.tsa.gov*. **U.S. Department of State.** ⊕ *www.travel.state.gov*.

▌ TAXES

The hotel tax in Belize is 9%, and a 12.5% Goods and Services Tax (GST) is charged on meals, tours, and other purchases at the hotel, along with most other purchases in Belize including car rentals, tours, and purchases at stores. The GST is supposed to be included in the cost of meals, goods, and services, but many businesses add on GST like a sales tax instead. Very small shops and street vendors are not required to collect GST.

When departing the country by international air, even on a short hop to Flores, Guatemala, you'll pay US$39.25 departure tax and fees. However, most international airlines include the departure tax in the airline ticket price. Don't pay twice—check your airline to see if the tax is included.

When leaving Belize by land to either Guatemala or Mexico, there's a border exit fee totaling BZ$40 or US$20. This may be paid in either U.S. dollars or Belize dollars, but not by credit card. For departures by boat to Guatemala, Mexico or Honduras, you pay a BZ$7.50 conservation fee, in U.S. or Belize dollars. Those in transit through Belize, staying less than 24 hours, can avoid paying the BZ$7.50 conservation fee but have to fork out other taxes and fees.

Some Guatemalan hotels and some tourist restaurants charge a 10% to 22% tourist tax, though others include this VAT in the price. The Guatemala airport-departure tax is US$30, plus about US$3 security fee. Guatemalan border officials in the past have asked for a Q20 fee (about US$2.50) when entering Guatemala at Melchor de Mencos. However, in 2016 this entrance fee was not being charged; there is no exit fee by land from Guatemala.

TIME

Belize time is the same as U.S. Central Standard Time. Daylight Saving time is not observed in Belize. Neither Guatemala nor the Mexican state of Quintana Roo currently observe Daylight Saving Time.

TIPPING

Belize restaurants rarely add a service charge, so in better restaurants tip 10%–20% of the total bill. At inexpensive places, leave small change or tip 10%. Many hotels and resorts add a service charge, usually 10%, to bills, so at these places additional tipping isn't necessary. In general, Belizeans tend not to look for tips, and Belizeans themselves tip sparingly, although with increasing tourism this is changing. It's not customary to tip taxi drivers or service station attendants. Guides at archaeological sites and fishing guides often expect a tip, around 10%–15% of the guide fee.

In Guatemala, restaurant bills do not typically include gratuities; 10% is customary. Bellhops and maids expect tips only in the expensive hotels. Guards who show you around ruins and locals who help you find hotels or give you little tours should also be tipped. Children will often charge a quetzal to let you take their photo.

TIPPING GUIDELINES FOR BELIZE	
Bartender	BZ$2–BZ$5 per round of drinks, or 10%–15% of the cost of the drinks
Bellhop	BZ$2–BZ$4 per bag, depending on the level of the hotel; none required if the hotel imposes a required service charge
Hotel Doorman	BZ$2–BZ$4 if he helps you get a cab
Hotel Maid	BZ$4–BZ$10 a day (either daily or at the end of your stay, in cash); nothing additional is required if a service charge is added to your bill, though some guests tip extra directly to the maid
Hotel Room-Service Waiter	BZ$2–BZ$5 per delivery, even if a service charge has been added
Porter at Airport	BZ$2 per bag
Taxi Driver	Not usually tipped, unless he or she carries your luggage or performs other extra services
Tour Guide	10%–15% of the cost of the tour
Waiter	10%–20%, with 15%–20% being the norm at high-end restaurants; nothing additional if a service charge is included in the bill
Fishing Guides	BZ$40–BZ$80 a day, with a minimum of 10% of the cost

TOURS

See also individual chapters for local tour guides and tour operators. Some of the recommended operators below, in addition to the categories they are listed under, offer multisport adventures and expeditions.

ARCHAEOLOGY

In Belize you can participate in a "dig" at a Mayan archaeological site, usually under the direction of a university archaeological team. Sessions run only a few weeks of the year, usually in spring or summer. Archaeological digs that accept volunteer workers are mostly in Orange Walk District. Some programs offer academic college credit. Prices don't include transportation to Belize or incidental personal expenses.

Road Scholar, a division of Elderhostel, offers a 15-day program in Belize, Guatemala, and Honduras on the history of the Maya, with insight into modern-day issues affecting their community. It also offers a 10-day Mystery of the Maya Program in Belize and Guatemala that combines snorkeling and visiting Maya sites. All the Road Scholar programs include accommodations, meals, guides, field trips, and in-country transportation, but not flights to and from Belize. The Maya Research Program, established in 1992, has two-week volunteer programs in the Blue Creek area of Orange Walk District. The Center for Archaeological and Tropical Studies (CATS) at the University of Texas-Austin accepts students and others for summer digs at its field station in the Rio Bravo Conservation area of Orange Walk District, located on Programme for Belize lands. Participants pay a fee for one four-week or two-week session. Fees cover room and board but not air fare to and from Belize. Participants live in a rustic dorm setting and learn the basics of field archaeology through lectures and hands-on experience. Students can gain class credits at the University of Texas.

Contacts Maya Research Program. ✉ *1910 E. Southeast Loop 323, #296, Tyler* ☎ *817/831–9011* ⊕ *www.mayaresearchprogram.org.* **Road Scholar.** ✉ *11 Ave. de Lafayette, Boston* ☎ *800/454–5768* ⊕ *www.roadscholar.org.* **University of Texas Center for Archaeological & Tropical Studies (CATS).** ✉ *J. J. Pickle Research Campus, Bldg. 5, 10100 Burnet Rd., University of Texas-Austin, Austin* ☎ *512/471–5946* ⊕ *www.liberalarts.utexas.edu/cats/.*

BIRD-WATCHING

Nearly 600 species of birds have been spotted in Belize, and every year five or more additional species are found in the country. Birders flock to Belize to see exciting species such as the jabiru stork, the largest flying bird in the Western Hemisphere; the harpy eagle, the scarlet macaw; the keel-billed toucan, the national bird of Belize; 21 species of hummingbirds; and endangered or rare species such as the yellow-headed parrot, ocellated turkey, orange-breasted falcon, and chestnut-breasted heron. Birding hot spots in Belize include Crooked Tree Wildlife Sanctuary, the Mountain Pine Ridge, the area around Chan Chich Lodge at Gallon Jug, and the Cockscomb Basin.

When selecting a bird-watching tour, ask questions. What species might be seen? What are the guide's qualifications? Does the operator work to protect natural habitats? How large are the birding groups? What equipment is used? (In addition to binoculars and a birding guidebook, this should include a high-powered telescope, a recorder to record and play back bird calls, and a spotlight for night viewing.) Trips can cost from BZ$1,600 per person for a six-day/five-night birding trip, including guides, lodging, and some meals. On an à la carte basis, short birding hikes with a local guide cost from BZ$30 per person, though at some jungle lodges such as Chaa Creek local birding hikes are free.

Victor Emanuel Nature Tours (VENT) has birding tours that combine visits to Chan Chich Lodge and Crooked Tree Wildlife Sanctuary. One-week tours in 2017 cost US$4,795 per person, not including airfare to Belize. Wildside Nature Tours has 8-, 10-, and 13-day birding trips that visit Crooked Tree, Cockscomb, and Cayo in Belize, and Tikal in Guatemala, from US$2,500 per person, not including airfare to Belize.

Contacts Victor Emmanuel Nature Tours. ✉ *2525 Wallingwood Dr., Suite 1003, Austin* ☎ *800/328–8368, 512/328–5221* ⊕ *www.ventbird.com.* **Wildside Nature Tours.** ✉ *241 Emerald Dr., Yardley* ☎ *888/875–9453, 610/564–0941* ⊕ *www.wildsidenaturetours.com.*

CULTURE TOURS AND HOMESTAYS

Homestays and village guesthouse stays in Mayan villages in Toledo District are offered by Toledo Ecotourism Association and Aguacate Belize Homestay Program, local organizations in the Punta Gorda area. These stays are very inexpensive, typically less than BZ$100 per day including meals and activities, but accommodations are basic.

Contact Aguacate Belize Homestay Program. ⊠ *BTIA, 46 Front St., Punta Gorda* ☎ *722/2531 BTIA office in Punta Gorda* ⊕ *www.aguacatebelize.com.* **Toledo Ecotourism Association (TEA).** ⊠ *TEA c/o BTIA Office, 46 Front St., Punta Gorda* ☎ *722/2531 BTIA Office in Punta Gorda* ⊕ *www.teabelize.org.*

FISHING

The best-known fishing lodges in Belize are high-end resorts catering to affluent anglers who, after a hard day on the water, expect ice-cold cocktails, equally icy air-conditioning, and Posturepedic mattresses. El Pescador on North Ambergris Caye, two lodges on Turneffe Atoll (Turneffe Flats and Turneffe Island Lodge), and several beach resorts in Placencia and Hopkins offer fishing with a touch of luxury—everything from guides to cold drinks included. Fishing travel companies like Rod & Reel Adventures typically book with fishing lodges.

If you want a less expensive fishing vacation, you can make your own arrangements for lodging and meals and hire your own local fishing guides in San Pedro, Caye Caulker, Placencia, Hopkins, Punta Gorda, and elsewhere. Destinations Belize in Placencia is a compromise between a total package and doing it all yourself. The owner, Mary Toy, an American lawyer from St. Louis, can help you arrange moderate accommodations, some meals, and guides for light-tackle or fly-fishing day trips (or for longer periods). She also puts together moderately priced packages for fishing in Placencia and elsewhere in Belize.

Contact Desinations Belize. ⊠ *General Delivery, Placencia Village* ☎ *523/4018 in Belize, 610/4718 cell phone in Belize* ⊕ *www.destinationsbelize.com.* **Rod and Reel Adventures.** ☎ *800/356–6982 in U.S. and Canada, 541/349–0777* ⊕ *www.rodandreeladventures.com.*

HORSEBACK RIDING

U.S.-based Equitours offers riding tour packages in the Cayo. A six-day, five-night trip is US$1,095 per person, not including airfare. Several lodges in Belize, including Mountain Equestrian Trails (MET) near San Ignacio and Banana Bank Lodge near Belmopan, specialize in riding vacations.

Contact Equitours. ⊠ *10 Stalnaker St., Dubois* ☎ *800/545–0019* ⊕ *www.equitours.com.*

KAYAKING

There are two types of kayaking trips: base kayaking and expedition kayaking. On a base kayaking trip you have a home base—usually a caye—from which you take day trips (or longer). On an expedition-style trip you travel from island to island or up mainland rivers. Typically, base kayaking is easier, but expedition kayaking is more adventurous.

Island Expeditions offers a number of complete expedition packages around Glover's Reef, Lighthouse Reef, and South Water Caye Marine Reserve. Several trips combine sea and river kayaking and base and expedition aspects. A six-night kayaking and paddleboarding lodge-to-lodge guided tour in the South Water Caye Marine Reserve is US$1,979 per person.

Contact Island Expeditions. ⊠ *4–1384 Portage Rd., Pemberton* ☎ *800/667–1630 in North America, 604/894–2312* ⊕ *www.island-expeditions.com.*

MULTISPORT

Multisport simply means that you can take part in a series of different activities—hiking, kayaking, cave tubing, birding, swimming, snorkeling.

Many Belize adventure trips include a bunch of different activities. For example, Adventure Life offers a variety tours, some combing jungle hiking, paddling, snorkeling, and visits to Mayan sites. Island Expeditions' 10-night Ultimate Adventure trip offers kayaking on the southern part of the Belize Barrier Reef, paddling on rivers in Toledo and caving and other adventures in western Belize. This tour is limited to 13 participants with up to 6 guides.

Contacts Adventure Life. ⊠ *712 W. Spruce St., Suite 1, Missoula* ☎ *800/344–6118, 406/541–2677* ⊕ *www.adventure-life.com.*

G Adventures. Formerly called Gap Tours, G Adventures offers 10 Belize multisport tours, including a 15-day tour from central Belize to Caye Caulker, involving canoeing, kayaking, light hiking, walking, biking, and rafting, with rates from US$1,495 per person, not including airfare to Belize. Other tours combine visits to Belize, Mexico, and Guatemala, and a couple add Costa Rica. ⊠ *19 Charlotte St., Old Town* ☎ *888/800–4100 in U.S. and Canada, 260–0999 in Canada* ⊕ *www.gadventures.com.*

PHOTO SAFARI

Nature Photography Adventure offers occasional photo safaris to Belize and Guatemala, with an emphasis on remote caves; participants must be reasonably physically fit to join this trip.

Contact Nature Photography Adventures. ⊠ *Box 1900, Ava* ☎ *417/683–6881* ⊕ *www.naturephotographyadventures.com.*

SPECIAL INTEREST

International Zoological Expeditions has 8- to 10-day trips, usually with an educational component such as ethnobotanical walks or mapping an island. IZE's trips combine time inland at Blue Creek in Toledo and at South Water Caye.

Contact International Zoological Expeditions. ⊠ *210 Washington St., Sherborn* ☎ *508/655–1461* ⊕ *www.izebelize.com.*

ONLINE RESOURCES

For information on Belize, your first stop should be the official site of the Belize Tourism Board. Belize Explorer is a private site that provides information on budget hotels—those priced under US$75

double. The Belize Tourism Industry Association's website also provides visitor information, mainly through information offices and monthly publications for visitors in Placencia and Punta Gorda.

The Belize Forums is an active online community of Belize visitors and residents; many regulars are happy to answer questions, though occasionally discussions become heated. Also, Lan Sluder, the co-author of this guide and many other books on Belize, has his own site called Belize First.

Belize Bus Blog has detailed and comprehensive information on bus, water taxi, shuttle, and other transportation in Belize.

There are numerous destination-specific websites, as well as dozens of personal blogs on living in and visiting Belize. Facebook also has many community and special interest pages on Belize. Increasingly, smaller restaurants and hotels often use Facebook pages rather than websites to promote their businesses.

For information on Guatemala, contact that country's tourist board, INGUAT.

Contacts Ambergris Caye. ⊕ *Ambergriscaye.com.* **Belize Tourism Board** (BTB). ⊠ *64 Regent St., Commercial District* ☎ *227/2420, 800/624–0686 in U.S.* ⊕ *www.travelbelize.org.* **Belize Bus Blog.** ⊕ *belizebus.wordpress.com.* **Belize Explorer.** ⊕ *www.belizeexplorer.com.* **Belize First.** ⊕ *www.belizefirst.com.* **The Belize Forums.** ⊕ *www.belizeforum.com/belize.* **Belize Tourism Industry Association** (BTIA). ⊠ *10 N. Park St., Commercial District* ☎ *227/1144* ⊕ *www.btia.org.* **Belmopan Online.com.** ⊕ *www.belmopanonline.com.* **Caye Caulker.** ⊕ *cayecaulker.org.* **Corozal.** ⊕ *corozal.com.* **Destinations Belize.** ⊕ *www.destinationsbelize.com.* **Go Caye Caulker.** ⊕ *www.gocayecaulker.com.* **INGUAT.** ☎ *502/2421–2800 general tourism information, 1500 in Guatemala dial this number for tourist assistance* ⊕ *www.inguat.gob.gt.* **Northern Belize.** ⊕ *northernbelize.com.* **Placencia.** ⊕ *www.placencia.com.* **Southern Belize.** ⊕ *southernbelize.com.* **Visit Hopkins Village.** ⊕ *www.visithopkinsvillagebelize.com.*

INDEX

Fodor's BELIZE

Design: Tina Malaney, *Associate Art Director*; Erica Cuoco, *Production Designer*

Photography: Jennifer Arnow, *Senior Photo Editor*

Maps: Rebecca Baer, *Senior Map Editor*; David Lindroth, *Cartographer*

Production: Angela L. McLean, *Senior Production Manager*; Jennifer DePrima, *Editorial Production Manager*

Sales: Jacqueline Lebow, *Sales Director*

Business & Operations: Chuck Hoover, *Chief Marketing Officer*; Joy Lai, *Vice President and General Manager*; Stephen Horowitz, *Head of Business Development and Partnerships*

Writers: Lan Sluder, Rose Lambert-Sluder

Editors: Margaret Kelly, Alexis Kelly

Production Editor: Carrie Parker

Copyright © 2017 by Fodor's Travel, a division of Internet Brands, Inc.

7th Edition

ISBN 978-0-14-754664-7

ISSN 1559–081X

SPECIAL SALES

This book is available at special discounts for bulk purchases for sales promotions or premiums. For more information, e-mail specialmarkets@penguinrandomhouse.com.

Printed in the United States of America

10 9 8 7 6 5 4 3 2 1

ABOUT OUR WRITERS

A former newspaper editor in New Orleans, Lan Sluder has been writing and reporting on this fascinating little country since 1991. He founded and edited the magazine, Belize First. Among Lan's 22 published books are more than a dozen on Belize, including *Easy Belize, Living Abroad in Belize*, and *Lan Sluder's Guide to Belize*. In the 1990s, he did the Belize section of Fodor's *Belize and Guatemala*. When Belize got its own Fodor's guide, Lan wrote the first edition and has been the sole writer until this edition, when daughter Rose Lambert-Sluder joined him as co-author. For this edition, Lan contributed the chapters on mainland Belize and the country overviews. Lan also has written books on the Carolinas and Georgia including *Amazing Asheville* and *Best Beach Vacations: Carolinas and Georgia*. He has contributed to two Fodor's guides on the region. His articles on travel, retirement, and business have appeared in magazines and newspapers around the world, including *Caribbean Travel & Life, The New York Times, Chicago Tribune, Canada's Globe & Mail, Bangkok Post, The Tico Times*, and *Where to Retire*. He currently writing a book on 25 great private eyes in novels, movies, and television.

Rose Lambert-Sluder has been kicking around Belize since she was three years old, when she started traveling with her dad in rental Jeeps. A freelance writer usually on the move, she has an MFA in Creative Writing from the University of Oregon and is currently writing a collection of short stories. Her favorite corner of the country is Caye Caulker, but Toledo is just as beautiful. She recommends chocolate with Belizean cacao—extra dark.